WAR AT THE TOP OF THE WORLD

THE STRUGGLE FOR AFGHANISTAN AND ASIA

ERIC S. MARGOLIS

KEY PORTER BOOKS

Library and Archives Canada Cataloguing in Publication

Margolis, Eric
    War at the top of the world: the struggle for Afghanistan and Asia/Eric S. Margolis.—
3rd ed.

Includes index.
ISBN 978-1-55263-910-8

1. Afghanistan—Politics and government. 2. Jammu and Kashmir (India)—Politics and government. 3. Tibet (China)—Politics and government—1951– . 4. China—Foreign relations—India. 5. India—Foreign relations—China. I. Title.

DS341.M373 2007   950   C2006-906430-X

This is a revised and updated edition of *War at the Top of the World: The Struggle for Afghanistan and Asia,* 2001, 1999.

The publisher gratefully acknowledges the support of the Canada Council for the Arts and the Ontario Arts Council for its publishing program. We acknowledge the support of the Government of Ontario through the Ontario Media Development Corporation's Ontario Book Initiative.

We acknowledge the financial support of the Government of Canada through the Book Publishing Industry Development Program (BPIDP) for our publishing activities.

Key Porter Books Limited
Six Adelaide Street East, Tenth Floor
Toronto, Ontario
Canada M5C 1H6

www.keyporter.com

Text design: Martin Gould
Electronic formatting: Jean Lightfoot Peters

Printed and bound in Canada

07 08 09 10 11 5 4 3 2 1

CONTENTS

Introduction to Revised Edition • vii

Introduction: Black Tuesday • xi

PART ONE **THE GREAT JIHAD**

1 Soldiers of Allah • 2

2 The Bravest Men on Earth • 10

3 Dodge City Meets the *Arabian Nights* • 28

4 Fadil the Kurd • 35

5 The Secret War • 41

6 Enter the Taliban • 53

7 Brother Osama • 79

PART TWO **KASHMIR: WAR IN PARADISE**

Prologue • 114

8 The Kingdom of Sikandar • 116

9 Revolt in the Mountains • 131

10 The Afghani • 145

11 Deconstructing South Asia • 154

12 The World's Most Dangerous Border • 158

13 Paradise Lost • 169

PART THREE **WAR IN THE DEATH ZONE**

14 The Road to Siachen • 178

15 Musa the Warrior • 193

16 The Hatred of Brothers • 211

PART FOUR **THE ROOF OF THE WORLD**

17 The Forbidden Kingdom • 238

18 India Awakes • 250

19 The Clash of the Titans • 267

20 China Under Siege • 275

21 The Fate of Asia • 285

22 War without End • 300

Postscript • 316

Index • 331

To Nexhmie Zaimi,
my mother,
to Henry Margolis,
my father,
and to L.C.

INTRODUCTION TO REVISED EDITION

February 2007

At the end of the 1990s, I proposed in my writings and commentaries a then unorthodox idea—some at the time even called it daft—that the world's newest crisis zones in the oncoming twenty-first century would be in the sweeping mountain region of South Asia and Central Asia where the fast-emerging power of China, recently freed from the fetters of Marxist economics by Deng Xiaoping, would clash with another emerging great power, India, and with two existing Asian powers, Japan, and the United States. However, I suggested that the most immediate threat would come in the Hindu Kush mountains, a southern arm of the great Himalaya chain, in the mountain states of Afghanistan and Kashmir.

At the time, I was sternly advised by a large number of editors and program directors that the world had absolutely no interest whatsoever in these remote places. Most Westerners, I was warned, would find mere mention of them alien and confusing. I sought to explain that I had written *War at the Top of the World* precisely in the rather immodest hope of trying to fill a lacuna in Western knowledge about a region I knew from my extensive travels and investigation was seething with anti-Western fury and ready to explode.

"Why should I be interested in what happens in Afghanistan, India or Pakistan!" snapped one caller. He was so angry with the topic on the morning talk show from Calgary, Alberta that he stopped his pickup truck on the roadside to call in and complain to the station.

"You should be interested because India and Pakistan are close to war—which could quickly turn nuclear. If that happened, God forbid, radioactive dust from what's left of their cities could begin showering down on your house, backyard, your ranch, and your kids within a week of a nuclear exchange."

India and Pakistan happily did not go to war, though they came very near a few times. But the region about which I had been warning abruptly confirmed my thesis about South Asia becoming the century's first crisis zone. On September 11, 2001, the United States came under surprise air attack by plotters who were believed to be based in the mountains of one of the world's least known nations, Afghanistan. Having covered the 1980's anti-Soviet struggle in Afghanistan and the ensuing civil war there, I knew this fascinating and captivating nation better than most Westerners and had developed a deep affection for this wild, medieval land. Decades in the Muslim world had given me unusual access to some of its more shadowy groups and a good understanding of their motivations and thinking.

After 9/11, I became a regular source for information and commentary on Afghanistan and what was called "Islamic terrorism."

"How did you know?" I was universally asked about my mostly accurate predictions.

There was no magic. I knew because I was watching and listening to a part of the world that we Westerners knew nothing about and cared about even less.

Six years later, most Westerners still understand very little about the themes of this book: Afghanistan, the struggle between India and Pakistan over the beautiful mountain state of Kashmir, the erosion of Tibetan culture, rivalry between China and India, and how China's emergence as a great power has upset the status quo in the strategic, volatile North Pacific.

In spite of being at war in Afghanistan since 2001, the only news most Americans and, more lately Canadians, get about that conflict is very biased, ill-informed, often ignorant reporting that parrots or paraphrases official military handouts. The politicians in Washington, Brussels, and Ottawa who plunged into this remote conflict have not much better understanding of it than do ordinary citizens.

Having been assured that military victory in Afghanistan would be swift, painless, and highly popular, the politicians readily embarked on a foreign adventure which, had they the least historic or cultural knowledge of the region, would wisely have chosen to avoid. The glorious imperial era when ill-armed mobs of unruly tribesmen could be mowed down by modern weapons without further complications is long gone. Today's troublesome tribesmen have learned to shoot back with relatively modern arms, and they have also learned that while Western armies are irresistible on the offensive, they are poor at holding ground and policing uncooperative populations, and horribly costly to maintain in the field.

Now, six years after invading Afghanistan, the U.S. and its NATO allies find themselves mired in an expensive, aimless conflict that is slowly turning against them. To understand why this has happened, one must study the record of the Soviet occupation of Afghanistan, which the U.S.-NATO occupation uncannily resembles.

One must have a basic understanding of the ferocious tribal politics that underlie everything in Afghanistan, and one most also have a sense of Pushtun tribal culture.

This modest political guidebook also explores India's rapid and overdue emergence as a new world power and why its more than half-century-old dispute with Pakistan remains the world's most dangerous political confrontation that could spiral into nuclear war.

It also looks deep into Pakistan, the only nuclear-armed Muslim nation that is at once a key ally of the U.S. in its "war on terrorism" while, at the same time, being a primary generator of anti-Western Islamic militancy. The insufficiently understood prospect of politically fragile, nuclear-armed Pakistan falling under a clique of radical Islamic officers, or dissolving into fratricidal chaos, should be an urgent concern of Western strategists. Whatever occurs in Pakistan over the next five years, this exceptionally important nation will play a key role in South Asia's and the West's security.

We are told the twenty-first century is Asia's century. This is almost certainly true, provided China and India retain their political integrity. As we increasingly turn our eyes toward Asian affairs, and away from our former Euro-centric view, understanding the roles played by Afghanistan, Islamic militants, and the rivalry between India, on one hand, and China and ally Pakistan on the other—the leitmotifs of this book—are basic to discerning where Asia is headed in the near to medium term.

Hopefully, this work will also give readers some of the sharp, unforgettable flavour of the vast, fascinating sweep of territory it covers and puncture some of the war propaganda, disinformation, and simple ignorance that has obscured our clear view of this, the world's most populous and volatile region.

INTRODUCTION: BLACK TUESDAY

I t all happened in a matter of hours, beginning on an otherwise typical Tuesday morning in early September. The outside world seemed to come out of nowhere and dealt the world's greatest power a massive blow. Four passenger airliners, hijacked by Mideastern terrorists and turned into cruise missiles, destroyed New York's World Trade Center, damaged the Pentagon, and shook America to its very core.

For the first time since the War of 1812, the continental United States had been seriously attacked. After a century of waging war in other nations' territories, Americans got a bitter taste of mass destruction and slaughter on their own soil.

In spite of the curious fact that the attackers appeared to have been Saudi Arabians and Egyptians, the Bush administration immediately laid blame for the kamikaze attacks on Osama bin Laden and his shadowy al Qaeda organization. America's wrath also fell on Afghanistan's ruling Taliban regime, which was sheltering and protecting bin Laden.

When the Taliban rejected an American ultimatum to hand over bin Laden, the United States swiftly organized an international coalition and launched massive air attacks on Afghanistan, followed by special forces operations on the ground.

America and the world, Bush proclaimed, faced the gravest peril from international terrorism—a code word for Islamic groups opposed to U.S. great power interests—which, warned the president in florid language drawn from World War II, was intent on destroying freedom, democracy, and America's way of life.

Americans abruptly found themselves in an undeclared war against a nation few could locate on a world map and even fewer knew anything about. The world's greatest military and economic power was battling one of the world's poorest, weakest, most ravaged nations that had already suffered through two decades of war and two million deaths. As U.S. warplanes bombed Afghanistan, at least five million of its people—a quarter of the population—was facing imminent starvation as a result of four years of drought.

War, as the Romans said, teaches geography. And so North Americans, who had only recently struggled to understand the difference between Croats, Bosnians, Serbs, and Albanians, were now confronted with a new, mind-numbing, tribal morass in one of the earth's remotest, most complex nations, into which the Bush administration had charged full speed in a quest for revenge, heedless of the many dangers of a land renowned as the nemesis of rulers and the graveyard of invaders.

In a remarkable turn of fate, the United States, which had abandoned South Asia in 1989 after the Soviet Union was defeated by an Afghan-Pakistani-U.S.-Saudi coalition, found itself drawn back into that region at the end of 2001. Equally ironic, the United States was compelled to invite the Russians back into Afghanistan through their proxy force, the Northern Alliance, as the price of Moscow's cooperation with the campaign against the Taliban, al Qaeda, and bin Laden.

In a further irony, after the overthrow of the unloved Taliban regime, Afghanistan slipped back into chaos and tribal rivalry, spurred on by outside powers that marked the period after the fall of the Afghan Communist regime in 1992, but this time made even worse by the spread of famine and huge numbers of internal refugees.

America's leadership found itself confronted by a new set of opportunities and dangers. On the positive side, virulently anti-U.S. groups had been crushed or dispersed, and the Taliban, which had become a favoured object of hatred and anger on U.S. college campuses over its medieval mistreatment of women, had been swept away. Perhaps most important, the United States now exercised important influence over Afghanistan, the shortest and most advantageous potential route for pipelines carrying Central Asia's vast energy resources, which America keenly coveted, south to the Arabian Sea port of Karachi.

On the negative side, however, was the danger that the United States might get mired in Afghan tribal politics and guerrilla warfare, a Lebanon or Somalia, writ large. U.S. troops might have to stay in Afghanistan to prop up a pro-American regime in Kabul—precisely the same problem faced by the Russians in the 1980s, when they ruled the cities while the mujahedin resistance forces controlled the countryside.

As a result of the course of events related to the September 11 attacks, the United States plunged into the murky political conflicts of South Asia, into the exceptionally dangerous nuclear confrontation over Kashmir between India and Pakistan, and into a tribal war in the mountains of the Hindu Kush. The twenty-first century's sole super-power thus found itself right in the middle of a quintessentially nineteenth-century colonial struggle.

In the mid-1800s, the British Empire and the expanding power of the Russian Empire began a long, bitter conflict as the Russians moved south towards the plains of India. Rudyard Kipling aptly termed the ensuing imperial rivalry, "the Great Game."

Today, a new Great Game is afoot at the top of the world. The chain of mountain ranges, plateaus, and valleys that begins in Afghanistan and Kashmir, and then sweeps 4,000 kilometres (2,500 miles) across the Indian subcontinent to Burma (now Myanmar), has become the globe's most volatile and dangerous geopolitical fault zone. Along this line of fragmentation, five nuclear-armed powers—the United States, successor to the British Empire; Russia; China; India; and Pakistan—and nuclear-aspiring Iran are engaged in a long-term rivalry that has already erupted in Afghanistan into the first important conflict of the twenty-first century.

Before the gruesome events of September 11, 2001, few Westerners, outside of those in the petroleum industry, spared any thought for South and Central Asia, or the Himalayas, a region generally dismissed as exotic, remote, and backwards, with impoverished, unstable soci-eties and obscure disputes that were of little concern to the rest of mankind. Such may have been the case a century ago when the first Great Game was played out along India's wild North-West Frontier and in Tibet between the British and Russian empires.

But America's war against Afghanistan suddenly brought the realization that South Asia, with fully a quarter of the world's population and great energy riches, is being shaken by a confluence of strategic, political, and economic tensions that threaten to ignite or worsen a series of interlocking conflicts whose effects may be felt around the globe.

According to a 1993 U.S. Central Intelligence Agency (CIA) study, the border of disputed Jammu and Kashmir, along which Indian and Pakistani forces have skirmished almost daily for the last half-century, is now considered the most likely place for a nuclear war to begin. Studies conducted by the RAND Corporation estimate such a nuclear exchange between India and Pakistan would initially kill two million people, cause one hundred million casualties, and contaminate South and Central Asia, as well as much of the globe, with radioactive fallout.

In May 1998, India shocked the world by detonating five nuclear devices, and testing intermediate-range missiles in an unmistakable assertion of its new, self-proclaimed status as a superpower. India's scimitar-rattling was aimed at cowing its old foe, Pakistan, and, even more significantly, as a clear warning to its new and now principal enemy, China.

Pakistan riposted by testing its own nuclear-capable missiles. China accelerated its numerous intermediate-missile programs and warned India against any aggressive actions. Russia sharply accelerated delivery of high-tech arms to India, its old Soviet-era strategic ally, while increasingly funneling weapons, military advisers, and intelligence agents into Afghanistan and Central Asia. Even Israel joined the contest by providing India with covert nuclear assistance, arms, technology, and military advisers.

Clearly, a new Great Game is under way, but this time one played for the very highest stakes by nuclear-armed rivals across a vast region of growing political and social instability, at a time when Asia's giants, India and China, haunted by the memory of the collapsed Soviet Union, are being shaken by deepening unease over their continued viability as unitary states.

I have covered or explored South Asia as a political journalist, war correspondent, and old-fashioned adventurer for the past twenty-six years. My many journeys across the subcontinent have taken me to the great Holy War in Afghanistan against the Soviets; to conflicts in Kashmir and atop the Siachen Glacier at 5,486 metres (18,000 feet); and to insurgencies in Punjab, Sri Lanka, and Burma. Frequent contacts with political leaders, intelligence agencies, and senior military figures in the region have afforded me particular insight into the tensions and rivalries beneath the surface of Asian geopolitics.

There is no other region on earth, in my view—not even the murderous Balkans or the ever-seething Middle East—that presents such a toxic stew of boiling religious, ethnic, political, strategic, and historical animosities, made all the more volatile by endemic poverty, illiteracy, and the sheer agony of daily existence. Nor is there any other part of our increasingly homogenized globe that is more unique, fascinating, and colourful than South Asia.

Two powerful and energetic forces—Islamic and Hindu political religious fundamentalism—have fanned the already flaring fires of South Asia. Both movements, a reaction to centuries of colonialism and backwardness, have released pent-up passions that are shaking the subcontinent and, most recently, have made themselves felt in North America and Europe.

The prospect of nuclear-armed states dominated by aggressive religious extremists is disturbing. Pakistan and India could go to war over Kashmir at any time, their fourth major conflict in half a century. This danger was dramatically illustrated by violent clashes in northern Kashmir that began in May 1999, the heaviest fighting in thirty years, in which India lost a number of warplanes and helicopter gunships. Indian and Pakistani nuclear forces were placed on high alert as the two old foes stumbled toward the brink of full-scale war along a 1,600-kilometre (1,000-mile) front.

Each nation has targeted the other's nuclear reactors and principal cities for potential nuclear attack. Growing internal political instability in both Asian powers, accentuated by powerful regional secessionist forces, raises the threat that chaos in either might tempt its neighbour to intervene or attack.

A war between India and Pakistan could very well draw China into the fray. Pakistan, which is constantly menaced by attack from India, is China's closest and most important ally. A full-scale war between Pakistan and India would most likely result in a major Pakistani defeat, unless China intervened in the Himalayas and Karakorams to support Pakistan. In fact, China has made clear it will not easily allow Pakistan, its sole "window on the West," to be defeated and, possibly, broken up or reabsorbed by India.

The festering problem of Tibet, and growing rivalry between India and China over Burma and the Indian Ocean, are other likely sources of potential conflict.

The collapse of the Soviet Union reminds us that China and India are also susceptible to a similar process of political and regional dissolution. Disintegration of either great nation-state seems almost unimaginable, yet so did the Soviet Union's stunningly sudden collapse. National instability in China or India would produce a geopolitical earthquake of enormous magnitude across Asia.

Even more ominous, India and China appear set on a collision course, as their regional interests and strategic ambitions come increasingly into conflict. Each superpower sees itself as the rightful dominant political and economic power in Asia. Both nations are developing intermediate-range nuclear arsenals clearly designed to fight a tactical or sub-strategic war. China and India are rapidly modernizing their huge ground forces, respectively the world's largest and second-largest, and making them more mobile, as well as expanding their air and naval arms. Naval rivalry between India and China is already under way in the eastern approaches of the Indian Ocean.

Any weakening of China's central government produced by the eventual decline or collapse of the ruling Communist party would almost certainly encourage secessionist movements and regionalism in China, most notably in Tibet and Sinkiang. Such a development would tempt India to seize the opportunity to intervene in Tibet, thus rectifying its disastrous strategic error in the 1950s when Delhi allowed China to annex and militarize the highly strategic Tibetan Plateau, which looms over North India and controls the headwaters of most of India's major rivers.

China and India's rivalry over Burma is also increasing. Burma's important strategic location and rich resources are coveted by both neighbouring powers. Delhi accuses China of seeking to forge a "strategic encirclement" of India through Pakistan, Tibet, Burma, and by naval expansion in the eastern reaches of the Indian Ocean. China, by contrast, sees itself encircled and challenged by an aggressive India, a resurgent Russia, and a hostile Vietnam, possibly joined at some later date by Japan or the United States.

Both China and India have long demonstrated hegemonistic behaviour toward their smaller Asian neighbours by demanding acceptance of their strategic diktat. As China and India continue to grow stronger militarily and economically, their demands for compliance and cooperation from their smaller neighbours are certain to grow apace. This, in turn, will bring China and India increasingly into contention as they vie to dominate South and Central Asia. Both powers will also increasingly compete for Asian oil, water, food, and mineral resources to fuel their expanding economies and sustain growing, increasingly urbanized populations.

History demonstrates that new powers, or resurgent older ones, invariably challenge the status quo, which we euphemistically term "stability." As new powers expand and flex their strategic muscles, they must clash with the old powers of the status quo, and, inevitably, destabilize the existing world order. In Asia, we see the unique spectacle of two ancient nations that are fast emerging as the newest superpowers in the midst of a fragmented, unstable region composed of small, weak states and a wounded, revanchist Russia.

This, and the fact that the two Asian superpowers are also uneasy neighbours sharing a long, disputed border, is a recipe for future conflict. War between China and India is not inevitable. But there are so many dangerous points of contention between them—a nuclear-weapons race, Pakistan, Kashmir, Tibet, India's eastern hill states, their disputed Himalayan borders, Burma, and the Indian Ocean—that a major military clash within the next decade between Asia's two titans, China and India, appears possible.

●●●

We must now add the conflict in Afghanistan to these simmering geopolitical tensions. To understand how one of the world's poorest, most remote, and once obscure nations has become the object of world attention, we must turn the clock back two decades to the remote mountains of Afghanistan, where a little-known tribal people who valued liberty more than their lives or fortunes joined battle in a seemingly hopeless struggle against the world's most powerful army.

PART ONE

THE
GREAT JIHAD

1
SOLDIERS OF ALLAH

Oh, Lord Shiva, save us from the claw of the tiger, the fang of the cobra,
and the vengeance of the Afghan.
OLD HINDU PRAYER

Speak not of those who are slain in the way of God as
dead; for they are alive.
KORAN

JALALABAD, AFGHANISTAN, May 1992

The first 107 mm rocket arced across a flat, arid plain of scrub and
rock toward the enemy position, a high, flat-topped hill, about
one kilometre (half a mile) distant from where we stood. The
rocket's fiery backblast produced a cloud of swirling black smoke and
a thunderous roar that seemed to advertise our exposed position to
everyone within the great amphitheatre-shaped valley surrounding
the besieged city of Jalalabad.

The missile hit the Communist position at its centre. First came an
elongated puff of grey-black smoke. Then, a few seconds later, there
was a loud explosion whose deep roar echoed off the dark mountains
towering over the Jalalabad plain. It seemed to me a good time to take
cover, but our leader, the venerable Hajji Ajab, and his nine men continued to stand proudly upright, and in full view of the enemy
position, unconcerned that we offered a splendid target to the now
aroused Communist garrison.

Curiously, the enemy remained silent. Hajji Ajab suggested in
strongly flavoured Pushtun that the Communist dogs were too frightened of the mujahedin to fight. The hajji was a grandfatherly
seventy-two, a tiny, frail-looking man with a gentle smile and a wispy
white beard that curled upward at the end. He had commanded mujahedin bands in battle against the Afghan Communists and the Soviets
for the past eleven years; he was also the imam (prayer leader) of his
small village, which was located some 15 kilometres (9 miles) south of
our position. Somehow, the ancient mountain warrior had twice

found time during the long struggle to make the hajj—or pilgrim-age—to distant Mecca. Hence his much-respected title, hajji, which gave him the right to wear a green turban and to lead his men both in prayer and in battle.

Hajji Ajab ordered another round to be fired. Selim, a skinny youth of eighteen who had been appointed our band's military technician on the basis of once having briefly worked in a Kabul garage, fiddled with the leads of a battered red car battery that he had wired up to the Chinese 107mm multibarrel rocket launcher.

A second rocket roared off, producing the usual dramatic pyrotech-nics. As it arced toward the enemy position, the mujahedin cried out, in unison, "*Allah Akbar!*" (God is great) the ancient Muslim war cry first heard in 622 CE when the Prophet Mohammed and his tiny band of companions were fighting for their lives against superior forces.

When the second rocket hit the Communist position and exploded, the old hajji cried out, "*Al-hamdililah!*" (Allah is praised). We joined him lustily, waving our arms, shaking our fists at the foe, yelling, "*Al-hamdililah!*" Thirteen hundred years seemed to vanish. The alchemy of battle had magically returned us to the time of the Prophet, as the holy warriors called upon the one, true God like the embattled companions of the Prophet Mohammed, to give their arms strength to smite the idolaters.

We fired off ten more rounds in rapid succession, alternating more cries of "*Allah Akbar*" when they were loosed, and "*Al-hamdililah*" when they exploded. The Islamic barrage finally produced an angry response from the Communist garrison. They opened up on us with mortars. White puffs of smoke burst around our position, but none of the shells caused injury. Then two T-55 tanks, dug in atop the enemy redoubt, opened rapid fire. The flat-trajectory tank shells made a sharp crack. While we could usually observe the mortar shells flying lazily through the air toward our position, the flat-trajectory, high-explosive tank shells came in too fast and level to be seen. Their explosions threw up big clumps of dirt, produced clouds of grey-black smoke, and sent red-hot shrapnel ricocheting off the rocks and boulders that lay scat-tered about us.

To my very great relief, Hajji Ajab finally ordered his men to squat down and take shelter behind the rocks. The blizzard of steel was becoming too much even for them. Adding to the danger, more enemy mortars took our position under fire. I crouched down and watched the explosions mushroom around us. Taking incoming artillery fire is one of life's more disagreeable, nerve-racking experiences. I attempted a Chinese meditation technique that I had recently learned in an effort to distance my inner self from the explosive outer reality around me. My meditation abruptly ended when a piece of hot shrapnel whistled by my right ear and ricocheted off a boulder.

After a half-hour that seemed to last for three days, the Communist barrage let up. Selim and two other gaunt mujahedin jumped up and began reloading the Chinese rocket launcher. The hajji stood erect and peered at the enemy position through his aged, watery eyes, thoughtfully stroking his beard in the manner of Islamic wise men. "Fire," he ordered. Once again, we jumped up and chorused, "Allah Akbar," as a ripple-fire of rockets flew toward the enemy redoubt.

There was a huge detonation that must have been audible in Kabul, 113 kilometres (70 miles) away. One of the rockets had hit and penetrated the redoubt's ammunition bunker. The entire Communist position was swathed in thick, billowing smoke, from whose centre bright orange flames shot skyward. It was an enormously satisfying spectacle. We hugged and kissed one another, laughing joyously and yelling, "Al-harndililahl" until we were hoarse and exhausted. There was no return fire from the Communist position: its garrison had probably fled for their lives from exploding shells in the ammunition bunker.

For the rest of the afternoon, we kept firing rockets at the smouldering Communist position and at supply depots located behind it. Our little victory must finally have galvanized the Afghan army command at Jalalabad, because, around 4 p.m. concentrated fire from two different batteries of highly accurate, Soviet-built D30 122 mm howitzers began to bracket our position. At the same time, we saw three T-54/55 tanks and four BTR armoured personnel carriers moving toward us about 3 kilometres (2 miles) away. The hajji's men had no anti-tank weapons. We were also down to our last wooden case of Chinese rockets.

"Mr. Eric," the hajji politely asked me through his son Jamal, who spoke some English, "would you like to stay and fight some more?" I didn't want to appear timid before these intrepid warriors, but I had to go back through the Khyber Pass night to get to Peshawar, from where I was due to take a plane to Lahore next morning to interview Pakistan's prime minister, Nawaz Sharif.

"Please inform his hajjiness that I think it would be better to go home now since I still have a long trip tonight." All this seemed very surreal, as if I were declining another cup of tea. Two 122 mm shells exploded just to our right, showering us with dirt.

Almost reluctantly, hajji Ajab and his band of holy warriors packed up their gear and manhandled the rocket launcher into the back of one of the white Toyota Land Cruisers—the favored vehicle of all Third World warriors—that had brought us to the battle. The investment of Jalalabad was a commuter's siege. The besiegers got up in the morning, drove or walked to the front lines, fought for four to six hours, and then often returned home for the night. The hajji's men had been blessed with Jeeps, thanks to the grace of Allah, and Saudi largesse.

This, however, was an exception. Many of the less fortunate mujahedin in other parts of the war zone were so poor they didn't even possess coats or shoes. Against the stabbing cold of the Afghan mountains, they had only thin wool shawls. The mujahedin would walk to battle barefoot, through deep snow, sometimes for two days and nights, carrying 40 kilograms (90 pounds) of mortar shells or rockets on their backs. Then they would trudge home, dodging inevitable counterattacks by Communist artillery, or the far more fearsome Hind helicopter gunships, which hunted the mujahedin across the open plains of Afghanistan, where the only cover was an occasional boulder or gully.

Off we drove, out of the depression in which the Jeeps had been hidden like so many docile ponies from an earlier age of war, and up into full view of the by now very angry Communist forces, who reopened a furious fire on us. Our drivers zigged and zagged across the rough ground as shells exploded around the racing Jeeps. Death from a broken neck in the violently jolting vehicle seemed as real a peril as being shredded by red-hot shrapnel. The Afghan warriors, however, seemed to find the death-defying ride a romp: they laughed with glee as the Jeeps careened perilously or hung on two wheels, as lethal white puffs of smoke from exploding shells blossomed around us. Finally, after what seemed hours, but was probably no more than five minutes, we rounded a knoll and moved out of the enemy's direct line of fire.

Ninety minutes later we arrived at the hajji's mud-walled village, which bore the scars of frequent enemy bombing and shelling. He invited me to stay for evening prayers and dinner, but I insisted that I must press on to Peshawar. I slowly embraced each member of the mujahedin band. One, named Gul Khan, a great strapping man with a ferocious-looking black beard, held my hand in both of his, Afghan style, and said, "Mr. Eric, please do not forget us." A knife twisted inside me. I felt a coward, a deserter, leaving these splendid fighters, my comrades-in-arms, to their holy war, while I returned, the satiated, to the relative security of Pakistan and then to my distant home.

Two Jeeploads of mujahedin bodyguards belonging to the renowned commander Abdul Haq met me at the hajji's village and escorted me on a long drive through blooming poppy fields to the border post at Torkham. This part of eastern Afghanistan was chaotic and extremely dangerous: bands of fighters from the seven different mujahedin factions roamed the countryside, sometimes clashing with one another; the Communist Afghan regime still had garrisons in the area and occasionally mounted offensive patrols; banditry and kidnapping were common, particularly among the wild, lawless tribes around the Khyber Pass.

The bodyguards had been arranged through the long arm of my friend, Lieutenant General Javid Nasser, director general of Pakistani intelligence. Two Jeeps are necessary to protect one vehicle in between: an ambush often knocks out the lead or tailing Jeep. The minute that firing begins, the men in the second Jeep can cover up those in the first and the centre vehicles with their fire.

Some miles outside of Torkham, I stopped to pay my respects to Abdul Haq, the senior mujahedin leader of the region. We sat, Afghanstyle, on delicate carpets in a long room without any furniture save bolster cushions placed along the wall, where the commander and his lieutenants reclined. The mujahedin sipped sweet tea and discussed the day's fighting, which had gone well.

Abdul Haq told me his forces were steadily outflanking the thick Communist defense lines around Jalalabad, which had for so long resisted their assaults. This heavily fortified city was the gateway to Kabul. Once it fell, the road to the Afghan capital would be open. The hated Afghan Communists were on their last legs. Now that their godless Soviet masters had fled Afghanistan, it was only a matter of time before the holy warriors would break the last enemy lines of resistance, march on Kabul, and hang Najibullah, the Afghan Marxist leader, from a lamppost, Allah willing.

We headed off for the Khyber Pass, which begins at Torkham. From there, I had to go on without my mujahedin bodyguards: they were banned from all Pathan tribal territory, including the Khyber Pass. So, too, were all Pakistani troops, except for the Khyber Rifles and the South Waziristan Scouts, who policed the turbulent Northwest Frontier from their high-walled medieval forts. An agent of Pakistani intelligence had warned me that Najibullah's Communist regime in Kabul had put a price on my head and had alerted tribal relatives among the Afridi to watch for my coming.

The Khyber Pass is a very narrow, twisting defile between 1,006-metre (3,300-foot) peaks that begins, at its southern terminus, outside Peshawar, Pakistan. The pass then snakes north for 45 tortuous kilometres (28 miles) over countless switchbacks and sharp curves to its northern end at Torkham, the first town one reaches in Afghanistan. Khyber is barren and bleak: its steep brown, grey, and black walls of broken rock and shale are devoid of vegetation or human habitation. The only sign of life on the pass is the large, rectangular fort of the Khyber Rifles, whose high, brown, crenellated walls and flag-surmounted towers lent it a wonderfully medieval flavour.

Though the pass seems uninhabited, Afridi tribesmen live atop the flat plateau on either side of the defile, and have made life miserable since the beginning of recorded history for merchants and armies seeking to transit Khyber. Alexander the Great and his Macedonian hoplites battled the Afridi when crossing Khyber in 327 BCE, on their way to invading the rich plains of Punjab. Every invading army since then has pushed south through the fabled pass, from the early Aryan invaders of India, the Turkic-Afghan army of Mahmud of Ghazni, and the Mongol "tumens" of Timur the Lame to the horse armies of Babur, the Mogul conqueror.

The armies of India's last invader, Britain, marched north through Khyber on their way to seize Afghanistan, battling the Afridi every bloodstained foot of the way. During the ferocious Afghan Wars of 1838–42 and 1878–80, battles between British forces and Pathans-mainly Afridis—raged the length of the pass, as well as at its southern and northern entrances. Afridis became rightly known by their British foes as among the bravest, and certainly the cruelest, of the notoriously cruel Pathan tribes.

The steel barrier gate at Torkham swung open to allow our Jeep to pass. I looked back out the window and, with a sinking feeling, waved farewell to my bodyguards. The Torkham gate shut behind us: we had now left the manifold dangers of Afghanistan for the even greater danger of the Khyber Pass.

My driver, a young Afghan named Ahmed, extinguished the Toyota's headlamps. It was necessary to make the run down Khyber in darkness: otherwise the lights of our Jeep would be visible for miles as we twisted and turned down the serpentine pass. Pakistani regulations did not allow us to carry automatic weapons, or, for that matter, even rifles—certainly a curious prohibition in a region where even twelve-year-old boys went heavily armed and Afghans treasured their guns, placing a higher value on them than on their wives. Our protection consisted of one revolver and two automatic pistols. I cocked my 9 mm, made sure I had a second clip handy, and wished mightily for an AK-47 and some grenades. We felt naked, and terribly vulnerable.

Ahmed accelerated to 113 kilometres per hour (70 miles per hour). Speed would have to be our main protection. The Jeep roared around the treacherous hairpin turns of the grim Khyber Pass, illuminated only by the weak moonlight, which was often obscured by thick, low-lying clouds. We swerved with neck-breaking force to avoid rocks that had fallen onto the road. The steep black walls of the pass seemed to be closing in around us. One turn taken too quickly and the Jeep would go into a fatal skid, plunging off the cliff into the dark abyss below.

After what seemed hours of death-defying driving, which was probably only about fifteen minutes, we heard bursts of automatic gunfire. We kept up our headlong descent of the pass. Once, at a particularly sharp turn, we came within inches of driving off the road. Falling rocks crashed into the top of the hurtling Jeep. We paid them no attention.

As we rounded a curve, we saw a cluster of shadowy figures standing on the black-topped road and along its shoulders. They were holding rifles and AK-47s and were very likely preparing to ambush us, but our speed was such that the Jeep was on them before they could even aim their weapons. The surprised ambushers scattered out of our way; we may have hit one or two, for I felt a strong jolt as we passed them, accompanied by cries. Shots rang out behind us, as the angry tribesmen opened fire at our Jeep, but by then we were rounding another bend in the road, and soon lost sight of the Afridis—if that is what they were. It was impossible to know whether these were the tribesmen Najibullah had sent to kidnap me or simply ordinary bandits—local tribesmen attempting to collect an impromptu road tax from whatever passing vehicle they might manage to stop.

I told Ahmed to slow down somewhat: better to shoot our way through another roadblock than go off the road into oblivion. If only we had our bodyguards, I mused, and a few G-7 anti-tank rockets—they are so handy for blasting one's way through roadblocks.

We hurtled through the night. The Jeep jolted violently, throwing us around the inside. I kept one hand on the dashboard and the other braced against the roof. I was afraid the shaking might make the pistol tucked into my belt accidentally go off. The Toyota skidded over a wet section of the road, lost traction, nearly rolled over, then righted itself.

Only the thought of falling into the hands of the vicious Afridis kept me from agonizing over the multiple dangers of our wild plunge down the winding pass. A relatively quick death caused by flying off the road or hitting a fallen boulder seemed much preferable to ending up an involuntary guest of the Afridis and then the Afghan secret police, both of whom had an unrivaled reputation for cruelty and sadism. My companions clearly shared my views. We hung on grimly, flying down the curves of the pass, tires smoking and squealing, pistols cocked, ready at each new corner for another ambuscade.

About an hour later we saw a bare light bulb ahead of us in the darkness, then a wooden barrier across the road, then a uniformed, turbaned sentry. We had reached the first checkpoint of the renowned Khyber Rifles. The guard saluted smartly as we drove through.

A little while later we rounded a corner and saw, spread gloriously below us, the twinkling lights of the frontier city of Peshawar—and safety. Armies since the beginning of time had marched down the Khyber Pass, but we may well have been the first to race through the pass in the dark of night. Ahmed looked at the city lights of Peshawar, gazed back at the dark mouth of the sinister pass, and spoke for all of us: "Allah be praised. Truly, it was His hand that guided us this night."

2
THE BRAVEST MEN ON EARTH

The warlike Afghan tribes were well known to ancient Greek historians, and even more intimately by the soldiers of Alexander the Great, who fought many bitter battles with them. Yet Afghanistan remained a geographical abstraction until the mid-eighteenth century, when a local warlord, Ahmad Shah Durrani, imposed a rough, transitory form of order over the nebulous region, and it began its gradual transformation into a coherent political entity.

Before that time, the Afghans had lived in splendid isolation, feuding among themselves, exacting tolls from caravans plying the trade routes to and from India, and joyfully launching bloody raids into neighbouring kingdoms. They acquired a reputation for cruelty, military prowess, and extreme unpredictability.

Afghan society has always been deeply divided by tribal, linguistic, religious, and regional loyalties, and so it remains today. Four principal ethnic groups dominated the country. South of the great natural divide formed by the Hindu Kush mountains—a name that means "crusher of Hindus"—dwell the mighty Pathans, the world's largest tribal group. Their lands extended as far west as Kandahar and the Iranian border, and as far south as the border of what is today Pakistan's North-West Frontier Province.

The Hindu term "Pathan" is actually a misnomer. A Pathan is very likely to take deep and violent offense at the term if you address him as such. I will continue to use "Pathan" because that is the name most familiar to western readers. These fierce tribesmen call themselves "Pakhtun" or "Pushtun," and their lands "Pushtunistan." Pathans are deeply religious Sunni Muslims, who regard Muslims from farther south as godless infidels, or *kufir*. They hold a special animosity for the Shia Muslims, who are a minority in parts of Afghanistan and Pakistan. The Pathans are divided into many tribes of varying sizes, of which four predominate: the nomadic Ghilzai, also known as "Kuchi", who roam the sweeping central plains of Afghanistan with their flocks; the imperial Durranis, traditionally the source of Afghanistan's royalty; the "free tribes" who are found straddling both sides of the British-drawn

Durand Line that separates Pakistan from Afghanistan; and the "settled" tribes who have been largely absorbed into Pakistani life, providing many of the army's senior officers and fiercest fighters. Pathans make up about 15 per cent of Pakistan's population and are concentrated in the autonomous North-West Frontier Province abutting Afghanistan.

Under the British Raj, Pathans were held to be one of India's six martial races, along with Sikhs, Gurkhas, Rajputs, Mahrattas, and Punjabi Muslims. All fit the British ideal of "grenadierism"—namely, admiration and preference for tall, sturdy soldiers of markedly aggressive nature who would form the army's elite offensive units. The Pathans embodied this ideal perfectly: they were tall, fair-skinned, and extremely warlike. These bellicose upland peoples formed the fighting core and finest units of the imperial armies of the Queen Empress of India.

The principal Pathan tribes are again divided into far more important subtribes, and then subdivided into powerful clans, known as *khels*. The most famous, or infamous, are the cruel, rapacious Afridis, guardians of the Khyber Pass, who inspired Kipling's admonition to British officers to, should they fall wounded on the North-West Frontier, save a last bullet for themselves lest they fall into the hands of Afridi and their women, whose exquisite sexual cruelties to prisoners were legendary on the frontier.

Best known of the *khels* are the proud Yusufzais; the cunning Shinwaris; those masters of raiding, Orakzais and Mahsuds; and the clever Bangash, ferocious Wazirs, and arrogant Mohmands. Beneath the *khels* are a bewildering, fragmented galaxy of clans and subclans linked by blood, though often divided by vendettas and bitter rivalries over water, pastures, booty, and women.

All of the many peoples of the northern Indian subcontinent know one thing as surely as they know not to touch fire: never cross an Afghan, for he, or his heirs, will surely exact revenge, even if it takes five hundred years.

In the lands of the Pathan, there is no law save the tribal code of Pushtunwali. This ancient code deals with disputes over "*zar, zan*, and *zamin*": gold, women, and land. At the heart of Pushtunwali is Badal— the Afghan's fearsome code of revenge. Pushtunwali, and the medieval code of Lek Dukagjin of the Gheg tribesmen of northern Albania, are remarkably similar. Under both codes, you can be shot dead for a disrespectful look, any slight to one's honour or female relatives, or simply because some gunman does not like the colour of your hat. But you must kill with care, since the right and duty of vengeance is enshrined in both groups of mountaineers' laws. However, women, children, and, above all, guests must be protected, and spared violence.

Highland Scots, and Gheg tribesmen of northern Albania, would feel quite at home in an Afghan raiding party, where the badge of Afghan manhood is the ubiquitous AK-47 automatic rifle. Feuding bands of Pathans often fight out their vendettas with heavy weapons, and even armoured vehicles. Pakistani authorities have learned not to interfere in these affairs of honour lest they provoke a general uprising among the hot-blooded Pathans.

North of the snow-capped Hindu Kush are Afghanistan's other main ethnic groups: the elegant, fine-featured Tajiks, whose ethnic roots, language (Dari), and culture are Persian; the nomadic, Shia Muslim, Hazara, a people of Tibetan-Mongol origin with pronounced Asiatic features; and the warlike Uzbeks of the northwest, a people of Turkic-Mongol origin who glory in the conquests of their great chieftain, Timur the Lame, or Tamerlane.

Tajiks traditionally formed Afghanistan's intellectual class and look down on the rustic Pathans as backward and uncouth. Add to this ethnic cocktail smaller numbers of Baluchis, Turkomen, and Nuristanis.

Fifty-seven years after the revelation of Islam in 622 CE, its followers split over the succession to the caliphate, which combined the powers spiritual and temporal of the Muslim *ummah*, or society. A group of Muslims broke away, insisting the mantle of leadership should have passed to the Prophet Muhammad's son-in-law Ali, and to his son Hussein, who were subsequently killed in battle at Karbala, and are venerated by all Shia as martyrs and virtual saints. Iran, which had been conquered by Islamic armies and converted to the Muslim religion, but which detested Arabs as desert primitives, quickly adopted Shiism as an expression of its nationalist spirit and individuality. In Iran, Shiism incorporated ancient Zoroastrian customs, the worship of saints, and mysticism to produce a faith that was very different from the austere Sunni Islam of the Arabian desert.

The Shia, who make up about 12 per cent of the world's one billion Muslims, are regarded as dangerous heretics by most orthodox Sunni Muslims. Today, Shia believers are concentrated in Iran, Lebanon, and

Iraq, where they form the majority; and in Pakistan and parts of Afghanistan, where they are a marginalized, widely disliked minority subject to occasional violent spasms of persecution. The Shia passion for martyrdom and self-sacrifice, and their deep sense of oppression, make them formidable fighters, as the Israelis learned to their dismay in southern Lebanon, where the Shia Hezbollah may become the first Arab force ever to defeat the Israeli Army in battle.

Imperial Britain attempted to invade and annex Afghanistan to its Indian empire, beginning in 1838. This ill-starred venture led to the First and Second Afghan Wars, which resulted in a series of bloody British defeats, or pyrrhic victories, which shocked Victorian England. The annihilation, in 1842, of an entire British expeditionary force of sixteen thousand men by the Ghilzai Pathans, immortalized by Lady Jane Butler's famed painting, *The Retreat from Kabul*, was one of the worst disasters in British military history, compelling the Raj to forsake its ambitions to conquer Afghanistan. On a wild mountain ridge, a lone rider, his head bandaged and bloody, struggles to stay astride his exhausted horse. Vultures wheel in the cold, blue sky above them. This was Dr. Charles Grant, one of the only survivors of the British army that had marched off from Peshawar, India, two months earlier to conquer Afghanistan. Having failed to hold Kabul, the defeated British had withdrawn south through the Khyber Pass, where the waiting Afridi had fallen upon them like wolves, and slaughtered the Queen's army almost to a man, inflicting unspeakable tortures upon those unlucky enough to be captured alive.

After this debacle, Britain contented itself with meddling, rather than intervening, in Afghan affairs, discreetly supporting the pro-British royal dynasty in Kabul. After Britain and Russia nearly went to war in northern Afghanistan in the 1870s, they agreed to leave it as a buffer zone between their two expanding empires. They also tacitly agreed, after some intrigues, to do the same with the remote Himalayan kingdoms of Tibet and Bhutan.

In 1885, Afghan rulers and Imperial Russia signed an agreement that defined Afghanistan's northern border as running along the Oxus River (the modern Amu Darya). Eight years later, Sir Mortimer Durand, representing the British Raj, signed an agreement in Kabul defining the border between British India and Afghanistan. The 1,930-kilometre (1,200-mile) border from the Pamir Mountains to Baluchistan, known henceforth as the Durand Line, became the de facto and de jure southern border of Afghanistan. For the first time, the land between the Durand Line and the Oxus came to be called "Afghanistan," rather than its previous names, "Afghan territory" or "Afghan region."

The modus vivendi between Afghanistan's chiefs and the Raj did not stop incessant clashes between British forces and various Pathan tribes on the northwest frontier, nor prevent a third Anglo-Afghan War in 1919. Fighting continued to flare along the border until the late 1930s. Nevertheless, Afghanistan was more or less left to its own devices. Remarkably, it was the only independent Muslim nation left on earth (besides secular, de-Islamicized Turkey): all others had been conquered, or absorbed, by Western imperialist powers, Russia and China.

Afghanistan thus remained in splendid isolation from the 1930s until the early 1970s, a *terra incognita* and geopolitical lacuna on the map of Asia. However, the world's new superpowers, the Soviet Union and the United States, both recognized Afghanistan's strategic importance, and, as part of their global rivalry, steadily increased efforts to spread their influence in the kingdom. The U.S.S.R. assumed an important role in arming and training the Afghan army, building roads and infrastructure, and in educational programs, which served as a vehicle for expanding the operations of the growing Afghan Communist party.

Afghanistan's royal family continued a tenuous, largely ceremonial rule over the fractious nation until 1973. In that year, King Zahir Shah, a feeble and much-disrespected monarch, was overthrown, while on a visit to Italy, by his scheming cousin Prince Mohammed Daoud, who proclaimed himself president. Daoud received powerful support from the underground Communist party, which the Soviets had been building up since 1965 in an effort to undermine the Afghan monarchy.

A period of growing instability ensued, during which the Soviet Union intensified its intrigues in Afghanistan to further the Russian historical grand strategy of eventually pushing south over the Hindu Kush, and then through Pakistan, down to the warm waters of the Arabian Sea. Communist organizers infiltrated the Afghan armed forces, the urban intelligentsia, and the many urban radical groups clamouring for various degrees of modernization.

The Communists were particularly successful in enlisting teachers, artists, physicians, and advocates of women's education, a success that was to provoke a vicious backlash against all four groups when the fundamentalist Taliban seized power in 1996. To the unwordly talibs, women's emancipation, music, art, and anything intellectual were the work of the hated Communists, who had slaughtered two million Afghans and tortured countless thousands. Under the Taliban, Kabul's tiny, Western-oriented elite was forced into seclusion, but not before telling their story to foreign aid workers and reporters. Though only a handful of urban women had been "emancipated" during the pre-1979 era, the mistaken view held abroad was that all of Afghanistan's women had been locked away by the Taliban and forced to wear the medieval head-to-toe burka. In fact, most Afghan women wore the burka, which was as much a symbol of protection as it was of repression. A woman could walk alone and unmolested provided she was covered up. The burka, like the veil in the Mideast, is a sign that the woman does not want to be disturbed or addressed.

The relegation of women to lower status was not unique to Afghanistan. Tribal regions of Iran, Pakistan, the Central Asian states, and parts of rural India have similar customs. But such nuances were lost on American and British feminists who preached a crusade against "sexist, repressive Muslims" that found willing ears on American college campuses and among U.S. congressmen looking for a safe cause to promote.

Meanwhile, Soviet military and civilian technicians poured into Afghanistan. In April 1978, two militant Afghan Communist leaders, Mohammed Taraki and Hafizullah Amin, mounted a coup in Kabul with planning and support from the Soviet KGB. Daoud was killed; Communist forces seized power. Thousands of anti-state opponents were liquidated in the notorious Pol Charki prison outside Kabul.

But in typical Afghan style, the Communist leadership, made up of intellectuals, journalists, teachers, and some mid-level army officers, immediately became locked in bitter ideological feuds and personal rivalries. Two powerful Communist factions—the Khalq, which was dominated by Pathans, and the Parchem, in which Uzbeks, Tajiks, and Hazaras were prominent—waged ferocious ideological battles that often led to outright combat.

Hafizullah Amin, Taraki's deputy, argued furiously with his nominal boss, who was a homicidal maniac. Their feuding deputies, Babrak Karmal and Najibullah, were packed off to Moscow.

In September 1979, Hafizullah Amin organized the murder of Mohammed Taraki, seized power, and began executing supporters of his late rival. In the finest tradition of baroque Soviet lies, and with delicious understatement, Radio Kabul announced the bullet-riddled Taraki had "resigned for health reasons." One version of events held that Amin had drawn a revolver in the course of a heated cabinet meeting and emptied it into Taraki. Another, that Taraki had been hustled from the meeting room and gunned down in the hall by Amin's guards.

Amin quickly proved to be an even more dangerous lunatic than Taraki. Completely misjudging his nation—as only an intellectual ideologue can—he embarked on a radical modernization and bloody Sovietization of the country that immediately provoked armed resistance from traditional, rural Afghans. Amin managed to combine the most vicious aspects of totalitarian Stalinism, and Pol Pot's demented social engineering, with Afghan ferocity, and an inability to compromise over the most minor issues. He instituted a reign of terror against all opponents, including the more moderate Communist Khalq faction, torturing and killing thousands of his victims by electrocution, burning, castration, impalement, slow freezing in giant refrigerators, acid baths, or by burying them alive.

The increasing turmoil and Amin's unspeakable cruelties were too much even for Moscow, which feared that its new socialist ally was about to collapse in chaos. The KGB warned the Kremlin that the Marxist regime in Kabul was drowning in a factional bloodbath.

In early December 1979, a seriously ailing Leonid Brezhnev, KGB boss Yuri Andropov, Defense Minister Dmitriy Ustinov, and a single Central Committee official decided, without consulting the rest of the Communist party or the government, to invade Afghanistan. In doing so, they invoked the Brezhnev Doctrine, which called for Soviet intervention whenever and wherever "fraternal" Communist regimes were threatened.

However, this venture was to have unimaginable, and ultimately catastrophic, consequences for the Soviet Empire. Whether these aged Communist leaders embarked on war as a reflex action, in response to the disorder in Afghanistan, or as the first step in a grand geopolitical drive to the Arabian Sea will be the subject of debate until the Kremlin archives are opened—if they ever are.

Adding to this debate, in 2001, Zbigniew Brzezinski, former U.S. national security adviser to President Jimmy Carter, claimed in an interview that he had ordered the CIA to begin arming anti-Soviet mujahedin forces inside Afghanistan before the Soviet invasion. Brzezinski, a fierce anti-Communist who, when I interviewed him, had a sort of shrine in his office to a fellow Pole who had fallen fighting the Soviets in Afghanistan, now claims he began the arms deliveries in order to lure the Soviets into a trap in Afghanistan, and thus get revenge for the catastrophic U.S. defeat in Vietnam.

Victory has a thousand fathers, and Brzezinski may be one of them. His claim to have begun arms deliveries to entrap the Soviets, even if true, seems to this writer unlikely to have provoked a full-scale Soviet invasion of Afghanistan since, in 1979, the intensity and effectiveness of anti-Soviet activity by the small bands of ragged mujahedin was minimal, no more than a nuisance factor in a fractious nation prone to tribal feuds, banditry, and local uprisings. Most of the anti-Communist resistance was armed with World War I Lee-Enfield .303 rifles and a scattering of automatic weapons for which ammunition was always in short supply. Hardly a threat worthy of the mighty Red Army.

On a frigid, snowy December night, a Soviet special forces unit from the elite Alpha group, which had covertly infiltrated Afghanistan on military cargo aircraft, raced into Kabul. The Soviet commandos stormed President Amin's palace, killed his surprised guards, burst into Amin's bedroom, and executed the cowering Afghan Communist leader with a burst of AK-47 fire.

Three Soviet motor rifle divisions immediately moved south across the border from Termez, in southern Uzbekistan, quickly occupying most of Afghanistan. The Soviet mechanized units took advantage of the modern trans-Afghan highway that the Soviet Union had thoughtfully constructed as part of its "fraternal friendship assistance" to Afghanistan. Ironically, in the spirit of benevolent coexistence, Washington had supplied most of the cash for the project, Moscow the materials and labour. The Americans failed to note that the highway was being built to support tanks and heavy armoured vehicles.

A more compliant Communist satrap, the ineffectual Babrak Karmal, was hustled back from Moscow and appointed president. The menacing Najibullah, known as "The Bull," was named his deputy. The United States and its NATO allies protested loudly, but without effect.

Far from settling the political imbroglio in Afghanistan, or assuring Communist domination, the brutal Soviet coup and subsequent invasion only made matters worse. The intervention was supposed to be a bloodless *coup de main*, like the highly successful 1968 invasion of

Czechoslovakia. But the Russians, who should have known better, disastrously miscalculated the response of their Afghan neighbours, who were nothing like the docile Czechs.

The arrival of Soviet troops suddenly diverted the natural bellicosity of the Afghans away from their usual feuds and focused it, full force, on a far more appealing target, a foreign invader. Religious leaders and local mullahs proclaimed a jihad (holy war) against the godless Soviet infidels from the north and their local Communist allies.

At first, the Soviets shrugged off the occasional guerrilla raids mounted by the poorly armed, hopelessly disorganized Afghan tribesmen, who were mostly equipped with antique arms, but as resistance to the Soviet occupation forces and their Afghan Communist allies intensified, it became increasingly clear the insurgency was taking root and would not be easily extinguished.

However, few nations outside Afghanistan, except for its immediate neighbours Pakistan, Iran, and India, cared in the least about this obscure conflict. In fact, in the newspaper business, an "Afghanistan story" was an editor's dismissive term for utterly unimportant, boring news that no one would ever want to read. The Soviets encouraged this obscurity by keeping journalists out of the parts of Afghanistan controlled by Communist forces—and by hunting down and trying to kill the tiny number of reporters bold enough to sneak in with the mujahedin from Pakistan. After all, the world had forgotten Tibetan resistance to Chinese invasion in the early 1950s; Moscow reckoned the same creeping amnesia would happen with Afghanistan, which, after a time, would simply vanish from the world's consciousness, and be absorbed, like the old Muslim emirates of Central Asia, into the Soviet Empire.

Besides, Afghanistan was a most inconvenient, difficult war for journalists. Places like South Africa or the Mideast had decent accommodation and good telecommunications. You could cover a battle, or the latest bloody outrage, and be back in your Intercontinental Hotel in time for a hot bath and decent dinner. Getting into Afghanistan usually meant trekking in from Pakistan through the mountains, an arduous and dangerous trip that could take weeks, during which hepatitis and food poisoning were as much a danger as Soviet bullets, rockets, or mines. And every step deeper into Afghanistan meant a longer, more perilous return voyage to the safety of Pakistan.

Equally discouraging, TV teams were far too expensive to send on lengthy, dangerous missions into a remote war in the mountains of the Hindu Kush. Besides, most Americans couldn't find Afghanistan on a map if their lives depended on it, nor could they register exotic foreign names in their minds. Afghanistan was a media-unfriendly war. The few Western news teams that ventured into Afghanistan usually penetrated no more than a few miles, had themselves filmed in Afghan garb beside a knocked-out Soviet tank, and then returned before dark to Pakistan. One prominent American TV newscaster, decked out in Afghan garb, even had a small fake battle staged for his benefit.

I followed this terrible war for three years, beginning in 1980, and tried to publish stories about the conflict in North American newspapers, but with infrequent success. Other journalists fared no better. Afghanistan's remoteness and the West's desire to avoid disturbing supposed detente with the U.S.S.R. for the sake of what one newspaper described as "a few Afghan mountain bandits" made people deaf and blind to the industrial-scale butchery in Afghanistan. Nevertheless, the Afghans fought on, heedless of the seemingly hopeless odds against them.

As Afghan resistance spread, the Soviets and their Afghan allies, unseen by the outside world, embarked on a ferocious scorched-earth campaign that combined the merciless destructiveness of Genghis Khan's Mongols with the calculated terrorism of Stalin. Villages that had sheltered mujahedin were razed. Crops were burned; farm animals machine-gunned. Tiny butterfly mines, no bigger than a tea saucer, but capable of blowing off a man's foot, were strewn by the millions. Booby-trapped toys were dropped from the air; Afghan children picked them up and had their hands blown off. Irrigation systems that had provided water for eight hundred years were destroyed; wells were poisoned. The dreaded Afghan KHAD secret police, trained and led by the KGB, imprisoned, tortured, and executed tens of thousands of Afghans. The horrors inflicted by the late, unlamented Hafizullah Amin on "enemies of the state" were continued, and even improved upon, by the KHAD. Gravediggers could not keep up with their workload, and complained bitterly to the authorities that their Stakhanovite quotas were impossible to meet.

The mujahedin confronted the Soviet war machine with the only weapons they had: raw courage, Islamic faith, and Lee-Enfield rifles. In one of those amazing trapdoors that sometimes open in history, a modern Soviet army, with armour, artillery, aircraft, and helicopter gunships, found itself pitted against a tribal force that, except for its rifles, could have ridden right out of the time of Harun ar-Rashid and the *Arabian Nights*.

Though the public and media were indifferent, consolidation of the Soviet invasion of Afghanistan had caused panic among governments in Washington, the Mideast, and Western Europe. The badly unnerved and deeply confused Carter administration was advised by the Joint Chiefs of Staff and the CIA that the Soviets would quickly pacify Afghanistan. Then, it was widely feared, the Soviets would advance their armoured units south through Pakistan, or southwest through the mountain passes of Iran, down to the oil-rich Gulf.

In August 1980, U.S. war planners advised Secretary of Defense Harold Brown and President Carter that there was "no other option" except the use of tactical nuclear weapons to prevent the Soviets from seizing the Gulf. The nearest U.S. ground forces were 11,300 kilometres (7,000 miles) away. Even if the U.S. embarked on a massive effort to rush troops and aircraft to the Gulf, the soonest it could deploy the first tank-equipped heavy divisions to the region would be D+30, at which time the Soviets would enjoy a 14–1 tactical advantage.

American planners had good reason to fear a Soviet attack on the Gulf, which at the time supplied 32 per cent of America's oil, 70 per cent of Europe's, and 77 per cent of Japan's. As a result of the August 1980 crisis, the United States steadily reduced its dependence on Mideast oil, which went from supplying nearly a third of its needs to only 7 per cent a decade or so later. Interestingly, the American public still is being told— and believes—that they depend on Mideast oil, which is essential to U.S. national security, though this is clearly not the case, at least economically.

The U.S. "security" presence in the Mideast is justified by the need to protect "vital" oil supplies. In reality, the continued U.S. military presence in the region is designed to prop up friendly regimes, protect Israel, and ensure that the United States keeps control of the oil supplies of key allies in Europe and North Asia. Domination of Mideast oil, the modern version of imperial Britain's control of the world's sea lanes, is a key component of the United States' "great power" status.

Soviet ground and air units in the backwater Caucasus and Turkestan military districts were normally maintained at "Category C," the lowest level of military readiness, and equipped with the oldest weapons systems. But in the seven months since the invasion of Afghanistan, the twenty-eight Soviet divisions based north of Iran had gone onto full war footing. Many units had left their garrisons and moved into the field. Soviet airborne divisions in Eastern Europe had been ordered on alert. Specialized communications, logistics, and Spetsnaz commando units were deployed in the region. Tactical air force units were reinforced and supplied with large stocks of munitions. Soviet units shifted to new radio frequencies, or maintained radio silence. The last time such activities were observed was just prior to the 1968 invasion of Czechoslovakia. By August 1989, the Soviets had massed 3,400 tanks, 8,000 armored personnel carriers, 370 combat aircraft, 350 helicopters, and 4,000 guns on Iran's border.

The distance from the Soviet border to the Gulf was 11,300 kilometres (700 air miles), or 1,600 kilometres (1,000 land miles). To reach the Strait of Hormuz, Soviet forces would have to cross the lofty Elburz Mountains, then skirt the uplands of the Zagros Mountains through narrow defiles, and over bad roads. Even so, the Pentagon estimated the Red Army's spearheads could reach the Gulf within ten or eleven days. Worse, Soviet armor based at Shindand in southwest Afghanistan was only 724 kilometres (450 miles) from the Gulf.

Secretary of Defense Brown estimated that a minimum of three U.S. divisions and five air wings would be required, just to slow a major Soviet attack; none was available. A lightning Soviet thrust could be delayed by sending in special forces to blow up bridges and block mountain passes, but Pentagon war planners concluded a determined Soviet thrust could not be halted without recourse to tactical nuclear weapons.

This option, it was clear, would almost inevitably escalate to all-out nuclear war with the Soviet Union. Even in the unlikely chance that it did not, any American action in Iran would certainly have provoked the Soviets to launch a blitzkrieg in Europe. At the time, the massed tank armies of the immensely powerful group of Soviet forces in East Germany were believed to be capable of reaching the English Channel in only six or seven days of round-the-clock fighting. The indecisive Carter administration watched all this, unable to decide on an effective response.

Most of the Muslim nations reacted similarly. Though always passionate oratorical champions of Islamic causes, in reality most Muslim nations followed a policy of every man for himself. The dictatorships and oligarchies of the Muslim world at this time were too preoccupied keeping themselves in power, or intriguing against their neighbours, to spare time or resources for less urgent matters. But when Soviet tanks rolled into Kabul, a shudder of fear coursed through the Arab world and Iran. Few in the Middle East believed Washington would risk nuclear war to prevent the Red Army from rolling into Tehran, Baghdad, or Kuwait.

But then, at this darkest of hours, two important events occurred that Moscow had not foreseen. First, Pakistan's leader, the tough former tank general Muhammad Zia ul-Haq, concluded early in 1980 that the Soviet invasion of landlocked, resource-poor Afghanistan, a nation of no intrinsic economic value, could have only one objective: as the first stage of a massive Soviet push through Pakistan to the Arabian Sea.

Accordingly, Zia launched a secret plan to defend Pakistan by covertly organizing resistance by the Afghan tribes to the Soviet invaders. As his chosen instrument of policy, Zia ordered his crack military intelligence agency, Inter-Service Intelligence (ISI), to arm, supply, and organize the Afghan resistance. Zia put this vast, complex undertaking under command of his right-hand man, one of Pakistan's most formidable Pathan officers, General Akhtar Abdul Rahman Khan, director general of ISI.

The second barely noticed event was the dispatch around the world of high-level delegations of Afghan notables. Their mission was to drum up political, military, and economic support among Muslim nations and Islamic communities for the growing holy war, and to counter Soviet propaganda that the only opposition to their occupation of Afghanistan was coming from bands of mountain bandits. The struggle for Afghanistan was to be internationalized.

President Zia secretly approached the United States in 1981 with his plan to mobilize and organize Afghan resistance, which the United States had previously dismissed as inept and doomed to failure. Zia's proposal came as a godsend to Washington and its frightened Arab oil allies: they immediately concluded an agreement with Islamabad to resist the Soviet occupation of Afghanistan. The CIA, Britain's M16, and Saudi Intelligence were ordered to cooperate closely with Pakistan's ISI and begin deliveries of arms to the Afghan resistance. The Pakistanis would run the war; the Western-Arab anti-Communist coalition would foot the bill.

While U.S. and British intelligence were still trying to sketch out a plan to provide limited aid to the Afghan resistance, Arab groups and individuals finally began to take action. Chief among them was the shadowy Muslim Brotherhood, a politically conservative Islamist organization that originated in Egypt, and later expanded into the Gulf and Levant. The Brotherhood had raised money and arms for an earlier jihad: the bloody, but little-known struggle by Libyans in the 1930s to free themselves of colonial rule by Fascist Italy. Now, the Brothers began sending sums of money and some arms through friendly Pakistan to the scattered bands of Afghan mujahedin. The Brotherhood would later go on to help found and fund other resistance groups in the Muslim world, including Hamas in Palestine.

In a remarkable departure from their usual parochial self-absorption, Muslims in various parts of the world became inspired and gripped by the remote struggle in Afghanistan. Whether it was guilt over abandoning the Palestinians, anger over Soviet atrocities in Afghanistan, or a yearning to show the world that Muslims were not a third-rate people, the Islamic world began to open its eyes and purses to the Afghans. What made this reaction even more noteworthy was that, at the time, the Soviets still wielded much influence over Algeria, Libya, Egypt, Syria, and Iraq.

Volunteers from across the Muslim world—at first a handful, then a growing stream that would eventually reach one hundred thousand men—went to Pakistan to enlist in the Great Jihad. Among them was a young man named Osama bin Laden, the son of one of Saudi Arabia's wealthiest contractors.

Realizing that money is the sinew of war, delegations of Afghan leaders set out to raise funds from the *ummah*, or Muslim communities around the world. The most senior of these eventually found his way to Toronto, Canada, home to a large Muslim community from India and Pakistan.

And thus, on a rainy fall day in 1982, I drove out to a school campus in the Toronto suburb of Mississauga to interview the visiting Afghan delegation. I had been invited because I was one of the few journalists who wrote and broadcast about Afghanistan and, I suppose, one of the even smaller number who actually seemed to care about the terrible tragedy in the mountains.

The vocational school appeared deserted; one of those innumerable academic breaks was under way. Fine, tall oak trees and birches grew in abundance around the low, modern buildings. A sharp fall wind gusted through the trees, producing a soft shower of wet brown and yellow leaves. Here was Canada at its loveliest: clean, bracing, filled with the scents of a gentle nature, peaceful, and as safe as your parents' home. A more surreal locale in which to meet the men who were leading the Afghans in a holy war could not be imagined.

I entered a dormitory building. Canada suddenly vanished before my eyes. A tall, burly, bearded Afghan barred my way. He wore traditional knee-length shirt called a kameez, and shalwar, (baggy pants); he had leather sandals on his bare feet, an empty bullet belt around his waist, and the round wool Chitral hat that all Afghans wear—even to bed—on his head. He looked ferocious, and obviously had some sort of weapon under the rough, brown wool shawl draped across his broad shoulders, though concealed weapons are illegal in Canada. The guard—for that is what he was—wordlessly frisked me and then showed me into a medium-size room whose main feature was an open-counter kitchen.

There, in a space only recently vacated by college students, five turbaned Afghan chieftains in full mountain garb stood about the stove, chatting and cooking up a steaming pot of pungent yellow curry. They dared not eat Canadian food for fear it might be contaminated by unclean pork.

The two most impressive and forceful men of the group were both amply bearded, and seemed in their fifties. Burhanuddin Rabbani was a man of considerable dignity, and a noted literary scholar. Like all his fellow Tajiks, who come from northeastern Afghanistan, Rabbani spoke Dari, a dialect of Persian. Before the Soviet invasion he had taught Islamic law at Kabul University; he had also written books on Persian poetry. His political party, the Jamiat Islami, had become a rallying point for non-Pathan anti-Communists. In the late 1990s, Rabbani's party would become the Northern Alliance, the main opposition to the Taliban.

The other significant presence was Sibgatullah Mojadidi, a short man with a long oval face, drooping eyes, and a downturned mouth that gave him a permanent look of deep melancholy, despite which his gaze was hard, intelligent, and sharp. Mojadidi was a respected Islamic theologian who had been educated at the Muslim world's leading religious institution, Cairo's Al-Azhar University; he was an authority on Sufism, a mystical branch of Islam. More important, Mojadidi was a

Pathan, a member of the dominant ethnic group in Afghanistan, who live south of the Hindu Kush mountains. I quickly fell into conversation with Rabbani and Mojadidi.

Among the others present was an Uzbek chieftain from the northwest, close to the border with the Soviet Union. This man was a hereditary saint, known as a *pir*, who said little. There was also a rather pompous royalist wearing a heavy gold Rolex. Completing the ethnic mosaic of Afghanistan was a notable of the Shia Hazara, a people of Mongol origin.

One of Rabbani's lieutenants translated for us. The Afghans had been raising funds in the United States and Canada. They had just come up the lake from Buffalo. In each city, Muslims had flocked to meet the mujahedin leaders and press into their hands whatever small sums these people of modest means could afford. I asked Rabbani how he could expect to defeat the Soviets, or even hold them at bay. Rabbani looked at me and smiled gently, as a father would at a young son asking a naive question. "Our faith makes us strong. We are in the right. Allah will show us the way."

"Yes," I persisted, "but how can you fight the Soviet Army with World War I rifles?"

Rabbani shrugged. "Allah will provide. What is important is that our faith be strong."

Mojadidi cut in, with a more worldly explanation. "We do have a few friends. Some, inshallah (Allah willing), will come to our aid. But even if they do not, you know we Afghan have defeated every nation that tried to conquer us. We defeated Alexander the Great, and the British. We will defeat the Russians too, Allah willing."

This time, however, the redoubtable Afghans were fighting a modern army equipped with armoured helicopter gunships, ground attack aircraft, poison gas, armoured vehicles, and artillery. Courage was not enough. And how, I wondered, could these proud, fractious tribal chiefs from an age long past wage a national struggle against a superpower whose ruthlessness was without equal in modern history?

I also saw in the Afghan leaders that same deficit of human talent that afflicts so many backward societies. All too often the leaders of such nations have no grounding in the processes of politics, administration, economics, finance, or industry. Their training is as country doctors, mission teachers, postal clerks, common soldiers, or rural clerics. This poor man's "intelligentsia" passes for an educated class in their threadbare post-colonial societies.

When the British, French, Italians, and Belgians gave independence to their colonial empires, or simply abandoned them, in many cases these clerks and teachers were the only people who could read or write, and so they became, by default, the new ruling class. You could tell them easily: they had soft hands; they wore ill-fitting suits, often blue and shiny, that were always too short and threadbare; they almost always displayed the primary status symbol of the Third World intellectual or senior bureaucrat, a fountain pen in their breast pocket.

This is how Patrice Lumumba came to power in the Congo and Ahmed Sukarno in Indonesia. Haiti's François Duvalier, that grandmaster of terror, began his bloody career as a humble country doctor combating yaws. Enver Hoxha of Albania, the Balkan Stalin, was a rural schoolteacher. Fidel Castro started out as a young lawyer with no clients, Idi Amin as a sergeant in the King's Uganda Rifles, and Anwar Sadat of Egypt as a passed-over major and an equally unsuccessful actor.

Most of these men burst from the profoundest obscurity onto the pages of history, propelled by cataclysmic historical events, the way the Himalayas were thrown skyward by the tectonic collision of a broken-off chunk of Africa with the land mass of Asia. The only thing they had in common was that lowest common denominator of political calculus: the instinct to cling to power at all costs.

Unfortunately, few of the men who would come to lead the Third World in the second half of the twentieth century had anything resembling what Russians term a "political culture." There was no tradition of compromise; no understanding of the need to accept dissenting views; no ability to accommodate different positions within one party; no comprehension that there could actually be such a thing as a loyal opposition party or that government or media critics might not all be agents of the CIA, KGB or MI6. None of them had any sense of political direction or purpose, or awareness of the need to build enduring institutions—courts, a free press, independent universities, or opposition political parties—and certainly they gave no thought at all to providing the public with the kind of political education that would allow them, one day, to assume a larger share of the management of their societies.

Standing before me in Toronto were just such men. However splendid their faith, determination, and courage against daunting odds, however unmistakable their will to defeat savage injustice, these Afghans clearly lacked any knowledge of what to do with their country if they by some miracle actually won the war. All of them certainly failed to understand a basic fact of history: that big wars change everything. A nation, once having fought a full-scale, total war, will be irrevocably altered, and can never return to the way it was in the past. Yet these men were fighting precisely to restore a society that was dying, or already dead.

They truly believed that, once the hated Communists were all killed or driven out, Afghanistan would simply resume its antique ways. The ungodly twentieth century, with its dangers that could not be killed by bullets, would be repelled. The old ruling class—warlords, religious leaders, local nobles, perhaps even the weak king, Zahir Shah—could revert to the familiar, constrained chaos that was Afghanistan before 1979.

I asked Professor Rabbani and the other leaders what form of government they would create in a liberated Afghanistan. None could answer more than to say, "Allah will guide our hands...we will build a government according to the sharia (Islamic Law)...we will be a nation of Muslims." Was there any Islamic nation that could serve as a role model? No. None. Egypt was corrupt; so was Pakistan. Turkey was not even a Muslim nation, having been "bought" by the Western infidels.

These answers left me uneasy, though at the time they did not seem particularly important. But in fact, they were a harbinger of the disaster to come to Afghanistan a decade later. A thousand tomorrows would be concerned with battle against the Soviets and their Communist satraps. Victory, if it were ever realized, was many years, or even decades, away. Ammunition was a far more pressing concern than political science. I told the Afghans I would do all in my power to make their cause known to the world.

As I was leaving, I said to Rabbani, "Inshallah, we will meet one day in Kabul." "Inshallah, my friend." He laughed with pleasure. "And perhaps in free Kashmir, as well," he added. The professor held my hand, and searched my face with his dark eyes for a long time. Muslims call this "reading the soul." In this manner, some Muslims have an uncanny ability to judge a person's motives and trustworthiness. I have had this done to me many times in my years among Muslim peoples, from Algeria to Indonesia, where studying a man's face, "reading his soul," is said to offer a surer bond than a battalion of lawyers or a library of contracts.

"You are now one of us," said Rabbani. "May Allah bless and protect you." I embraced each of the Afghan leaders. I walked outside, from one world into another. The time-lock snapped shut behind me: I was again back in the twentieth century. The wind off the lake had picked up, and it had grown much colder. Leaves flew up in spirals around the birches. Afghanistan again seemed two planets away.

Yet as I drove home, I kept hearing "Afghanistan" echoing in my mind. A great jihad had begun. I could not say precisely why, but I knew without a doubt that I had to go and join this war in the mountains at the top of the world.

3
DODGE CITY MEETS THE
ARABIAN NIGHTS

PESHAWAR, 1986

Peshawar, capital of the North-West Frontier Province (NFP), the wildest city on earth, the borderline between the Middle Ages and the twentieth century. I loved Peshawar the minute I laid eyes on its slim minarets, its bulbously domed palaces, its dark, mysterious souks, and still darker alleyways. Take away the cars and vans that clog the city's narrow streets, and Peshawar has changed not a whit since the days of Kipling. Dust, incense, car fumes, sweet spices, and the reek of rotting garbage infuse its sultry air. A great din assaults the senses: honking horns, Pathan music, angry disputes, hawkers offering their wares, occasional bursts of gunfire, the muezzin's call to prayer. Women, veiled from head to toe in black, move like silent wraiths through the raucous crowds.

Walk down the Street of Leather, across the Street of Silver; wend your way through a barrel-vaulted gallery illuminated by shafts of dusty sunlight filtering down from the vaulted stone roof; and then go up the Street of Daggers. Cheap consumer goods from China trucked down from Kashgar along the Karakoram Highway, the world's highest and most treacherous road, are piled high. So are crates of Russian air conditioners, Japanese stereos, Korean rice cookers, French perfume, and un-Islamic brandy. Great woven baskets heaped with vermilion, jade-green, purple, saffron, and ocher spices. Rice of many hues, plump nuts, a cornucopia of dried fruits. Steaming, fly-covered goat carcasses putrefying in the rising heat of the day. Open sewers snaking down the long, winding streets, filled with black sludge and unspeakable refuse.

Tall noblemen—sirdars and zamindars—swaggering haughtily down the crowded alleys. Tough Pakistani soldiers. Chinese traders from beyond the great Taklimakan Desert. Fair-skinned Kashmiris. Belligerent Sikhs with bristling black beards and orange turbans, always ready to take offense at the least slight. Tibetan lamas and Ladakhi herdsmen. Shifty-eyed Iranians and regal Baluchi tribesmen who might have stepped out of the Old Testament. And even a group of petrified Japanese tourists in pastel polyester leisure suits, cowering together in abject terror of all the germs and wild men surrounding them.

At the point where the Khyber Pass debouches onto flatter land rises the ancient city of Peshawar: guardian of the pass, one of Central Asia's most important trading centres, and, since the dawn of history, a renowned nexus of intrigue. To this day, Alexandrian coins are routinely unearthed around Peshawar. At almost every sharp turn of an alley, or in the maze of the covered souks, you encounter fair-skinned, blue-eyed men who might be Swedes or North Germans, yet they are Pathans.

Though Peshawar is within Pakistani territory, such political geography is only notional. The Pathans do as they please within the NFP, which Pakistan calls "Pakistani-administered tribal territory." The only reminders of the central government in Islamabad are a few nineteenth-century forts dotted along the border with Afghanistan, whose garrisons struggle to keep the Pakistani flag flying over a region that knows no political loyalty, and to maintain the often disturbed peace among the fractious Pathans.

In the first quarter of the twentieth century, two wonderfully colourful figures appeared out of the barren mountains of the North-

West Frontier. First, a fiery holy man, with a delightful name: the Fakir of Ipi. The old fakir rallied the Pathans against the infidel farangi and came within a turban's length of taking Peshawar back from the British, who spent the better part of a decade chasing the elusive Fakir of Ipi through the mountains of Waziristan. Then there emerged an even more fearsome figure, the "Mad Mullah," who rode own from the Malakand Pass at the head of twenty thousand savage horsemen, determined to put the impious city of Peshawar to the sword. Only British aircraft and heavy guns managed to save Peshawar from the Mad Mullah and his holy warriors. The British press railed against these "Islamic fanatics" with the same passion as that found in the *London Telegraph* today, still denouncing the modern versions of such troublesome Islamic malefactors, Muammar Gadhafi of Libya, Saddam Hussein of Iraq, and Osama bin Laden.

Peshawar was to serve for nearly a century as the British India's main army garrison on the permanently rebellious North-West Frontier. From Peshawar, the British launched forty-seven major military expeditions into Afghanistan. All proved fruitless. In the end, not even the world's greatest power, Imperial Britain, could subdue the warlike, feuding Afghans.

I slipped into Peshawar after dark, to elude the many watchful eyes of the Soviet and Afghan Communist intelligence services. I spent the night at the inappropriately named Pearl Hotel; in the lobby, a large sign proclaimed, "Hotel Policy: Arms cannot brought inside the hotel premisis [sic]. Personal Guards or Gunmen are requested to deposit their weapons with the Hotel Security. We need your cooperation. The Management." Who could not like Peshawar? It was a combination of Dodge City and the *Arabian Nights*.

I visited the vast Afghan refugee camps that sprawled outside the city, where some of the 3.5 million civilians who had been driven from their homes by the war had sought shelter. This was a place of dislocation and squalor, but a more horrifying experience awaited. An Egyptian Islamic Red Crescent doctor took me on a tour of two hospitals for wounded mujahedin. "Up north"—that is, inside Afghanistan—there were no field hospitals for the wounded fighters. The admirable international group Medecins Sans Frontières had set up a few aid posts. These excepted, any of the tens of thousands of mujahedin or civilians who were wounded, and could not crawl or be carried to Pakistan, would simply be left to die.

The Peshawar hospitals, as I had feared, were gruesome beyond belief. They stank of putrefying flesh and gangrene. Bloody bandages and rusted bedpans were strewn across the floors. Beds, often shared by two men or three children, were soaked with brown dried, blood and green or yellow pus. Every third bed held an amputee. Many men and boys were missing both legs. They showed me their stumps and managed to smile or whisper a greeting. Others had shattered limbs wired up with clamps, or lay in traction. Many of the bodies of the patients had been peppered by scores of tiny steel darts from exploding anti-personnel bombs, shredded by shrapnel, or horribly burned.

What stunned me about this hospital was that not one patient, no matter how horribly maimed, made so much as a whimper. Even the nightmare burn victims of napalm uttered not a cry. As I came to each bed, an injured Afghan holy warrior would struggle to sit up and grasp my hand in both of his, wishing me *"Salaam aleikum"* (Peace be unto thee). Those who could not speak would smile at me, and silently try to move their lips in greeting.

I remember one great bearded man who had lost both legs above the knee to a Soviet tank shell. What did he need? I asked. "Please, sir, get me a pair of artificial legs so I can go back and fight the Communists," he replied. Time and time again I heard this same answer. And I actually saw a one-legged mujahedin painfully...unbelievably...setting off from the hospital to make the long journey back to the war zone—on crutches. To another wounded Afghan with gangrene, I offered to go to a local pharmacy and buy antibiotics for him. "No, no," he insisted. "Get me my gun!"

These were the soldiers of Allah, the bravest men on earth. They had no material possessions save their ragged clothing and their rifles, but they had vast reserves of pride. They feared no man, and certainly not death. Each man believed that Allah stood at his right shoulder; Allah who was all-merciful, in spite of the cruel world that He had inexplicably created; Allah who would carry him to his final rest as a parent would wrap a sleepy child in his arms and take him off to bed. Afterwards, I stood in front of the hospital and wept, not just for the horrors I had seen there, but also for the heart-wrenchingly courageous, burned, broken, shattered men who lay so silently within. It was the most noble and the most painful thing I have ever seen.

That night, a curtained Jeep took me on a long ride through Peshawar's unlighted alleys, changing direction and doubling back to throw off pursuers, until we came to a low concrete villa in a quiet residential zone. Mujahedin guards prowled outside, their AK-47s at the ready.

In an anteroom, Professor Burhanuddin Rabbani greeted me with arms tread wide, and a smile of welcome on his weathered face. We embraced. He had aged since I last saw him in that university apartment in Mississauga: his beard was now more white than black.

The "hopeless" war, Rabbani explained to me as we sat cross-legged on a fine Kerman carpet, sipping small glasses of sweet mint tea, was no longer hopeless. The Afghan people had risen en masse against the Soviets and their hated satrap, General Najibullah. His own forces, the moderate Islamist Jamiat Islami, had spread as far north as Mazar-e-Sharif, near the border with Soviet Uzbekistan, and west to Herat and Kandahar.

Professor Rabbani, a traditionalist who would later become president of Afghanistan, had become closely allied with the Americans, while his bitter rivalry with the mujahedin leader favoured by Pakistan, engineer Gulbuddin Hekmatyar, grew in intensity. Meanwhile, Rabbani's chief lieutenant, Ahmad Shah Massoud, a fellow Talik, was fighting the Red Army to a standstill around the strategic Salang Tunnel north of Kabul. In the south, Hekmatyar's Pathan Hizbi Islami forces were beleaguering Communist garrisons between the Pakistani border and the approaches to Kabul.

Most important, the "friends" that Mojadidi had told me would come when we first met four years earlier had finally arrived, and were hard at work. You could see them in Islamabad, around the vast Ojhri arms depot run by the Pakistani Inter-Service Intelligence (ISI); and in Peshawar, particularly a few miles out of town, at the old American U-2 air base known as "Kanada," from which Gary Powers took off on his final, doomed spy mission over the U.S.S.R.

Tall, fit, gum-chewing North American men with sunglasses, crew-cuts, and nothing to say were all around Peshawar. There were some tough-looking British SAS types, and a motley collection of young Mideasterners: mainly Egyptians, Iraqis, Algerians, Saudis, and Jordanians. A contingent of armed Chinese "merchants" discreetly patrolled a large warehouse on the outskirts of Peshawar. Every night, unmarked military transport aircraft flew in from the south; landed at remote, heavily guarded sections of the airports at Islamabad and Peshawar, and disgorged concealed cargoes under cover of darkness.

The secret war was under way. Britain's MI6, the CIA, Saudi intelligence, Chinese military intelligence, and Pakistan's ISI were in full swing with their covert campaign to train, organize, arm, coordinate, and supply the various mujahedin factions. The arms pipeline had opened, and through it flowed hundreds of millions of dollars of small arms, munitions, and war supplies.

"We can win this war, inshallah," Rabbani told me, as the hot light of a kerosene lantern played on the silver threads woven into the fabric of his grey silk turban. "But we must find some way to fight the Hinds. We can do nothing...nothing...against those terrible machines."

The much-feared Hinds were really flying tanks: even the big 12.7 mm heavy AA guns supplied by China couldn't penetrate the Hinds' thick armour plate. The gunships could deliver devastating fire on fixed or moving targets, using advanced optical sighting systems to target their 23 mm Gaffing guns, and the pods of anti-personnel rockets, packed with thousands of needle-sharp flechettes, slung beneath their stubby wings.

In addition to the Hinds, the Soviet and Afghan air forces had large numbers of highly effective SU-25 Frogfoot armored ground attack aircraft, as well as squadrons of older MIGS and Sukhoi fighters. The open, treeless terrain of Afghanistan provided little cover for mujahedin bands. Once located, they were pursued relentlessly by a combination of Hinds and jets. If the mujahedin holed up in rocks or caves, special Soviet commando units would be air-assaulted in by helicopter, to first surround and then kill them all, sometimes using poison gas.

By mid-1986, the Soviets had perfected their counter-insurgency tactics, sharply reducing the flow of Western arms to the mujahedin, and threatening the very survival of the jihad. Infantry backed by heavy artillery positioned in fortified fire bases would garrison all urban areas and larger villages. Armoured units would keep the main roads open. Elite hunter-killer teams, using Hinds and aircraft, would then track down and liquidate the mujahedin in the field.

Rabbani looked profoundly sad and spoke with immense pain in his voice. More than a million of his people—one in fifteen—had been killed, and his country laid waste. Three and a half million were refugees. Victory was still only a dream. And a new danger had crept into the Afghan war: tribal rivalry and growing animosity between the mujahedin commanders.

Unbeknownst to the mujahedin, Soviet KGB teams that specialized in stirring ethnic or tribal conflict were committing provocations designed to turn the seven mujahedin groups against one another. The KGB staged carefully calibrated assassinations, ambushes, and raids, complete with faked evidence left behind, that convinced mujahedin leaders they were being attacked by other allied mujahedin groups.

Tragically, four years later, just as victory in Afghanistan appeared to be at hand, the various mujahedin factions, riven by ethnic, tribal, and personal rivalries, fell to fighting among themselves. This evil development would shape the course of Afghan affairs for the next decade, plunging the nearly destroyed nation into a bitter civil war that inflicted yet more suffering and misery on its people.

Equally important, the civil war would eventually draw Russia back into the fray, engage Afghanistan's Central Asian neighbours in the conflict, and lay the groundwork for the appearance of the Islamic fundamentalist Taliban movement. The seemingly unquenchable chaos and strife in Afghanistan would come to destabilize the entire region, nearly cause a major war with Iran in 1998, spill over into Kashmir in the 1990s, and provoke the United States to launch a war against Afghanistan in the fall of 2001. U.S. intervention in Afghanistan in 2001 changed the nature and importance of the conflict, just as America's intervention in the Indochina War after France's defeat had transformed a regional conflict into a war with international ramifications. What began as a swift U.S. "surgical operation" to overthrow Afghanistan's Taliban regime and hunt down Osama bin Laden, the alleged perpetrator of the 9/11 attacks on New York and Washington, gradually evolved into a six-year low-intensity conflict with no end in sight.

4
FADIL THE KURD

My friend," Fadil the Kurd said to me, grinning broadly, "you must come with us into Afghanistan. We will shoot the Stinger missile together. We will shoot down many Russian planes and helicopters!"

I had met Fadil in the early 1980s. We had kept up our friendship over the years, meeting in Peshawar and Islamabad. Now we were again in Peshawar, which hummed with the excitement of the war next door.

Fadil was a handsome man in his mid-thirties, broad-shouldered, erect, and of medium height, who wore his dark blond hair short and never appeared without stubble on his square jaw. His eyes were a striking blue-grey. He spoke fluent Arabic, Turkish, good Farsi, better English, some Urdu, and of course his native Kurdish.

After the Pathans, the Kurds are the world's second-largest tribal people. And like the Pathans, they are fierce, quarrelsome, and untamed, a fair-skinned people among those of darker hues, a nation of warriors seemingly destined to battle for all eternity.

History has been exceptionally cruel to the Kurds. There are twenty-five million, possibly even thirty-five million of them. No one knows for sure. Nomads to the bone, they will not sit still long enough to be counted—or killed.

Kurds, like the Pathans, are an Indo-European plains people whose Aryan ancestors migrated to the mountains of what is now eastern Turkey, Iran, southern Russia, Iraq, and Syria during the Bronze Age. Converted to Islam in the sixteenth century, the Kurds are ardent Sunnis, but have guarded their tribal culture and generally avoided mixing with their lowland neighbours. Throughout the centuries, they have fought endless wars to defend their mountain pastures, as often feuding with their own tribes as with Arabs, Turks, Armenians, Iranians, or Mongols.

Kurdish military prowess is legendary. Salah ad-Din, or Saladin, the great general who defeated the Crusaders, was a Kurd. Like the Pathans, all Kurdish males are warriors from youth and bear arms as a matter of course. Their enemies have justly learned to fear the ferocious Kurdish war bands, the peshmergas.

Kurds tribes never in their long history possessed a national state. They were scattered across the uplands of the Fertile Crescent, living a precarious existence in nations that refused to recognize their distinct identity and often treated them as backwards mountaineers or worse, bandits or rebels. The great oilfields of Kurdistan at Mosul and Kirkuk were exploited by others. As the Kurds are wont to say, they have no friends but the mountains.

The U.S. invasion of Iraq in 2003 and the overthrow of the Sunni regime in Baghdad changed the fortunes of the Kurdish tribes. For the first time, they found themselves in a more or less autonomous state under American military protection. They could thumb their noses at Baghdad with impunity and trade with whomever they chose.

The only danger to the new autonomous Kurdish mini-state—many Kurds called it the nascent independent Kurdish state they had long sought—was the constant threat of military assault by Turkey, which repeatedly vowed to prevent the emergence of an independent Kurdish republic that would ignite secessionist passions among its own restive Kurds.

Fadil had come from one of the peshmergas that had battled both Iraq and Iran. In the 1970s, the CIA, Israel's Mossad, and Iran's SAVAK secret police secretly trained and armed Kurds in an effort to destabilize Iraq. Fadil learned his English and his mastery of weapons from CIA instructors in northern Iran.

Later, he drifted away from the endless war against Iraq, and went to Egypt to study engineering at Cairo University. There, he became involved with the Muslim Brotherhood, the powerful underground Islamic organization that was politically conservative and intensely anti-Communist. In the early 1980s, the Brotherhood began organizing aid for the Afghan mujahedin.

Soon after that, the CIA and the Brotherhood began discreetly co-operating to oppose the Soviets in Afghanistan. The CIA supplied money and East Bloc arms, covertly acquired through international arms merchants and China; the Brotherhood provided skilled fighters and also opened doors for the Americans in the Islamic underground from the Gulf to Peshawar. Saudi Arabia, eager to oppose the Soviets and to channel Islamic ferment away from its borders, joined the CIA in financing the Brotherhood.

Fadil was sent to Pakistan to train mujahedin to operate Chinese-supplied heavy infantry weapons. His sharp mind, natural authority, and strong personality quickly resulted in his being given command of a mujahedin combat unit. He would often slip with his men across the border to mount night assaults on Soviet or Afghan Communist targets, or join larger offensives against important enemy bases.

Later, Fadil joined a carefully selected group of volunteers from various Middle Eastern nations for training by the CIA and ISI to become instructors in the use of the Stinger missile. This long, slim, shoulder-launched anti-aircraft missile was to prove as decisive to the Afghan war as the English longbow was at Crécy and Agincourt.

Finding some means of countering Soviet air power—above all, the deadly Hind armoured helicopter gunships—was absolutely essential; otherwise the war would be lost. Britain sent in teams of SAS men to train mujahedin in the use of their Blowpipe anti-aircraft missile. Like so many British-made mechanical products, it was heavy, cumbersome, too complex for the mujahedin, and virtually worthless in combat. So was the Chinese portable anti-aircraft missile that had been supplied to the mujahedin, a copy of the Soviet SAM-7.

The American-made Stinger, however, proved exactly the opposite.

The shoulder-fired Stinger could track a manoeuvring target up to about 3,350 metres (11,000 feet). Most important, the Stinger's extremely sensitive infrared seeker could lock on and hold a target at different angles, unlike less sensitive missiles that needed to be fired directly at the enemy aircraft's engine exhaust. Tracking fast-moving targets with the Stinger was still difficult, and required considerable skill, but even so the missile was remarkably deadly and proved the first effective man-portable anti-aircraft weapon. It provided infantrymen in the open the same decisive defensive capability against the danger of close air attack that bayonets and pikes had given them against cavalry attacks in the past.

The first teams of Arabs sent into the field by the CIA and ISI shot down a number of Soviet fighters and transport aircraft. Most important, their Stingers hit and destroyed two heavily armoured Hinds. The course of the war changed abruptly. The Red Air Force and the fearsome Hind flying tanks would no longer be able to dominate the battlefields of Afghanistan.

•••

Fadil had invited me to join his CIA-trained hunter-killer team, equipped with the new Stinger missiles. We crossed the Pakistani border at dusk and marched north for four days into Lowgar Province to provide anti-aircraft cover for a band of mujahedin attacking a group of important Afghan army posts.

We stood on a vast, beautiful plain. It was as flat as a table and covered by a delicate fuzz of green produced by recent spring rains. At the extreme horizon, encircling the plain on three sides, rose a great wall of majestic, snow-capped mountains. The warming air shimmered. Insects hummed about the red and gold flowers that dotted the plain.

Fadil pointed. "There, there, at about two o'clock." Squinting against the sun, I could just make out dark shapes approaching us from the north, moving fast in the cobalt-blue sky.

There was no cover anywhere. The dark shapes drew closer. Fadil watched them calmly through his field glasses. "Sukhoi-25s. Three!" These were Soviet-built, heavily armoured attack aircraft, probably flying out of the huge Bagram air base near Kabul. The 25s were configured for ground attack, carrying cannon, rockets, and anti-personnel bombs.

The Sukhois were coming because another group of mujahedin had just shelled and were assaulting an isolated Soviet outpost a mile to the west of us. Fadil and his team were in an overwatch position, providing air defense cover for the attack.

Intent on the besieged outpost, the Soviet pilots failed to see our group. They deployed their dive brakes, slowed down, and prepared for a strafing run on the mujahedin attacking the outpost's heavily wired perimeter. Fadil directed two of his men who held Stingers on their shoulders. He carefully adjusted their aim points: "Five degrees left, Selim .... Lead more, more wait, wait, wait ...."

"Fire," Fadil said, his voice flat and emotionless. The two Stingers launched with an intense backblast. They flew toward the three Sukhois, corkscrewing slowly. Their progress toward the Soviet warplanes seemed agonizingly slow. Surely the aircraft would be gone by the time the missiles reached their original aim point.

We heard an explosion in the distance, then a saw puff of black smoke where the Sukhois had been. The first Stinger had found its mark. The other one continued its flight, disappearing from our sight. Moments later, we saw a wing tear off one of the Sukhois. It nosed up, then began to cartwheel down, until it smashed into the earth. The two other Soviet aircraft immediately went to full military power, pulled maximum-G turns, and fled the scene at great speed. Soviet pilots were quickly learning to fear the deadly Stingers.

"*Allah Akbar! Allah Akbar!*" Fadil and his men cried out, shaking their fists at the fleeing Soviet warplanes.

•••

Fadil and I celebrated our small victory over the Sukhois at my hotel in Peshawar with a group of Muslim volunteers who had come to fight in the jihad. We laughed and joked, sharing the uniquely intense camaraderie and ease of soldiers. The petty squabbles and jealousies that divide the Muslim world into warring tribes were temporarily forgotten.

These were men of the Islamic International Brigade. Some ten thousand volunteers from every corner of the Middle East, and some from places as distant as Indonesia or Mali, had volunteered or had been recruited by the Muslim Brotherhood and various Saudi religious or welfare organizations to go and fight the jihad in Afghanistan.

They were not mercenaries. The great Arab oil rush was still on and educated workers of every sort were in great demand across the Mideast. Many members of the International Brigades had in fact given up good jobs and left their families to go on the jihad, just as young, idealistic Americans, Canadians, and Europeans had done for another International Brigade in Spain half a century earlier.

What moved men from deeply selfish Arab societies, where loyalty normally extends no further than family, clan, and tribe, to head off to war in the distant and dangerous mountains of Afghanistan against the world's largest and best-equipped land army? For some, the motive was no deeper than a youthful desire for adventure. But most of the volunteers were driven by two more potent forces: their faith in a militant, activist Islam, and their determination to avenge the humiliation and shame suffered for so long by the Muslim world at the hands of its two greatest modern foes, the Western powers and the Soviet Union. These Islamic volunteers aspired to undo on the battlefields of Afghanistan the defeats, disgraces, failures, and follies of a thousand years of Muslim history.

A decade later some of these same men, by now battle-hardened and scarred, would go to neighbouring Kashmir to join the battle against Indian rule. Another "Afghani" (in reality a Saudi) named Osama bin Laden, would embark on a quixotic one-man crusade to drive the United States from its Mideast raj.

Before going off to war, the men of the International Brigade were trained by military instructors from the United States, Britain, and Pakistan. Imams in the camps filled their ears with prayers and their hearts with the passion of Islam, teaching that being a true Muslim means actively advancing Allah's will on earth.

Many—certainly thousands—died in battle, or later of their wounds. Others succumbed to hepatitis, malaria, pneumonia, and a legion of other diseases. After the fall of the Communists, some stayed on in Afghanistan, mainly around Peshawar, where they joined religious schools, called "madrassas," devoting themselves to theological studies. Others, unwilling to leave their new fraternity of Islamic warriors and determined to advance the cause of militant Islam, went off to fight in Indian-ruled Kashmir.

The rest, seasoned warriors infused with the spirit of Islamic revolution, returned to their homes: to Algeria, Morocco, Iran, Lebanon, Egypt; to Jordan, Arabia, and the Gulf. Fadil, who as a Kurd had no homeland, returned to an adopted one, Egypt, where he vanished into the teeming slums of eastern Cairo to carry on his personal jihad. In all these places, whatever their origins, the veterans quickly became known as "Afghani": men of honour and courage whose faith had defeated the mightiest foe. They were spearheads of the Islamic renewal, the scourge of oppressors—soldiers of Allah.

•••

The Americans, Soviets, and Indians all agreed that they desired a weak, divided Afghanistan rather than a united one that might become the launching pad for Islamic nationalism in Central Asia. The great powers determined that Afghanistan was to return to its former status as a neutral buffer state.

The Islamic revolution had served its purpose, at least for the United States. Once the Soviets had been driven from Afganistan, and the threat to the oil-rich Gulf accordingly removed, Washington cut off all arms and money to the mujahedin. The Islamic warriors who had been America's ally, and surrogate army, were now denounced as

"Islamic terrorists." The United States and the Soviet Union/Russia quietly joined forces to combat the spread of political Islam. The evil Muslim genie was to be put back in its bottle.

5
THE SECRET WAR

RAWALPINDI, PAKISTAN

I'm an optimist," Pakistan's then-president Zia ul-Haq said to me in 1986, "but the situation could not be worse." Sitting in the den of his unassuming house in the Rawalpindi military cantonment, Pakistan's embattled leader looked remarkably calm and relaxed. The room was cluttered with books, newspapers, and toys that had been left scattered about by his grandchildren.

Dressed in a white shalwar and kameez, Zia looked like a mid-level Pakistani civil servant on his day off. The former tank general was of medium height, rather stocky, but muscular and fit from the tennis and golf he so dearly loved. His pomaded hair, just beginning to grey, was combed straight back. Zia's smile, which revealed flawless, gleaming white teeth, was intense, and notoriously infectious.

When recalling Zia, I always picture his powerful smile. But what struck me even more forcibly were his eyes and his hands. Zia's deeply indented eyes were surrounded by dark-pigmented circles, almost like a harlequin's domino mask. They would quickly shift from warm to steely cold; from, friendly and sparkling to hard and ruthless. His hands were like two chunks of rough-hewn marble, thick and strong; they attested to the tough, even brutal side of the general-turned-president. But then, no one with soft hands or a soft heart could possibly rule Pakistan, one of the world's most turbulent, maddeningly fractious, and unstable nations. Zia would make a marvellous friend, I concluded, and an exceptionally dangerous enemy.

Zia was also an extremely modest man, and a genuinely religious one. Among pious Muslims, modesty in appearance and behaviour is considered a cardinal virtue. Zia had none of the hand-me-down pomp of the British Raj; adopted by India's Gandhi dynasty and its successors; none of the ludicrous, nouveau-riche ostentation of Iran's vainglorious shah; and none of the demagoguery, hard drinking, and wenching of his predecessor, Zulfikar Ali Bhutto.

Zia was widely respected, even by many of his bitterest critics, as an honest man. This was a rare attribute for a politician in Pakistan, a nation steeped in the most pervasive and corrosive corruption, where political office was the golden staircase to self-enrichment. Almost unique among Pakistan's leaders, Zia died without leaving his family a fortune.

His mood that day in Rawalpindi was exceedingly grim. India and Pakistan were on the verge of war. Four hundred thousand Indian troops had massed on the border with Pakistan. Under the late Indira Gandhi (who had been assassinated in 1984, two years before), India had become the U.S.S.R.'s closest ally and the largest recipient of Soviet arms. The two enjoyed a "special relationship" akin to the old U.S.-British entente, and their alliance meant that all the best units of the Pakistani army were tied down defending the long, vulnerable border with India. Only two weak infantry divisions were left to guard against Soviet incursions across the long Afghan frontier.

By the mid-1980s, Soviet troop strength in Afghanistan had risen to 140,000 men. Resistance to the occupation, though fierce, was fragmented and had largely been contained to rural areas. The Soviets were busy building major bases in remote southwestern Afghanistan at Farah and Shindand: their purpose could only be to support a major military thrust into western Pakistan and the Gulf. At Shindand, the Soviets had also set up highly sophisticated electronic warfare systems and medium-range missiles.

"Shindand," Zia explained to me, "is only 500 kilometres [300 miles] from our port at Gwadar—maybe four days, at most, by tank." Gwadar lay on the Arabian Sea, next to Iranian Baluchistan, west of Pakistan's main port, Karachi. The warm waters of the Arabian Sea gave onto the Indian Ocean, and thence to all the world's seas.

Russia's—and now the Soviet Union's—historic grand strategy is to expand to all of its potential maritime borders, Zia continued. Five hundred years earlier, the U.S.S.R. had begun as Rus, a collection of landlocked principalities around Kiev and Novgorod.

Ever since Tsar Ivan IV (the Terrible) united the Russian state in the sixteenth century, it had pressed relentlessly outward: down the Volga to conquer the lands of the Muslim Mongol Golden Horde around Astrakhan and the Caspian; south to Rostov, to Kerch on the Black Sea, and to the Muslim Khanate of the Crimea; then northwest, to the shores of the Baltic, and east across Siberia to the distant Pacific Ocean. In the 1840s, the Russian Empire again began to expand southeast, into Muslim Turkestan, a vast area of steppe and mountain stretching from the Caspian to China. And on into the wild Caucasus, where warlike Muslim mountaineers—Dagestanis, Chechen, Ingush, Cherkess—rose in a holy war against the Russian invaders. Their heroic resistance continues to our own day.

Zia took a piece of triangular red plastic from his bookcase and held it flat against the wall map, point upward. "This is the course of Russian expansion into our part of the world over the past two hundred years. Moscow's expansion into Muslim Central Asia has been relentless. Look at the dates of the fall of the Muslim Khanates: Bukhoro 1848, Tashkent 1851, Samarkand 1853, Balkh 1865, Khiva 1868." Each year, the Czar's armies moved closer to the Himalayas, to India, and to the Arabian Sea. It took the Afghan tribes and the power of the British Indian Raj to finally halt—or delay—the Russian drive south, the long, hard-fought struggle for Central Asia that Kipling called the "Great Game."

Russia could wait years, even a century, to attain its strategic goal, said Zia. "One day, Russia will reach the southern shore." The general went to a bookcase and extracted a slim volume. "This book—it's a statement of Soviet foreign policy—was given to me by the ambassador. He said to me, 'Your Excellency, this is our foreign policy. You can take this book and read it one hundred years from now, and nothing will have changed. Your American friends change policy every year. Russia's policy never alters. You should remember this!' "

As a writer on naval strategy, I immediately understood Zia's argument. By the early nineteenth century, the fleets of the Russian Empire had managed to secure access to all the world's great oceans and seas save two: the Mediterranean and the Indian Ocean. And for these two great bodies of water, Russia's czars ached with desire, knowing that when Russia finally reached its historic goal of the "warm waters," the

Third Rome would truly rule the world. The collapse of the Soviet Union in 1991 delayed this grand strategy, but it has no way changed Russia's historic quest to reach all its ultimate maritime borders.

Russia's four great fleets—Northern, Baltic, Black Sea, and Pacific—suffered from a fatal disadvantage: they could not concentrate. Their bases and operational areas were all widely separated. In time of war, none could support the others. As the 1904 Russo-Japanese War disastrously showed, enemy fleets could, by concentration, gain tactical superiority over each separate Russian fleet, and defeat them in detail, before they could join forces. To make matters worse, the Pacific fleet guarding the distant, thinly populated Far East was dependent on two vulnerable rail lines of the Trans-Siberian and Baikal-Amur railways for its supplies and communications.

Here was the classic military predicament of operating on exterior lines. The grand geopolitical solution to this problem was clearly understood by past Russian strategists.

First, seize Istanbul and the Dardanelles; then join with Serbia, a loyal ally, to gain the Adriatic coast, seizing the strategic Albanian deep-water ports of Vlorë and Durres. Successful execution of this plan would turn the eastern Mediterranean into a Russian lake.

Second, complete the drive to the south through Central Asia by reaching the shores of the Arabian Sea. The next step: establish a Soviet Gibraltar at Gwadar, in Baluchistan, or outside Karachi, and link this new naval base complex to the Soviet rail system at Tashkent. Such a coup would allow the U.S.S.R. to create the logistical base for a powerful Indian Ocean fleet, which would be the strategic nexus between the Pacific and Northern fleets and could dominate the Western world's oil artery from the Gulf.

Reaching the coast of the Arabian Sea would open all East Africa and Arabia to Soviet influence; then, once the strategic alliance with India was cemented, Singapore and the Strait of Malacca would be brought under Soviet naval guns. This final act in the historic Russian expansion would alter the entire geopolitical balance of the world, transforming Russia from a primarily land power into a genuine naval superpower, breaking the stranglehold on maritime commerce and naval power held by the Anglo-American affiance.

The occupation of Afghanistan was a breathtaking geopolitical gamble, the first step of a master plan that would ultimately mean the attainment of Russia's profoundest historic ambition. It was a move that could shake the world and make the Soviet Union master of both the land and the seas. The timing was ideal: the West quailed before Soviet power. President Carter might be ready to cede the Middle East without a fight. From southern Afghanistan, the Russians could almost smell the warm, salty waters of the Arabian Sea: only some poorly armed Afghan tribesmen, a thousand kilometers of Pakistani territory, and General Zia ul-Haq stood in their way.

"We decided," Zia said in his usual unassuming way, "that the Soviets would destroy Pakistan if we did not act." Pakistani military intelligence, was convinced Moscow and its ally India would invade Pakistan as soon as the Afghan resistance had been crushed. "The only reason the Soviets didn't invade sooner was that they had to secure their supply lines through Afghanistan from attack by the mujahedin." An invasion of Pakistan would not be possible until Soviet communications from Tashkent to the Khyber Pass were secured.

Abandoned by the United States, assailed by supporters of the executed Zulfikar Ali Bhutto, and threatened by a joint Indian-Soviet invasion, Zia and his right-hand man, General Akhdar Abdul Rahman Khan, decided the only way to save Pakistan was to confront the Soviets head-on in Afghanistan. Pakistan, an impoverished, backward nation of 130 million, would launch a covert war against the world's greatest land power.

General Akhdar Abdul Rahman Khan was one of the most intimidating men I had ever met. The director general of Pakistan's ISI agency briefed me on the course of the war and Pakistan's growing involvement. Pakistani army officers, seconded to the jihad, provided most of the technical services for the mujahedin: radio, logistics, medical support, ordinance, combat planning, and intelligence. I was shown films of ISI men in Afghan garb blowing up Soviet oil pipelines and microwave relay towers, firing heavy weapons, servicing arms and equipment, or directing tactical and staff operations.

Logistics were the single most important element in the war. Every bullet, every mortar shell or rocket, that was fired in Afghanistan had to be transported by trucks, then on horses, mules, and, finally, men's backs from secret ISI arms depots in northern Pakistan. Without the efficient ISI logistics network, the jihad would have been crushed by 1985.

Pakistani covert assistance turned the war from an inevitable defeat for the mujahedin into a bloody stalemate that halted the Soviet *Drang nach Suden*. Mideastern and American money continued pouring into ISI coffers to support the war. The CIA and MI6 quickly became allies of the ISI in the secret war. At its peak, in 1988, more than $600 million annually was flowing through the ISI to the mujahedin. And it was through the ISI and the Muslim International Brigade that the deadly Stingers were deployed, altering the course of the war and so greatly contributing to the ultimate Soviet defeat.

I asked Zia where he found the courage to face the incessant, furious Soviet threats to invade and "punish" Pakistan. "I stay calm. I am a Muslim. I believe that Allah defends the just, and our cause is just." Coming from a Western political leader, such words would cloy and reek of hypocrisy. But Zia was a passionate Muslim who ardently believed in what he said and truly thought of himself as a Muslim soldier whose duty, as the Koran says, is to defend the Muslim community when it is attacked. "My faith and my people's faith gives me strength to fight against odds that are"—Zia smiled his big smile—"impossible."

Zia and Akhdar made the impossible happen. Thanks to them, and to the heroism of the mujahedin and the Afghan people (of whom 1.5 million became shahi (martyred) in the Great Jihad), and thanks also to the Stingers, the Islamic Brigades, and Western and Muslim money, the Red Army—the most powerful military force on earth—had been stopped in its tracks.

When the U.S.S.R.'s new leader, Mikhail Gorbachev, came to power, he ordered a complete review of the Afghan war and its mounting economic cost to the foundering Soviet economy. Appalled by the stalemated war's expense, and bowing to widespread public anger over losses in Afghanistan, Gorbachev called an end to the conflict. By mid-1989 the last units of the Soviet army crossed out of Afghanistan over the bridge at Termez.

Defeat in Afghanistan shattered the myth of Soviet military invincibility in the most humiliating possible manner: the ever-victorious Red Army had not been beaten by the redoubtable Germans, or even by high-tech Americans, but by primitive tribesmen, and even worse than that, by Muslims, who are to Russians the most hated and despised of people. It would be as if a ragtag army of Puerto Ricans and Mexicans had defeated America in a war.

The demoralized Soviet soldiers who returned from Afghanistan also brought back with them a political virus that would soon infect and then destroy the entire Soviet Union. The Communist empire was bankrupt, corrupt, frozen rigid by incompetence, laziness, cynicism, and despair. On the outside it seemed virile and aggressive. But like *The Wizard of Oz*, it was all sound and coloured smoke. As the Russians retreated from Kabul, a great wind arose and raced across the Russian heartland, sweeping all before its fury.

The storm from Afghanistan blew down the Potemkin village that was the Soviet Union. It blew away the ingrained, pervasive fear that had held the rickety Soviet system together. When the fear was dispelled, the many peoples of the U.S.S.R. opened their eyes and saw that they lived not in a bountiful, heroic state, but in a vast, dilapidated ruin, a modern version of the moribund Ottoman Empire. The U.S.S.R.'s subject races and nations saw Moscow humbled by primitive Afghans and promptly decamped from the union, no longer terrified of a punitive invasion by the Red Army, or midnight arrests by the KGB. Local chiefs and party bosses in the republics—collectively known as "mafias"—concluded they were better off without Moscow, and could keep their wealth at home instead of paying it into the Kremlin's coffers. The generational revolution that was sweeping Eastern Europe hit the Soviet Union full force, bringing down its elderly, discredited power structure.

Three years after the last Soviet troops left Afghanistan, the Soviet Union and the once mighty Communist Party, having run out of lies, and no longer able to inspire fear, simply collapsed from internal rot and oozed away into the gutter of history.

The Soviet Union and communism probably would not have fallen so soon without the blows struck by Zia ul-Haq, who decided to draw his sword and stand almost single-handedly to face the world's greatest and most ruthless land power. The heroic Polish uprising, secretly organized and financed by the Vatican, and President Ronald Reagan's decision to engage the U.S.S.R. in a massive and ultimately ruinous arms race, had undermined Soviet power. Zia and the mujahedin delivered the death blow to the Soviet Empire.

Without Zia, there would have been no victory in Afghanistan. Had the secret war not been waged, the Soviets might have reached the warm waters of the Arabian Sea by 1988. In many ways, the victory of

Zia and the mujahedin in Afghanistan was as great a historic triumph as the defeat of 110,000 Byzantine troops on the banks of the Yarmuk in 632 CE by fifty thousand Arab holy warriors of the great general, and first Saif-ul-Islam (sword of Islam), Khalid ibn al-Walid. In our day, another Saif-ul-Islam, Zia ul-Haq, helped bring down an evil empire that was the worst oppressor on earth of Muslims and non-Muslims alike.

Modest to the end, Zia kept the details of Pakistan's epic resistance a secret. In spite of having been fully briefed in 1986, I never revealed this remarkable story until the war was over, for fear of endangering the jihad and Pakistan's secret role in this epic victory.

The last time I saw Zia, I asked him if he planned to retire. "By 1990, I will have contributed enough." He paused, and then produced his trademark dazzling smile: "I will then concentrate on improving my golf and tennis."

But he would not have the opportunity. In June 1988, the Soviet proconsul in Kabul, Yuli Vorontsov, openly threatened that Zia and Akhdar would "pay personally" for the looming Soviet defeat in Afghanistan.

On August 17, 1988, a C-130 military transport carrying Zia ul-Haq, Akhdar Abdul Rahman, thirty of Pakistan's most senior military officers, and U.S. ambassador Arnold Raphael took off from Bahawalpur, in central Pakistan. Minutes later, the C-130 went out of control and crashed into the desert, where it exploded and burned. All aboard were killed.

Pakistan's government investigated the crash, aided by U.S. Air Force accident investigators. The FBI was brought into the investigation because the American ambassador to Pakistan and a senior U.S. general were aboard the doomed flight. The inquiry concluded that Zia's C-130 had been sabotaged by the introduction of a poisonous, incapacitating gas into the cockpit. Just as the FBI was about to open its own detailed investigation, the State Department intervened and blocked the FBI investigation, leaking claims to the media that the crash was caused by mechanical malfunction. This was to become the official American version of events, even though U.S. Air Force investigators flatly contradicted the claim.

The new Pakistani government of Benazir Bhutto moved swiftly to cover up or destroy evidence from the crash. The flight crew's bodies were never autopsied, but quickly buried. Key components from the aircraft vanished. Records were "lost." Senior officials appointed by Zia were purged en masse. It was as if a giant eraser had wiped away the memory of the general who had faced down the Soviets in Afghanistan.

Pakistani air chief Marshal Hakimullah, who chaired the inquiry, told me it was also his own personal view that the aircraft had been sabotaged, and the ensuing investigation short-circuited by both Washington and Bhutto's government. "I am afraid we will never find out the true story," he told me in 1996—eight years after the crash.

Zia had many enemies. Which of them murdered him?

In 1988, I had been one of the first Western journalists to gain access to KGB headquarters in Moscow. I asked two senior KGB generals if their agency had been involved in the Zia assassination. They denied any involvement, but suggested the Afghan KHAD had "played a role." This is unlikely. KHAD was a faithful satrap of the KGB and would not have mounted a major assassination without full approval from Moscow. In any case, it lacked the expertise and technical capability to sabotage Zia's aircraft by the sophisticated method that was used. India's intelligence agency, the Research and Analysis Wing (RAW), was also an unlikely candidate, being in a similar position.

This process of elimination leaves three possibilities. The first is General Mirza Aslam Beg, who was the sole senior officer to escape the crash, and other senior officials, acting in collusion with a foreign power.

The second possibility is the KGB. Over the past decade, I have heard from ex-KGB officers that the assassination may have been mounted by technical experts from Department 8 and "wet affairs" teams from Directorate S, using special unidentifiable gases perfected by KGB laboratories, like the cyanide compounds used to assassinate Ukrainian nationalists in West Germany. More recently, Ukraine's new reformist, anti-communist president, Viktor Yushchenko was poisoned with highly toxic dioxin. A defector from KGB, Alexander Litvinenko, was murdered in London in November 2006, with radioactive polonium-210. Livinenko has claimed the Moscow apartment bombings in 1999 used to justify Russia's second invasion of Chechnya were staged by KGB/FSB agents.

According to the reports I heard, three KGB assassination teams had been assigned to kill Zia. They were ordered to stay in a constant of readiness, waiting for an opportunity to strike. Shortly after Volontsov's threat against Zia, Soviet foreign minister Eduard Shevardnadze warned

Pakistan that its continued support for the mujahedin would "not go unpunished." Shevardnadze denied in a 1994 interview with me that he had had any part in Zia's assassination.

Six weeks after Zia was killed, Vladimir Kryuchkov was promoted to chairman of the KGB by Mikhail Gorbachev. Kryuchkov was head of the KGB's first chief directorate, to which Department 8 and Directorate S belonged.

The third and last possibility: a majority of Pakistanis believe to this day that Zia was murdered by the United States. Zia had ambitions for Pakistan to dominate Afghanistan, and then to go on to assume the leadership of the Muslim peoples of Central Asia. Neither Moscow nor Washington wanted to see a Pakistani-led Islamic Risorgimento to in Asia. The victorious Zia clearly threatened the tacit agreement between the United States and the U.S.S.R. to demilitarize and isolate Afghanistan, as well as to leave the ex-Soviet republics of Central Asia within Moscow's sphere of influence.

In short, Zia had become a dangerous inconvenience. Pakistan and the mujahedin had served their purpose and were no longer needed. If FBI investigators discovered that Zia had, in fact, been murdered by the KGB, the trail of guilt would lead right to the man who would have had to authorize the murder: Mikhail Gorbachev. But Gorbachev was now ending the Cold War and dismantling the once menacing Soviet Empire. Accusing the Soviets of involvement in Zia's assassination might very likely derail START arms-reductions negotiations.

No one in Washington wanted to embarrass or undermine the new Soviet leader, or endanger the fragile détente between the superpowers.

After the assignation attempt on Pope John Paul II, U.S. and European investigators had similarly shied away from following the evidence trail that led, via Bulgaria, to Moscow.

The investigation of Zia's murder has gone cold. I asked former Pakistani prime minister Benazir Bhutto why her government had not continued the investigation and had apparently destroyed evidence relating to it. "It was an accident, that's all. There was no point in investigation further," she told me, adding a curious epilogue about Zia's body having been found in a river and a box of stones being buried in his grave.

My own view is that the most probable cause of Zia's assassination was a secret compact between Washington and Moscow to eliminate the Pakistani leader, made during U.S.-Soviet negotiations at Geneva, Switzerland, in the spring of 1988, to end the war in Afghanistan.

Zia was immediately replaced by the U.S.-educated Bhutto, darling of the Western media, enemy of Islamic forces, and a compliant ally of Washington. She could be counted on to keep the Pax Americana in South Asia. Rarely has there been a neater or more complete transfer of power than that between the Zia regime and Bhutto.

Another ISI director, General Hamid Gul, who had directed secret operations in Afghanistan, told me a decade later he was convinced the United States had assassinated Zia ul-Haq, probably with help from the Bhutto family and other senior officials. Zia, claims General Gul, had to die because he refused to obey directives from Washington, and kept insisting the Soviet Union still remained determined to dominate Afghanistan and, eventually, Pakistan.

So, having served his role and become an inconvenience, Zia ul-Haq was "surgically" removed. Some day, the sordid details of his murder will emerge. As Henry Kissinger noted in another context, it is far safer being an enemy of the United States than an ally.

•••

The Soviet Union had suffered its first military defeat. While the West rejoiced in this historic victory, Afghanistan was left in ruins. Large parts of the country were devastated: villages had been reduced to rubble; bridges and irrigation systems destroyed; wells poisoned; farm animals slaughtered. Many of the ten million anti-personnel mines scattered by the Soviets remained active, rendering much of the nation's agricultural land lethal and unusable.

At least twenty-five thousand Islamic mujahedin and twenty thousand Afghan Communist troops died in the struggle. An estimated 1.5 million civilians, about 10 per cent of the total population, were dead. Five million Afghans were refugees in Iran and Pakistan.

The psychological damage inflicted on Afghanistan equalled the enormous physical destruction. Before the war the multiethnic Afghans had coexisted reasonably successfully, but now the fragile regional religious, ethnic, and linguistic mosaic of pre-war Afghan society was shattered. None of the Afghan leaders or warlords knew how to reassemble the jagged, jumbled pieces of what had once been a country.

Unseen by the West, the Soviet KGB's campaign to promote tribal turmoil had been a deadly success. The result was violent civil war in which all Afghanistan's neighbours, including Russia, intervened. After a decade of war against the Soviets, Afghanistan was plunged anew into bloody conflict and chaos. The Afghans won the war against the Soviets, but lost the peace. Jealousy, tribalism, and the lust for power had replaced the holy war. It was a demoralizing spectacle, humankind at its lowest ebb: politics as usual. Victory had been thrown away; the Russians and their Communist Central Asian allies were worming their way back into Afghanistan. The world regarded the once heroic mujahedin as dangerous wild men and fanatics. Many Americans would even foolishly claim they should never have aided the anti-Soviet resistance.

The fragile mosaic of Afghanistan had been shattered by twenty years of war; it could not be put together again. The great powers used Afghanistan as a battlefield for their proxy wars, then left this once beautiful nation a smoking ruin, covered with millions of active mines, ruined villages, and warring factions.

Disgusted by the bloody mess in Afghanistan, many mujahedin, both Afghan and foreign, turned their attention to neighbouring Pakistan and Kashmir. A year after the Soviets withdrew from Afghanistan, rebellion erupted in Indian-held Kashmir. The explosion in Kashmir was spontaneous, but there is no doubt the Islamic victory in Afghanistan ignited the new intifada. Muslims across the world were elated, emboldened, and made proud by the victory over communism in Afghanistan.

If the world's leading conventional military power could be beaten in Afghanistan by Islamic faith and ardor, many Muslims reasoned, they could just as well liberate themselves from oppressive regimes everywhere else, be it from Egypt's pro-Western military regime, the Israeli occupation of southern Lebanon, Saudi oil oligarchs, Indian misrule in Kashmir, Catholic oppression in the Philippines, or Russia's brutal repression of the Caucasus.

Accordingly, small numbers of battle-hardened mujahedin left their bases around Peshawar and made the short voyage from Afghanistan to the Pakistani portion of Kashmir. Next door, in Indian-held Kashmir, Muslims were being ferociously repressed and abused by the infidel Hindus. It was the duty of all good Muslims to succor them in their hour of need.

A new jihad had begun.

6
ENTER THE TALIBAN

Almost everyone expected the Communist regime of Najibullah to collapse immediately after Soviet military forces withdrew from Afghanistan in 1989. But it did not. The Afghan Communists clung to power in Kabul and other major cities, uncannily resembling the isolated, moribund South Vietnamese regime after President Richard Nixon withdrew U.S. troops and "Vietnamized" the conflict.

Najibullah's troops, backed by a steady flow of arms, spare parts, and supplies from the U.S.S.R.; pilots, mechanics, and advisers from India; and air support from the Soviet air force managed to hold back the mujahedin forces. In 1992, the CIA and the ISI rushed the mujahedin into a final assault against the Communists dug in around the strategic city of Jalalabad, which controls the road to Kabul. The result was a serious defeat for the mujahedin, whose forces proved hopeless at a conventional battle that required planning, coordination, and cooperation.

Nevertheless, support for the brutal Najibullah was fast eroding.

Key Communist army commanders went over to the mujahedin, followed by pro-Kabul tribal leaders. The final blow to Najibullah came when one of the pillars of his regime, the brutal Uzbek warlord and Communist stalwart Abdul Rashid Dostum, changed sides after the promise of substantial bribes from the ISI and the CIA.

The triumphant mujahedin finally entered Kabul, proclaimed victory, and soon after broke into the UN compound where Najibullah had taken refuge, castrated him slowly, stuffed his genitals into his mouth, and hanged him and his brother in public. A cruel end, but one richly deserved by the Communist dictator who had murdered and tortured so many of his countrymen. Then, the mujahedin fell to squabbling amongst themselves.

For the next two years, the mujahedin managed to at least maintain an uneasy truce in Afghanistan. The nation quickly disintegrated into a patchwork of fiefs and armed camps, ruled by local tribal chiefs, religious leaders, warlords, and former Afghan army officers. After an interminable traditional tribal council, known as a *loya jirga*, the various mujahedin parties and other local leaders succeeded in cobbling together what looked, at least to outsiders, like a national government.

The mujahedin chiefs agreed to share power through a rotating presidency. My old friend, Professor Burhanuddin Rabbani, head of the Tajik Jamiat Islami Party, became president. The Pathan leader, Gulbuddin Hekmatyar, was named to the powerless role of prime minister. Behind the scenes, they and their tribal factions continued to plot and manoeuvre against one another, while Pakistan, India, Iran, and Russia sought to aid their respective Afghan clients. When Rabbani refused to step down from the rotating presidency at the end of his two-year term in 1994, fighting erupted in Kabul, and then across Afghanistan.

Rabbani and his military commander-cum-strongman, Ahmad Shah Massoud, held Kabul and Tajik territory in the northeast. They were backed by General Dostum and his ferocious Uzbek troops. The principal opposition to the northerners came from the Pathan Hizbi Islami, led by Hekmatyar, a favourite of Pakistan's ISI boys and the most effective field commander in the war against the Communists.

Gulbadin Hekmatyar, whose name means "Mr. Fix-it" in Pushtun, was a unique figure in Afghan politics. Unlike other Afghan leaders—mainly tribal chiefs, mullahs, or generals who wanted to return their nation to its pre-Communist past—Hekmatyar, a former engineering student at Kabul University—sought to modernize his nation by kicking out the old feudal, reactionary order and bringing in a form of Islamic democracy. He was also a devout Muslim and a nationalist.

Hekmatyar was certainly a mysterious figure. Tall, gaunt, and sallow, with big, sad eyes, and always sporting a black turban, he looked like a cross between Rasputin and a Goya saint. I recall vividly the first time I met Hekmatyar. I was standing quite alone at the end of a bare room in an ISI safe house in Peshawar, waiting for the Pathan leader. I looked away for a moment, and then back at the doorway. Standing in the corner of the dimly lit room was a silent Hekmatyar, smiling at me. Somehow, he had opened the door, entered, and closed it again, and all without a sound. He quite literally materialized like a phantom before me.

Not content with this trick, he produced one of my newspaper columns from North America and said, in quite good English,

"Welcome, Mr. Eric, I read all your articles on Afghanistan." Besides being the most effective military leader of the Great Jihad, Gulbuddin was also one of the most hated of all Afghans, on whose turbaned head lay innumerable warrants of death. The Soviets and Communists, of course, detested and feared him. But his greatest foe was Ahmad Shah Massoud, Rabbani's military commander, known to the adoring, fawning Western press as the "Lion of Panjshir."

Massoud was a charismatic, dashing figure who immediately charmed Westerners. He was educated, spoke decent French, was a well-educated Tajik, and looked a bit like the actor Robert De Niro in some North-West Frontier epic. Massoud told Western reporters all the right things: he wanted democracy, education, and women's rights. Gulbuddin spoke of holy struggle and the continued Soviet threat.

The Israelis, who then provided the outside world with much information on Afghanistan and Islamic affairs, early on targeted Hekmatyar as a potential Islamic menace. Gulbuddin was accused of being a drug runner, mass murderer, Islamic fanatic, and even a homosexual. While not personally involved in drugs, there is no doubt that many of Hekmatyar's men were. All factions were steeped in the drug trade, Afghanistan's only real source of money.

When Gulbuddin refused to comply with CIA demands over Afghanistan's political future and refused to renounce plans to bring Islamic revolution to the Central Asian Communist states, he became the target of American hostility. Hekmatyar claimed to me that the CIA had tried to assassinate him on three occasions, once exploding a powerful truck bomb in Kabul that caused numerous deaths and casualties.

While the Western media extolled Massoud as the hero who won the war against the Soviets, the facts were otherwise. As the conflict was still raging, Massoud suddenly announced a cease-fire with the Soviets that was to last until the war's end. His abandonment of the anti-Soviet coalition was a major blow to the resistance. Massoud controlled the southern end of the strategic Salang Tunnel, the main artery from the Tajikistan border to Kabul, and the most important Soviet supply route in Afghanistan. The ISI had repeatedly tried to blow up the tunnel, but failed. Massoud's surprise deal with Moscow assured the safety of Salang and vital Soviet supply lines.

Massoud's defection to the Soviets had been caused by personal animosity and jealousy between him and Hekmatyar, and by an ominous series of gunfights, ambushes, and killings between Tajik and Pathan mujahedin. The Soviet KGB got wind of this growing ethnic animosity and cleverly played upon it, staging provocations and offering to make Massoud their main ally and ruler of Afghanistan. As far as the Pathan mujahedin were concerned, Massoud was a traitor. They would spit on the ground at the mere mention of his name. Massoud's defection was to have important consequences for Afghanistan in the mid-1990s, and again in 2001. Memories of Soviet KGB officers and generals have by now confirmed that Massoud closely collaborate with Soviet and intelligence in an effort to become the leader of Afghanistan. He was also discreetly aided by France's intelligence service.

Massoud's assassination by agents of Osama bin Laden in September 2001, was hailed by most non-Tajik Afghans as extermination of a notorious traitor who was the tool of foreign powers. His bitter rival, Gulbuddin Hekmatyar, went on to become Afghanistan's postwar prime minister, then a major opponent of the U.S. occupation and a key ally of Taliban in its anti-Western resistance. He remains marked for death by CIA, which has twice failed to kill him by means of Predator missile-firing drones.

The failure of Rabbani's Jamiat Islami to share power with other tribal factions plunged Afghanistan into civil war. The Tajiks and Uzbeks, led by Massoud and Dostum, battled Gulbuddin's Pathans in and around Kabul, turning the capital, which had thus far been spared, into a battleground. All sides, heedless of civilian casualties, used artillery and rocket batteries to blast their opponents out of sections of Kabul and other key cities.

Dostum unleashed his wild Uzbek tribesmen on an orgy of rape, pillage, and murder. Kabul was thoroughly looted and largely destroyed. Many thousands of Afghan women were raped, often repeatedly. At least thirty thousand civilians died, perhaps fifty thousand—the majority at the hands of the Uzbeks and Tajiks—but many, too, in rocket bombardments launched by Gulbuddin's Pathan fighters besieging the city.

The rest of Afghanistan dissolved into chaos and banditry. The only law was the law of the gun. In some places, tribal chieftains and warlords held sway; in others, rival bands of outlaws and feuding mujahedin. The chaos that engulfed Afghanistan provided fertile ground for opium growers and traffickers.

Before 1979 almost all of South Asia's opium crop was grown in Iran. But during the decade the Soviets occupied Afghanistan, many Afghan farmers, unable to sow their crops due to fighting and land mines, or profiting from internal disorder and lawlessness, began growing opium poppies. So did Pathan tribesmen in Pakistan's autonomous North-West Frontier Province. The technology to transform raw opium into refined heroin was quickly learned. In short order, Afghanistan equalled Iran's opium production of about eight hundred tons per annum and became the world's largest grower and exporter of opium and morphine base, the precursor to refined heroin. By the time the Taliban cracked down on opium growing, over two hundred thousand acres of Afghanistan were being devoted to poppy cultivation.

While being driven from Torkham to Jalalabad one day in the early 1990s, I was dazzled by a sea of bright carmine that blanketed all the fields and hills around us, as far as the eye could see. "What are those beautiful flowers?" I innocently asked, the quintessential New Yorker whose knowledge of flora and fauna came from Central Park. A large, hugely bearded Pathan laconically replied, "Opium, Mr. Eric." I shut up.

Afghan morphine and heroin poured into Pakistan, creating two million addicted heroin smokers, and passed through the great port of Karachi on the way to Europe and the United States. Afghan heroin soon captured over 60 per cent of the American market.

The heroin trade brought addiction, crime, and rampant corruption to Pakistan, which some began to call a second Colombia. Drug lords bought police, narcotic agents, and politicians wholesale. They lived in garish palaces, protected by scores of gunmen and, in some cases, small private armies. Corruption infected all branches of government up to the highest levels. The surging drug trade also afflicted the U.S.S.R. and later, Russia: a steady stream of opium, heroin, speed, and hashish was brought north from Afghanistan by Russian soldiers and gangsters, spreading addiction—and then AIDS—across the nation.

The CIA and the ISI—the mujahedin's patrons—inevitably became tainted by the drug trade. American intelligence officials were perfectly aware of the opium trade, but did nothing to discourage it. U.S. drug enforcement officials based in Pakistan were powerless to do anything.

The war against the Soviets took precedence over the war against drugs. In Southeast Asia, the CIA had quickly learned that opium was an essential rural commodity and mainstay of the economy. Guns and opium were the real currencies of the mountain regions where the CIA raised anti-Communist guerrilla fighters among the Humong peoples.

The CIA, like their French predecessors, were soon compelled to begin dealing in opium within Southeast Asia in order to finance their irregular armies. Many of South Vietnam's and Thailand's leading politicians and generals—America's closet allies—were also deeply involved in the opium and heroin trade. Drugs were an inextricable part of power, politics, and commerce in Southeast Asia.

Such became the case in Afghanistan and Pakistan, and later in Central America, where the CIA-backed anti-Communist Contra movement and the agency's star client, Panama's dictator Manuel Noriega, were also deeply involved in the cocaine trade.

The total breakdown of order in Afghanistan from 1992 to the present allowed the drug trade to flourish. Local Afghan warlords, backed by the various Pakistani police and security forces, and elements of the Pakistani Army, battled for control of opium fields, processing laboratories, and export routes down to Karachi. The 2.5 million Afghan refugees in Pakistan cornered a substantial portion of the drug and gun trade. Karachi, the heroin terminus, quickly turned into the "Chicago of South Asia," as local gangs fought for control of "brown gold."

Today, Afghanistan supplies over 90 per cent of the world's heroin. In 2005, its heroin exports surged by over 20 per cent. Certain members of the U.S.-installed government in Kabul, and many of the warlords that support it, are deeply involved in the drug trade. Taliban all but eliminated poppy growing. The U.S. invasion ironically revived the drug trade.

The "war on drugs" met the "war on terrorism"; the war on drugs lost.

•••

In 1993, while Afghanistan was racked by banditry, the drug trade, warlordism, and rape, a Pathan mullah from a remote, mud-walled village in southern Afghanistan assembled a handful of talibs (religious students) and sought out a group of bandits who had raped girls and women from a neighbouring village. Mullah Omar captured the rapists and executed them on the spot. He became overnight a hero and savior.

Omar, a tall, eagle-faced Pathan, was already a renowned mujahid, or holy warrior. He had lost an eye and suffered numerous grave wounds while fighting the Soviets. Mullah Omar was an Islamic and Pathan traditionalist, like many of his fellows, who believed in an ultra-strict interpretation of the Koran and the wisdom and immutability of tribal customs.

His assembled band of talib seminarians and ordinary tribesmen quickly grew into a significant fighting force. They soon imposed law and order over a growing region of southern Afghanistan, ending rape and banditry, and enforced the sharia, Islamic law, which calls for severe punishment of murderers, drinkers of alcohol, thieves, rapists, child molesters, adulterers, and fornicators.

The talibs' remarkable success in bringing law and order to southern Afghanistan soon came to the ears of the Pakistani government and just as soon became mixed up in Pakistan's internal politics. In 1994, Bhutto's government decided that the talibs—or Taliban—might be useful auxiliaries in Afghanistan.

The boys from the ISI controlled some of the mujahedin groups—notably Gulbuddin Hekmatyar's Hizbi Islami. The ISI was counting on Gulbuddin to kick the Tajiks and Uzbeks out of Kabul. Bhutto detested the ISI, a sentiment fully returned by Pakistan's spooks and generals, so she assigned her interior minister, Naseerullah Babar, to begin supporting the Taliban as a counterweight to the ISI's mujahedin. For the record, Bhutto denies having done so. The able Babar armed and equipped the talibs in Afghanistan. His men also began recruiting for the Taliban in the Pathan tribal territory in Pakistan's North-West Frontier Province where there were large numbers of Pathan refugees and Islamic religious schools.

•••

The struggle against the Soviet Union killed two million Afghan civilians and left countless orphans. Many of these orphans were taken in and sheltered by these Islamic schools, known as "madrassas," which were funded by charitable donations from across the Islamic world, particularly Saudi Arabia and the Gulf. It is the duty of all Muslims to give *zakat*, a percentage of their annual income, to charity. Many millions of dollars of *zakat* flowed to the victims of the murderous war in Afghanistan.

Education in the madrassas was basic: memorizing the Koran and learning the rudiments of reading and writing. At least the orphans were fed, clothed, and cared for; without the madrassas, many would have starved to death, become serfs to the poppy growers, or been sexually abused.

Some of the Saudi and Gulf-funded madrassas were staffed by Saudis mullahs and teachers from Arabia, the cradle of Islam. These brought with them Wahhabism, a little-known Islamic sect from Arabia that was to play an important role in Afghan affairs from the early 1900s to the present.

Mohammad ibn Abd al-Wahhab was born into an Arabian Bedouin family in 1703. Wahab became an important religious teacher who developed and preached an austere, uncompromising version of purist Islam that harked back to the early Muslim era. Wahhab believed the Arabs and other Muslim peoples had become dangerously corrupted by their Turkish and European occupiers. Modern Islam, Wahhab preached, was weak and degenerate because Muslims had fallen away from the strictures of their original faith. The Islamic world would find renewal only in a return to the strictest interpretation of the Koran, total adherence to the sharia, and absolute rejection of all foreign influences.

Wahhabism is significant because it was the first religious and political manifestation of an awakening and renewal, after a millennium's sleep, of the backwards, mouldering Islamic world. A century later, two other Islamic puritan, revivalist, nationalist movements— the Dervishes of Sudan and the Senussis of North Africa—would raise the green banner of Islam and struggle to drive the British, French, and Italian colonial invaders from their lands. In both cases, the raw courage and burning faith of the Dervish and Senussi tribal warriors could not overcome the machine guns, artillery, and aircraft of the European invaders—no more than the Taliban's tribal warriors could withstand the onslaught of American B-52s in late 2001. Other Islamic uprisings against Western colonialism occurred in India, Egypt, Indonesia, the Horn of Africa, Afghanistan, Central Asia, and the Philippines. All were crushed.

Abd al-Wahhab formed an alliance with the ruling family of the Nedj region, the ibn Sauds, and converted them to his creed. Saudi-led tribal forces emerged from their remote hinterland and captured the holy cities of Mecca in 1803 and Medina two years later. In both cities, and in the now Iraqi city of Karbala, an important centre of religious pilgrimage for Shia Muslims, the Wahhabis destroyed all shrines, in keeping with Islam's anathema against idolatry. Interestingly, nearly three hundred years later, this same iconoclastic zeal would lead the Taliban to blow up three famed Buddhist statues in northern Afghanistan, an act that led to enormous worldwide outrage and consternation. This act in many ways sealed the fate of the Taliban, which was then declared an outlaw regime by most nations—the same nations that had watched unconcerned as Serb troops and irregulars dynamited Muslim mosques across Bosnia and Kosova.

At the heart of the Wahhabi movement was the Ikhwan, a body of warrior-preachers who resembled the medieval Christian crusading orders, such as the Teutonic Knights and Knights of Malta. The Ikhwan was modelled after the Ansar, the small band of devoted warriors and companions who accompanied the prophet Mohammed in his early struggle to bring Islam to Arabia. The Ikhwan was to continue spreading Wahhabism across Arabia until the twentieth century. These zealots considered all other Muslims to be *kufir*.

One of the modern Mideast's most colourful personalities, the British-born commander of Jordan's Arab Legion Sir John Bagot Glubb—known to one and all as "Glubb Pasha"—recounts in his memoirs how earlier in his career he had commanded the Iraq Border Constabulary fighting raiding bands of Ikhwan from Saudi Arabia. In a touching admission that still stirs my emotions to this day, Glubb wrote that of all the many decorations he received during his long and glorious military career, the one he most prized was "Defender of the Shepherds of Iraq."

By 1932, the Ikhwan finally conquered the entire Arabian Peninsula for Abdul-Aziz ibn-Saud, who then proclaimed the Kingdom of Saudi Arabia. The victorious Saudis drove out their bitter rivals, the British-backed ibn Rashids. The ibn Rashids—or Hashernites, as they came to be known—fled the peninsula but were given the crowns of the newly created states of Transjordan (later Jordan) and Iraq in consolation by Imperial Britain.

The Ikhwan rejected peacetime life and sought to continue its crusade by invading apostate Iraq, Transjordan, and French-ruled Syria.

King ibn Saud, who feared the men who had brought him to power, finally destroyed the Ikhwan, using armoured cars and aircraft purchased from the West.

But the Ikhwan's dour militancy lived on in rural Saudi Arabia and helped shape the Muslim Brotherhood, which was to play such an important role in the future of the Mideast. Wahhabism—sans the Ikhwan—became the state creed of the new kingdom and gave the upstart Saudis a political-religious legitimacy to which they cling to this day. Equally significant, a latter-day Ikhwani, Osama bin Laden, would declare a one-man holy war against Western powers involved in the Mideast and against Muslim rulers whom he deemed un-Islamic, corrupt, and hypocritical. Many talibs were inspired by the example of the Ikhwan's holy warriors.

For all the Saudis' current ostentation and often vulgar consumerism, the royal family still holds power and internal legitimacy as defender of the faith, defender of the holy places, and champion of the Wahhabi creed. In terms of modern Saudi society, this means the strict application of sharia law, segregation of the sexes, veiling of women, enforced religious observances, and rejection of corrupt Western influences. Wahhabism also means that the ruling family—as defenders of the faith—are the ultimate political authority so long as they are so consecrated by the assembly of religious scholars, or ulema, which they always are.

The Wahhabi missionaries in the Afghan and Pakistani madrassas thus inculcated into the orphans and other students their harsh, purist desert creed. Another key reason for the lavish Saudi funding of religious schools was their deep fear of Iran's political and religious proselytizing in Afghanistan.

•••

Ever since the 1979 Islamic revolution that overthrew the shah of Iran, Saudi Arabia had waged a covert war against Iran. Terrified that Iran would incite revolution in their kingdoms, and equally frightened that Iran's revolutionary forces might invade the Gulf, the Saudis joined the United States and Britain in urging Iraq's Saddam Hussein to invade Iran and overthrow its Islamic regime. Forty billion Saudi dollars, and secret supplies of arms, chemical/biological weapons, and intelligence from the United States and Britain, allowed Iraq to fight Iran to a standstill.

After the stalemated First Gulf War, Iranian agents dispersed into Afghanistan and Central Asia in a campaign to spread Shia Islam and win influence for Tehran. The United States, Pakistan, Turkey, and Saudi Arabia took great alarm: the Saudis were given the task of countering the spread of Iranian revolution. They poured money into Afghanistan, building mosques, madrassas, and funding numerous anti-Iranian guerrilla groups there, as well as fanatical anti-Shia militants in Pakistan. The Iranians amply financed their missionaries and Shia guerrillas inside Afghanistan, and militant Shia groups in Pakistan. An ugly little Islamic war raged—and continues—inside Afghanistan and Pakistan, producing yet more chaos and religious fanaticism. The bitter Saudi-Iranian rivalry grew steadily, roiling the affairs of the Mideast and South Asia. Today, Iran's growing power, and the current Sunni-Shia civil war in U.S.-occupied Iraq have added another dangerous dimension to this conflict, which threatens to spark a general Shia-Sunni war in the heart of the Mideast. Sunnis now speak of "Persian Safavid" imperialism, a reference to attempts by eighteenth-century Iran to convert Sunnis to Shia Islam. Many Muslim militants look in horror at the growing conflict between the two branches of their faith, calling it the product of Western divide-and-rule machinations and the historic prejudices of narrow-minded Iraqis.

In 1994, the success of Mullah Omar in bringing order to his territory led Pakistani Interior Minister Babar to ask the talibs to rescue an important trade caravan headed for Central Asia that had been held up near Kandahar. Mullah Omar and his men rescued the caravan and opened the trade route north. Support, in the form of weapons and cash, flowed from Pakistan's Interior Ministry.

This development both annoyed and intrigued the Interior Ministry's rival, the ISI. The spooks at the ISI were convinced that Bhutto was trying to do an end run around them in Afghanistan by creating a new guerrilla force that would supplant the Pakistani-backed Pathan mujahedin. This was probably quite true.

The ISI lost no time in befriending the Taliban and cultivating Mullah Omar and other clerics in the madrassa movement. Islamabad was also increasingly worried by the Tajik-Uzbek-Hazara alliance holding Kabul, which had become bitterly anti-Pakistani and was increasingly in cahoots with the Russians and Iranians. The ISI decided that the youthful, idealistic talibs would be more effective than the tired mujahedin, whose efforts were being devoted to squabbling, gun-running, and opium growing. Pakistan's Islamic religious parties also lent their political and financial support to the Taliban movement. So, too, did Pathans of Pakistan's North-West Frontier.

In short order, the ISI elbowed aside the Interior Ministry and fielded a force of talib militants, which was primarily composed of young male religious seminarians in their teens or early twenties, along with former mujahedin grown disillusioned with events in Afghanistan. The new Taliban was an improbable fighting force. Its raw recruits were orphans, outcasts, and unworldly tribesmen with no real military training and an extremely primitive, even medieval, view of the world. Most were from Pathan tribes of the deep interior and remote mountains, the most backward of Afghanistan's not very evolved people, steeped in medievalism and xenophobia.

Somehow, the Pakistanis turned this unmartial assemblage into what looked like a fighting force of about ten thousand men. A small number of old tanks, artillery, and even a few MIG and Sukhoi fighters were miraculously took provided the seminarians, who promptly ceased their devotions and took up arms. According to popular legend, the talibs advanced with a Koran in one hand and an AK-47 automatic rifle in the other, guided by the hand of Allah and the irresistible power of their pure faith.

A miracle did, in a sense, occur, though thanks more to the ISI than divine intervention. Led by Mullah Omar, the talibs marched on one town after another, sweeping all resistance before them. There was some fighting, but most of the Taliban's successes were gained through Afghanistan's traditional mode of warfare: the judicious payments of bundles of cash and guns to tribal leaders and warlords. Truckloads of cash from the opened the way for the Taliban advance. Kandahar fell, then Herat, then Jalalabad. The Taliban's foes seemed to melt away before the Islamic host. Small numbers of ISI men, and Pakistani commandos in mufti, helped the Taliban with communications, logistics, planning, and, on occasion, combat.

In late 2001, ISI agents, this time working for the United States, which was then attacking Afghanistan, bought tribal chiefs away from the Taliban, using bundles of much-coveted U.S. dollars, resulting in the rapid disintegration of Taliban forces in the north and defections among southern Pathan tribal leaders.

The Taliban swept all before it and took Kabul in September 1996. Mazar-e-Sharif fell when the Taliban took advantage of splits within General Rashid Dostum's Uzbeks. He fled to Turkey, which gave this major war criminal asylum in the hope of one day asserting its influence in the Uzbek region of Afghanistan and in Uzbekistan. Pan-Turkish nationalists, or pan-Turanians, claim these were part of the greater Turkish nation that stretches from Anatolia to the Great Wall of China—the region that used to be called Turkestan before it was invaded and annexed by Russia and China.

Ahmad Shah Massoud's Tajiks were driven back to their tribal homeland in the Panjshir Valley, north-northeast of Kabul. Massoud was saved by the timely arrival of arms, munitions, supplies, and cash from Russia and Iran, but his forces were eventually compressed into a remote corner of Afghanistan.

The triumphant Taliban had managed to more or less unify and bring order to Afghanistan after seven years of chaos and civil war. The Tajiks and Uzbeks were steadily driven back. By mid-1997, the Taliban had won control of 85 percent of Afghanistan. Mullah Omar proclaimed the new "Islamic Emirate of Afghanistan," though he modestly kept the humble title of mullah—small town holy man—rather than the far grander emir. Ominously, only three nations recognized the new emirate: Pakistan, its patron; Saudi Arabia; and the United Arab Emirates. All other nations, and the UN, maintained the fiction that President Rabbani's Jamiat Islami Party was the legitimate government of Afghanistan.

Once in power, the Taliban proved stunningly inept and heavy-handed. Watching the backcountry talibs try to govern from "modern" Kabul reminded me of that brilliant scene in David Lean's *Lawrence of Arabia*, in which Emir Faisal's army of illiterate Bedouins occupied Damascus. Unable to run or even begin to comprehend an urban complex, they first argue bitterly over loot and power, then withdraw into the remote desert, an environment that they understood. "At least the desert is clean," says a Bedouin leader as he rides out of Damascus. He could as well have been speaking for the Taliban, which feared and distrusted urban life.

The rural mullahs and their idealistic teenage warriors were intimidated by the big city, which was whispered to be a den of sin, debauchery, and idolatry. They were outraged and offended by Westernized middle class, particularly the women, who went about brazenly unveiled, in contravention of tribal custom.

The Taliban's retro-medievalism was a reflection of traditional Pathan tribal custom and a direct reaction to the communist era. To the naive talibs, any city dwellers who were too educated or adopted Western ways, and particularly "liberated" females, had to be communists. During the 1970s, the Soviet-directed Afghan Communist Party had successfully infiltrated the small Afghan middle and intellectual classes by championing social modernization, education, and women's equality.

Communist Afghan men shaved their beards; communist Afghan women went unveiled and worked in offices, stores, schools, and hospitals. They were thoroughly modern Marxists. In Kabul, leftist intellectuals drank whiskey and vodka, which traditional Muslims view with as much disapproval, or even horror, as Westerners do the public consumption of addictive drugs.

The Afghan Communists proclaimed that they were bringing modernity and equality to their nation. In fact, the Communists did promote education and better treatment for women, but not so much to help society as to advance the interests of the party. Much of the tiny Afghan intelligentsia, which included doctors, teachers, and artists, became Communists or supported the militant left. Kabul became a hotbed of leftist thinking and agitation. But the Afghan Communists were split between two factions: the primarily Pathan rural Khalq faction and the more urban Parcham faction that included many Tajiks, Uzbeks, and a few Hazaras. Feuding, and later outright warfare, between the Parchami and Khalqi was to tear apart the Communist camp and fatally weaken it.

After the coup that brought the Communists to power, Afghan Marxists filled the ranks of the new regime, as well as its armed forces and secret police. Attempts by the new regime to spread educational and social reforms to the countryside—and promote communism were met with outrage and bitter opposition from traditionalists. Local mullahs fiercely denounced the "godless Communists" and called on all good Muslims to fight them tooth and nail. In short order, education and women's improvement came to be synonymous with the evils of communism, which was responsible for the deaths of two million Afghans.

When the Taliban consolidated its power, it ordained that women in the cities were to work only in the home and had to be covered head to toe in the tent-like burka when they went out, lest they cause good men to sin by rousing their lust. Men had to wear beards to show they belonged to the faithful and were not sissified, Westernized Afghans, or, worse, communists. Music, films, TV, and magazines were banned by the Taliban's dour puritans.

Mullah Omar preached a medieval creed that often employed Islamic terminology to foster the most archaic customs of tribal Afghanistan, some of which dated from pre-Islamic days. Educated Muslims everywhere were deeply embarrassed by the Taliban's behaviour.

Educated Afghans, NGO aid workers, and, increasingly, the outside world protested loudly. Muslim nations that should have supported the new regime shied away in embarrassment. Even the Taliban's few foreign friends found it extremely difficult to explain or justify the behaviour of the obscurantist talibs.

But the Taliban did not give a hoot for foreign opinion or diplomatic niceties. These wild mountaineers did as they pleased and told the rest of the world, in particular Western aid agencies and their idealistic workers, to go straight to the devil. In fact, they clearly revelled in shocking foreigners and showing off their independence.

Few of the talibs could speak anything but Pushtun. Even fewer had any concept of the outside world or the need to project a positive image abroad. They were grim, sullen, inarticulate, and, often, simply dim-witted. To outsiders, the Taliban appeared to be struggling to comprehend the eleventh century, never mind the twenty-first.

While the world was put off by the Taliban's little Savonarolas, their medieval theocracy became a magnet for numbers of young Islamic idealists, restless Pakistani teenagers, disillusioned Mideast youth— many from the working class—and Muslim adventure-seekers, just as idealistic young European and American leftists had flocked to Spain in the late 1930s to fight for "freedom" and "social justice," only to discover that they were really cannon-fodder for Stalin. The Taliban appeared to offer the promise of a true Islamic state, Islamic social justice, and a pure society free of the foul corruption that infuses the entire Muslim world. To many Muslim militants, Afghanistan under the Taliban was, as they termed it, the only "free space" in the entire repressive Islamic world.

Unlike most of Afghanistan's other political and tribal parties, the Taliban was a genuine religious movement based on a narrow definition of Islamic law. The Taliban enforced public prayer and fasting during the holy month of Ramadan. People who committed minor violations of religious law were whipped. Adulterers and thieves were publicly executed, usually by stoning, hanging, or shooting, according to the harsh penalties of Islamic law.

Under sharia law, it is considered preferable to openly and severely punish criminals as an example, rather than to lock men away to rot in jail, as other societies do. In nations that enforce Islamic law, crime rates are extremely low, often less than a tenth of those in Western states. But such draconian practices horrified foreigners and brought international condemnation on the Taliban. Curiously, Saudi Arabia, which conducts similar public punishments, including decapitation, escaped world outrage.

In spite of its zealous excesses, the Taliban brought peace and order to most of Afghanistan. Rape was halted, so was banditry and prostitution. The crime rate plummeted. Corruption decreased sharply. A majority of Afghans, particularly rural dwellers, welcomed the Taliban's rule, which, though harsh and backwards, was at least honest. Better the peace of the mullahs than chaos.

The Taliban even made the momentous decision, based on religious conviction, to wipe out poppy cultivation and drug trafficking. This was a very perilous undertaking: in dirt-poor Afghanistan, many farmers only managed to eke out a subsistence living by growing poppies. Producing morphine base and transporting it to laboratories in Pakistan was a major source of employment in Afghanistan.

In spite of predictions that the anti-drug campaign would fail, the Taliban surprisingly succeeded. According to the United Nations Office for Drug Control and Crime Prevention, by 2001, poppy, opium, and heroin production in Taliban-controlled parts of Afghanistan had fallen to near zero.

The only regions where opium was still being produced were in territories controlled by the opposition Northern Alliance. This was the first time in the nation's history that the drug trade had been largely stopped. The United States, still waging its "war on drugs," quietly gave the Taliban $43 million in May 2001. Additional U.S. funds are said to have been given covertly to the Taliban. The United States congratulated the Taliban for crushing the drug trade. Five months later, when the United States was preparing to attack Afghanistan, as it claimed—falsely—that the Taliban was running the Afghan drug trade when it was in fact Washington's ally, the Northern Alliance, that was operating and rapidly expanding the narcotics business to pre-Taliban levels. In Washington's view, the war against Osama bin Laden and the Taliban took precedence over its much ballyhooed war on drugs. One crusade had pre-empted another.

Still, the talibs were grand masters of negative public relations. They were unsurpassed in modern history for bringing trouble down on their own heads. Their overt brutality, narrow-minded beliefs, and ugly behaviour quickly turned them into international pariahs. Behind the scenes, "moderate" talibs argued furiously with hard-liners. One such factional debate led to the dynamiting of the ancient Buddhist cave statues at Bamiyan.

The Taliban's mistreatment of women—veiling and confining them to home in the cities (but not in rural areas)—differed very little from the way females are treated in rural regions of Pakistan, Iran, eastern Turkey, much of Central Asia, and India—not to mention Saudi Arabia and the Gulf states. But to outsiders, the Taliban alone was the "Great Satan" of female abuse. Foreign aid workers, some of them undercover missionaries, and drop-in journalists with no understanding of the region often exaggerated the Taliban's bad deeds while ignoring its positive accomplishments.

In August 2001, a young Hindu boy and Hindu girl were publicly lynched in rural India, while a crowd, including their parents, applauded. Their crime: they had become engaged. The girl was of a slightly higher caste than the boy. For this transgression against India's caste system, they were put to death. While the world was lustily condemning the Taliban, three hundred million dark-skinned Indian untouchables were living a life of hunger, racial oppression, and ceaseless abuse. No one in the West seemed to care that untouchable women were being routinely gang-raped by higher caste men or murdered if they dared protest. No one cared about ten-year-old Hindu child brides or wives being murdered, often by being burned alive, to clear the way for another dowry-laden spouse, nor that an Indian untouchable woman dared not allow her shadow to fall on a Brahman, lest he be polluted. No American women's groups protested the lynchings nor the plight of untouchable women.

Mistreatment of Afghan women by the Taliban became a favourite campus cause. U.S. and European media jumped on this issue and so did politicians, who saw an easy way to win female votes. The flood of indignation blended nicely into long-held Western popular belief that Islam was cruel, sadistic, anti-female—in short, the world's leading oppressor of women. People who could not locate Afghanistan on a map were nevertheless seething with fury against the brutish, bearded Taliban.

After launching its war against Afghanistan, the Bush administration tried to whip up anti-Taliban fever in the United States by claiming that the campaign was in part designed to liberate Afghan women from the clutches of the Taliban and free them from the veil. No mention was made, however, of the plight of women in nations allied to the United States. Most Americans were confused when they saw TV clips of Northern Alliance tanks—supposedly U.S. allies and the "good guys"—whipping their burka-clad women, just like the "bad" Taliban.

The Taliban's enforcement of the wearing of the burka had inflamed females in the West and brought their wrath down on the talibs. Ironically, when the Soviet Union and its Afghan Communist allies killed one million Afghan women in the 1980s, there was hardly a peep of protest from women's groups, the UN, or university campuses. Making women wear the veil, it seems, was a worse crime than killing them.

Nor was there any international outcry in the mid-1990s when thousands of Afghan women were raped by General Rashid Dostum's Uzbek troops, a crime wave that was ended by the Taliban. The Taliban equalled male abuse, went the thinking in North America and Europe. Afghan women had to be saved. Few foreigners, however, spared any Afghan thought for the veiled women in other Islamic countries, or, for that matter, Detroit's Muslim enclave. Even fewer understood the idea that many Muslim women prefer to go covered—both as a symbol of piety and as a sign for men to keep away.

The West's simplistic outrage against the Taliban was underlined when U.S. TV teams interviewed a spokesman for the Northern

Alliance—America's new Afghan ally—who proclaimed his movement was fighting for the liberation of women. The Tajik-Uzbek Alliance, at least, was smart enough to tell the farangi TV crews what they wanted to hear. Standing in the background while this interview was in progress was a group of "liberated" Tajik women, covered from head to toe in blue burkas, just like Taliban women. The Taliban was too thick-headed and unworldy to attempt to counter either the wave of negative feminist publicity that was rushing down on it or anti-Taliban propaganda films, some made by Afghan Communists and widely aired in Europe and North America.

The tsunami of female outrage against the Taliban made the Clinton administration very nervous. When the Taliban first came to power, the United States was not at all displeased. The Sunni Muslim Taliban had a hatred for the Shia Iranian regime that was surpassed only by the loathing held by Iran's mullahs for the Taliban. And the talibs were friends of friends, the Saudis.

Iran was immediately convinced that the Taliban regime had been put into power by its blood enemies, the Americans, Saudis, and Pakistanis. The Taliban was a dagger aimed at Iran. The CIA, Tehran believed, was engaged in a nefarious scheme to "out-mullah" its own fire-eating mullahs.

The Iranians, no amateurs themselves when it comes to plotting and scheming, were certainly right about the Saudis and Pakistanis. The Taliban would scotch Iran's influence in Afghanistan and might open the way south for energy pipelines from Central Asia to Karachi. However, the United States, which had watched approvingly as the Taliban was assisted into power by Pakistan, remained uncertain about how to deal with the wild men of Kabul.

The Taliban, the United States realized, was a useful weapon against Iran and could open a second front against the anti-American regime in Tehran. The Taliban's fiery mullahs would draw extremist Muslims away from Tehran. Most important, America's big oil lobby was urging Washington to cozy up to Kabul in order to clear the way for its long-sought pipelines. Iran offered a shorter route, but the Israel lobby had mobilized Congress to block any attempts at a rapprochement with Iran, so Afghanistan remained the best alternative.

•••

The United States also had warily flirted with the Taliban for another interesting strategic reason: China. In the late 1990s, the People's Republic was being increasingly seen by the White House, the Pentagon, and the U.S. foreign-policy establishment as a future geopolitical rival—and possibly overt enemy—of the United States and a growing threat to America's sovereignty in the western Pacific. In spite of Osama bin Laden's presence in Afghanistan, Washington was tempted to use Afghanistan to vex and monitor both Iran and China.

In Sinkiang—formerly Eastern Turkestan, China's highly sensitive, westernmost province—the Muslim majority, known as Uighurs, had been resisting growing Han Chinese colonization for decades. Armed rebellion broke out in the mid-1990s. The United States considered intensifying the anti-Chinese uprising in Sinkiang by arming and aiding Uighur rebels. Stoking rebellion in Sinkiang would distract China from its confrontation with the United States and Taiwan and could serve as a useful bargaining chip in future negotiations.

The United States saw Afghanistan as an ideal base from which to promote a major anti-Chinese rebellion. Small numbers of Uighur fighters came across the narrow, mountainous Wakhan Corridor, which connects Sinkiang with Afghanistan, and trained in Taliban camps. At the time, these Uighurs, and other Central Asian insurgents, were classified by Washington as freedom fighters. By 2001, however, the CIA's project to fuel a large uprising in Sinkiang was put on hold, pending new developments. The Central Asian liberation movements were reclassified as terrorists.

Meanwhile, as the anti-Taliban furor grew in the media, on campuses, and in Congress, and as Taliban guest Osama bin Laden began to loom larger in the public's imagination, the U.S. government backed away from any further support for the fierce mullahs in Kabul. Afghanistan was increasingly referred to in the United States as a "pariah" or "rogue" state, and the Pentagon began contingency planning for military action against Afghanistan.

The Taliban as a movement was also feared and distrusted by most of Afghanistan's unloving neighbours. The Taliban's leaders, strongly believing in the Koranic admonition to assist Muslims wherever they were oppressed, provided sanctuary and training facilities to a variety of Islamic fundamentalist forces.

The largest and most active groups were Pakistani-backed Muslim militants fighting for the independence of Indian-ruled. Kashmir. At the time, only Russia backed India's claim that these separatists were terrorists. Most other nations saw the Kashmiri insurgents as legitimate fighters in an obscure war no one cared about—at least until September 11, 2001. To Pakistan, they were heroic freedom fighters.

There were also mujahedin from Central Asia who sought to overthrow the neo-communist, totalitarian regimes of these Russian satellite states. The most active group was the Islamic Movement of Uzbekistan, which was battling the Uzbek dictator Islom Karimov, whose regime has killed, jailed, and tortured tens of thousands of political opponents, both Islamists and those calling for democratic government.

Other Islamic and non-Islamic groups based in Afghanistan opposed the equally nasty regime in Tajikistan, a Russian protectorate, where twenty-five thousand Russian troops are fighting a few thousand Muslim insurgents. There was also a sprinkling of militants from Kazakhstan and Kyrgyzstan. All were branded Islamic terrorists by Russia and its Central Asian satraps. Only gas-rich Turkmenistan maintained good relations with the Taliban. A handful of Islamic separatists from the southern Philippines also took up residence in Kabul.

The Taliban proudly gave refuge to small numbers of Muslim Chechens. They had waged a desperate, ten-year struggle against Russian attempts to crush this tiny nation of 1.5 million. Most of these Chechen mujahedin were children or grandchildren of Chechens who had survived concentration camps in Siberia and Central Asia, the victims of Stalin's attempted destruction of the entire Chechen people.

The Chechens had resisted Russian colonialism for three centuries and were fighting on against impossible odds. Afghanistan was one of only two nations that opened its doors and hearts to the valiant Chechens, who had been abandoned or ignored by the rest of the world, most shamefully by the Muslim nations.

The Kremlin routinely slandered the Chechen independence movement as Islamic terrorists and later sought to smear them as allies or agents of Osama bin Laden, a claim that resonated in America. Russia's new leader, Vladimir Putin, had come to power after a wave of apartment bombings that killed three hundred people and terrified the nation by vowing to crush the Islamic (Chechen) terrorists. Intriguingly, a Moscow TV news team actually caught a team of undercover federal security agents planting a bomb in a building. Soon after, Russia invaded Chechnya—to which Russia had granted de facto independence—"to stamp out Islamic terrorism." The Kremlin claimed Osama bin Laden was aiding the Chechen terrorists. After the September 2001 World Trade Center and Pentagon attacks, the Bush administration would use the same language to justify its war against Afghanistan.

Boris Yeltsin's soldiers and air force killed up to one hundred thousand Chechen civilians and leveled the capital, Grozny, during the first Chechen war from 1994 to 1997. President Bill Clinton actually had the effrontery to compare Yeltsin's slaughter to Abraham Lincoln's actions during the American Civil War. Russia killed another eighty-seven thousand civilians in the second Chechen war, which has been largely crushed by the most brutal means while the world turned its back on genocide in the Caucasus. The United States initially condemned Russia for its brutality and war crimes in Chechnya. But after September 11, President Bush abruptly hailed President Vladimir Putin and Russia for fighting terrorism in Chechyna. Such was the price for Russia's so-called support in the campaign against Afghanistan.

•••

India had long opposed the Taliban, which it saw as a cat's paw for its hated neighbour, Pakistan, and helped the Northern Alliance, in league with its regional strategic allies, Russia and Iran. As previously noted, Iran loathed and feared the Taliban.

After Taliban warriors killed a number of Iranian "diplomats"—actually military advisers aiding the Northern Alliance—Iran mobilized seventy-five thousand troops on its eastern border and threatened—until tempers in Tehran cooled down—to invade Afghanistan.

China also watched the Taliban nervously, concerned by Kabul's links to Uighur separatists and wary of Islamic agitation, but also aware that the Taliban was a close ally of its closest ally, Pakistan, and an enemy of its enemy, India.

After the Pakistani-supported Taliban movement seized much of Afghanistan in 1996, its neighbours—Russia, Uzbekistan, Tajikistan, and Kazakhstan—delivered arms, munitions, and military supplies to the Uzbek forces of former Communist warlord General Rashid Dostum, in Mazar-e-Sharif and, later, to Massoud in the Panjshir Valley.

Russian military advisers served with Dostum's forces and piloted his small air force. It was noteworthy that, while Russia was begging loans from the West, it managed to find $2.4 billion to spend on the war in Chechnya, and at least $1 billion to battle the Taliban in Afghanistan.

Russia viewed the Taliban as a grave threat to the neo-Communist rulers of Central Asia. These newly independent states were still reliant on Moscow for military protection; their feeble economies remained linked to Russia's and dependent on trade with the Russian federation. As far as the leadership in Moscow was concerned, the Central Asian states had merely decamped temporarily from the union in 1991. Once Russia was restored to political and economic stability, Central Asia would fall back into Moscow's orbit.

Russia's strategy in Central Asia was thus to prop up the region's post-Communist dictators, universally known to locals as "the mafia"; keep Islamists and any other revolutionary political movements out; repress Islam and prevent its spread; and ensure that the United States and its allies did not push their way into Moscow's backyard, or as Russians called it, "our near abroad."

In a highly significant statement of policy that was totally ignored by the West, Moscow made clear in the mid-1990s that its strategic borders were identical to the old borders of the U.S.S.R. Any threat to Central Asia or the Caucasus would be considered a threat to Russia. In military terms, Russia's "near abroad" was still part of the motherland. Substantial numbers of Russian troops remained at bases in Central Asia and the Caucasus, where they were frequently employed to combat Islamic rebels. Twenty-five thousand Russian troops were based in Tajikistan to combat local Islamic rebels and guard the border with Afghanistan.

Afghanistan under Taliban rule threatened Russia's security and energy plans for Central Asia. The Taliban annoyed India and China. Kabul became a "mecca" for anti-American militants. It was only a matter of time before Afghanistan's enemies would take action to squelch the irksome Taliban. That moment came in September 2001.

•••

The attacks on New York and Washington were presaged, though it was not known at the time, by an attack against Ahmad Shah Massoud at his base in the Panjshir Valley. Two assassins, posing as Arab TV cameramen, were interviewing the Tajik leader when they exploded a bomb hidden in their camera. The assassins died; Massoud was gravely wounded and died soon after in a Russian helicopter that was rushing him to a Russian Army hospital in Tajikistan. Subsequent investigation led back to plotters in Britain and Europe, and strong suspicions that the attack had been mounted by Osama bin Laden's al Qaeda organization in order to decapitate one of the Taliban's most dangerous foes. After a period of shock and confusion, the Tajik arm of the Northern Alliance found a new military leader, General Muhammed Fahim, formerly a senior official of the old Communist KHAD, who was assisted into the leadership by the Russians.

Meanwhile, the Taliban signed its own death warrant in the fury-filled days after September 11. The United States, thirsting for vengeance, demanded that the Taliban hand over Osama bin Laden. Mullah Omar refused. Kabul had twice previously offered to send bin Laden to an Islamic court in a Muslim nation to face America's charges, but the United States rejected the offer. "Dead or alive," Bush demanded. Such colourful Wild West language delighted Americans, but Europeans cringed with embarrassment and worry that America was being led by one rustic into a war against another.

Looking back on America's invasion of Afghanistan and the overthrow of the Taliban, it seems incredible that Mullah Omar didn't accept the inevitable and hand bin Laden over to the enraged Americans. His failure to do so meant the end of his religious regime and the reoccupation of Afghanistan by the Russians through their proxy forces, the Northern Alliance.

But Afghans, and particularly Pathans, are notoriously stubborn and dig in their heels when backed into a corner. Mullah Omar reacted in true Pathan style, telling the world's greatest power to go to hell.

But why?

First, because bin Laden was a true hero to most Afghans. The Saudi militant had given up a life of ease and luxury to come wage jihad to liberate Afghanistan. He had been wounded many times in the holy struggle. Bin Laden had built tunnels and shelters for the mujahedin. He had used his fortune to construct hospitals and orphanages, help war widows, and feed the poor. In short, bin Laden was regarded as something of a saint by Afghans.

Second, the code of the Pathans—Pushtunwali—makes protecting a guest sacrosanct. Mullah Omar, who deeply admired bin Laden, often took his counsel, and refused to betray his guest. In the cynical outside world, however, no one understood this antique act of honor. American media pundits, who knew nothing about Afghanistan, wrongly claimed that the Taliban depended for survival on bin Laden and his small band of supporters.

Frantic attempts by Pakistan's president, General Pervez Musharraf, to convince Mullah Omar to bow to Washington's demands proved futile. Musharraf was a blunt-spoken soldier, not a politician, as I discovered when I interviewed him in 1999 (shortly after he seized power), but he was wise enough to understand that the United States was determined to attack Afghanistan and would destroy Pakistan if he did not accede to Washington's demands for base rights and political support. Musharraf had to take the fateful decision to fire his friends and fellow generals who had brought him to power, abandon his ally Mullah Omar, and join Bush's so-called crusade against terrorism.

In his memoirs, published in 2006, Musharraf claimed that after 9/11, the U.S. deputy secretary of state threatened war against Pakistan if it did not immediately abandon Taliban, cut off its supplies, and allow U.S. forces to use three Pakistani bases for operations against Afghanistan. This claim coincides with information that I received from other high-level Pakistani sources, including ISI. Musharraf even claimed he evaluated a possible war against the U.S. but decided to give in rather than see Pakistan "bombed to rubble."

The Taliban might still have saved its skin by claiming bin Laden had left Afghanistan and by placing an anonymous call to a newspaper in Somalia, Nigeria, or Sudan saying, "This is bin Laden. I am here with you to continue my jihad." This stratagem would at least have bought some time or wrong-footed the Americans. The United States had no evidence that the Taliban was involved in the September 11 bombing. Without bin Laden, the Americans may have lacked a *casus belli* to attack Afghanistan.

A Taliban spokesman did claim bin Laden had left for destinations unknown, but two days later another spokesman contradicted him, foolishly admitting bin Laden was still "our guest" in Afghanistan.

Had the situation not been so tragic and fraught with danger, the Taliban's behaviour would have been highly comical. Its "foreign minister," a twenty-something turbaned dolt who barely spoke English, muttered statements that made no sense. Next to him, in full view of TV cameras beaming out the scene to the world, was his interpreter, a monster of a man with bulging muscles, a huge bushy black beard, a piratical skullcap, and a black eye patch—an apparition straight out of the *Arabian Nights'* "Ali Baba and the Forty Thieves." All this sinister talib lacked to complete the image of Muslim malevolence was a giant scimitar in his beefy hands.

This public relations catastrophe and the inability to issue a cogent defense of its position in any recognizable language sealed the Taliban's fate. While the Northern Alliance's slick, shaved, business-suited, PR-coached spokesmen were winning the war of the air waves, the ignorant and foolish talibs managed to convince any doubters that they were public menaces and primitive ruffians who richly deserved to be carpet-bombed back to the first century BCE.

So unworldly were these hillbillies that when the first U.S. B-52 heavy bombers appeared over their trenches, they shook their fists at the impending doom from above and proclaimed that their courage would overcome the weapons of the new farangi, just as it had the hated, godless Soviets.

Blasted and assailed by the Americans and the Northern Alliance, the Taliban abandoned Kabul and retreated into the vastness of Pathan tribal territory around Kandahar, hotly pursued by the Northern Alliance and U.S. forces. Seven years after the Taliban erupted on the stage of Afghanistan, it evaporated with equal speed into the mountains of the Hindu Kush. Mullah Omar was being hunted by American Special Forces and Marines. The Islamic Emirate of Afghanistan was no more. But the Great Game to control the top of the world was certainly not over. A new act had begun.

7
BROTHER OSAMA

Deserts, as T.E. Lawrence observed, produce men and faiths that are fierce, austere, and uncompromising. Four decades after "Lawrence of Arabia" fought to free that region of the world from Turkish rule, another messianic, would-be liberator from the desert peninsula was born, in 1957, to a wealthy family in Saudi Arabia's capital, Riyadh.

Osama bin Laden was the seventeenth son of Mohammed Awad bin Laden, one of Saudi Arabia's wealthiest commoners. Mohammed bin Laden had come to Saudi Arabia in the 1930s from the Hadramaut, region of Yemen, once the fertile land of the Queen of Sheba, the ancient world's principal source of perfume. Osama bin Laden's mother was Syrian, a people noted for intelligence and quick wits. In all, bin Laden Senior produced some fifty-three offspring from a number of different wives. They all lived together in a typical Arab extended family compound.

At that time, oil was just being discovered by American prospectors in the new kingdom created by Abdul-Aziz ibn-Saud, and large sums of money were beginning to flow into the royal coffers. Mohammed bin Laden, like many emigrants from impoverished, overpopulated Yemen, worked as a cargo porter at Jiddah, Saudi Arabia's steamy port on the Red Sea. In a remarkable rags to riches story, the elder bin Laden managed to start a small construction firm, which grew in a mere twenty years, thanks to the kingdom's oil boom, into the nation's largest construction company. A decade later, bin Laden enterprises had become a multi-billion-dollar conglomerate with interests in construction, housing, hospitals, pharmaceuticals, and consumer goods.

Like many other business success stories in Saudi Arabia and the Gulf, the key to bin Laden's remarkable accomplishments lay in his intimate relations with the Saudi royal family. Mohammed bin Laden built numerous palaces for King Saud, a weak, dissolute monarch. But bin Laden also cultivated the able, highly intelligent Prince Faisal, who succeeded the ailing Saud to become king.

King Saud had bankrupted the kingdom by squandering its vast income on foolish projects, casinos, and expensive courtesans.

Finances were in such a desperate state that government officials and civil servants could not be paid. Mohammed bin Laden saved the day by paying almost all government salaries from his own purse for eight months, just as the famed American financier J.P. Morgan had personally saved the U.S. government from bankruptcy after the crash of 1893. King Faisal decreed that all future major government construction projects would go to the bin Laden Group.

In the late 1960s and early 1970s, the bin Laden Group was put in charge of the highly sensitive task of rebuilding and modernizing the Islamic holy sites at Mecca and Medina. Bin Laden also set up numerous joint venture corporations with the royal family, whose operations and profits were shrouded in secrecy. In the oil kingdom, it was normal, indeed expected, for successful businessmen to allot part of the shares in their firms to the six thousand-plus Saudi princes who comprised the royal family. There were rarely any contracts or even written agreements governing such joint ventures: all business was concluded, desert style, by a handshake, and assured not by lawyers and deeds, but by honour and reputation.

This is a common practice throughout the Arab world, Africa, and parts of Asia, where tax collection is, at best, spotty. The ruling family always expects to receive at least 20 per cent of all new business ventures. In many cases, trusted businessmen front for kings and presidents. No one can expect to conduct a sizeable business in Arabia or the Gulf without allocating a large share of the profits to the ruling dynasty. It is thus virtually impossible to determine where the bin Laden Group leaves off and the royal family's interests begin.

Bin Laden Senior had a well-deserved reputation as a model Muslim: pious and humble, simple in dress and speech, generous to the poor and needy, and free of the ostentation that quickly engulfed the nouveau riche oil kingdom. The elder bin Laden brought up his children strictly, and forced them to marry early and learn the nuts and bolts of his businesses from the shop floor up. The bin Laden home was often filled with visiting Islamic scholars and notables making the annual hajj (pilgrimage) to Mecca.

Mohammed bin Laden died in 1970, when his son Osama was only thirteen. But the strict family tradition of piety, humility, and hard work continued. Osama married his first wife—there would eventually be four—at the age of seventeen, and attended university in Saudi

Arabia, where he studied engineering and public administration. The young bin Laden travelled during these years to other Arab nations, Afghanistan, and Pakistan. Meanwhile, Mohammed bin Laden's already huge fortune kept expanding after his death. By the 1990s, the bin Laden business empire, now controlled by his numerous sons, was producing an estimated $5 billion in annual revenue.

Many young, wealthy Saudis of Osama bin Laden's generation went to high school and university in Europe or the United States, then embarked on a carefree, adolescent life that revolved around sports cars, Riviera discotheques, power boats, premium scotch, and luxury prostitutes. Once an upper-class Saudi youth had sown his wild oats abroad, he was expected to return to the kingdom, marry, and begin his own family. However, to avoid the boredom of family life and Saudi Arabia's strictures against alcohol and carnal entertainment, Saudi men would routinely head off with a group of friends for long "business" weekends of wine, women, and song in London, Paris, Copenhagen, or—as had become fashionable—Warsaw, where the blonds were less expensive and somewhat "friendlier."

This idyllic existence was not the path chosen by Osama bin Laden, though his family's wealth could have lavishly supported any of the usual excesses in which young Saudis routinely indulged. To the contrary, the young bin Laden was noted for his serious, often somber, rather intense nature, shyness, devotion to religion, and pursuit of a reserved lifestyle that was in keeping with traditional Islamic practice.

Bin Laden immersed himself in Islamic studies and came to be profoundly influenced, emotionally, intellectually, and politically, by two important modern Islamic thinkers: Mohammed Qutb and Abdullah Azzam.

Mohammed Qutb was a prominent leader of the Egyptian Brotherhood, the conservative, Islamist-nationalist movement that sought renewal of Muslim society through adoption of Islamic principles and law. Though he grew up in cosmopolitan Egypt and was well educated, Qutb became one of the first modern Islamic absolutists.

The earth, he wrote, was divided into Islamic and non-Islamic parts: the *dar al-Islam*, or house of Islam, and the *dar al-Harb*, or house of hostility. True Islam could only flourish in a wholly Islamic land, the *dar al-Islam*. Muslims could not be complete and receive full divine mercy unless they dwelled in a land ruled by Islamic sharia law. Unlike most

Muslims, who believe Jews and Christians are people of the book and part of the system of Islamic faith, Qutb advanced the novel and alarming notion that they were not in any way the lineal predecessors of the Muslim religion. He denied Jews were the "chosen people" and called them evil. Muslims, Qutb pronounced, were the "chosen of God."

Most important, Qutb called for Islamic revolutions from Morocco to Indonesia to overthrow secularist and Western-dominated regimes, such as the "brown Frenchmen" who ran Morocco, Algeria, and Tunisia and the "brown Englishmen" who ruled Jordan, Iraq, and the Gulf states. Only in Islam could exploited Muslim peoples find a government based on morality, principle, and human dignity, Qutb preached.

Predating Samuel Huntington's overwrought theory about the inevitable clash of Christian and Muslim civilizations, Qutb called for a "war of civilizations" between Islam and other religions. He personified what the American thinker and poet Peter Viereck aptly termed "bloody-minded professors" in his brilliant analysis of the roots of Germany's National Socialist Party, the kind of extremist, ivory-tower theorists who brought so much suffering to the twentieth century.

•••

The young bin Laden was inspired by Qutb's revolutionary ideas, as was a young Iranian mullah, Ruhollah Khomeini. In 1966, the Muslim Brotherhood attempted to assassinate Egypt's strongman, Gamal Abdel Nasser, whom it denounced as a godless socialist and enemy of Islam. Qutb was arrested and hanged, thus gaining the fame of martyrdom he would not have enjoyed had he lived. Ironically, at the time, Nasser was the hero of the Arabs and a champion of the Third World, while Qutb was little known. Three decades later, Nasser would be dismissed as a failure, while Qutb's theories would inflame and inspire Islamic militants from Morocco to Indonesia.

Osama bin Laden's frequent references to the Muslim world's need to struggle against the West and Russia—the *dar al-Harb*—and his calls for jihad against "Christian crusaders and Jews" echoed Qutb's absolutist philosophy.

Sheik Abdullah Azzam was the second important intellectual influence on the young bin Laden. Azzam was born in Palestine in 1941. His family was driven by Israeli forces in 1967 from their ancestral home in the West Bank and fled to Jordan. Azzam joined the Palestinian strug-gle against Israeli occupation but had to flee to Jordan. He studied extensively in Egypt, earning a Ph.D. in religious law from the world's leading Islamic university, Cairo's venerable al-Azhar.

Azzam returned to fight in the intifada against Israel, but soon grew disillusioned by his fellow Palestinians' lack of religious ardor. To his dismay, Azzam realized that the PLO and other Palestinian liberation groups were secular movements interested in power and land, not in building pure Islamic states. Azzam moved to Saudi Arabia where he devoted himself to the goal of creating the caliphate (Islamic rule), around the world. His slogan: "Jihad (struggle) and the rifle alone: no negotiations, no conferences, and no dialogues."

Soon after, Azzam moved to Peshawar, Pakistan, where he founded the Bait al-Ansar, or Mujahedin Services Bureau, to aid mujahedin fight-ing the Soviets in Afghanistan and help foreign volunteers prepare for the war. Sheik Abdullah then joined the mujahedin inside Afghanistan, one of the first Arab volunteers to do so, earning great distinction for his organizing skills and bravery in combat. He waged a ceaseless but unsuc-cessful struggle to unit the feuding mujahedin groups.

But Azzam's most significant contributions to the jihad were as a spokesman for the struggle and as the leader of the International Islamic Brigades. Azzam's books, articles, and broadcasts spread news and knowledge of the hitherto unknown Afghan jihad across the Arab, and later, the entire Muslim, world. "We Muslims are not defeated by our enemies," he wrote. "Instead, we are defeated by our own selves." Given enough faith, Muslims could defeat any oppressor, no matter how powerful, promised Azzam. His pan-Islamic thinking gave rise to what would come to be known as the Muslim International.

Azzam's writing and taped interviews aroused the passions of young men across the Mideast. The exiled Palestinian became the quintessential mujahid—holy warrior—fearlessly confronting impossi-ble odds and ready at any time to face death.

Arab and other Muslim volunteers, who would eventually number a total of one hundred thousand between 1979 and 1989, flocked in ever-growing numbers to Peshawar, in northwest Pakistan, thanks to Azzam's calls to holy war and discreet cash subsidies paid by Saudi Arabia and the CIA. During this period, the CIA made extensive use of Islamic preachers and authority figures to recruit for the anti-Soviet jihad in Afghanistan, including the blind Sheik Abdul Rahman, who was jailed for the first bombing of New York's World Trade Center. Whether Azzam cooperated with the CIA or Saudi intelligence during this period is uncertain, though this writer has heard of possible connections between the sheik and U.S. intelligence.

By the mid-1980s, Azzam was renowned as leader of the foreign mujahedin and a leading apostle of worldwide jihad to free Muslims from foreign occupation or oppression. Afghanistan, Azzam preached, was just the beginning of the holy struggle, and proof from God that miracles could happen if faith was sufficiently strong and mujahedin were prepared to accept martyrdom. His words did, in fact, impart great moral strength to the International Brigades; they went on to inspire the Lebanese mujahedin of Hizbullah, who eventually drove another modern, high-tech army, that of Israel, from their soil.

Sheik Abdullah's final contribution was to begin formation, through his Peshawar bureau, of a cadre of dedicated, professional Muslim revolutionary fighters, who, like the Ansar, or companions of the Prophet, would fight oppression, spread the word of Islam, and combat what he saw as the greatest enemies of the Muslim peoples: the United States, Israel, and Russia.

I met Dr. Abdullah Azzam in his small, cluttered Peshawar office in 1986. The dingy room was filled with dusty stacks of poorly printed brochures about jihad and the Afghan cause. He was mild-mannered and hardly impressed me as an Islamic firebrand, but people in Peshawar always spoke of him with deep respect. At the time, I could not imagine that this very modest operation would play such a decisive role in transforming an unknown struggle into an Islamic crusade. What I recall most vividly about the Palestinian mujahid was his quiet determination and optimism. He spoke as if he were convinced a miracle would come to pass. One, of course, did: victory over the world's greatest land power. A farangi skeptic like me simply lacked the faith to understand the inevitable will of Allah.

In November 1989, nine months after the last defeated Soviet troops left Afghanistan, Sheik Abdullah and two of his sons were killed in Peshawar by three powerful roadside bombs. Azzam's assassins have never been found, but suspicion points at the Soviet KGB seeking vengeance, as in the case of President Zia ul-Haq, for its defeat in Afghanistan. But there are also claims that Azzam was killed by the same operatives hired by U.S. intelligence who had tried, unsuccessfully, to assassinate Gulbuddin Hekmatyar; by Saudi agents; or by Pakistan's ISI. The only fact we know for certain is that Azzam's calls for jihad in other nations after the victory in Afghanistan were not welcomed by the United States or Saudi Arabia. This Islamic genie had served his purpose and had to be sealed back into the lamp.

•••

Soon after the 1979 Soviet invasion, Osama bin Laden, inspired by Sheik Abdullah Azzam's writings, went to Peshawar where he sought to aid the anti-Communist jihad that had just begun. He met with mujahedin leaders Professors Rabbani and Abdul Sayaf, whom he had previously encountered in Saudi Arabia when they visited the bin Laden home. Bin laden returned to Saudi Arabia, spending the next two years raising money and supplies for the Afghan jihad. Thanks to his family's connections, bin Laden was able to raise millions of dollars for the holy war.

Growing ever more dedicated to the jihad, in 1982 bin Laden brought some of his construction firm's technicians and machinery to Afghanistan, where they constructed a series of redoubts, tunnels, and cave complexes to shelter the mujahedin and their supplies from Soviet air bombardment. The Soviets, and later the Americans, would make these caves a primary target of attack. I visited some near Jalalabad: they were low, dank, and claustrophobic, but they proved quite effective against Soviet bombs and artillery. These "bin Laden caves," as some called them, had an important strategic role: all supplies for the mujahedin—every bullet and every mortar shell—had to be transported into Afghanistan from secret ISI depots in Pakistan by horse or mule. Protecting these vital supplies from Soviet attack was essential. Without such shelters, the war could not have been prosecuted. Bin Laden and his construction crews—the "Seabees" of the Afghan War—quickly and efficiently built a network of such vital bases, earning bin Laden a heroic reputation among the Afghan and foreign volunteers.

Two years later, bin Laden noticed that foreign volunteers—by now known as Afghani—arriving in Peshawar did not have a formal reception centre. No record was being kept of their arrivals, departures, or deaths. Bin Laden opened a combination of guest house and jihad administrative office to serve this function. He devoted particular effort to notifying the families of fallen mujahedin. Bin Laden and Sheik Abdullah Azzam agreed to coordinate the jihad bureau and bin Laden's guest house, which soon came to be known as al Qaeda, which means base or headquarters in Arabic. How bin Laden rose from running a seedy guest house in Peshawar to being the world's most notorious malefactor is one of the fascinating tales of our time.

As the war progressed, bin Laden and a small band of devoted followers—rarely more than a score of fighters—were increasingly involved in various combat zones within Afghanistan. Bin Laden is said to have participated in at least six major battles against Communist forces, and numerous skirmishes. He lived in the field and, in spite of his wealth, shared the same filthy clothing and meagre rations as his fellow mujahedin.

By now in his thirties, bin Laden gained even more fame for bravery during this period of intensive combat. He was seriously wounded in combat against the Russians at least twice, and injured on three other occasions. He gained a reputation for utter fearlessness in the face of death, not even flinching, it is said, when a Scud missile exploded quite close to him. Bin Laden, like many other mujahedin, may also have contracted hepatitis during this time, a serious occupational hazard for all who spent time in Afghanistan. I often felt safer facing Communist shelling than eating the food offered to be by the famously hospitable but often unhygienic Afghans. One could at least take shelter from artillery; one could never refuse food proffered by a host.

•••

I encountered bin Laden toward the end of the war near Jalalabad, in the walled residence of a powerful Pushtun warlord, Hajji Kadir, who had become both my host and protector, providing me with two Jeeps filled with heavily armed bodyguards. Hajji Kadir became vice-president of Afghanistan under the Karzai regime, and was assassinated in Kabul in a still unsolved killing that many believe was linked to Afghan drug lords. We were a score of men in a large, empty room, furnished only with colourful tribal carpets and green bolsters on which we leaned while sipping sweet chai tea. Bin Laden sat at the far end of the room from me. I noticed him because of his stature, over six feet five inches, and his gaunt body. He was dressed as a simple fighter and spoke softly to the men around him.

There was nothing else exceptionable about the man. To me, he was just another Afghan, one of thousands who had come to fight the hated Communists. And, at that time, Osama bin Laden was not the "world's most sought-after terrorist" (U.S. media 2001), but merely another "heroic freedom-fighter" (U.S. media 1988). In fact, I forgot about the encounter until the late 1990s, when bin Laden burst upon the scene as the world's leading Islamic menace.

Claims that bin Laden had been recruited by the CIA or worked as one of its agents are false. There is not a shred of evidence that bin Laden had any connections to the CIA in spite of its key role in recruiting, financing, and arming the International Islamic Brigades. However, bin Laden did have some contacts with the ISI, which worked in liaison with the CIA, as did most of the mujahedin, who relied on the ISI for arms, munitions, logistics, and communications support.

Bin Laden survived the war and returned in late 1989 to Saudi Arabia. Like his fellow Afghanis, bin Laden was infused with the passions of victory: they had defeated the world's leading military power, liberated a Muslim nation from oppression, and shown the world that Islam was a force with which to be reckoned. If faith and courage could liberate Afghanistan, then why could they not be directed against other regimes that oppressed the Islamic world, pillaged its wealth, and denied true Islam?

As Sheik Abdullah Azzam said to me in 1986, words I vividly recall to this day, "When we have driven the Soviet imperialists from Afghanistan and freed its people, we will go and liberate Saudi Arabia, and then Palestine, from Western imperialism."

Azzam's view of the United States as the leading persecutor and exploiter of the Muslim world was quickly and wholly adopted by Osama bin Laden and his fellow mujahedin. I spent many nights struggling to convince members of the Islamic International Brigade in Peshawar and Afghanistan that the United States was not an oppressor of the Muslims, but had been misled into self-defeating policies by enemies of the Muslim world. It was up to them, I kept repeating, to make Americans understand their cause to overthrow western-sustained despotic regimes in the Mideast, eradicate endemic corruption, and bring about a era of renewal for the Muslim world.

So long as America sustained the jihad in Afghanistan, Azzam's anti-Western philosophy was mostly ignored, but once the U.S. abandoned the Afghan cause, made a deal with Russia, and quickly became a perceived enemy of Islamic renewal, the men who fought in the great jihad came around to Azzam's thinking, most notably, Osama bin Laden. Azzam's assassination in 1989 was widely believed to have been committed by either CIA or KGB, both of whom had now become enemies of the Muslim cause.

•••

Saudi intelligence, which was very active in wartime and postwar Afghanistan, actively monitored bin Laden and his followers. There was nothing secret about the al Qaeda operation, and bin Laden was well known to Saudi security. Long-standing Saudi policy called for buying off or funding Islamic militants, provided they stayed far away from the kingdom. In fact, the Saudis had been delighted to use the Afghan war as a safety valve through which youthful Islamists could blow off pressure. But when these firebrands came home, the Saudi security police were waiting for them.

Bin Laden was too prominent to be arrested, but he was watched. He began calling for Saudi Arabia to loosen its ties with the United States and do more to help the Palestinians. Most of his wrath, however, he directed at Iraq, which, in 1990, had really just emerged victorious from the bloody, eight-year war against Iran in which at least five hundred thousand Iraqi and Iranian soldiers had died. Iraq's pyrrhic victory was due to secret aid from the United States, Britain, Saudi Arabia, and the Gulf emirates. While the United States and Britain armed Iraq and provided it—as I discovered in Baghdad in late 1990—with chemical and biological weapons programs, Israel was secretly selling $5 billion of arms to Iran. Iraq's invasion of Islamic Iran in 1980—at the urging of Washington and London—had proven a human, political, and financial disaster for Muslims and a bonanza for the United States and Israel. The stalemated war cost the oil-rich Arabs over $120 billion, left Iraq bankrupt and deeply in debt, and set the country back a decade.

Bin Laden warned the Saudi royal family that Saddam Hussein (then still a close American ally at the time) planned to invade oil-rich Kuwait. The Saudi princes dismissed bin Laden's warnings. Soon after,

Iraq surprised everyone but bin Laden by invading Kuwait. Saddam Hussein may have simply reacted to an exceptionally crude insult from the Kuwaiti crown princes; he may have had a master plan for absorbing Kuwait—once a part of what became Iraq; or he may have been lured into a trap by the United States, whose ambassador to Baghdad seemingly gave the Iraqi leader a green light to invade Kuwait.

Osama bin Laden volunteered to recruit mujahedin from Afghanistan to help defend Saudi Arabia from an Iraqi attack. He was politely refused. In fact, we now know that Saddam Hussein had no plans whatsoever to invade Saudi Arabia. But the U.S. government showed Saudi leaders satellite photos of Iraqi armoured and mechanized divisions massing on their border for a full-scale invasion.

These photos were clever fakes. They worked perfectly. The Saudi royal family panicked and, for the first time, gave the United States the right to base large numbers of warplanes and troops in the kingdom. The United States had been pressing the Saudis for years to station a heavy division and one or two air wings in Saudi Arabia. But the royal family feared that the presence of U.S. troops in the Muslim holy land would be denounced as a sin and an affront to Islam by the kingdom's Wahhabi-dominated ulema and by militant Islamists. Iran, Saudi Arabia's bitter enemy, would crow that the royal family had sold out to the Americans.

The United States was grudgingly allowed to build a huge air base and command centre in Saudi Arabia that could be furnished quickly with warplanes and headquarters personnel in an emergency. Protection of the royal family was assigned to American rapid response forces and units based at sea and in Bahrain. This mission had previously been performed by Pakistani troops. The Saudis, in true Mideast style, did not trust their own army (which was usually denied ammunition) to protect them from either outsiders or their own people.

Bin Laden has told interviewers that the arrival of U.S. troops on sacred Saudi soil was a horrible shock that became a turning point in his life. He began to loudly denounce the presence of American *kufir* as a defilement of Islamic holy land and a threat to Islam. Arabia was not being defended by the Americans, he fulminated; it had been militarily occupied and turned into a colony. Many Saudis agreed with bin Laden, so many, in fact, that the government tried to muzzle him and confined bin Laden to his home. The National Guard—the tribal militia maintained by the Saudis as a counterweight to their small, ineffective army—raided his home and threatened his followers.

In mid-1991, bin Laden managed, with the help of powerful relatives and friends, to escape from Saudi Arabia, and sought refuge in Afghanistan. The Saudis sent agents to kidnap or assassinate him. They also paid the ISI to hunt him down and kill him. These attempts failed, thanks to timely warnings from highly placed friends in Saudi Arabia and from his many admirers within the ISI. Deciding that Afghanistan was too dangerous for him, bin Laden fled to Sudan, another remote and marginal Muslim country that barely existed as far as the rest of the world was concerned.

Bin Laden's primary reasons for settling in Sudan were security for himself and his family, which by then grown to four wives and ten children, and the desire for some peace and quiet after a decade of fighting and agitating. Backward, impoverished Sudan was out of the way, had an Islamic government, and offered many opportunities for business, to which bin Laden decided to devote himself, at least for a while.

The Sudanese were happy to have bin Laden, who brought them sizeable investments from Saudi businessmen and his own extended family. Sudan was a huge, undeveloped nation with large resources of oil, agricultural land, water, wood, and minerals, all but the first lacking in Saudi Arabia. Sudan's poverty and backwardness—as well as a complex, festering tribal war in the south that was supported by various foreign nations and Christian religious charities—had frustrated previous plans to develop one of Africa's largest nations.

Bin Laden devoted himself to managing construction projects for the Sudanese government and investing his personal funds in various agricultural schemes. He bought a large but unimpressive villa in Khartoum, where he lived with his growing family. In spite of maintaining a low profile, bin Laden continued to be a magnet for militant Islamists and kept up his numerous contacts with Afghani across the Arab world.

During this period, members of militant Egyptian Islamic groups based in Sudan staged attacks on U.S. and Egyptian interests in Yemen and Somalia. An unsuccessful assassination attempt was made by Sudan-based exiles of Islamic Jihad, led by Dr. Ayman al-Zawahiri, against Egypt's strongman, General Hosni Mubarak. Bin Laden was not involved in any of these incidents, but his prominence and reputation as a firebrand made him a target of U.S., Saudi, and Egyptian wrath. His assets were quietly frozen by Saudi Arabia; he was declared an enemy of the kingdom and stripped of his citizenship. The United States demanded that Sudan expel bin Laden or face economic and political sanctions. Egypt threatened to attack Sudan.

As pressure mounted against him, bin Laden openly denounced the Saudi regime through communiqués and videotapes. He accused the Saudi royal family of having sold their nation and its wealth to the Americans. Saudi Arabia was virtually giving away their oil to the West, bin Laden charged, echoing similar accusations made a decade earlier by Libya's leader, Muammar Gadhafi, in exchange for U.S. military protection from its own people. Arabia was under U.S. military occupation, thundered bin Laden, and its holy sites defiled by Christian American soldiers who violated Islam's bans on alcohol, mixing of the sexes, pornography, degenerate music, and crass consumerism.

Arabia's oil, said bin Laden, echoing Iran's Islamic revolutionaries of the 1980s, did not belong to the six thousand princes of the Saudi royal family; it was the gift of Allah that belonged to all Arabs and needy Muslims, and should have been spent on social development and education rather than being thrown away in European casinos and bordellos or wasted on billions' worth of useless U.S. and British arms that the Saudi military could barely operate.

By "selling" Saudi Arabia to Western interests and allowing the holy land to be defiled, the family of Saud had affronted Islam and lost all claim to be "defender of the faith" and "keeper of the holy places." This was a grave charge, since the legitimacy of the Saudi regime was based on its politico-religious role as defender and guardian of Islam.

Stung by these accusations, which found much support in Arabia and the Arab world, the Saudis intensified efforts to apprehend and silence bin Laden. For the first time, U.S. intelligence began to see the Saudi exile as a danger to America's Mideast interests—American-supported Egypt and the oil monarchs and emirs of Saudi Arabia, Kuwait, and the Gulf states.

•••

In 1995, a car bomb was set off in Riyadh. Anonymous callers claimed it was to protest the U.S. presence in Saudi Arabia. The regime blamed it first on Iran, then on bin Laden. Four Saudi Afghani were tortured until they confessed, and then they were quickly beheaded.

The following year, a powerful truck bomb shattered U.S. military barracks at the al-Khobar base in eastern Saudi Arabia, killing nineteen American airmen. The Saudis initially blamed Iranian-supported Shias from the region, but then claimed that Afghani were involved. U.S. intelligence distrusted the Saudi version and favoured the view that Iran was behind the bombing. Osama bin Laden is still blamed by the Americans for the al-Khobar attack. No one ever claimed responsibility for the attack, an ominous and sinister precedent for the series of anonymous terrorist attacks that were to come.

After learning the Sudanese regime might expel him or hand him over to the Saudis, Osama bin Laden and his small entourage fled Khartoum in mid-1996 and again sought refuge in the Afghan city of Jalalabad. Bin Laden's confrontation with Saudi Arabia and his precipitous flight from Sudan cost him a large portion of his fortune. Saudi authorities had frozen bin Laden's bank accounts and assets. The bankrupt Sudanese regime reneged on tens of millions of dollars owed to bin Laden's construction firm and defaulted on millions more in loans. Bin Laden lost all of his investments in Sudan.

Claims by the U.S. media that bin Laden was worth at least $300 million were wrong. By 2000, the former millionaire had spent most of his fortune supporting jihad activities and charities in Afghanistan. He lost the rest in Sudan. After the flight from Sudan, bin Laden was largely supported by modest donations from admirers around the world, by some of his relatives, and by a small number of wealthy Saudis and Gulf Arabs.

Soon after arriving in Afghanistan, bin Laden issued a long, rambling document that amounted to a one-man declaration of war against the Saudi royal family. He demanded that American forces based in the oil kingdom be expelled. Only the Saudis paid any real attention to this Arab Don Quixote. They redoubled efforts to bribe Afghan leaders to hand him over to Saudi agents, and tried to assassinate him once again.

Meanwhile, Taliban forces were sweeping all opposition before them. By the fall of 1996, they reached Jalalabad, and soon after, took Kabul. The Taliban's supreme spiritual leader, Mullah Omar, sent a delegation to bin Laden offering him the religious movement's protection.

Bin Laden readily and gratefully accepted. Mullah Omar was undoubtedly motivated by bin Laden's renown in the war against the Soviets and status as a national hero. Bin Laden's strong religious convictions, his conservative Wahhabi beliefs, and his image as a humble Muslim mujahid fighting oppression appealed to the Taliban's leaders, who shared similar views.

The nervous Saudis tried once again to assassinate Osama bin Laden, this time in early 1997, using gunmen hired through Pakistan's ISI, which was cooperating with the Saudis, a major financial benefactor of Pakistan. But, as in the past, bin Laden admirers inside the ISI tipped him off and the assassination attempt failed. Mullah Omar, by now aware that his "guest" might bring a great deal of trouble down on Afghanistan and the Taliban, requested bin Laden keep a low profile and avoid antagonizing the Saudis, as well as the Americans, who were then flirting with the Taliban regime.

Bin Laden's growing name in the Muslim world turned him into an important symbol of resistance against the status quo, and made his new headquarters in Kandahar a gathering place for Islamic militants. At that time, Afghanistan was one of the few places in the Muslim world where those opposed to the current order of things could safely meet.

The rest of the *ummah* (Muslim community) was ruled by medieval feudal monarchies and military or civilian dictators kept in power by soldiers, ruthless secret police, and an American security umbrella. The few Muslim nations that were not under American, French, or British political domination—such as Syria, Libya, Yemen, Sudan, Iraq, Iran, and, to a far lesser degree, Pakistan and Malaysia—were run by regimes that were equally as undemocratic and repressive as America's Mideast satraps.

Nearly all Muslim regimes at the time—from Colonel Gadhafi's bizarre socialist Libya, to neo-Stalinist Uzbekistan, to feudal Saudi Arabia—saw Islamic militancy as a dire threat to the existing social and economic order and, of course, to their hold on power. Most political and many religious activities by Islamic parties, whether moderate democrats or militant fire-eaters, was branded "Islamic terrorism" and viciously suppressed. Islamists were jailed in large numbers, routinely tortured, and frequently executed.

The assassination by Islamic militants in 1981 of Egypt's U.S.-backed leader, Anwar Sadat, was the opening salvo of a long struggle that would culminate two decades later in the 2001 U.S. war against

Afghanistan and form the basis for the long so-called war on terrorism waged by Washington against a wide variety of Islamic and nationalist or anti-Western resistance groups that continues to this day and shows no signs of ending.

Sadat—and Jordan's King Hussein—had been virtually sanctified by the U.S. media as "good Arabs" who had made peace with Israel and were staunchly pro-American models of reason. Americans were never informed by their media that Sadat—and, for that matter, Jordan's King Hussein—had been paid CIA "assets" since the early 1950s and were faithfully executing U.S. policy directives in the Mideast.

While Americans loved Anwar Sadat and New York's media elite feted him, to ordinary Egyptians he was a deeply corrupt opportunist. Many called him a clown and a traitor who had sold his nation's interests to the Americans and Israelis. Besides the billions in baksheesh (bribes) promised to Egypt to sign the Camp David Accords with Israel, Sadat and his family were reported to have received many millions in undercover payments from the CIA and from international Jewish groups. A few years later, Sudan's leader, General Ja'afar Numayi, would also be bribed by Jewish organizations to allow so-called Ethiopian Jews, or Falashas, to be airlifted from his nation to Israel.

Sadat, in the view of most Egyptians—excluding the tiny, wealthy, deeply corrupt ruling class—had not only betrayed his nation, but also stabbed the Arab cause in the back. By pulling out of the confrontation with Israel, Sadat made it impossible for the other weak Arab states ever to fight Israel. Sadat literally sold the Palestinians down the river. Tales of his family's rampant corruption and lavish living, disdain for Islamic custom, and evident passion for Western ways outraged ordinary Egyptians who lived from hand to mouth. The very same tide of popular revulsion had swept Iran before the overthrow of the U.S.-backed shah and his parasitic family.

In mosques across Egypt—the only place where Sadat's U.S.-advised secret police dared not enter—the Egyptian ruler was denounced as an apostate, a thief, and a "new Pharaoh."

But Sadat was kept in power by the large Egyptian Army, which was paid, armed, and supplied by the United States, and by his various security agencies, closely advised by the CIA and the FBI. In fact, Sadat was protected by a cadre of U.S. agents; his generals were watched, their phone calls and conversations intercepted by U.S. National

Security Agency staff in Cairo. Washington was determined to protect Sadat against the fate of the late shah of Iran.

In September 1981, during a grandiose military parade in Cairo, a small group of Egyptian soldiers belonging to a hitherto unknown organization, Islamic Jihad, crying "Death to Pharaoh" and *"Allah akbar!"* rushed Sadat's viewing stand, and riddled him with gunfire. America's most cooperative and important Mideast "asset" was dead; the war between the United States and Islamic revolutionaries had begun.

A long, bitter, extremely violent struggle then ensued between Egyptian security forces and underground groups of Islamic militants. The two most prominent Islamist groups, Islamic Jihad and Gamma al Islamia, tried to bring down the U.S.-backed Cairo regime by assassinating cabinet ministers and staging bombing attacks. Sadat's successor, General Hosni Mubarak, who was helped into power by the CIA, waged a bloody, merciless war against the Islamists, who were branded terrorists, whether violent or non-violent. Many Islamists were secretly executed or disappeared. Intelligence and security agents helped the Mubarak regime break the Islamists, even reportedly participating in torture of suspects, as they had in the shah's Iran. Dr. Ayman al-Zawahiri, a respected, non-political Egyptian surgeon, was apparently framed by a neighbour and arrested as an Islamist by the Egyptian secret police. His brutal, repeated torture in prison is believed to have turned him into a ferocious enemy of the Mubarak regime and its main supporter, the United States. Zawahiri went underground and soon became leader of Egyptian Jihad. In 1997, Egyptian Jihad murdered fifty-eight foreign tourists in cold blood at Luxor in an attempt to wreck Egypt's vital tourist trade.

After more than a decade of brutal, dirty urban warfare, the Mubarak regime managed to repress, but not wholly eliminate, the Islamists. Many of the Islamist leaders fled Egypt, or went deep underground, determined to carry on the fight against Mubarak's regime and its protector. A number of Egyptian Islamists sought refuge in the United States, among them the blind sheik Abdul Rahman, thanks to help from his old friends at the CIA.

By getting so deeply involved in Egypt's bitter civil war, by acting defender of its unpopular, repressive regime, and by increasing its already substantial support of Israel, the United States had placed itself squarely in the Mideast's firing line and had become a regional and global combatant, a fact few Americans understood until after September 11, 2001.

Dr. Ayman al-Zawahiri, the Egyptian Jihad leader, sought refuge in Afghanistan, where he soon met Osama bin Laden. Other Egyptian revolutionaries followed, notably Muhammed Atef, a former police officer, who later ran the military wing of al Qaeda and was indicted by U.S. federal authorities in the East Africa embassy bombings. Atef became bin Laden's right-hand man and then in-law: bin Laden's son married Atef's daughter. Mohammed Atef was killed in Afghanistan by American bombing in November 2001, but the roots of Islamic Jihad and al Qaeda would remain buried deep in Egypt.

Bin Laden and al-Zawahiri became instant friends. Small numbers of other foreign Islamic militants also came to bin Laden's headquarters. This ragtag group of revolutionaries was aptly dubbed by one writer as "Che Guevaras in turbans." Senior members of Pakistan's small but vociferous Islamic parties also met with bin Laden and gave him financial backing and open support. Afghanistan became the Havana of the 1990s, a haven and gathering place for angry revolutionaries united by their hatred of the United States.

Afghanistan's conservative clergy, the ulema, also supported bin Laden, a fact that encouraged him to begin making pronouncements couched in Islamic terms. Afghanistan's Sunni mullahs were pleased by bin Laden's fierce denunciations of heretical Shia Muslims, a position shared by the Taliban's leadership.

●●●

In 1998, Osama bin Laden issued a fatwa calling on all Muslims to fight to free Palestine, expel the United States from Saudi Arabia, and end the punishment of Iraq. He announced the formation of an international alliance to oppose "U.S. imperialism" and "Zionism," both of which he lumped under the name of "crusaders." In the most ominous part of his quixotic declaration of war, bin Laden sanctioned killing Americans and Jews by the new international jihad. Whether he meant Americans and Jews everywhere, or only in the Mideast, remained unclear. Bin Laden's ally, Dr. Ayman al-Zawahiri—known to all as "the doctor"—co-signed the fatwa.

A fatwa is a binding religious decree, rather like a medieval papal bull, that is issued by the Islamic religious leadership. Most Muslims rejected bin Laden's right to pronounce on religious matters since he had no credentials as an Islamic scholar or leader. But a small minority of fundamentalists, who support a return to early Islamic ways and strongly oppose any authority role for scholars or clergy, maintain that any good, respected Muslim has the right to issue a religious decree.

Bin Laden's fatwa was ignored by Western media but it was noticed by U.S. intelligence and Israel's Mossad, which maintained a wide agent network in Central Asia. Bin Laden was moved up a notch on the West's threat list, but was still regarded as just another angry Islamic fanatic—what the French term an *enrage*. Even so, by calling for jihad against the West and Israel, bin Laden had signed his own death warrant.

Still, the Western powers took no action against bin Laden. Their attention was still focused on oil. At the time, the United States was still being friendly to the Taliban regime in hopes that it would allow the American oil firm Unocal to build pipelines across Afhanistan to export Central Asian oil through Pakistan. France was courting Ahmad Shah Massoud's Tajik Northern Alliance. Britain was ready to follow the American lead.

American and European firms believed that they could take advantage of the Taliban's naifs, who had no knowledge of the outside world and no sense whatsoever of commercial matters. Osama bin Laden, experienced in contracting, big business, and finance, provided invaluable commercial and legal advice to the Taliban on dealing and contracting with foreign business firms. He in a sense became by default their leading business agent. In 1998, bin Laden advised the Taliban to give the pipeline contract to an Argentine firm, which had offered Afghanistan a better deal. Unocal lost out. Washington was furious, cut off aid to Kabul, and almost immediately turned on the Taliban and branded it an "outlaw regime."

Bin Laden's relative obscurity in the world media ended on August 7, 1998. Two huge truck bombs exploded almost simultaneously, shattering the U.S. embassies in Nairobi, Kenya, and Dar es Salaam, Tanzania. The Nairobi bombing killed 200 Kenyans and 12 Americans; 4,650 people were injured, most by flying glass. The explosion in Dar es Salaam was far less lethal: 11 people were killed and 72 injured.

The twin attacks were clearly intended as a major blow to America's prestige and authority. The deaths of so many innocent Kenyan civilians showed that the bombings' perpetrators had a total disregard for human life, lacked any sense of humanity, and clearly didn't care that most of the victims were totally innocent Africans.

The U.S. government was outraged by the bloody attacks, but average Americans less so, no doubt because most of the victims were Kenyans. Few Americans could find Kenya or Tanzania on a map. The Clinton administration almost immediately blamed Osama bin Laden and offered a $2 million reward for the bombers.

Two weeks later, the Clinton administration, which invariably favored theatrics over action, struck back in an attack that proved both farcical and tragic. More than twenty Tomahawk missiles were fired from U.S. Navy vessels in the Arabian Sea at what was described by Washington as a "terrorist complex" outside Khost, Afghanistan. U.S. intelligence reported that bin Laden was holding a meeting there with his senior staff. In fact, bin. Laden was far away. The terrorist complex was actually a collection of ramshackle huts and a training course that was being used by Kashmiri mujahedin fighting India. Some twenty people were killed at Khost, and six civilians by an errant Tomahawk that crashed in Pakistan.

Seventeen Tomahawks were fired at the al-Shifa pharmaceutical plant outside Khartoum, Sudan. The White House insisted it had conclusive proof that the plant was being used by Osama bin Laden to produce deadly vx nerve gas. U.S. National Security Council director Sandy Berger claimed U.S. agents had found soil samples at al-Shifa that contained the last precursor chemical to vx. The U.S. media faithfully lapped up leaks from the White House and the Pentagon that bin Laden, and perhaps Saddam Hussein, were churning out poison gas in Sudan.

The "smoking gun" turned out to be smoke. UN chemical inspectors examined the plant and found no trace of chemical weapons or their precursors. The American attack killed a watchman and destroyed a vital pharmaceutical plant that produced 50 per cent of Sudan's human and veterinary medicines. Washington shrugged off accusations it had committed an act of international terrorism.

After receipt of large amounts of cash from the U.S., Kenyan, and Tanzanian police, discreetly aided by FBI agents, arrested a group of

Muslim men, charged them with involvement in the bombings, and handed the men over to U.S. authorities. The chief witness, and main source of evidence that the East Africa attacks were linked to bin Laden, was a defector from al Qaeda, who had fled after being co discovered stealing. The three other defendants all claimed their confessions had been extracted in East Africa during extensive and repeated torture.

After a long trial in May 2001, all four were convicted of murder and criminal conspiracy involving Osama bin Laden. Circumstantial evidence produced by the prosecution suggested an international plot leading back to al Qaeda. Osama bin Laden, however, denied any involvement in the embassy attacks, though he applauded them. The United States raised its reward for him to $5 million.

•••

The American media quickly zeroed in on bin Laden as a world-class menace. Thus began a symbiotic relationship between bin Laden and the U.S. media in which one fed off the other. Like Muammar Gadhafi, Osama bin Laden seemed to relish provoking outrage and consternation in the West, and revelled in the image of Muslim bogeyman. The U.S. media, fuelled by leaks from the U.S. government, Egypt, Saudi Arabia, and Israel, ascribed all sorts of nefarious plots to bin Laden—nuclear, chemical, and biological weapons among them—so that he came to resemble a sort of Islamic Dr. Fu Manchu or Dr. No, hidden away in the forbidding mountains of Afghanistan, plotting his revenge on the Western world.

The media sensationalism that turned bin Laden from an obscure Islamic enrage into a global menace is a common phenomenon of Western reporting on the Muslim world. During the Victorian era, the British press vied to produce the most lurid reports of the Muslim threats to Her Majesty's Empire.

In India, the notorious Tippu Sultan led a national rebellion against the British Raj and was branded a "bloodthirsty monster" by the press. Jules Verne even wrote a book about him. Out of the wastes of Sudan came the dreaded Mandi and his Dervish army, who outraged Christian Britain by storming Khartoum and killing its imperial defender, General "Chinese" Gordon. There were the "Mad Mullah" and the "Fakir of Ipi," our old friends from chapter 3, who nearly ran the British out of Peshawar; and a second "Mad Mullah," who battled British imperial rule over the Somali coast.

In our own era, a new Muslim menace appeared in every new decade to challenge America's geopolitical interests in the Muslim world: Egypt's Gamal Abdel Nasser; PLO leader Yasser Arafat; Libya's Muammar Gadhafi; Iran's Iman Ruhollah Khomeini; Iraq's Saddam Hussein; Osama bin Laden; and, most recently, Hezbullah's clever Sheik Hassan Nasrallah, and Iran's gasconading president, Mahmoud Ahmadinejad.

Personalizing the complex politics of the Muslim world into a single hateful, malevolent individual has always been the West's way of dealing with events in that region. Demonizing those who oppose Western imperial interests as "fanatics, madmen, or terrorists" has been standard procedure for two centuries. As bin Laden became known around the world, the Americans, British, and Israelis found it extremely useful to portray him as the incarnation of Muslim hostility and resistance to Western military, political, and economic domination. Those who resisted Western policies were terrorists, or at least supporters of terrorism, pure and simple.

Osama bin Laden was very sensitive to his image and the need to wage his own struggle in the media. In the nineteenth century, war was conducted on land and at sea; in the twentieth century, air power became the dominant dimension of warfare. In the twenty-first century, the most important component of war would be the airwaves. Bin Laden carefully monitored the Western media and, unlike many other Mideasterners and South Asians, he developed a keen sense of the United States and American politics and society. Most of his communications were aimed at Arabic-speaking audiences, and thus couched in the flowery, often bombastic language of the Arab world. Bin Laden's speeches, usually poorly translated into English, made him sound lunatic, or at least very bizarre, with their obscure references and allusions to early Islamic history. Muslims, however, understood bin Laden's message quite well.

Bin Laden's growing fame, or notoriety, drew increasing numbers of disaffected or adventurous Muslims to his banner. Al Qaeda had been portrayed by the Western media as a vast, international organization somewhat like the old twentieth-century Communist Party. In this sense, al Qaeda and other Islamic militant groups finally came to fill the role of super-enemy, formerly played by the now defunct U.S.S.R. After a decade of futilely searching for a new foe after the Soviet collapse in 1991, the Pentagon at last found in al Qaeda an enemy against which it could wage war and test new weapons systems, and a compelling reason for expanding defense spending.

In reality, al Qaeda's hard core, based in Afghanistan, probably numbered fewer than one thousand men. Some estimates put it at under three hundred. This was bin Laden's immediate entourage, which included his senior staff, their families, and bodyguards.

I have long believed that al Qaeda has been exaggerated out of all proportion by the U.S. government and media, which desires a single, unified theory of evil to explain numerous anti-American incidents and movements around the globe. In my view, bin Laden acted largely as a figurehead who rallied anti-American forces and publicized their cause to the world. Think of him of as a chief franchiser granting local agreements and providing marketing support to a small groups of like-minded partisans spread across many nations.

In fact, while Osama bin Laden was certainly aware of many anti-American activities, his role in the September 11, 2001, attacks against the United States still remains cloudy. At first, bin Laden, who prizes his reputation for veracity, denied being behind the attacks. But in recent years, he and deputy Ayman al-Zawahiri have dropped broad hints that they at least knew about plans for the attacks, or even approved them. The real mastermind of the attacks may have been al-Zawahiri. In December 2001, Saudi Arabia's senior security official, Prince Nayef, one of the ruling family's most powerful figures, asserted that bin Laden was merely a "tool" of al Qaeda, not its true leader. The real mastermind of the attacks may have been the Egyptian al-Zawahiri. However, the origin and centre of the September 2001 plot more likely lies in Egypt and Saudi Arabia, not in Afghanistan. U.S. security authorities still believe that Khalid Sheik Mohammed, who is in U.S. custody in the Guantánamo prison, was the architect of the plot, for which he sought approval and likely financing from Osama bin Laden. The actual jihadist cell that carried out the attack was based in Hamburg, Germany, and did not have direct links to Afghanistan. In fact, it did have links through a Moroccan member to North African Salafist groups.

There were also some five thousand to seven thousand foreign mujahedin in Afghanistan from Pakistan, India, Kashmir, Uzbekistan, and the Middle East, and a handful from the Philippines and Chechnya. Even a few Americans joined up. These fighters were not al Qaeda followers, though the United States always lumped them into the al Qaeda total, and ruthlessly hunted them down when the United States attacked Afghanistan. Most, if not all, had come in response to the Taliban's offer of safe haven for non-Shia Islamic. Some were ideologically sympathetic to bin Laden, though many were not at all interested in his anti-U.S., anti-Saudi crusade, but rather in their own national struggles. Afghanistan offered them refuge and training bases.

Al Qaeda ran a small number of training camps for its guerrillas and other Third World revolutionaries. These camps were little more than a few wooden or mud buildings, some storage caves, and firing ranges.

I saw identical mujahedin training camps during the 1990s around Jalalabad. Of the forty to sixty terrorist training camps ascribed to al Qaeda by the Pentagon, the majority were used by other, non–al Qaeda groups, mainly mujahedin fighting in Indian-ruled Kashmir.

•••

Al Qaeda's "World Islamic Front Against Jews and Crusaders" was not a tightly knit international organization. It was a loose federation of like-minded groups and individuals that dotted the Islamic world and had small cells in Europe, North America, Latin America, and Southeast Asia. Al Qaeda is believed to be vertically integrated, with bin Laden as supreme leader. Beneath him was a majlis, or council, to which four committees reported: military, finance, religious-legal affairs, and, unusually for any Muslim organization, media.

Below this headquarters were cells in many nations made up of few—often less than six—supporters. Al Qaeda was highly compartmentalized and decentralized, which made it extremely difficult for Western intelligence agencies to monitor and even harder to penetrate. In fact, al Qaeda was not an organization in the usual sense. The movement was really an amorphous collection of like-minded individuals who, outside of the small headquarters unit inside Afghanistan, hid behind the facade of normal life. There were almost no regular communications between al Qaeda cells, and only sporadic movements of money. Western claims that bin Laden was financed by a vast, underground financial network that used banks and Islamic charities are wildly overblown. In reality, small amounts of cash were transferred, when necessary, through the *hawala* system, an ancient "banking" network based on trust that used small money exchangers spread across the globe. Overseas Chinese use a similar system. Today, 70 per cent of cash transfers from South Asia to North America and Europe go through the *hawala* system and are unrecorded.

Al Qaeda members lived simply and were motivated by ideology, not money. Anti-U.S. operations, whether done by al-Qaeda or other organizations, cost very little. The World Trade Center bombings are estimated to have cost a mere $250,000 to mount, the cost of a luxury car. Al Qaeda could also count on emergency, ad hoc donations from sympathizers. Laden often stated the only way to drive U.S. influence from the Muslim World was by attacking America's Achilles heel, its finances, trade, and general economy. Interestingly, compared to the minor estimated cost of mounting the 9/11 attacks and subsequent terrorist incidents, the U.S. response has been prodigiously expensive. The direct costs of economic disruption and repairing damage caused by the attack on New York City is estimated at well over U.S. $100 billon, a figure that supporters of bin Laden note is roughly equivalent to U.S. overt financial aid to Israel since the 1950s. The ongoing hunt for bin Laden in Afghanistan employs some twenty-two thousand U.S. troops, and a small army of CIA, NSA, DIA, and FBI agents. The combined effort costs around $1.5 billion monthly, or some $108 billion by the end of 2006. Pakistan has captured some seven hundred al Qaida "suspects" and handed many over to the U.S. for millions in cash rewards. Washington believes it has killed or captured about three-quarters of al Qaida's leaders and senior field officers.

Communications were usually handled by trusted couriers. Al Qaeda was aware that it was being incessantly monitored by the CIA, the U.S. National Security Agency, electronic intelligence, and optical satellites of the U.S. National Reconnaissance Office, as well as other intelligence agencies from Britain, France, Germany, Israel, Saudi Arabia, Egypt, Turkey, Jordan, Iran, Pakistan, India, and Russia.

Bin Laden was acutely aware of the dangers posed by modern communications equipment. Their emissions act like a beacon for electronic intelligence systems. On April 21, 1996, the Chechen leader,

General Jokhar Dudayev, was negotiating with Russian leader Boris Yeltsin for his nation's independence. Dudayev made a call on his satellite telephone. Moments later, two 240 mm artillery rockets slammed into the Chechen leader and his party. Dudayev was assassinated by the Russians using a new, secret electronic system (supplied by the Clinton administration to Moscow specifically for that purpose), capable of homing rockets and missiles in on specific telephone transmissions. As a result, bin Laden avoided all radio transmissions and refused to be around any electronic equipment, even a simple quartz watch.

In many ways, al Qaeda was similar in structure to Israel's justly renowned intelligence agency, Mossad. A small headquarters operation was able to quickly mobilize manpower, money, and logistic support from Jewish supporters, known as *sayanim*, spread across the globe. *Sayanim*, who are all unpaid volunteers, can be called upon at any time by Mossad to provide information, money, and services—without questions being asked. This gives Mossad a huge pool of no-cost "assets," many of them highly placed, influential members of their national governments and communities, including the United States.

Like Israel's spy system, al Qaeda was bound by powerful ideological links. Bin Laden and al Qaeda members were uniform in their belief that the West had become the leading enemy and oppressor of Muslim peoples, and that they were the vanguards who would purify the earth of Western corruption.

In their view, which was widely shared across the Islamic world, the United States was a hegemonistic superpower determined to bring the entire globe under its control. After the collapse of the Soviet Union, the Muslim world became the main centre of opposition to American political, commercial, and cultural domination. While many Muslims were captivated by America and everything it represented, others— many of them young people—rejected its crass commercialism, Hollywood's violence and sexual exploitation, the pillaging of their dwindling energy resources, and Washington's relentless support of corrupt, vicious, self-serving regimes. They hated the way Americans treated them, with a combination of ignorance, arrogance, and thinly disguised contempt.

Bin Laden's catechism of hatred has three pillars. First, Israel. To bin Laden, and indeed, to most of the Muslim world's 1.2 billion people, Israel is an illegal, colonial imposition—the product of the West's guilt over the Nazi extermination of Europe's Jews, paid for by the Arabs. Israel is seen as a cruel, ruthless persecutor of five million Palestinians, 70 per cent of whom remain refugees.

After the September 2001 attacks, Osama bin Laden warned, "There will be no peace or security in America until there is peace and security in Palestine."

Thanks to Al Jazeera satellite TV—the Arab world's first uncensored TV broadcasts—the entire Muslim world each night can see the spectacle of Palestinian children and adults being gunned down by Israeli soldiers. They see teenage Palestinians throwing rocks at Israel's U.S.-supplied tanks, or being blasted by Israel's U.S.-supplied helicopter gunships—all courtesy of American taxpayers. The agony of Palestine has become the agony of the entire Islamic world. Muslims are as horrified watching the bloody repression of Palestinians by Israeli tanks and soldiers as Jews would have been in the 1940s watching the crushing of their valiant uprising in the Warsaw ghetto.

The Muslim world's outrage was further deepened by Israel's well-televised 2006 assault on Lebanon in retaliation for the capture of two Israeli soldiers in a routine border skirmish with Hezbollah fighters. Both the ferocity of Israel's retaliation, the killing of many civilians, America's thwarting international efforts to end the fighting, and its hurried supply of bombs to Israel reverberated from one end of the Muslim world to the other, making a mockery of Washington's efforts to improve its image in Islamic nations and generating a whole new generation of anti-American jihadis.

In the prevailing Muslim view, amplified by bin Laden, America's government and media have been virtually taken over by the Jewish lobby. Anyone in Congress or the media who dares oppose America's total backing of Israel faces professional oblivion. Many Muslims believe that the Israel lobby has grown so powerful that it now merely transmits orders direct from Jerusalem to Washington. They are not alone. In the words of noted Israeli writer and peace activist Uri Avnery, if Israel ordered the U.S. Congress to repeal the Ten Commandments, the entire Senate would vote in favour.

Ironically, American supporters of Israel have laboured for decades to align America's foreign policy with that of Israel, and to make Israel's foes those of America. They have been so successful that foreigners can rarely tell where American policy leaves off and Israel's begins. A former head of the Israel lobby was taped by a contributor, boasting that his organization, American Israel Public Affairs Committee, had "our man" in every key decision-making organ that ran U.S. Mideast policy.

Under the Clinton administration, almost every portfolio dealing with the Mideast was staffed by long-time, well-known supporters of Israel, some of whom had lived there or worked for the Israel lobby. Imagine the outcry if such positions had been filled by militant American Muslims. Non-Americans had trouble understanding how Jewish Americans could favour Israel but still try to retain some balance in dealing with the Arabs. In short, America and Israel have blended together, at least in the view of Mideasterners, and have become one and the same.

The ultimate and terrifying culmination of this mistaken perception came on September 11, 2001 when Muslim terrorists struck at the symbols of U.S. power—the World Trade Center and the Pentagon— and the alleged symbol of Jewish power, Wall Street. America had now become a co-belligerent in the Mideast and was, for the first time, paying the price. Israelis had endlessly suffered from Arab terror attacks, and the Arabs had suffered from Israeli terror attacks. Now it was America's turn to join the Mideast's madness.

•••

The second object of Osama bin Laden's hatred was captured in the person of Iraq's dictator, Saddam Hussein. To bin Laden, Saddam was the incarnation of the despotic rulers denounced in the Koran and a disgrace to the Arabs. Iraq's ruler, fulminated bin Laden, was a long-time henchman of the West and its local enforcer. As noted, bin Laden even offered to send his mujahidin to defend Saudi Arabia against any Iraqi attack.

However, America's crushing defeat of Iraq and subsequent sanctions forced bin Laden to modify his stance by delineating between Saddam and Iraq's increasingly tormented people. After the First Gulf War against Iraq, America's strategy was to totally isolate it and inflict such punishing sanctions and suffering on its citizens that they would revolt and overthrow President Saddam Hussein and replace him with a pro-U.S. regime.

Washington's postwar strategy in Iraq failed miserably.

President George H.W. Bush called on Iraq's Shia and Kurds, who mad up nearly 80 per cent of the population, to rebel and overthrow Saddam's Sunni regime. When the Shia and Kurds did so, expecting at least some U.S. military support, President Bush turned his eyes away and allowed Saddam's still largely intact military forces to brutally crush the uprisings, massacring large numbers of rebels. Saddam Hussein claimed that he had every right to put down dangerous revolts during wartime.

The ensuing U.S. trade sanctions and embargos imposed on Iraq were so draconian that Iraq's Ministry of Education was banned from importing pencils for schoolchildren because the lead they contained might somehow by used in non-existent strategic weapons programs. These sanctions also denied Iraq imports of chlorine necessary to purify drinking water and every sort of medical imaging devices, surgical equipment and supplies, many basic medicines, including antibiotics and painkillers.

Declassified Pentagon documents from the 1991 war show that the United States purposely targeted and destroyed Iraq's sewage treatment and water purification facilities and then largely prevented their post-war reconstruction.

As a direct result, most of the five hundred thousand Iraqis—mostly children—whom the UN reported to have died as a result of U.S. sanctions succumbed to water-borne diseases. Iraqis were forced to drink water from their highly polluted rivers and canals, all of which were infused with raw sewage. When queried about this frightful number of dead Iraqis, then U.S. Secretary of state Madeleine Albright famously retorted, "It is a price worth paying." Her statement reverberated across the Muslim world, forming a frequent quote in Osama bin Laden's speeches.

Albright's remarkably callous and stupid statement reverberated across the Muslim world and reinforced its widely held view, however mistaken, that Israel was directing U.S. foreign policy and had driven the Bush Administration into an all-out attack on Iraq because it was a military threat to Israel and had dared challenge the Jewish state's Mideast nuclear monopoly. Belief in the Muslim world that Israel was controlling U.S. Mideast policy was further intensified by President George W. Bush's invasion of Iraq in 2003, and Vice-President Dick Cheney's quoted remark that the war against Iraq had been launched "primarily for the benefit of Israel."

Muslim anger against the U.S. rose even more when it was revealed that during the early 1980s the United States supplied Iraq with feeder stocks of anthrax, botulism, plague, Q fever, and tularemia for its covert bio-weapons program. British technicians sent by Her Majesty's government—as I discovered in 1991—produced chemical and biological weapons for Saddam Hussein in the 1980s that were acceptable, so long as they were used against Muslim Iranians. Afterward, Iraq would be branded a "terrorist state" for producing such weapons. Saudi Arabia helped fund Saddam Hussein's nuclear weapons program.

The Muslim world has come to hate the United States for its long, self-serving crusade against a detestable regime that they reluctantly support only because Iraq, unlike its neighbours, refuses to give in to American demands and continues to defy the world's greatest power.

•••

The third pillar of hate is bin Laden's homeland, Saudi Arabia. As noted earlier, he has become the nemesis of the Saudi royal family, which he and many other critics regard as a wicked, corrupt, selfish "kleptocracy" that is looting Arabia's wealth and has sold Islam's holy land to the Americans. The only way to be rid of the Saudi feudal system, according to bin Laden, is to drive its American protector and sustainer from the peninsula by making its continued garrisoning prohibitively expensive—strategically, the same way U.S. Marines were driven from Lebanon.

All three of these issues—Palestine, Iraq, and Saudi Arabia—are legitimate political questions. But Osama bin Laden took these issues and distorted them into a religious struggle between pure Islam and the West. His bizarrely named "World Islamic Front Against Jews and Crusaders" was clearly intended to ignite religious uprisings across the Muslim world, with perhaps bin Laden as its ultimate leader and spiritual guide, in short, a second Mandi.

Very few Muslims accepted bin Laden's fanciful idea of a titanic religious crusade against the West, or even couching their struggles in religious terms. Even fewer took the self-proclaimed Saudi "guide" seriously—with the notable exception of the unwolrdly Taliban, some of whose more backwards members saw him as a saintly prophet. Even so, the Taliban kept bin Laden at arm's length and never fully integrated his al Qaeda fighters into their ragtag forces, though bin Laden's men sometimes joined the Taliban fighting against Tajik forces.

Osama bin Laden was regarded as a dangerous outlaw by most governments of the Muslim world, but by 1998 he had become a hero—in fact, the hero—to most ordinary people from Morocco to Indonesia. The reason was simple: bin Laden had become the personification of resistance to American political, economic, and cultural hegemony. At a time when no nation on earth dared directly challenge America's global power, a single man had stood up to Washington and thrown down the gauntlet. It mattered little that bin Laden might be a mass murderer, a deranged fanatic, or a warped Muslim. To his millions of admirers, Osama was the man who kept defying the American Goliath.

The same phenomena occurred with Saddam Hussein on the eve of the 1990 Gulf War. He, too, defied the United States and refused to bow to its dictates. Like bin Laden, Saddam challenged the United States to a test of wills, daring Washington to fight him mano-a-mano. Such defiance, even though it came from a brutal tyrant, thrilled many Muslims who were profoundly disgusted by their own government's craven subservience to America's often arrogant, bullying behaviour.

Muslims were desperately in need of heroes. While the world was. racing into the high-tech twenty-first century, much of the Islamic world was stuck back in the early twentieth century. There was very little of which modern Muslims could be proud. The majority of Muslim nations were ruled by monarchs or dictators of varying sorts, and their societies were plagued by endemic corruption, malfeasance, and pervasive selfishness. They were technologically backward, politically impotent, socially stultified, and culturally comatose. No Muslim nations had come to the aid of the suffering Palestinians. No Muslims—save a few Afghan and Chechen mujahedin—had gone to rescue the Muslims of Bosnia and Kosovo from rape and slaughter.

But what Muslims really needed was not a Great Jihad against the West and Israel led by bin Laden, but a jihad against their own rotting, corrupt governments co-opted by the West to ruthlessly exploit them politically and economically.

Fifty per cent of the population of the Islamic world today is under eighteen years old. They are inheriting a legacy of failure, futility, and shame. Muslims are widely regarded by non-Muslims as second-class citizens, or worse, natural-born terrorists or violent primitives. After the

Arab defeats in the 1948, 1956, 1967, and 1973 Arab-Israeli Wars, after Pakistan's defeats at the hands of India, and after Saddam's defeat in Kuwait in 1991 and again in 2003, Muslims saw nothing but an unbroken record of military and political disasters. The only exception was the glorious jihad in Afghanistan, the first time in modern history that Muslim arms had triumphed.

Out of this unique success came Osama bin Laden. Not only was he cloaked in the mantle of an epic victory; he was continuing the jihad against what Muslims saw as oppression—both from the United States and its own American-supported rulers, whom he called "hypocrites." He was defending the rights of persecuted Muslims and striking back at the enemies of Islam. Among ordinary Muslims, bin Laden was increasingly called "Brother Osama."

To North Americans, Osama bin Laden was a ruthless killer and a madman. By the time of the World Trade Center and Pentagon attacks, this reputation was already cast in the public mind. Bin Laden was a mass murderer for killing innocent Americans; nothing could justify such monstrous behaviour.

This view was correct. But few Americans—and certainly not the media—paused to consider how many innocent foreigners had been killed by the U.S. bombs and missiles in the previous decades.

After the September 11 bombings, Americans were appalled and enraged by TV clips of Palestinians cheering the slaughter. None seemed to recall how Americans would cheer and laugh as they watched the U.S. smart bombs and the occupation pulverize Iraq, killing an estimated fifty thousand–one hundred thousand civilians; nor how the Israeli invasion of Lebanon in 1982—approved by the U.S. government—killed eighteen thousand Lebanese civilians; nor how the 1980 Gulf War, encouraged by the United States, killed five hundred thousand Iraqis and Iranians; nor how the endless Arab-Israeli conflict has killed untold thousands.

Bin Laden, wrongly or rightly, was seen by militant Muslims as the avenger of these slaughters, the deliverer of overdue retribution that America so richly deserved for wars and overthrown governments across the Mideast. From 1980 to 2001, the United States had committed acts of war against these Muslim nations: Iraq, Iran, Libya, Syria, Lebanon, Sudan, Iran, Somalia, and Afghanistan. In this period, the United States overthrew or tried to bring down governments of Egypt,

Syria, Iraq, Iran, Lebanon, Sudan, Libya, and most lately Afghanistan. The United States sought to assassinate numerous Muslim leaders, including Egypt's Gamal Abdel Nasser, Iraq's Saddam Hussein, Libya's Muammar Gadhafi, Iran's clerical leadership, the leadership of the Taliban, and Iraqi's Saddam Hussein.

The United States has not been an innocent bystander in the Mideast, but rather the central figure in the region's murderous politics since World War II, a nation that has made and unmade regimes, armed and financed wars, and shaped events for its own great power interests: oil and geopolitics.

It now seems inevitable that one day such powerful intrusion from the United States would ignite lethal retaliation against America. Militant Muslims could finally say, "Now they know what we've been through for years." To them, Brother Osama was the long-awaited instrument of America's punishment.

KASHMIR: WAR IN PARADISE

PROLOGUE

Fight in the way of God against those who fight against you,
but do not yourselves be aggressors; for verily, God does not love
aggressors....Fight against them until there is no longer
oppression and all men are free to worship God.

KORAN

KASHMIR. LINE OF CONTROL. 0243 HRS.

Two star shells drifted slowly down from the moonless sky, blazing an intense, sharp-edged magnesium light over the pine forests below. Off to our left, beyond the next hill, Indian border guards began firing shimmering volleys of tracer bullets. From somewhere farther behind the fortified Line of Control (LOC) that divides Kashmir, a battery of Indian 81 mm mortars opened fire.

Rashid laughed. "They are frightened. The Indians are firing at ghosts again." Indeed, Indian troops guarding the ceasefire line in Kashmir were jumpy and trigger-happy. Small bands of mujahedin were slipping across the hilly, wooded border each night to join the national uprising in the Indian-held portion of Kashmir. The nervous Indians fired at every sound, at anything that moved in the night.

We were huddled down behind a small knoll, shivering slightly as the damp cold of the Kashmir mountains penetrated our olive-drab field jackets. After a few minutes, the firing abated, then ceased completely. The rising wind stirred the tall pines around us. Rashid rose to his feet and began surveying the Indian positions below us through a pair of powerful German field glasses. He had come up to the front line that night to study Indian defenses. I had joined him on the reconnaissance mission, eager to have a close look at the barrier defenses on the Indian side of the LOC, a series of strong points behind a lethal barrier of thick razor wire, minefields, and delicate sensors that detected movement and sound.

Rashid had made, as I had, a very long, arduous journey to join the intifada in Kashmir. At some time in the distant past, Rashid had been an engineering student in Iraq. He showed me an old, dog-eared photo of himself: youthful, beardless, and slim. Now, many years and more pounds later, the burly Rashid looked the picture of a modern Islamic holy warrior, with his thick black beard, regulation pakul knitted hat from Afghanistan, green field outfit and combat boots, AK-47 Kalashnikov, and a brace of Chinese-made grenades.

Soon after graduating from university in Baghdad, Rashid went off to Pakistan to join the great jihad (holy war), which was being waged against the Soviet army in Afghanistan. For Rashid, and thousands of other idealistic young Muslim men and women, the struggle against the Communists in Afghanistan was not merely a crusade against evil and oppression; it seemed, at the time, a path that would lead the downtrodden Islamic world to renewal and dignity.

Rashid had joined the Islamic International Brigade and fought the Communists for four years in the 1980s in Afghanistan, where he was trained by the CIA as a heavy weapons specialist.

We heard a series of rapid explosions about a mile off to our left. Rashid told me Indian howitzers were firing at a nullah, a narrow, dry gully that intersected the border at a right angle, and that provided a sheltered corridor along which mujahedin units slipped across the border between the Indian and Pakistani parts of Kashmir. Indian patrols were either using newly acquired night-vision devices to spot and then bring fire down on a group of holy warriors who were trying to penetrate the minefields and wire along the LOC, or were merely interdicting a known crossing point with random shelling.

The Muslim uprising in the two-thirds of Kashmir occupied by India had been under way for more than four years. After nearly half a century of Indian rule that was as inefficient and capricious as it was corrupt and brutal, Kashmiri Muslims had unexpectedly exploded in rebellion. The uprising surprised everyone, not least the Kashmiris themselves, who had long had a reputation for passivity, and wholly lacked the martial reputation of their other northern neighbours.

But the victory in 1989 by Islamic forces over the mighty Soviet Union and its Afghan Communist satraps had galvanized the entire Muslim world, including the Muslim majority in neighbouring Kashmir. For the first time in memory, Muslims had defeated a mighty colonial power, the U.S.S.R., which was also the world's leading oppressor of Islam.

The struggle to free Muslim lands from European and Russian colonial rule had been going on for sixty years. In the 1930s, bands of Libyan mujahedin had breached barbed wire and minefields laid by the

Italians along the border with Egypt. Twenty years later, Algerian mujahedin had fought their way across the minefields and electrified wire of
the lethal Morice Line, built by the French to halt infiltration and the
re-supply of the rebel forces. In the 1950s and '60s, Palestinian feday-
een had been cut down trying to breach to the wire and minefields
defending Israel's border. Now it was Rashid's turn lead his holy warriors across a new line of death on a new jihad.

8
THE KINGDOM OF SIKANDAR

The fabled state of Kashmir lies in majestic isolation amid the
towering mountain ranges separating the overpopulated plains
of India from the endless steppes and deserts of Central Asia.
Kashmir has long been called the "jewel of India," "the Switzerland of
Asia," and the "abode of the gods."

The noted nineteenth-century geopoliticians Sir Halford Mackinder
and Baron Karl Haushofer described this region as one the world's primary
strategic pivots—the nexus of continents, empires, and civilizations.

Kashmir is surrounded by a great bowl of crags: the Himalayas
and Karakorarns. Its borders are disputed but Kashmir's total. area is
approximately 239,000 square kilometres (92,200 square miles),
roughly the size of Great Britain. With a population of eleven million, Kashmir is larger than half the world's nations. Eight and a half
million Kashmiris live in the Indian-held sector, 2.5 million in the
Pakistani portion, or Azad Kashmir. Another million people of
Kashmiri origin live in the Pakistani-administered Gilgit-Baltistan
region, or Northern Territories, an area claimed by Kashmiri nationalists as part of their nation. A further million live in Pakistan, or are
scattered in the diaspora around the globe.

The majority of Kashrniris are tall, slender, fair-skinned people of
Aryan, Indo-European origin. A minority, concentrated in Ladakh, the

Gilgit Valley, and Baltistan are Mongol-Tibetans, short, dark-skinned people little different in physical appearance from the tribes of Tibet. Kashmir also has two small groups of nomadic mountaineers: the Gujars and Dards. Culturally, Kashmir's peoples have traditionally looked northward to Central Asia and Tibet, rather than south to India.

Unless you are a yak or a bird, there are only two ways of getting into the Indian-ruled portion of Kashmir. The first is an interminably long, physically excruciating, and often perilous 700-kilometre (435-mile) road voyage from New Delhi, India, over rising hills and steep mountain passes, which are often blocked by snow or landslides, to Srinagar, Kashmir's lake-girded capital.

A flight into the Kashmir Valley from New Delhi on one of India's internal airlines is also rather risky: their pilots are notorious for drink and incompetence; maintenance is shoddy; and aircraft are old, tired, and often suffering from advanced metal fatigue. Indian air carriers are almost always late; flights are frequently cancelled because of mechanical problems or for other, more mysterious reasons.

Weaving and bobbing in a small Indian airliner between snow-capped mountains and around huge banks of cumulus clouds is a grandly hair-raising experience, even for the most phlegmatic or jaded traveller. But however dangerous flying inside India may be, it is quicker and considerably safer to take a plane than to brave the sustained terror and intense discomforts of road travel.

The Pakistani portion of divided Kashmir, called Azad (Free) Kashmir, can be reached only by a long, tortuous journey over evil mountain roads, a trek that begins at Pakistan's capital, Islamabad, in northern Punjab, where the foothills of the mighty Karakoram range start to rise. Islamabad itself is no easy destination to attain. I had decided to go to Azad Kashmir to follow the new jihad in the Indian-ruled part of the divided state, and to renew my contacts with some of the mujahedin I had met during the Afghan conflict.

•••

Custom-made capitals are disturbing, sterile places, unnatural creations that are half ghost town, half Potemkin village. Their awkward locations are determined not by the natural evolutionary logic of urbanism, geography, and trade, but by fear of foreign invasion, desire to escape the evils of commercial contamination, the need to be in friendly tribal territory, or, worst of all, rampant megalomania.

Think of Brasilia, a sort of bureaucratic Devil's Island, preposterously sited in the middle of a vast nothingness, a good 1,600 kilometres (1,000 miles) from the inhabited coastal regions of Brazil; of Romanian tyrant Nicolae Ceausescu's monstrous megalomaniapolis of neo-Stalinist palaces, built on the bulldozed ruins of elegant old Bucharest. Abuja, the new Nigerian capital, fallen into semi-ruin and slipping back into the jungle even before its construction was completed. Or the latest folly of would-be grandeur, the new Kazakh capital at Astana, a windblown former caravan stop on the empty Central Asian steppe.

Islamabad, Pakistan's capital, was created in 1954 for all these bad reasons by its then president, Field Marshal Ayub Khan, a tough Pathan soldier from the North-West Frontier. Ayub sought to remove government from the nefarious clutches of corrupt, wicked Karachi; to move away from unfriendly Sind Province to his political, military, and tribal power base in the north; and, of course, to leave a grandiose monument of his enlightened rule.

Five decades later, Islamabad remains a monument of sorts to Ayub, with its squat, uniform blocks of banal, white marble government buildings set among leafy trees and lush gardens. Streets are laid out in an eminently logical grid pattern, and numbered, appropriately, like so many office files. The city is whistle-clean, orderly, tranquil, and odour-free, a leafy bureaucratic oasis carefully set apart from the otherwise ubiquitous squalor, tumult, and disorder of South Asia. Islamabad looks and smells nothing like the rest of Pakistan. The capital is a brain detached from the nation's body, floating, as in a B-grade science-fiction film, in a sterile, liquid-filled container called Islamabad.

After two steamy nights in Islamabad, I set off for Azad Kashmir, wedged in the back of a Japanese car whose features included exceptionally bad springs, a struggling motor, and an impaired braking system. My ultimate destination was Chokoti, a village that lies at the apex of a sharp salient along the mountainous ceasefire line between Indian and Pakistani forces in Kashmir. The road to the north is deceptive. You first leave Islamabad along a smooth-surfaced highway with four luxurious lanes, bordered by impressive white curbstones. Once out of sight of Islamabad, however, this Pakistani autobahn soon deteriorates into a two-lane potholed road that winds laboriously upward to the hill station of Muree, a famous refuge of colonial British from the murderous summer heat of the Indian plains.

Muree, a cluster of low wooden buildings atop a steep hill, has little to recommend it save its 2,286-metre (7,500-foot) altitude and panoramic views of the Karakoram Mountains to the north. Any pretense at modern arterial communications ceases at Muree. Beyond, the road hugs the side of the Jhelum River, one of the five main tributaries of the great Indus River. The road, by now a narrow strip of intermittent asphalt punctuated by deep potholes, interrupted by water courses, and liberally peppered with fallen rocks and branches, wound down through narrow gorges.

Overladen trucks, threatening to capsize at any moment, careened perilously around blind corners. Animals and pedestrians ambled along the road, as heedless of danger as if it were a country lane. Gaily painted buses, known as "flying coaches," navigated with an equal disregard for safety, as if eager to deliver their tightly packed human cargoes into the hands of Allah the Merciful. In fact, each year numerous flying coaches miss turns and fall into the Jhelum or the even mightier Indus, vast torrents of roiling, vicious, grey water filled with an aqueous avalanche of rocks, boulders, and logs. The unfortunate charabancs and their passengers are ground to unidentifiable bits in this lethal Himalayan slurry.

As the road again rose, the air grew steadily cooler. The torrid heat of the plains below was forgotten as we climbed through thick forests of spruce, beech, and pine. Clouds and mist hung low, grey and moist. Freshets of icy water poured down the mossy sides of the ever-steeper cliffs banking the road and river.

Wet, muddy, and unstable, the road grew more perilous as we progressed. Each hairpin turn threatened either a watery grave in the Jhelum River or instant pulverization by a hurtling truck or bus. Road travel seems to be Pakistan's natural form of population control.

One quickly gets what I call "Pakistani road terror," a condition that combines utter helplessness with panic, flashes of fatalism, and nervous frenzy. It's impossible to close your eyes for a second, even during a twenty-hour ride, lest you fail to see your last moments on earth. Screaming at the drivers, who keep their pedals to the floor and horns blaring, is pointless. They shrug, laugh at the foolish farangi, mutter curses in Baluchi or some obscure dialect, and go even faster. You cling desperately to the seat back, or straps, brace your battered body and pray to Allah, Vishnu, Buddha, and the Holy Virgin of Santiago that you will survive the next mile.

After six hours of this unrelenting torture, we arrive at Muzafarabad, the grandly named capital of the third of the mountain state controlled by Pakistan, Azad Kashmir. The city is very far from impressive. It is a dismal collection of mouldering concrete buildings and wooden shacks set in a dreary valley, with the usual Indo-Pakistani urban backdrop of broken-down vehicles, stray animals, street urchins, refuse heaps, ugly overhead power lines, and squalid shops lit by a single, dim fluorescent bulb giving off a funereal blue glow. I was not impressed. Could this truly be the gateway to fabled Kashmir?

I was escorted, with much solemnity, to meet the prime minister of Azad Kashmir, a soft-spoken, venerable gentleman with a very white beard, neatly attired in a grey Nehru jacket and a high karakul fur hat. Very politely, in his gentle voice, he denounced the impious, godless Indians who were raping and pillaging his beloved Kashmir. "You must study the Holy Koran," he admonished me gently, wagging a finger and showing grandfatherly concern for the visiting non-believer. "Allah will guide us to the true path in Kashmir, and smite the ungodly." Brave words, but there were nearly one billion "ungodly" Hindus across the border.

The high official seemed to have little else of note to say. We exchanged platitudes, and drank milky tea. Known as "chat," this form of tea is unique to the Asian subcontinent. To make it properly, you must take a battered, blackened, greasy aluminum pan; add contaminated water, two or three tablespoonfuls of insect-infested sugar, raw, unpasteurized milk, and black, perfumed tea; then boil it all up into a sweet white drink that will either cure whatever ails travellers to these parts or, more likely, leave you with Q fever, cholera, and assorted parasites. In these parts, tea cannot be refused when offered, which it always is. I discreetly gulped down an antibiotic capsule I had learned to always keep secreted in my pocket for just such social occasions.

I was relieved to bid the venerable prime minister farewell and continue our journey to see the refugee camps in Azad Kashmir and continue on to the front at Chokoti. We left town, and crossed the rushing river over an old, groaning Bailey bridge left over from World War II. There was a large flag-decked stone arch surmounting its far end, bearing a sign proclaiming "Welcome to Azad Kashmir." We drove through, leaving melancholy Muzafarabad well behind.

As before, the narrow, wet, crumbling road followed the sinuous gorge hewn by the raging Jhelum River into the heart of the granite mountains, ever deeper into Kashmir. Sprays of water from the raging river washed over the road and our car. Occasional clusters of hovels and orchards clung to the side of the road. Otherwise, we were alone in the great vastness of soaring mountains, rushing water, and winding defiles.

By now, the mountains had become taller and more jagged, so that their serrated peaks seemed to shred the thin white clouds scudding over them. We were awash in green: thick stands of trees and bush; lichen-covered rocks; and broad slopes blanketed with tall, damp, glistening grass. A sea of welcome luscious green after the endless aridity of the dun-coloured plains. And everywhere precious water, worth more than human life in the dry south, gushing forth from rocks, running like quicksilver down granite slopes, collecting in sparkling pools, cascading with abandon into the Jhelum River. This seemed an outrageous, criminally extravagant waste of precious water, like gold coins thrown into the sea for the entertainment of children. I recalled an old love poem of the Gujar nomads: "I am thirsty; you are my water..."

At that precise moment, I suddenly understood why Indians and Pakistanis were willing to kill for Kashmir, why they had warred fifty years over this kingdom in the clouds. Kashmir aroused the most ferocious and unique passions in everyone, passions that brooked neither compromise nor concession. The place quite simply was heaven. And no one was about to hand over heaven, of all places, to a hated enemy. To dwellers on the flat, sere, furnace-like plains of north India and Punjab, Kashmir was a dream: inexhaustible sweet water; cool air; lush, dark soil; trees, flowers, fruits; and beautiful, fair-skinned women. No matter that few Indians had actually seen Kashmir. It was truly the jewel of India, the guardian of the holy rivers, the abode of the gods.

To comprehend the importance of Kashmir to the Indian psyche, one must first understand the role played by race in India's ancient culture. Few outsiders understand how important caste and skin colour are in Hindu society.

The linguistic origin of the word "caste" comes from the Portuguese and Spanish term for race, *casta*. Rightly so, because the caste system discriminates by race and enforces social stratification; one of its prime goals in India is to keep the darker-skinned lower orders, in particular, Dravidians, from mixing socially or sexually with the lighter-skinned higher orders. The caste system has become so fragmented into sub-castes, and so much a part of India's social fabric, that its racist origins have come to be widely ignored or forgotten. India, for example, became a leading foe and constant critic of South Africa's apartheid system, unconscious of the irony that its own caste system was just as racially driven and pervasive as that imposed by the regime it so ardently denounced.

At the apex of India's caste pyramid are Brahmans, who believe themselves to be defiled if any of the food they consume has been touched by a lower-caste person, or if even the shadow of such a person falls upon them. Economics reinforces caste for the large numbers of Indian peasants who are condemned to permanent indentured servitude, unable ever to escape the crushing debts and accumulating interest they owe to rapacious moneylenders. Indebtedness passes from one generation to the next, ensuring the permanence of their near slavery. At the bottom of the caste system are 160 million untouchables, today known as Dalits, a group whose original function was menial chores and the sweeping up of feces deposited in the street by higher-caste defecators. Some years ago when I was in India, sociologists were amazed to discover an unknown subcaste of untouchables who had never previously been identified because they were not allowed to appear in daylight. These wretches lived exclusively in garbage dumps, where they fed on refuse, emerging only at night to do washing for slightly higher-caste untouchables.

The Brahmin caste has long provided Hindu India's ruling elite. Brahmins and other high castes are generally of Indo-European, or Aryan, blood. Groups of nomadic Aryan tribes from Western Asia—the progenitors of Europe's Indo-European settlers—came down into north India through the Khyber Pass around 1500 BCE, spreading rapidly across the subcontinent as far east as Bengal. The religion of these Aryan tribes, based on the holy books of the Veda with their pantheon of warrior sky deities, spread in the wake of the invaders; by 1000 BCE it had developed into Brahmanism, a more complex, nuanced faith, the precursor of today's Hindu faith.

Hinduism divides society into four basic castes: Brahmans (priests), Kshatriya (nobles, warriors), Vaisya (merchants or farmers), and Sudra (workers). Over the centuries innumerable subcastes have developed.

The only way for a Hindu to rise from a lower to a higher caste is through the process of reincarnation.

The Aryan Hindus were racially and linguistically akin to the early Germanic tribes that migrated into Europe. This link can easily be distinguished by the word for "king." In Europe's languages, *roi, Rex*, and *rey*, all share the same ancient Aryan linguistic root as the Indian term, "raja." The Aryans displaced India's indigenous Dravidians, a smaller, dark-skinned people, pushing them down into southern India. Today, skin colour and language are the great divide of India: in the north, Hindi-speaking Aryans; in the south, dark-skinned speakers of Dravidian languages such as Tamil, Kannada, Malayalam, Telugu. A northern Indian from Punjab or Uttar Pradesh is as distinct racially and linguistically as a Norwegian is from a Sicilian.

Brahmins from Kashmir, who held the highest rank on this racial-religious-social scale, are held in great esteem for their fair skin, fine features, and aristocratic ways. To Hindus, Kashmir is a repository of the pure essence of Aryan Hindu culture. Jawaharlal Nehru, India's first prime minister and founding father, was a Kashmiri Brahman. Brilliant, haughty, and imperious, Nehru was the embodiment of Hindu hereditary royalty.

Legend has it that the light-skinned peoples of Kashmir, Gilgit, the Hunza Valley, and Baltistan are descendants of the soldiers of Alexander the Great. Those who know Rudyard Kipling's "The Man Who Would Be King," or the superb film that was made of it, will recall how the local tribes awaited the return of Sikandar, Alexander's son. There may, in fact, be substance to this charming legend. Alexander fought his way through the Khyber Pass and entered northern India via the Indus valley in 327 BCE. The following year, Alexander won a major battle against the local king at Hydapses, but his army refused to march any deeper into India.

Alexander returned to Persia, but he left behind many thousands of his elite Macedonian troops, with orders to marry local women and found Greek satrapies. In classical times, Macedonians and most Greeks were a fair-skinned, blue-eyed people who showed their Germanic roots—a far cry from today's Hellenes, who are the product of centuries of racial mixing with multiethnic Ottoman Turks, Slavs, and other Balkan peoples.

Cut off in Kashmir from India and Afghanistan by the ramparts of the Karakorams and Himalayas, the Greco-Kashmiri gene pool remained relatively isolated until modern times. The result is a people who appear strikingly different from their neighbours, rather like marooned survivors from a lost ship—wrecked, beached, and forgotten long ago on a strange, uncharted island.

On my way from Gilgit I passed through the fabled Hunza Valley, the ancestral home of the Aga Khans, the powerful hereditary Imam of one branch of Shiism. Stopping for chai at a tea shop at the crest of a long, winding pass, I saw a blond man in a parka, about 1.8 metres (6 feet) tall with very fair skin and blue eyes, and taking him to be British or north German, I addressed him in English. He could not understand me. The shop owner said, "Sahib-sir, he only speaks our local language." I was stunned and abashed. Later, I was to see many natives of Hunza, Kashmir, the Swat Valley, and Chitral who looked as Aryan as the man in the blue parka. The Kafir Kalash, a little-known non-Muslim tribe with the interesting custom of picking the strongest man in the village to mate with all its virgins, look as if they had just flown in from Hamburg. Where did these fair-skinned people come from, if not Alexander's hoplites?

For Muslims, passions over Kashmir run even deeper. Kashmir is the only Indian state that has a Muslim majority; it had been a stronghold of high Islamic culture for centuries. More important, Kashmir's famous gardens, shimmering lakes, snow-clad mountains, waterfalls, beautiful women, and Alpine climate seem to embody the Koran's description of Muslim paradise. For 260 million illiterate but deeply pious Muslims in Pakistan and India, Kashmir is literally heaven on earth.

To politicians and generals on both sides, Kashmir has always been of such enormous strategic importance that its loss simply cannot be contemplated. To bitter enemies India and Pakistan, Kashmir plays the same inflammatory role as Alsace-Lorraine did between France and Germany from 1870 to 1945, a jealously disputed territory that arouses fierce irredentist hatreds and exaggerated fears in both nations.

•••

The region today known as Kashmir was a Buddhist kingdom that paid fealty to Tibet until the seventh century CE, when it fell under Hindu rule. Muslim rulers ousted the Hindus in the fourteenth century. The great Muslim Mogul emperor Akbar conquered the valley in 1586 and made it his summer residence. In 1757, wild Afghans overran Kashmir. Then in 1819 came the warlike Sikhs, until they in turn were defeated in the Sikh Wars by the army of the British East India Company, which annexed Punjab and Kashmir.

In 1846, the British East India Company sold Kashmir to Gulab Singh, the Hindu maharaja of Jammu, giving him the status of an independent princely ruler under the Raj, to which the maharaja paid annual tribute. Supported by the British, Gulab Singh annexed the neighbouring regions of Gilgit, Hunza, Nagar, and Chitral to his kingdom of Kashmir and Jammu, creating the region today termed Kashmir. Muslim Kashmiris rebelled repeatedly against their new Hindu ruler, but the revolts were put down by the maharaja's forces, aided by troops of the British Indian Army.

At the time of India's partition by Britain in 1947, today's Indian-ruled part of Jammu and Kashmir was about 77 per cent Muslim, 20 per cent Hindus, and 3 per cent Sikhs and Buddhists. What was to become the Pakistani portion, or Azad Kashmir, was 100 per cent Muslim. The Indian-controlled state was ruled by Gulab Singh's descendant, Hari Singh. Economically, Kashmir was closely linked to the eastern Punjab, the region that was to become Pakistan after partition. Poor roads, high passes, and landslides made communication with India difficult, even in clement summer weather. The roads leading northwest from Pathankot to Jammu and Poonch in southern Kashmir were often closed by rockfalls, or snow. Srinagar, Kashmir's capital, was four times closer to Islamabad than to Delhi.

Though an independent united India extending from Iran to Burma was the most cherished dream of the Congress Party, led by Mohandas K. Gandhi and Jawaharlal Nehru, by the end of World War II it became clear the subcontinent was headed for partition. The leader of the powerful Muslim League, Muhammad Ali Jinnah, pressed relentlessly for creation of a state for India's minority Muslims that would offer them a haven from frequent persecution by Hindus, and the opportunity to create the world's first nation guided by Islamic thinking.

By the eve of India's independence in 1947, Britain's new socialist government was eager to wash its hands of colonialism and India, and Lord Louis Mountbatten, the British viceroy, hastily agreed to Jinnah's plan to create a separate Muslim state out of predominantly

Muslim regions in Bengal, the western Punjab, and Sind, though the latter two areas were separated from the former by an entire continent. Nehru and Gandhi protested bitterly, prophetically warning that the decision to split the British Raj in two (or three) would destabilize the subcontinent and lead to future strife. Mountbatten and his advisers rebuffed these warnings and made few plans to deal with any breakdown of law and order.

India was partitioned on August 15, 1947. Communal violence between Hindus, Muslims, and Sikhs immediately erupted. In one of modern history's largest population transfers, seventeen million Hindus and Muslims fled their homes. An orgy of mass killing, rape, arson, and looting ensued that the confused British authorities proved powerless to prevent or suppress. Estimates of the number of people who died in the bloodbath range between five hundred thousand and one million.

India's five hundred-odd princely states, which had formerly been vassals of the British Raj, were left to decide on accession to India or Pakistan. The largest such state, Hyderabad, with a large Muslim population, elected to join India, which surrounded it. But Kashmir, which lay between India and Pakistan, presented a unique problem.

The terrible trauma of partition hit Kashmir with full force: it quickly became the focus of ferocious Indo-Pakistani rivalry. Lord Mountbatten went to Kashmir shortly before partition and advised the maharaja, a reactionary and dissolute potentate, to determine whether his people wished to join India or Pakistan—or whether they preferred a third option, to remain an independent princely state. Gandhi hurried north to Kashmir and convinced the maharaja to accede to India and dismiss his prime minister, who favoured independence. Muslim Kashmiri leaders, notably Sheik Abdullah and Ghulam Abbas, were thrown into prison by the maharaja.

Mountbatten advised that the Kashmiri majority be allowed to choose their own allegiance, and Nehru publicly promised to respect their wishes, but in the end both advice and promises were ignored. Mountbatten's strong-willed wife, Edwina, who was openly carrying on an affair with Nehru, may well have influenced her wavering husband to tacitly favour Indian rule over Kashmir—or, at least, not to impede it. Britain's socialist government failed to ensure that its pre-partition assurances were observed. Kashmiri Muslims, who overwhelmingly desired to join Pakistan, were ordered to surrender their arms, and promptly revolted. In September 1947, in the southern Kashmir regions of Poonch and Jammu, which had and still have sizeable Hindu majorities, mobs of Hindus and Sikhs, aided by the maharaja's Sikh soldiers, began slaughtering Muslims. Muslim sources claim two hundred thousand of the region's total Muslim population of five hundred thousand were killed, and the rest driven as refugees to Pakistan. Muslim mobs turned against Hindus and Sikhs, slaughtering thousands.

As communal fighting spread across Kashmir, Pakistani leaders organized a "spontaneous" counterattack in October 1947 by Pathan tribesmen from the North-West Frontier. The war-loving Pathans proclaimed a holy war, and promptly attacked the maharaja's small ragtag personal army of Hindus and Sikhs. The fierce Pathans routed the maharaja's troops, and advanced swiftly to within 30 kilometres (19 miles) of Srinagar, the Kashmir' capital, and were poised to seize its vital airfield, the only one in Kashmir. The panicky maharaja appealed to Delhi for immediate military aid. Nehru agreed to succor the beleaguered Hindu ruler, but only if he would immediately join India. Hari Singh quickly agreed to Nehru's demand, and signed the Instrument of Accession to India on October 26, 1947, but with an important proviso: Kashmiris could decide on the future of their state once the military emergency was over. Lord Mountbatten confirmed this in a letter to the maharaja on the following day.

Meanwhile, in typical tribal fashion, the Pathans delayed their attack on Srinagar and its airfield in order to devote themselves to looting and pillage. This delay allowed India time to mount an air bridge to Srinagar. The Indians used their entire inventory of thirty Dakota military transports to airlift a battalion of Sikhs, blood enemies of the Pathans, to Srinagar's airfield. A three-thousand-man army brigade was rushed up the terrible roads from the plains to Kashmir. After a month of chaotic fighting, the Pathans and Muslim irregular forces were pushed westward by arriving Indian Army troops. Further inconclusive fighting, which was joined in 1948 by regular Pakistani army units, sputtered on until the United Nations imposed a ceasefire in January 1949 between India and Pakistan.

When the fighting ended, two-thirds of Kashmir was in Indian hands, and a third in Pakistan's. The ceasefire line between the warring forces (the LOC) became the de facto border, along which both sides constructed field fortifications and deployed large numbers of troops and artillery—and there they remain today, half a century later, in a state of constant skirmishing and occasional major clashes. The lush Kashmir Valley, Srinagar, and mountainous Ladakh remained in Indian hands. In addition to the western third of the Kashmir Valley, Pakistan ended up in possession of the more northern Kashmiri regions of Gilgit and Baltistan, which it terms the "Northern Territories."

The border up to the top of Kashmir, which abuts China and Tibet, a rampart of soaring, snow-capped mountains and the great Baltoro and Siachen glaciers, was left undemarcated—it was judged that no one could have any possible interest in such an uninhabitable, lethally high range of frozen crags. Such common sense would later fall victim to the poisonous hatred between Indians and Pakistanis, driving them to fight ferociously over utterly remote, absolutely worthless peaks that even mountain goats would not inhabit.

Beginning in 1948, the UN Security Council passed a series of resolutions calling for the status of Kashmir to be decided by a free, impartial plebiscite under supervision of the UN. Pakistan readily agreed, knowing the outcome would favour it. But Delhi refused to accept the UN's will, and set about integrating Kashmir into India. Subsequent UN resolutions reaffirming the original call for a plebiscite were also ignored or dismissed by India as non-binding, irrelevant, and an unacceptable intrusion into India's internal affairs. Pakistan refused to withdraw its forces from Azad Kashmir.

Kashmir remains the oldest, longest-running world dispute before the UN, predating even the Arab-Israeli conflict and the intractable dispute over Cyprus and shows no sign of being resolved.

After 1949, riots by Kashmiri Muslims were put down ruthlessly, and Kashmiri Muslim leaders were repeatedly jailed, bribed, or intimidated into silence. In 1957, after years of creeping legal and administrative expropriation, India officially annexed Kashmir. Delhi was also subsequently to annex the former Portuguese territory of Goa, and turn the remote, but strategic, Himalayan states of Bhutan and Sikkim into Indian protectorates. Aside from protests by Pakistan, Portugal, and, ominously, China, all three annexations were greeted by the outside world with deep indifference. Few observers at the time noted that India, a vociferous champion of non-alignment and self-proclaimed scourge of Western colonialism, had itself become something of a regional colonial power.

•••

Another important element in the interlocking conflicts at the top of the world lies in a region deep in the vastness of the Karakorams. Remote Ladakh, known for centuries as "little Tibet," occupies an area on the northern shoulder of Kashmir. It is India's only region with a Buddhist majority. Ladakh's people are of the same ethnic and linguistic group as Tibetans, and in fact form part of historic ethnic Tibet.

Ladakh is one of the earth's least-known places, a long, lonely series of desolate, arid valleys, girded on the southwest by the Zanskar Mountains, to the northeast by the Ladakh Range and the Karakorams, and the southwest by Kashmir. Geographically, it forms the extreme western end of the Tibetan Plateau.

A single narrow military road, open only six months of the year, leads up from Srinagar, across the Zoji La (*la* means "pass"), at 3,529 metres (11,578 feet) to Kargil. Then the road struggles over a series of even more vertiginous passes to the capital, Leh, which lies near the upper reaches of the mighty Indus River, Pakistan's principal source of groundwater. Leh, which has twenty thousand inhabitants, resembles a miniature version of pre-1950 Lhasa in culture and language. In fact, today Ladakh looks much more like traditional Tibet than the neighbouring Chinese-occupied state. Harsh Chinese rule and immigration by some two million Han Chinese settlers have permanently altered the ethnography and character of Tibet; Ladakh, by contrast, still retains some of its original Tibetan culture, Buddhist-Lamist religion. The Indians have fortunately done less to alter Ladakh's way of life.

Like the rest of Kashmir, Ladakh has been the frequent victim of invasions by neighbours, including Tibet. The Dogra maharajas of Jammu and Kashmir established their rule over Ladakh in the mid-1800s. At partition, in 1947, India forces occupied Ladakh, keeping on its king as a figurehead. The Chinese occupation of Aksai Chin, and the 1962 border war between China and India, spurred Delhi to build the military road linking Srinagar to Kargil and Leh, and to deploy large numbers of troops in Ladakh, parts of which are permanently restricted as sensitive military zones. When the Dalai Lama fled to India from Tibet after the Chinese invasion, he sought permission to settle in Ladakh. Fearing his presence would kindle Ladakhi nationalism and pro-Tibetan sentiments, India denied the request.

The failure by the nineteenth-century British Raj to clearly demarcate borders in the Himalayas, the Karakorams, and Kashmir would come back to haunt twentieth-century India, China, and Pakistan. As an Arab diplomat told me, "Most of the problems today in Asia and Africa are the fault of British imperialism." An exaggeration, to be sure, but one that contains an important kernel of truth.

China holds Ladakh to be an extension of Tibet, and thus part of China. Tibetans insist Ladakh is part of their ancient kingdom. Pakistan contends Ladakh is part of Kashmir, which is claimed by Pakistan. India insists Ladakh is part of the Indian union; Delhi has possession, of course, and troops on the ground, to support its claim.

The little mountain state of 130,000 people is of great strategic significance to India: its northwest border runs along the notional ceasefire line with Pakistani-held Baltistan, from the region around Kargil to the enormous Siachen Glacier on the border of Tibet. Its northeast frontier abuts the strategic Aksai Chin plateau, annexed by China in the 1950s. Leh is filled with Indian military personnel, producing an uncomfortable comparison with Chinese-occupied Lhasa.

India has long restricted visits by foreigners and journalists to Ladakh, citing military security. Another reason may be reported unrest by Ladakhis against heavy-handed Indian rule. India is extremely sensitive to potential accusations that it may be suppressing or illegally occupying Little Tibet, just as China suffers international rebuke and protest over its seizure of "Big" Tibet.

Like two other, similar mountain kingdoms, Bhutan and Sikkim, Ladakh is a historical orphan, caught between two of the world's largest nations, and destined, inevitably, to be absorbed by them.

•••

While India and Pakistan were fighting over the Kashmir Valley, China quietly took advantage of the confusion to advance its own territorial claims on the remote eastern end of Kashmir. Northeast of Ladakh, abutting Tibet, lies Aksai Chin, another chunk of disputed Kashmir that was of enormous strategic interest to China. Aksai Chin is a vast, arid, almost uninhabited plateau of icy lakes and frozen peaks, averaging 4,572 metres (15,000 feet) of elevation, on the western extension of the Tibetan plateau. China seized Aksai Chin in the 1950s because the region offered the only possible route for a planned military road that would provide a vital southern link between Tibet and strategic Sinkiang, China's westernmost province.

Aksai Chin was so remote, Indian intelligence didn't even find out China had driven a strategic road across it until early in the 1960s. Pakistan gave tacit approval to this annexation because it badly needed Chinese political and military aid in its long struggle with India. Delhi insists to this day that Aksai Chin is Chinese-occupied Indian territory. Tibetans say Aksai Chin is part of historical Tibet, which it most likely is. No one has ever bothered to ask the opinion of the few yak herders of Aksai Chin who scratch a precarious living from this vast, forbidding wilderness of clouds, snow, and ice.

9
REVOLT IN THE MOUNTAINS

In 1963, growing anger at India's often brutal, corrupt rule over Kashmir, and the theft of a sacred hair of the Prophet from the famous Hazratbal Mosque in Srinagar, ignited widespread protests and riots by Muslims. The protests raged on for two years, and were brutally suppressed, with heavy bloodshed, by Indian security forces.

The surging violence in Kashmir finally sparked a second full-scale war between India and Pakistan in 1965. The two nations battled for seventeen days before the UN imposed a ceasefire. Each tried to cut off the other's access roads to Kashmir through northern Punjab. Both the Indian and Pakistani armies soon bogged down along the long front from Kashmir to the Arabian Sea, quickly exhausting their inadequate stores of munitions and supplies. Like nearly all Third World armies, neither side could mobilize rapidly enough to sustain or provide logistical support for a fast-moving armoured offensive. As so often happens in Indo-Pakistani wars, *blitz*krieg soon turned to *sitz*krieg.

Pakistan, which had believed its superior armour, its pilots, and the fighting spirit of its renowned "martial races"—Punjabis and Pathans— would overcome Indian numerical and material superiority, was forced to realize it lacked the military or economic power to decisively defeat seven-times-larger India. In addition, it was clear that, in any conflict, India held the important advantage of strategic depth, which allowed it to trade territory for time to mobilize and concentrate its superior forces. Narrow, wasp-waisted Pakistan had no such luxury.

During 1970–71, India's aggressive leader, Indira Gandhi, emboldened by her new strategic alliance with the Soviet Union, took advantage of an uprising in East Pakistan (today Bangladesh) against harsh rule by West Pakistan. Indira Gandhi had special Tibetan troops of the Indian armies, disguised as Bangladeshi rebels, infiltrate into East Pakistan to begin guerrilla warfare. As the revolt spread, Gandhi sent her rearmed, expanded army to conquer indefensible East Pakistan, which was easily overrun in three weeks by the very able Indian commander-in-chief, General Sam Maneckshaw.

Once again, Pakistani forces in the west, supported by heavy air attacks, hurled themselves against Indian deployments in Kashmir, northern Punjab, and the Thar Desert of Rajasthan. After initial dramatic successes, Pakistani attacks petered out. A major Pakistani armoured thrust against Pathankot and Jammu threatened to isolate Kashmir from India. But it was halted before its objective. So was a second major thrust toward Poonch, in southern Kashmir. Pakistan lacked adequate air cover, strategic reserves, or supplies to sustain its offensives.

Superior Indian forces, concentrated in two corps commands, counterattacked in the north, driving toward Sialkot, attempting to isolate Azad Kashmir from the rest of Pakistan. In the south, an Indian strike corps thrust into the Thar Desert, with the objective of cutting the narrow, vulnerable 1,600-kilometre (1,000-mile) rail and road lines between northern Punjab and Sind. Intense air and land battles raged as India gradually gained the upper hand. Both sides fought with gallantry and élan, but the tide of war turned relentlessly against Pakistan, which was forced onto the strategic defensive. For a while, it seemed Indira Gandhi would heed calls by nationalists to crush Pakistan once and for all. But heavy American pressure, including threats that the Seventh Fleet, which rushed a carrier battle group into the Arabian Sea off Pakistan, might intervene in the war, the exhaustion of Indian war stocks, and stiffening Pakistani resistance forced negotiations that ended hostilities.

Pakistan had suffered catastrophic dismemberment, losing its eastern half, which became the independent state of Bangladesh, but the impasse in Kashmir remained unchanged. Pakistanis emerged from the war badly shaken, militarily, morally, and politically.

In July 1972, India and Pakistan conducted lengthy negotiations at the old British hill station at Simla, under the aegis of their respective patrons, the U.S.S.R. and the United States. Moscow and Washington, concerned they might be dragged into the Indo-Pakistani war, and thus face the risk of a direct clash, pressed Islamabad and Delhi to reach a negotiated settlement.

After much haggling, India and Pakistan agreed, first, that they would settle all their differences by peaceful means through bilateral negotiations; second, that neither would take any action to upset the status quo, or aid any forces seeking to do so; and, third, that the Line of Control in Kashmir would form the temporary border between India and Pakistan until Kashmir's final status was resolved.

India, basking in its successful war, regarded the Simla Agreement as a final end to the long dispute. Pakistan, in India's view, had accepted the permanent division of Kashmir and recognized Delhi's rule over two-thirds of the state. Equally important, according to Delhi's interpretation, Pakistan had agreed that Kashmir was to remain a wholly bilateral issue, not subject to any outside intervention or mediation, particularly that of the UN. Kashmir was now an entirely internal Indian matter; no UN interference, notably a plebiscite, would be legal under the Simla Agreement. Delhi adamantly maintains this position to this day.

Pakistan, negotiating from a position of weakness at Simla, portrayed the accords in a different light. Though on rather shaky legal ground, Islamabad held that the pact left the door open for UN intervention, and did nothing to preclude a referendum. Ever since 1972, Pakistan's diplomatic strategy has been to get India to admit that Kashmir remained "disputed" territory, and to involve the UN and friendly foreign powers in the issue. India has just as resolutely used its considerable diplomatic power to keep the United Nations and foreign powers out of the Kashmir dispute.

In effect, Simla resolved nothing. Unrest continued to flare up in the Kashmir Valley; Indian and Pakistani forces skirmished along the LOC. India continued a rapid increase of its armed forces, using new Soviet armour, artillery, and aircraft to develop a much-enhanced offensive capability against Pakistan.

Then, in 1974, India detonated a nuclear device in the Thar Desert, shaking Pakistan to its foundations and forcing Islamabad to embark on a long, covert, financially ruinous nuclear program. Pakistan's fiery leader, Zulfikar Ali Bhutto, announced his people would "eat grass" to pay for the arms race between two of the world's poorest nations. A very senior Pakistani diplomat, who attended a meeting between U.S. Secretary of State Henry Kissinger and Bhutto, told me that Kissinger had warned Bhutto the United States would "hold him personally responsible" if Pakistan went ahead with development of nuclear arms. Bhutto supporters were later to call his overthrow and execution by General Zia ul-Haq "Kissinger's revenge." Coincidentally, in the summer of 1988, the U.S.S.R. used precisely the same phrase, threatening to hold President Zia "personally responsible" for engineering a Soviet defeat in Afghanistan. Like Bhutto, Zia met an untimely end. After Simla, India's leaders almost convinced themselves the Kashmir problem had been permanently resolved by Pakistan's defeat in 1971. They also believed that continuing opposition by Kashmir's majority to Indian rule was wholly the result of Pakistani intrigues and subversion. Bloody Pakistan's nose, the thinking went, and the Kashmir problem will go away.

But it did not. Behind a facade of tense calm, a spirit of revolt was surging among Kashmiri Muslims. On July 13, 1989, a march in Srinagar by Kashmiris to commemorate Islamic martyrs, including Muslim leaders executed by India, turned violent and was crushed, with heavy casualties. Five months later, Kashmiri militants kidnapped the daughter of the home minister; she was released in exchange for the freeing of five jailed Kashmiri leaders.

This bizarre incident released a wave of nationalist emotion, violent protests, and bloody rioting across Kashmir. Both India and Pakistan were completely surprised by the sudden Muslim intifada, which, contrary to Delhi's mantras about foreign subversion, was in fact an indigenous, popular revolt by a people who could no longer bear Indian repression. Far from instigating the rebellion, Pakistan's intelligence service (ISI) was sharply rebuked by its political masters for failing to predict it.

On January 19, 1990, India proclaimed a state of siege in Kashmir: the compliant, pro-Indian Muslim chief minister, Farouk Abdullah, was forced to resign. Direct federal rule was imposed by Delhi, and the constitution and laws protecting individual rights were suspended in Kashmir. Delhi empowered its security forces to arrest and interrogate Kashmiris at will. Tens of thousands of troops and paramilitary police were rushed to Kashmir with orders to put down the rebellion by any means. Journalists were banned, so they could not report on what was to come.

Indian security forces had gained extensive experience in counter-insurgency and urban guerrilla warfare during the long, bitter battle that took place in the 1980s against Sikh secessionists in Punjab. Sikhs are followers of a warrior religion founded in the sixteenth century by Guru Nanak. Though only 2 per cent of India's population, the industrious Sikhs of Punjab produce almost 50 per cent of the nation's wheat, and fill many middle and senior positions in the armed forces and police.

In the early 1980s, groups of young Sikh fundamentalist militants began demanding independence from India and the creation of a Sikh state in Punjab, to be known as Khalistan, which would border rebellious Kashmir to the southwest. Rebellion against Hindu rule spread quickly: Indian security forces were put on the defensive and seriously demoralized by increasingly effective Sikh guerrilla groups and urban street fighters. The militant Sikhs devoted as much energy to killing their own fellow Sikhs who wanted to stay within India as they did attacking Indian security forces.

Delhi was losing the battle against Sikh fundamentalists until Indira Gandhi put an utterly ruthless, highly skilled police general, K.P.S. Gill, himself a Sikh, in charge of Punjab security. She gave Gill carte blanche, ordering him to smash the Sikh rebels, no questions asked. Gill reorganized the poorly led, disorganized, deeply demoralized security forces, and initiated a comprehensive intelligence program to understand, identify, and then penetrate the various Sikh secessionist factions.

Delhi chose the right man to crush the Sikh rebellion. The Sikh police general was tall, ferocious, and immensely impressive, with his perfectly wound turban, bristling mustache, neatly trimmed beard, and clipped, military speech. When I interviewed him, Gill answered Politely enough, but his hard, fierce eyes bored into me, telegraphing the message that all journalists, particularly Western ones, were meddling scum. Gill spoke of eradicating the Sikh separatists as if he were casually discussing exterminating lice. Sikhs are renowned for their bravery, fierceness, tenacity, and love of revenge. Delhi had cleverly set a Sikh to catch its Sikh foes.

The only other man I had met who commanded such instant respect and fear was Pakistan's director general of intelligence, General Akhtar Abdul Rahman Khan, who died in 1988 with President Zia in the mysterious crash of their C-130 transport aircraft. Akhdar made people tremble with fear; Gill looked as he was about to rip your skin off.

Gill counterattacked Sikh separatists, using summary executions and mass arrests; routine torture; intimidation of families; informers; and bribery. He flooded Punjab with regular army units and paramilitary police. Thousands of Sikh "miscreants" simply disappeared after being arrested "for questioning." Some were guilty of sedition, many others were innocent. Anyone denounced by informers, or whose name was uttered under torture, was arrested and, in turn, interrogated. Those suspected of being active militants were shot, and their bodies hidden.

In this manner, Gill and his men relentlessly broke each link in the chain of Sikh separatists. Indian security forces also used "false flag" agents, disguised as Sikh militants, to provoke factional battles by attacking other, genuine Sikh militants, or to commit atrocities that were then blamed by the media on the Sikh nationalists.

Gill finally crushed Sikh separatism, trampling on India's constitution, laws, and civil rights in the process. The outside world turned its back on this bloody drama. Canada, where there was a large, very militant Sikh expatriate community, became embroiled in a covert struggle between agents of India's intelligence service (RAW) and cells of Sikh extremists, one of which may have planted the bomb that destroyed an Air India 747 aircraft in flight, killing hundreds of people. Canada's security services apparently shared considerable information on Sikh militants with RAW and allowed a large number of its agents to operate in Canada under cover.

But Sikhs, it is said, never forget a wrong, and will always have their vengeance. After the Sikhs' holiest place, the Golden Temple at

Amritsar, was stormed by Indian troops, Indira Gandhi's own Sikh bodyguards shot her dead. Death was a fitting retribution, said Sikhs, for her cruel suppression of the Punjab.

Having only recently pacified the Sikhs in Punjab, Indian security forces and the military were totally surprised and dismayed by the 1989 explosion of protests by Muslims across Kashmir. But once over the initial shock, Delhi gradually marshalled its security forces and sent them to Kashmir, where the repressive methods perfected by General Gill in Punjab against Sikhs were immediately put to use against an even more dangerous foe: Muslims.

•••

Though it was unseen by the outside world, the 1989 revolt in Kashmir had been brewing for decades. Delhi ruled Kashmir through a group of compliant Muslim politicians, just as Moscow ruled over Central Asia by means of local Communist satraps, or "Red sultans." Both ruling groups resembled traditional mafia organizations, monopolizing illegal business, and subcontracting or franchising out areas of criminal and legal commercial activities. Corruption, extortion, and bribery were rampant, often surpassing even the outrageous levels common to lowland India. India's Muslim henchmen made themselves very rich and deeply hated.

Any Kashmiri who dared agitate for independence or union with Pakistan, including journalists and academics, was quickly jailed, often under the most brutal conditions. Occasional attempts by India to increase the Hindu population of Kashmir by moving settlers into Jammu inflamed Muslim passions, and brought attacks against the Hindu newcomers.

Blatantly rigged elections in 1987 further fanned outrage against Indian authorities. A year earlier, a handful of Kashmiri militants, grandly named the Jammu Kashmir Liberation Front (JKLF), had taken to the mountains and begun a modest guerrilla insurrection. The JKLF's academic and intellectual leaders were deeply inspired by the Algerian war for independence against French rule, and sought to emulate the successful guerrilla warfare strategy and patriotic national mobilization achieved by the Algerian Front de Libération nationale (FLN).

Muslim Kashmiris were themselves a haughty lot, notoriously rich in self-esteem, and they found Indian hegemony intolerable. Kashmiri Hindus and the proconsular establishment from Delhi treated Muslim Kashmiris with contempt, rapacity, suspicion, and disdain. All the stereotypical hatreds between Muslims and Hindus common to the plains of India became inflated to twice life-size in the rarefied mountain atmosphere of Kashmir, and eventually they exploded into violence.

The eruption was a genuine, spontaneous popular protest. Ill-trained Indian security forces panicked, opened fire on crowds, and savagely beat demonstrators. The inevitable result was renewed protests, this time with increased violence, as Muslims began fighting back with the few weapons they possessed.

Delhi rushed divisions of mountain troops and large numbers of paramilitary police to Kashmir. A new proconsul, Girish Saxena, seconded from the intelligence service RAW, was sent up from Delhi in the hope he would become a second K.P.S. Gill. A statewide crackdown began: thousands of Kashmiris were arrested, beaten, and tortured. Some, identified by informers as the protest's ringleaders, were summarily executed. Indian forces looted and burned, treating Kashmir like occupied enemy territory.

India's brutal reaction to popular protests in Kashmir sparked the formation of a number of resistance groups. At first, they amounted to no more than a handful of men, amateur fighters armed with bird guns, pistols, and knives. Some operated in Srinagar and the larger towns; others took to the wooded mountains. The Indian paramilitary forces were cowardly and undisciplined—little more than uniformed thugs; they committed growing outrages against the civilian population: rapes, robbery, arson, beatings. Their savage behaviour, driven by anti-Muslim hatred, alienated more and more Kashmiris, causing many young men, and entire families, to flee across the Line of Control into Pakistani Kashmir.

Many Muslims stayed on in Azad Kashmir as permanent refugees; but a growing number of the young men took military training, and returned to fight Indian occupation forces. Veterans of the jihad in Afghanistan, both native Afghan mujahedin and foreign "Afghani" who had remained in and around Peshawar, went to Kashmir to train and assist the fighters of the new intifada. The Afghan veterans brought the Kashmiri mujahedin a wealth of combat experience and badly needed training in logistics, communications, and planning. Equally important, they infused the Kashmiris with Islamic fervour, and provided living proof that faith, courage, and determination could overcome seemingly overwhelming odds.

In the years from 1990 to 1995, Kashmiri resistance forces were estimated to number between twenty-five thousand and thirty thousand fighters, divided into a score of different groups. Some of the rebels received military training in Pakistan from the ISI, and automatic weapons, mortars, and munitions were supplied to them across the border. This assistance, combined with help from Afghan mujahedin advisers, transformed the Kashmiris from a ragtag Maquis into moderately effective guerrilla fighters, well able to put Indian security forces on the defensive.

The resistance ambushed Indian patrols, cut up convoys, killed stragglers, and staged frequent grenade and bomb attacks to make life miserable for Indian military personnel in the crowded cities and towns. Mountainous Kashmir was far better suited to guerrilla warfare than largely flat Punjab: its forested hills and high ground offered ample refuge for irregular forces who easily eluded the slow-moving Indian forces pursuing them. Large-scale anti-guerrilla sweeps by ponderous Indian regular forces proved equally ineffective.

Though India has gained the upper hand militarily in Kashmir, its repression continues to be criticized by Indian and international human rights organizations such as Amnesty International, Asia Watch, and Physicians for Human Rights. Indian authorities have long banned many rights groups and journalists from Kashmir, using the excuse that "the time is not right for a visit." India simply does not want the world to see what it is doing in Kashmir.

Pakistan acted similarly in 1971 when its military proconsul, General Tikka Khan, the "Butcher of Dacca," attempted to ruthlessly crush the Bengali nationalist movement in secessionist East Pakistan, later Bangladesh. Pakistan's brutality in Bangladesh was brief and erratic. India's harsh behaviour in Kashmir, by contrast, has been sustained and unwavering since late 1989.

Indian security forces have adopted the crude expedient of arresting, torturing, and killing anyone suspected of being a militant. Whenever mujahedin activity or unrest is reported in an area, Indian forces stage what they call a "crackdown." Indian troops cordon off an area, then parade its inhabitants before hooded informers. Men identified as militants by the informers are immediately taken away to Indian bases, where they are repeatedly tortured until they divulge information, real or made up. Then they are usually executed and their bodies returned to their families.

Detainees were routinely savagely beaten, often on the feet, a favourite Turkish punishment known as the "bastinado." Feet are a remarkably sensitive part of the body; repeated beating there produces intolerable pain after a short time that courses from the lower extremities to the head. Numerous detainees have had their feet amputated after post-beating gangrene set in. Indian security also uses heavy wooden or metal rollers on the back of victims' backs and thighs. Muscles are crushed, and kidneys are damaged, releasing toxins into the bloodstream. Suspects are also given electric shock; brought to near drowning in tubs of filthy water; semi-suffocated by wet rags; constrained or suspended in excruciatingly painful positions; burned with cigarettes and lighters; and rectally violated with iron bars, bottles, or pieces of wood.

Suspected militants have been dragged from hospital beds, and even operating tables, by Indian forces. One doctor estimated that 60 per cent of all hospitalized Kashmiris suffered from trauma caused by gunshots, explosions, or torture. Other injured suspects in jail are denied even basic medical attention. Many men arrested are simply shot at night and dumped into rivers; others have been doused with gasoline and burned alive.

The brutality of India's security forces, notably the police and paramilitary gendarmes, is not unique to Kashmir, though it is far more intense and widespread in the mountain state. Human rights organizations have long accused police across India of torture, summary executions, and pervasive violence toward detainees, which has occasionally even included blinding. Muslims and other minorities in particular are victims of India's savage police, who are unconstrained by law, political control, or any notion of decency.

Arson remains a favourite weapon of Indian security forces in Kashmir, where most dwellings are made of wood. Villages suspected of aiding or having harboured militants are frequently burned to the ground. Villagers suspected of aiding the intifada would be lined up, beaten, and robbed. Homes would be first looted then burned. Domestic animals were slaughtered; wells were poisoned. Indian reporters and cameramen trying to document such cruelties have been beaten and, in a few reported cases, they, too, were doused with fuel and set alight.

Muslim women became the particular target of the paramilitary, and occasionally the regular forces. Rape became a constant feature of repression. In many cases, all of the young women of villages would be gang-raped, often repeatedly. The Indians understood full well that, in Muslim culture, rape is one of the most abominable crimes possible. A Muslim woman who has been raped is considered permanently defiled and unclean. In Bosnia and Kosovo, Serb forces raped thousands of Muslim women, sometimes even girls as young as nine, in an organized effort to break the Muslims' will to resist, or drive them from their homes. Rape was a double tragedy and curse for Muslim women: not only were they assaulted and brutalized, but afterwards they would be outcasts among their own people. Often, women who became pregnant from the rapes would commit suicide.

I spoke to a survivor of one of India's "crackdowns," a shy middle-aged woman with a deeply lined face and strikingly blue eyes, who had fled to Azad Kashmir after her small village was incinerated by Indian troops. "They took all of our men away and beat them," she told me in a trembling voice. "My husband and son were put into a truck and driven off. I have never heard from them since."

There was more, but her Muslim modesty and deep shame would not allow her tell me. A female journalist travelling with me took her aside and, through an interpreter, over many cups of tea, learned the woman's story. The Indian troops divided the younger women and girls from the older ones. They marched the younger women behind some stacks of fodder. The Indians, many of whom were drunk, tore off the women's clothing, threw the victims on the ground, and proceeded to gang-rape them repeatedly, including three girls under nine years of age. Those who resisted were beaten, and one was shot. After vaginally raping the women and girls, the Indian paramilitary police raped them again anally, spat on them, and called them "Muslim whores."

After relating her horrifying story, the woman, unable to face us, vanished into a tent, alone with her misery and shame. A Kashmiri man of the camp told me, "She is defiled. No man will ever touch her again after what the Hindus have done to her."

The cruelties inflicted on Kashmiris by Indian troops have not provoked a national outcry in India. The public has ignored frequent reports of such savagery and the protests of Indian rights organizations. The Indian government and press have managed to demonize Muslim Kashmiris, branding them "subversives" and "terrorists."

Kashmir is presented as a place where Indian troops bravely try to keep order under incessant attack by heavily armed, well-organized Muslim fanatics, armed and directed by Pakistan and a worldwide Islamic conspiracy. The killing of women and children by Indian forces is excused; these "unfortunates" are said to have been caught in the crossfire of gun battles initiated by terrorists making use of civilian cover.

In fact, Kashmiri militant groups and assorted jihadists from across the LOC in Pakistani Kashmir have waged their own typically dirty urban guerilla war, murdering Hindu and Sikh civilians and Muslims friendly to the Indians or those considered informers. Their attacks have killed considerably more innocent civilians than Indian forces and have become increasing brutal and often indiscriminate, perfectly fitting into the United State's new definition of "terrorism."

In the West, the Kashmiri mujahedin groups have been ignored, or regarded as terrorists. The latter view came after a well-publicized incident in which four Westerners, oblivious to political events, went trekking in Kashmir. They were kidnapped by a then unknown mujahedin group, al-Faran, and have never been seen since. The severed head of one of the unfortunate trekkers was later found on a rock, accompanied by a note from the shadowy al-Faran. The British and Australian press had a field day with this grisly story and heaped abuse on Kashmiri Muslims. On July 4, 1998, another Kashmiri resistance group, al-Fateh, told relatives the missing hikers were confirmed dead, and charged that the al-Faran kidnappers were actually set up and run as a false-flag operation by Indian intelligence to blacken the name of the Islamic resistance.

It is impossible to reach a reliable count of civilian casualties in the Kashmiri intifada. Resistance groups claim at least eighty thousand people have been killed by Indian forces since 1990. Delhi insists no more than a few thousand have died, mostly in crossfire, or, in many cases, at the hands of the "terrorists." Hundreds of Kashmiris deemed collaborators have been killed by the insurgents. In addition, some two hundred thousand Kashmiri Hindus, mainly from the Jammu region, have fled their homes for the safety of India. Indian military and police casualties are a closely guarded secret, though the number may exceed ten thousand.

•••

As the intifada in Kashmir intensified, Srinagar was transformed from a pleasant, easygoing lakeside vacation resort into a grim, dangerous place, where every alley and corner threatened Indian patrols with ambush or sniping. Indian soldiers and paramilitary troops guarded intersections and high ground from the safety of heavily sandbagged bunkers.

Indian regular troops, untrained in guerrilla warfare, conducted large, usually fruitless sweeps; alerted by civilian supporters, the guerrillas usually had time to slip away. When Indian soldiers managed to close with guerrillas, or encountered surprise attacks, the Indians responded by heavy, indiscriminate firing, often with heavy weapons, killing or wounding large numbers of civilians caught in the crossfire.

Delhi rushed more regular troops to Kashmir. By 1998, their number was to rise to over three hundred thousand, or a third of the army's total force, putting a severe strain on logistics. Units were brought in from the Himalayan border with China and the eastern sectors, where a rebellion in India's extreme eastern regions in Assam and the hill states bordering Burma had long simmered.

India's professional soldiers were fairly well disciplined and competently led (though as the revolt continued, they committed an increasing number of atrocities). But the large number of paramilitary forces also deployed in Kashmir, today about three hundred thousand men, became notorious for poor discipline, brutality, looting, and trigger-happy behaviour. While regulars manned most checkpoints and guarded important installations, the Border Security Force, Central Reserve Police Force, Indo-Tibetan Border Police, and Jammu and Kashmir state police took the lead in rooting out rebels and punishing their civilian supporters, real or imagined.

Counter-insurgency operations are always a dirty business. Indian forces in Kashmir found themselves in an alien environment far from their home, surrounded by a hostile population, never knowing when they would be attacked. Demoralized and frightened, the Indians became ever more savage as their hatred for Muslim Kashmiris grew. Muslims who had not favoured the intifada were driven into its arms by the increasing violence and ferocity of Indian repression.

Indian intelligence and security forces embarked on a campaign, patterned on operations against Sikh militants in Punjab, to identify, infiltrate, and destroy the urban networks of the various Kashmiri resistance groups. Informers, coerced by threats to their families, torture, or bribery, would single out resistance operatives. They would be arrested and subjected to the most brutal tortures. A favourite torture, developed in Punjab, was ramming a kilo of fiery hot chili powder up a victim's rectum. Children of suspected rebels would sometimes be tortured and raped in front of their parents.

In this manner, Indian security agents relentlessly uprooted the rebels' underground structure. Thousands of suspected militants, including journalists, academics, and intifada supporters, were arrested and many executed; their bodies were secretly buried. In March 1999, Amnesty International called for India to end the "nightmare" of disappearances, which the London-based organization claimed had amounted to eight hundred people since 1990, including children, the elderly, and those with no known links to secessionist groups.

By the end of 2005, the Indian Army had managed to seal the long Line of Control with Azad Kashmir by implanting dense belts of anti-personnel mines, listening devices, motion-detectors, and barbed wire along the border. Large numbers of troops were permanently stationed on the LOC in fortified positions. Israeli counter-insurgency advisers secretly aided the Indian Army in creating a lethal barrier along the entire length of the frontier, which reduced to a trickle the previous flow from Pakistani territory of fighters, munitions, and supplies. The mountainous, forested terrain still permitted some small mujahedin bands to slip across, but the fighting effectiveness of the resistance was seriously degraded by India's intensified security measures along the border with Pakistani Kashmir.

The virtual sealing of the LOC and intense anti-insurgent operations inside Kashmir brought the insurgency to its lowest ebb since 1990. According to the Indian Army, no more than four thousand insurgents are still active in the field, through the true figure was almost certainly higher. India still claims that most of the mujahedin in Kashmir are foreigners, meaning volunteers from other Islamic nations or Pakistani infiltrators.

Meanwhile, the various insurgent groups, some advocating continued struggle, others favouring a negotiated settlement, have increasingly battled among themselves, and murdered Muslims deemed to be traitors.

Indian intelligence agents, advised by Mossad experts from Israel, skillfully played on these divisions, as they had learned to do with feuding Sikh militants in Punjab, by staging false-flag attacks and spreading fake documents to provoke fighting between mujahedin factions. Indian casualties dropped sharply.

The state was literally blanketed by huge numbers of Indian security forces: by 1997, there was one Indian soldier or paramilitary policeman for every thirteen Kashmiris. The urban infrastructure of the various mujahedin groups had been shattered by torture, executions, mass arrests, and defections. In the field, the Indian Army developed more effective and aggressive counter-insurgency techniques, abandoning mass, non-productive sweeps in favour of small-unit hunter-killer missions, supported by air surveillance and the extensive use of helicopters with night-vision devices. Indian military and security forces learned to cooperate and to share information. The mujahedin were everywhere on the defensive. Delhi felt sufficiently confident to proclaim that the end of the insurgency was in sight.

But it was not.

10

THE AFGHANI

It is thankless—and dangerous—to be a Muslim Kashmiri who wants to stay part of India, but a small minority of Kashmiris, mainly wealthy merchants and tourist operators who have seen their once-thriving businesses dwindle to nothing, distrust the mujahedin and prefer civic calm, even under Delhi's rule, to endless insurrection or an independent state that they fear would be run by erratic Islamic radicals.

However, Muslim fundamentalists are a minority in the numerous resistance groups, and their political appeal to civilians is modest. Urbane Kashmiri Muslims have never been noted for fundamentalist ardour, and are a reasonably open-minded people.

Pro-Indian Muslims had rallied under the banner of Dr. Farouk Abdullah, a sixty-one-year-old doctor who is the son of the famed and often-jailed nationalist Sheik Mohammed Abdullah, known as "the Lion of Kashmir," the leader of Kashmir's Muslims at the time of partition. The younger Abdullah lived for many years in England; he returned to Kashmir and was elected state prime minister in 1996 in an election that was crudely rigged by Indian authorities. However, India claimed the vote gave full legitimacy to the new government and to Kashmir's future as an Indian state.

Most Kashmiris dismissed the vote as a fraud, and Dr. Abdullah as an Indian puppet. Algerians used to have a zesty expression for tame politicians who collaborated with the French: *beni-oui-ouis*. Even Delhi regards Abdullah and his government—who live and travel under constant heavy guard by Indian troops—with condescension.

Still, India and its local supporters keep insisting the choice was between Abdullah and malevolent Islamic radicals, who, if Kashmir ever attained real independence, would emulate Afghanistan's ultra-reactionary Taliban movement by imposing medieval Islam on the sophisticated Kashmiris. If India's *jawans* (soldiers) stop defending Kashmir, claims the pro-Indian faction, hordes of primitive Islamic warriors will sweep over Kashmir and down into India, like the Muslim Moguls of centuries past.

However, the idea that the Taliban or any other Afghan group could invade Kashmir was preposterous. While a few Taliban volunteer mujahedin may slip across the LOC, there is no real threat from Afghanistan.

A far more serious challenge to Indian rule over Kashmir is posed by the largest and one of the oldest Kashmiri resistance movements, the Jammu Kashmir Liberation Front (JKLF). The party, based in England and Rawalpindi, Pakistan, is currently led by sixty-five-year-old Amanullah Khan, a veteran warhorse and Kashmiri nationalist who was born in the Gilgit-Baltistan region.

The hanging of JKLF leader Maqbool Butt in Delhi in 1984 enraged Kashmiris and was an important factor in the nationalist explosion of 1990. The JKLF advocates total independence for Kashmir and the formation of a federal state with a two-legislature parliamentary government. It would be a non-sectarian, secular state in which the members of parliament would be elected by direct representation, and the rights of all religions and ethnic groups were guaranteed. After five years of independence, the UN would organize and supervise a national referendum to determine whether Kashmir wished to remain independent, or to join India or Pakistan.

This sensible plan deeply worries both India and Pakistan. For Delhi, the moderate JKLF platform directly contradicts its claims that all the opposition are dangerous Muslim radicals bent on creating an Islamic theocracy under the influence of Afghanistan and Iran—the latter nation being cleverly thrown in by the Indians to set off alarm bells in Washington. The JKLF proposals also make Delhi very nervous because they sound too close to existing UN Security Council resolutions over Kashmir and could be adopted as a basis for an international settlement.

The JKLF makes Pakistan almost as nervous. The movement calls for an independent Kashmir to be formed from the five provinces that more or less made up pre-1947 Kashmir: the Kashmir Valley (the Srinagar region); Jammu; Pakistan-held Azad Kashmir; Indian-held Ladakh; and Gilgit-Baltistan, which Pakistan calls its "Northern Territories."

Pakistan says it would immediately cede Azad Kashmir, a region of no intrinsic value, to an independent Kashmiri state. But Pakistan long ago grew deeply attached to the mountain region of Gilgit and Baltistan, which extends from Afghanistan to Ladakh and Tibet. The two great valleys are important earners of tourist income, and occupy a vital strategic location in the Himalayan-Karakoram system. Equally important, the Karakoram Highway, the sole road link between Pakistan and its principal ally, China, begins in Gilgit, and extends up the Hunza Valley over the Khunjerab Pass, into Chinese Sinkiang.

If an independent Kashmir were to reclaim Gilgit-Baltistan, a large section of Pakistan's beautiful north—its own version of Kashmir—would be wrenched away. Islamabad has sought since the 1950s to erase the region's image as part of Kashmir, and recast it as an extension of Pakistan. The JKLFS troublesome leader, Amanullah Khan, has found himself thrown into Pakistani jails more than once for raising this contentious issue.

In 1990, the JKLF declared itself a government in exile, which led to a serious split in its ranks. Amanullah Khan's attempts to stage two marches of JKLF civilians across the LOC in February and March 1992, which could easily have sparked war with India, enormously annoyed Islamabad, which very nearly proscribed his movement. The Pakistanis cannot seem to decide whether the JKLF is more of a threat to them, or to India. Meanwhile, JKLF claims Islamabad is secretly in cahoots with Delhi to maintain the status quo by sabotaging Kashmiri independence.

There may be substance to this cynical view. India and Pakistan have grown used to the status quo of Kashmir, which, if not comfortable is at least familiar. Any change would unleash unpredictable forces and threaten to upset the region's political geography. The situation has been frozen since 1947, and states, like people, do not like change. Listening to the disgruntled Kashmiris reminded me of similar statements by Palestinians, who claimed their Arab brothers were secretly conspiring with Israel to deny them a state that would, inevitably, alter the Mideast map. Similarly, India and Pakistan, for all their recriminations, have grown accustomed to the existing order of things.

Islamabad much prefers other pro-Pakistani Kashmiri resistance groups, such as the Harakat-ul-Ansar, the Hezbollah (no relation to Lebanon's Hezbollah), the Harakat-ul-Mujahedin, Jihad Islami, Gujjar Tigers, al-Barq, and eighteen other colourfully named organizations. Most of these number no more than a few hundred to a few thousand active supporters, and even many of these are split into inimical factions that occasionally fight among themselves over territory, money, and personal or ideological rivalries. Some of these Kashmiri resistance groups represent bourgeois, urban elements; others call for creation of an Islamic state in Kashmir run under sharia law. The only thing all have in common is their intense hatred of India.

One thing is certain. India will never relinquish its portion of Kashmir without ensuring that Pakistan must give up its part, the Northern Territories, as well. Cynical Indians are counting on equally cynical Pakistanis never to do this.

•••

India constantly claims that Pakistan finances, trains, and arms the Kashmiri resistance organizations, which it always brands "terrorist groups." India has long blamed Islamabad's machinations for the revolt in Kashmir. In truth, Pakistan has discreetly sustained some, though certainly not all, of the Kashmiri resistance forces. Lately, Islamabad's support has been more discreet and somewhat reduced, particularly after the U.S. occupation of Afghanistan. Pakistan's ISI has aided and armed at least eight of the Kashmiri freedom groups, including, at various times, the problematic JKLF.

As recounted in the first part of this book, ISI managed the long war in Afghanistan against Soviet occupation in close cooperation with the CIA, providing logistical support, training, arms, communications, and staff planning to the seven Afghan mujahedin groups. ISI officers served in the field, leading attacks and conducting sabotage missions against Soviet forces. Without ISI support, and its provision of U.S.-supplied Stinger missiles, the medieval bands of Afghan warriors could never have fought the Red Army to a bloody stalemate.

Just as Indian security forces mastered counter-insurgency tactics in rebellious Punjab, the ISI has drawn on its long, successful experience in the Afghan war to assist and, at times, direct the Kashmiri resistance. A small number of combat-hardened Afghan mujahedin and volunteers from other Islamic nations, the remnants of the Islamic Foreign Legion who battled in Afghanistan, joined the Kashmiri resistance as advisers and fighters. However, Indian claims that nearly all Kashmiri resistance fighters are foreigners—mainly Afghans, or Arab mercenaries—are simply untrue: most of the insurgents are native Kashmiris, though a cadre of foreign holy warriors has played a key role, and ISI supplies key logistic support.

In one of the refugee camps along the Jhelum River, I was greeted by an old comrade-in-arms, Commander Nadji. Tall, skinny, and bearded, he wore the knitted, round pakul hat beloved by all Afghans that has become a badge of honour worn by veterans of the Great Jihad. We had met in Peshawar, Pakistan, in 1986, while the war raged in neighbouring Afghanistan.

Nadji was an Egyptian descended from the band of six hundred Albanian soldiers of fortune who, in 1805, had conquered Egypt under their chief, the great Mehmet Ali Pasha. He gave up his engineering studies in Cairo, and went to join the Islamic International Brigade in the great Afghan jihad.

Nadji and his fellow legionnaires had been discreetly financed by the Saudi royal family, which was always ready to fund Islamic militancy, provided it was as far away as possible from their kingdom. The Saudis also saw in the Islamic Legion a useful counter to the growing influence of their bitter rival Iran, which was intriguing among the Shia Hazara tribes of central and western Afghanistan.

Nadji fought for three years in central Afghanistan, and was wounded in the leg by shellfire shortly before the Soviet withdrawal. By the time he recovered, civil war between the Afghan factions had replaced Soviet occupation. Like most other members of the Islamic Legion, Nadji soon grew disgusted by the sordid tribal melee that replaced the once glorious jihad. Embittered and disillusioned, like so many other past youthful revolutionaries, he returned to Egypt. But there he became a wanted man: the Egyptian government regarded the Afghan veterans, or "Afghani," as dangerous troublemakers who were training the growing Islamic underground in Egypt in urban guerrilla warfare.

Soon after we first met in Peshawar, Nadji had told me that once he and his friends had liberated Afghanistan from Soviet imperialism, they would go on to free Egypt from American domination. Why not? In the eyes of Islamic militants, Egypt's military ruler-turned-president, General Hosni Mubarak, was no less a puppet of the Americans than the Afghan military dictator, General Najibullah, was of the Soviets. There was no difference, in their eyes, between Soviet and American imperialism. But neo-colonial powers were bent on occupying the Muslim world and exploiting its rich resources. Commander Nadji's words to me were to be repeated, almost verbatim, in 1998 by the militant anti-American mujahid, Osama bin Laden.

When rebellion erupted in Kashmir, Nadji fled Egypt and returned to Peshawar. He and hundreds of other "Afghani" rushed to Azad Kashmir to offer their services to the neophyte Kashmiri guerrillas. The ISI eagerly encouraged the restless Afghan veterans to leave Peshawar and betake themselves to Azad Kashmir. The Afghani had joined local Islamic fundamentalist parties in loudly accusing Benazir Bhutto's government of being American stooges. These charges made Islamabad very nervous, not least because they held a good measure of truth. The American government made no secret that it far preferred the malleable Bhutto to the iron-fisted Zia ul-Haq. Bhutto had no pan-Islamist or Greater Pakistan pretensions; she was content to cooperate at all times with American policy, repress Islamic forces, "modernize" Pakistan, and maintain "stability." These were Western code words for keeping Pakistan firmly in America's strategic orbit and responsive to Washington's diktat.

The United States strongly backed the Western-educated Bhutto as a "moderate" and—that famous term of approval for cooperative Third World leaders—"someone we can do business with." Yet, while overtly supporting the Bhutto regime, Washington was getting ready to scupper Pakistan. The powerful Israel lobby, Washington's most effective special-interest organization, had grown alarmed by Islamabad's nuclear potential, fearing Pakistani nuclear weapons might find their way into the hands of Israel's Arab enemies, such as Syria, Iraq, or Libya. Though there was absolutely no evidence of this happening, Israel and its Washington lobby engineered a change in U.S. policy toward Pakistan.

Pakistan, once hailed in the United States as a heroic ally during the Afghan conflict, was swiftly and ruthlessly downgraded to the status of "Islamic threat," and summarily denied by Congress, through the Pressler Amendment, the military and economic aid that had long sustained it.

The cutoff of U.S. military aid, spare parts, new weapons, and economic assistance brought Pakistan close to economic collapse, and caused a very serious decline in its military power just at a time when India was issuing increasing threats and beefing up its offensive forces on the border. Ironically, the U.S. embargo of conventional arms to former loyal ally Pakistan had the counterproductive result of compelling Islamabad to accelerate its covert nuclear program and rely increasingly on nuclear weapons for defense against India.

•••

Nadji chain-smoked and coughed as we spoke, his lanky, gaunt frame shaken by chronic bronchitis brought on by endless cigarettes, stress, the dust in Egypt, and now Kashmir's cold, damp climate. "At first (in the mid-1990s), we could move across the LOC easily. We'd go over at night, and attack Indian patrols or watch posts with mortars, RPGS (rocket-propelled grenades), and automatic weapons. The Indians usually panicked, and fired everywhere.

"The Hindus made the Afghan Communist soldiers look brave." He laughed scornfully. "We killed a lot of them. Many just ran away." News that fierce Afghan mujahedin veterans, who showed no mercy and took no prisoners, were operating in Kashmir demoralized Indian troops and kept them hunkered down in their fortified positions.

"But you know, my friend, the same evil thing happened here as in Afghanistan," Nadji continued. "The many resistance groups each ended up with a different sponsor, and they spent as much time fighting each other as they did the infidel. We cursed Muslims are always better at fighting our brothers than the unbelievers." His body shook from a spasm of coughing.

"By now," he continued bitterly, "the Indians have learned to fight better. They are more aggressive. Kashmiris are becoming afraid to help us, or they even inform on the mujahedin—to prevent their villages from being burned down and their women raped." Nadji shrugged, and stroked his uneven beard. "We don't have enough men, or arms. This time, there are no Stinger missiles to use against Indian helicopters. The war, my old friend, is getting very difficult. We are really alone."

But what about support from the Islamic world? I asked. Nadji spat on the ground and lit another cigarette. "Support? We have been abandoned. Only Pakistan gives us any real help. A little baksheesh (money, tips) comes from the Gulf emirates—less, for sure, than the money the emirs spend each week on their European whores. Other than that, the Muslim world completely ignores the Kashmir Intifada.

"Those bastard Muslim sons of dogs won't even give us diplomatic support. And the Indians are clever, very clever at buying off the Arab states and other Muslim nations. Some trade, vacations to Bombay, gold rings and jewels, that's all it takes. Muslims can be bought for very little."

Nadji was right. India's skillful diplomacy, and its sheer size, made even Islamic nations unwilling to support the Kashmiri struggle for independence. What benefit could be gained by antagonizing mighty India for the sake of a little-known people who seemed unlikely to ever gain independence? Delhi cleverly played another diplomatic card by making it very clear to Arab states that its long-time support, of Palestinian rights would depend on their silence over Kashmir. Delhi apparently saw no contradiction in steadfastly advocating self-determination and statehood for Palestinians on one hand, while denying the same right to Kashmiris on the other—or by regularly condemning Israel in the UN for its repression in Palestine, while insisting the UN had no business whatsoever in Kashmir.

We sat and sipped tea, watching the steam from our dented tin mugs rise up in the cool, moist air. We had drunk tea many times before in Peshawar, and inside Afghanistan as well. Those days seemed very distant: we young optimists had hoped the brutal Russians and their local Communist henchmen would be driven from Afghanistan and replaced by an Islamic government, guided by the Koran's principles of equal justice, social welfare, equality, and the active democracy practiced during the early, golden days of Islam.

"We killed Afghanistan to make it free. Maybe we'll do the same for Kashmir," observed Nadji dejectedly. "By God, we beat Russia, the world's biggest military power, and now we're being asked to go beat India, with almost one billion people. How many miracles can we do in one lifetime, in the name of Allah. How many?"

More tea and cigarettes brightened Nadji's mood. "But what else can we do? The Holy Koran tells us it's the duty of all good Muslims to go fight injustice wherever it occurs. Every man must fight his own jihad, both against his own internal devils, and against the world's wrongs."

Such earnest and pious professions may sound romantic, even theatrical, to Western ears. In our world, consumerism and movie-star worship long ago replaced religion. But among Muslims it is still common to "live by the book" and be guided by its commands. Young, militant Muslims, like Nadji, reject Western values and have sought to rebuild a psychological foundation for themselves in the rediscovery of their grandfathers' beliefs and customs. There must have been many young men in the International Brigades during the Spanish Civil War who spoke just like Nadji, their hearts filled with the fresh optimism of youth and the incandescent passion of certainty and faith.

Nadji stood, embraced me repeatedly, and put his hand over my heart, in the manner of the Afghans. He waved farewell as our Jeep departed. I looked back at him as we bounced away along the dirt track, a lone holy warrior from distant Egypt, waging his own lonely struggle against the world's second most populous nation for the sake of oppressed fellow Muslims, whose alien Indo-European language he could not even speak.

A year later, I learned that my old friend Nadji had been shahid, martyred. He had been killed in action against Indian forces during a nighttime firefight. His men had to leave his body on the field. Commander Nadji's jihad was over. The news of his death shook me. I recalled the Koranic phrase, "Those who fall in the holy struggle are not dead, but live on," and I prayed that it was true.

11
DECONSTRUCTING SOUTH ASIA

Kashmir evokes deep existential fears in Delhi that go far beyond concerns of day-to-day politics, or even the swollen Hindu nationalist pretensions of the opposition Bharatiya Janata Party. Though India's exquisitely rich culture and history date back more than four thousand years, it has been a nation for only the past sixty years. As a political entity, modern India was the creation of British imperialism, a bittersweet legacy to which Indians cling as a source of national legitimacy and cohesiveness—as well as a totem of foreign oppression on which they blame many of their ills.

Though few Indian leaders will ever admit to it, their darkest unspoken fear is that the complex, fragile, often maddening diversity of modern India will some day unravel, just as another great, cosmopolitan, multiethnic empire, the late Soviet Union, did in 1991.

That India functions at all as a unified state is something of a daily political miracle. Its one billion people speak some two hundred languages and major dialects, follow eight major religions and myriad cults, and represent a bewildering jumble of races and ethnic groups. The languages of north and south India are mutually incomprehensible, necessitating the use of English as a national lingua franca. India has the world's third-largest Muslim population, after Indonesia and Pakistan. Poor land communications, vast distances, and natural obstacles combine to divide, and then subdivide, India into semi-isolated regions.

Economically, India looks like an Asian colossus. But on closer scrutiny one discovers the amazing fact that India's economy is slightly smaller than that of Holland, which has a mere 15.5 million people. The misapprehension by Western politicians and businessmen that India's newly opened markets promise an Asian gold rush led the U.S. government to wink at India's nuclear program, thus avoiding confrontation with Delhi. In 2006, the Bush administration gave formal blessing to India's civilian and nuclear programs by concluding a pact to supply Delhi with nuclear fuel, which it badly lacked, the latest U.S. arms, and extensive nuclear technology. This startling *volte-face* in U.S.

nuclear non-proliferation policy allowed India to use its existing nuclear fuel in its weapons-making rectors while the U.S. supplied India's power generating nuclear plants. The accord also clearly established a new U.S.-India strategic accord aimed directly at China and Pakistan. Beijing lost no time in denouncing the pact as a weapon aimed at China.

India is really an agglomeration of diverse nations held together from the centre, at Delhi; this feat is achieved by a vast bureaucracy, powerful security forces, political inertia, and sheer deadweight—rather what a united Europe might one day aspire to resemble. Even India's much-vaunted democratic system is being relentlessly eroded by endemic corruption, graft, and violence.

Local warlords, powerful feudal landowners, caste-based party bosses, and gangsters known as "goondas" have come to dominate the political process. India's huge internal paramilitary security forces (some 1.1 million strong) and its local police are notorious for extortion, corruption, and brutal misconduct.

India has been afflicted by secessionist movements ever since independence. The Kashmir independence movement and Sikh separatism in Punjab have been the greatest challenges to a united India.

But other, more obscure independence movements have flared for decades in the northeastern state of Assam, in the hill tracts of India's far east (abutting Burma), and in the Andaman Islands of the Indian Ocean.

From time to time, there are rumblings of potential secession in the twenty-five states that make up the Indian union, notably the southern state of Tamil Nadu, whose population outnumbers that of France. Some Indians even believe that all of predominantly Dravidian South India may one day decide to escape what is seen as economic, political, and cultural domination by the Hindi-speaking north.

India's leaders have long worried that the secession from the union of either Indian-ruled Kashmir or Sikh Punjab could trigger a process of gradual national dissolution. The dramatic disintegration of the Soviet Empire in Eastern Europe, and then the collapse of the U.S.S.R. itself, horrified India's political establishment. They were all too aware that the Soviet Union's final demise was begun by miners' strikes in Poland, followed by the Afghan War, and, finally, popular uprisings in East Germany. None of these events taken separately appeared to threaten the existence of the Soviet imperium; but together they combined to break the sinews of Soviet power, producing an earth-shaking, historical revolution.

Thus, for most thinking Indians, Kashmiri independence or, worse, its accession to Pakistan is an intolerable, mortal threat to the integrity of their nation. To Hindu nationalists, even the continued existence of Pakistan constitutes a threat to the Indian union, as well as a painful affront to their sense of national importance and a galling reminder of their hated historical enemy, the Muslim Mogul Empire.

Pakistan reflects the mirror image of these deeply ingrained political and psychological fears. India's ceaseless fulminations and blood-curdling threats against Pakistan, its growing anti-Islamic rhetoric, its new strategic alliance with Israel, frequent pogroms against Indian Muslims, and the steady growth of Indian military power deployed against Pakistan have convinced most Pakistanis that India is a mortal danger, and intends to dismember their nation.

Pakistanis fear, with some reason, that India's repression of Kashmiri Muslims and Sikh nationalists is an evil foretoken of what awaits them if their nation is ever reabsorbed into Greater India.

India's invasion of East Pakistan, and attempts by agents of India's powerful intelligence service, the Research and Analysis Wing (RAW), to destabilize Pakistan's Sind Province and North-West Frontier by fomenting communal violence are seen by Pakistanis as final proof of India's determination to dismember their nation.

Ironically, Pakistan's leaders have tried to promote the same policy of destabilization in India. The Pakistan's intelligence service, has been intermittently active in aiding secessionist rebellions in Kashmir, Punjab, and, to a far lesser degree, in eastern India. Though they would never say so publicly, Pakistan's strategists have long held the view their nation's sole salvation would be the breakup of India, an event that would also leave Pakistan the dominant military power on the subcontinent China, India's other powerful rival, would be no less happy to see the Indian union dissolve into a patchwork of weak, feuding states. China's cautious official position has been that long-strained relations with India are gradually improving. But in private, China regards India's growing military capability with mounting con-cern. India, for its part, has raised alarms over the alleged threat of strategic encirclement by China, and used the issue to justify its nuclear tests.

Chinese military intelligence expressed just such concerns about India in deep background talks with me in 1983, at a time when China was principally focused on the strategic threat from the Soviet Union. I had been invited to Beijing to exchange views with Chinese strategic analysts because of my close relations with the Afghan mujahedin, who were resisting the Soviet occupation of Afghanistan. In exchange for my assessment of the various Afghan resistance groups and the general course of the war, the Chinese shared with me some of their strategic thinking about India and the Soviet Union. Shortly after, China began discreetly supplying weapons and munitions to the Afghan resistance.

The Chinese security officials told me that they anticipated a military clash with India in the Himalayas or Karakorams early in the twenty-first century, or perhaps even sooner, as part of either an Indo-Pakistani war or a struggle to control Tibet or Burma.

Chinese strategists, who take a far longer view than their Western counterparts, believe India will eventually come under serious centrifugal strains that may cause it to splinter. China's leadership is probably torn between encouraging this process, with all the risks that involves, and attempting to postpone what they see as an inevitable clash with India until after Beijing has completed its lengthy process of military modernization at the end of the first decade of the twenty-first century.

The view expressed to me in Beijing, and subsequently repeated by other Chinese military sources, is that the growing power of India and China will be unlikely to coexist in harmony. The two great powers, divided by an uncertain mountain border and small, unstable states would one day vie for mastery of Asia. For now, however, Asia's two titans are content to hold guarded talks aimed at lowering tensions and seeking mutual trade opportunities, though the Sino-Indian pattern of trade is ten to one in China's favour and deep suspicions remain between them

12

THE WORLD'S MOST DANGEROUS BORDER

Chokoti, the last village on the Pakistani side of the Line of Control, was a cluster of dilapidated wooden buildings, shacks, and teahouses that bore evident scars of frequent Indian shelling. The LOC lies a couple of miles east of Chokoti. The invisible line snakes between heights held by entrenched Pakistani and Indian forces, their ultimate positions when the 1949 ceasefire came into effect. The Jhelum River, heedless of politics or war, cuts a right angle across the LOC, flowing east toward the city of Barmula, just behind Indian lines, and then, a mere 40 kilometres (25 miles) farther east, to Srinagar.

At first, the mighty Jhelum Gorge, surrounded by steep, scrub-clad hills, and clumps of trees, was silent save for the rushing of the grey waters below. A vast panorama of mountains with distant snow-capped crags beyond them offered a tourist-brochure scene of idyllic Kashmir. A Pakistani army camp in a sheltered depression was the only sign of human habitation. A group of subalterns of the 180th Mountain Brigade sat around a green table, playing bridge, sipping lemonade, and complaining in clipped English accents about the terrible heat. They could have been bored young officers of the British Raj in the Queen Empress's army a century ago.

"Be careful," they warned cheerily, "the bloody Indians are shooting again. Keep your heads down!"

We climbed up a very steep ridge over broken rocks and scree, sweating profusely in the blistering 49°C (120°F) weather. A heat wave had struck northern India and Pakistan, killing hundreds on the plains below. Our military escort ordered us to keep low and stay alert. As we reached the top of the ridge, a series of sharp reports echoed around the valley, sending flocks of birds into panicked flight. A stream of tracer bullets sprayed over our heads. From somewhere across the valley, a medium machine gun had opened up on our position.

"Take cover, take cover," yelled the Pakistani captain who was guiding us. We dove into a line of sandbagged trenches, and headed into the shelter of a large bunker. Mortars on the Indian side began firing at our position, and other points along the LOC. Pakistani machine guns and mortars returned fire.

The heavy exchange continued for about five minutes. After the guns fell silent we observed the Indian bunkers and trenches across the valley through field glasses, but detected no sign of movement. Off to our right, beyond our field of vision in the direction of Poonch, Pakistani and Indian artillery began to exchange salvos of 122 mm and 155 mm shells. Two of the world's poorest nations had just expended tens of thousands of dollars' worth of ammunition, for no better purpose than to vent the hatred, frustration, and boredom of the frontline soldiers on either side.

Indian and Pakistani troops have been skirmishing along the LOC since 1949. They usually snipe at one another's positions and lob occasional shells. But, from time to time, particularly when tensions rise sharply between Delhi and Islamabad, the fighting becomes generalized along the LOC, as brigade—or even division-sized units—go into action. When this occurs neither side knows for certain whether the bombardment is merely another demonstration or the opening of a major offensive. As a result, nerves stay frayed; both sides keep their forces on the alert along the LOG, and supporting divisions in a state of high combat-readiness farther behind the front.

I watched the two sides trade fire, wondering if the exchange marked the beginning of an all-out Indian invasion of Azad Kashmir. Tensions between India and Pakistan were running high in the spring and summer of 1992. Both sides were at hair-trigger readiness after two months of mounting threats. India had massed a number of new divisions in Kashmir behind the LOC. Just south of Kashmir, in northern Punjab, elements of two Indian armoured "strike corps" were concentrating between Pathankot and Amritsar for what could become a major offensive against the strategic Pakistani city of Sialkot, the gateway to southern Azad Kashmir.

Frustrated and enraged by the rebellion in Kashmir, India was loudly threatening to "teach Pakistan a lesson." Reserve units were being activated and mobilized in India and Pakistan. Troops were moving into forward positions, and behind them long truck convoys of war supplies, Indian armour, and artillery had left their cantonments and adopted offensive deployments. Indian and Pakistani air bases were on high alert, with aircraft armed and fuelled up, many prepared to take off on two or three minutes' notice. Both air forces had gone to war-readiness reconnaissance and combat air patrols.

Reports were coming from South Asia and abroad that India had deployed a number of nuclear weapons to forward air bases near the Pakistani border for its precision-strike Jaguar fighter-bombers. Pakistan, it was rumoured, had a number of F-16s with nuclear bombs ready to take off at a moment's notice at Chaklala air base. Though Delhi and Islamabad denied they had nuclear weapons, and thus had not gone to full nuclear alert, the CIA was later to report to Congress that the two foes had in fact been activating their nuclear arsenals.

This confrontation over Kashmir was the closest the world had come to a full-scale nuclear war since 1973, when Israel had armed and deployed its top-secret arsenal of nuclear-tipped missiles and nuclear bombs, and was getting ready to use them to destroy advancing Syrian and Egyptian armoured divisions on the Golan Heights and in Sinai. Fortunately, the Egyptian and Syrian attacks both petered out before the panicky Israelis had unleashed their nuclear weapons. The Syrians, in fact, deliberately halted their advance just before reaching the western edge of the Golan Heights, not wishing to give Israel any excuse to launch a nuclear attack.

Standing in a bunker in the middle of what might become a general, or even a nuclear war, was not a comfortable feeling. Having covered some ten wars or conflicts, I was used to being under fire. From the relative safety of a bunker, it was even rather entertaining. But the idea that a nuclear war might actually occur, with me sitting at ground zero, was unsettling. Wars often begin as much by mischance and miscalculation as by plan. Localized clashes that got out of control could quickly escalate into division-level, then corps-level fighting, then to all-out war along the 1,600-kilometre (1,000-mile) front from the Arabian Sea to Tibet. And, according to the CIA, the Indo-Pakistani border, on which I was currently positioned, was the most likely place for a nuclear war to erupt.

Fortunately, India decided not to attack Pakistan. The highly professional generals of India's armed forces restrained the war fever of their civilian masters, who, like politicians everywhere, misjudged or misunderstood the implications, conduct, and true costs of war. Fighting in Kashmir's mountainous terrain would be primarily infantry combat, and much of it World War I–style frontal attack, allowing the defending Pakistanis to fight from strong, prepared positions on high ground. India would rot be able to make use of its considerable advantage in armour, artillery, and aircraft. A stalemate was likely to ensue after bloody, inconclusive combat.

But even a military stalemate presented great danger, for Indian generals would then be driven to seek victory by broadening the scope of their operations to other sectors, where India's mobile forces could be used to better profit. To decisively defeat Pakistan, India would have to attack farther south on the plains of Punjab, and strike across the great Thar Desert of Rajastan into Sind, just north of the great port city of Karachi. This would mean a total war between the two huge nations, with the possible threat of a nuclear exchange. India's leaders wisely declined the battle. Still, it was a close-run thing, and a harbinger of what might come in the future.

Movements by Kashmiri rebels across the LOC also heightened these simmering tensions. Pakistani forces often give mujahedin units covering fire when they run into Indian patrols, or come under fire from Indian positions. Indian generals repeatedly warn they may exercise the right of hot pursuit to follow the mujahedin back to their bases in Azad Kashmir, or even launch offensives to destroy the insurgents' bases there. The widely held belief among Indians that the Kashmiri intifada would crumble if its roots in Pakistan were torn out constantly tempts Delhi to launch a punitive attack into Azad Kashmir, just as Turkey's generals have considerably degraded the combat-effectiveness of Kurdistan Workers' Party (PKK) guerrillas by repeatedly mounting air and ground offensives against their operating bases in northern Iraq.

In the summer of 1999, Kashmiri guerrillas and Pakistani special forces made a daring incursion into the Indian-controlled mountains of the Kargil region. Dug in to heights of 4,570-metres (15,000-feet) altitude and higher, the Pakistanis were able to direct artillery fire onto the only road to Leh, effectively severing Indian military communications in Ladakh. India launched a major counter-offensive using troops, artillery, and warplanes. After more than two weeks of heavy fighting, India drove back with guerillas and Pakistani forces, but at a heavy cost of some five thousand casualties and two aircraft.

During the fighting, Indian commanders reportedly pleaded with Delhi to allow them to launch a general offensive against Pakistan in the plains of Punjab and the Thar Desert, where India's advantage in manpower, tanks, and artillery would have proved decisive. Such an offensive could have sparked nuclear war. According to U.S. intelligence, the two hostile powers were only three days away from a full-scale conflict.

Hot pursuit of rebels into Azad Kashmir by the Indian Army could quickly escalate into a bigger war, particularly if the attackers were threatened with Pakistani counterattacks. To rescue the stalled attacking force, Indian commanders would have to rush in reinforcements, initiate diversionary assaults at other points on the line, or, if these measures failed, open a broader offensive in northern Punjab. Such actions could spark an all-out war along the entire 1,600-kilometre (1,000-mile) front from the Siachen Glacier to the Arabian Sea.

Experts at the Pentagon consider this possibility to be the most likely scenario for triggering a major Indo-Pakistani conflict, one that neither side wants, but from which they could not withdraw without serious political and military loss. One senior Pentagon official described the hot-pursuit scenario as "our constant nightmare."

A full-scale war with India would threaten Pakistan's very existence, and present its general staff with the almost impossible task of defending their strategically vulnerable nation. Pakistan resembles Egypt: a great river flows down from remote mountains, on whose banks, and great southern delta, live the majority of the population. On the map, both nations look large; but when desert, arid land, and unpopulated areas are deducted from the picture, what remains is a relatively small nation clinging precariously to a narrow river valley.

Pakistan's population and defenses are concentrated in two important provinces, Sind in the south, and Punjab in the north. Its other regions—the North-West Frontier, the Northern Territories, and Baluchistan—are geographically remote. Between the southern port of Karachi and the Punjab's most important northern metropolis, Lahore, lies about 1,000 kilometres (600 miles) of desert and scrub on either side of the Indus valley.

Halfway between these two cities is a large salient that juts into Pakistan. From this point, Indian mobile forces need race over only 80 kilometres (50 miles) of flat terrain to reach the cities of Sukkur, Rahimyar Khan, or, farther north, the important Bahawalpur-Multan nexus, in order to sever the road and rail lines that link Punjab and

Sind. If these vital spinal communications were cut, Pakistan would be divided, isolated, and paralyzed. Indian forces could isolate Punjab, preventing Pakistani reinforcements from moving south, while they conquered Karachi and Hyderabad at their leisure.

Keenly aware of Pakistan's strategic weakness, India's defense planners have created a group of highly mobile "strike corps," composed of powerful armoured and mechanized units, supported by mobile artillery and highly capable units of engineers. Much of the army's strength-1,400 modern T-72 tanks, BMP-1/2 armoured fighting vehicles, and modern, self-propelled or mobile guns—is concentrated in these strike corps, which are deployed in Punjab, the Thar Desert, and above the marshy Rann of Kutch, just north of the Arabian Sea coast. Their mission, in time of war, is to penetrate deeply into Pakistan, sever its communications, and defeat the divided Pakistani army.

On paper, India's forces on its western front appear to be only slightly stronger than Pakistan's. While confronting Pakistan, India must also maintain large numbers of troops on the borders with Chinese-ruled Tibet, and garrison rebellious Kashmir, Assam, and the tribal states of India's far eastern border with Burma. In wartime, India's huge, million-man paramilitary forces could perform some of these functions, relieving army troops for duty on the front with Pakistan. But the very real threat that China might threaten India's northern borders in support of its ally, Pakistan, forces India's high command to maintain substantial air and ground forces to cover the remote north.

This strategic drain on troops leaves India with a significant but hardly overwhelming superiority on its western front. There, India deploys three armoured, four mechanized, and thirteen or so infantry divisions or division equivalents (two of them armoured), as well as large numbers of artillery formations. In Kashmir, India fields at least five of its nine mountain divisions.

Pakistan, by contrast, need only use light infantry units to watch its borders with Afghanistan and Iran, concentrating its best forces on the Indian front. Pakistan can deploy two armoured divisions, and about fourteen or fifteen infantry divisions or division equivalents.

In armour, Pakistan is outnumbered three to two by India; in artillery, three to one. Pakistan's artillery is less modern, and has a shorter range than India's. The bulk of Pakistan's tanks, old U.S. M48s and Chinese Type59s, 69s, and 85s, are obsolescent, undergunned, and poorly equipped, particularly compared with India's far more modern and effective Soviet/Russian-supplied T-72 tanks.

In the air, India long ago outclassed Pakistan's air force, which has been crippled by a long, punishing American embargo of arms and spare parts. India not only outnumbers Pakistan's air force by nearly two to one, its state-of-the-art Russian MIG-29s and SU-30s and French Mirage 2000s technologically outclass Pakistan's only fairly modern fighters, thirty-two F-16s. The rest of Pakistan's 410 combat-aircraft force consists of elderly French Mirages, and a collection of obsolescent J-6 and J-7 Chinese fighters, modernized versions of the venerable MIG-21 and Chinese Q-5 ground attack aircraft, based on the late '50s model MIG-19.

The military embargo imposed on Pakistan by the United States at the end of the Afghan war in 1989–90 seriously weakened Pakistan's air force: it could not obtain the new F-16s it badly needed, spare parts for its existing American-made equipment, or AWACS capability for the command and control of modern air combat. As a result, the combat capability of the once formidable Pakistan Air Force was cut in half. Pakistan was compelled to shop the world's arms markets for used equipment, finally acquiring from France, after many delays, a batch of old, refurbished, 1960s-vintage Mirage-Vs. A squadron of F-16s that Pakistan had ordered in 1988–89 was embargoed by Washington, even though Islamabad had paid some $650 million for the aircraft. But in 2006, Washington finally agreed to supply a squadron of older model F-16s to General Pervez Musharraf's government in recognition of his service in Afghanistan and vital role in fighting America's jihadist foes. Opponents of the military regime grumbled that Pakistan was being thrown military crumbs for which it had long ago paid.

Pakistan's air force still produces better pilots than India's air arm, which has one of the world's highest accident rates, but modern Russian equipment, advanced electronics and radar, and improved command and control have lessened Pakistan's once substantial quali-tative edge.

India's other advantage is that its economy is almost six times larger than Pakistan's. In three previous Indo-Pakistani wars, both sides quickly ran out of munitions and war supplies, but over the past twenty years India has ensured this failure will not happen again by developing a powerful military-industrial base and an extensive chain of well-stocked military depots close to the Pakistani border, designed to support sustained offensive operations by its mobile strike corps.

By contrast, Pakistan lacks this strategic logistic base, and must import from abroad many of its war stocks, spares, and basic supplies. In time of war, this grave imbalance means Pakistani forces would soon run low on armour, aircraft, missiles, engines, electronics, spare parts, and heavy munitions, while Indian forces would be able to sustain combat for a considerably longer period—perhaps long enough to attain decisive victory. In fact, India's logistic supplies and spare parts reserves give it the capability of fighting for eight to twelve weeks longer than Pakistan.

Once hostilities began, India's powerful navy, which includes modern submarines and one aircraft carrier (with a second under order), would immediately blockade Pakistan's only two seaports at Karachi and Gwadar in Baluchistan, cutting off all of Pakistan's maritime trade. The only way beleaguered Pakistan could obtain strategic supplies of oil, heavy weapons, and munitions would be from Iran, by means of a vulnerable, extremely difficult, 1,600-kilometre (1,000-mile) supply route across the vast deserts and mountains of Baluchistan. In time of war, once Pakistan had exhausted its reserves of fuel and munitions, it would be unable to replenish its vital war stocks because of an effective blockade by the Indian Navy. Pakistan's smaller navy would challenge the Indian blockade, but would be unlikely to actually break it and reopen maritime trade.

India also has the advantage of size. With few targets of strategic importance in the border areas, India could comfortably withdraw before any Pakistani offensive without risking defeat, then counterattack, and cut off over-extending Pakistani forces. India, like Russia, is simply too large to conquer. The only way for Pakistan to win a strategic victory would be to surround and destroy all of India's mobile strike corps along the border in under ten days of sustained combat. But such an outcome is most unlikely, given Pakistan's weakness in armour, logistic support, and air cover.

In a war with India, Pakistan would be much more likely to remain on the strategic defensive: its best hope would be to grab and hold portions of Indian territory along the border to be used as bargaining chips when the war had ended. However, Pakistan's logistical weakness means that, in a lengthy war of attrition, India would be bound to win. Delhi's refusal to be intimidated by the U.S. embargo imposed after its nuclear tests suggests strongly that India might be equally resistant to foreign diplomatic and economic pressure to quickly end a war against Pakistan.

For Pakistan, in the event of a major war, simply defending the long line from Kashmir to Karachi will be an almost impossible task. All of Pakistan's cities, large towns, and communications between Islamabad and Karachi are compressed into the Indus Valley. Modern, mechanized warfare demands ample manoeuvre space, and fluid defense in depth. Having the advantage of the strategic offensive, India can choose where and when to launch its powerful strike corps, concentrating them for inevitable breakthroughs where Pakistani forces are stretched thin, or are absent. After slicing through brittle Pakistani defenses, India's mechanized forces could then defeat the Pakistanis in detail, opening the way to the great port city of Karachi, and to Lahore.

India has another important advantage that becomes crucial in desert warfare: spy satellites that can deliver fairly rapid data on the location of Pakistani forces to the Indian high command in Delhi. During the Iran-Iraq War, data secretly supplied to Baghdad by U.S. reconnaissance satellites played a decisive role in the conflict. According to reliable intelligence sources, the United States actually gave Saddam Hussein's regime a ground station through which it could receive real-time down-linked data from American recon satellites.

In the 1991 Gulf War, Iraqi units in Kuwait's deserts were under constant microscopic examination by U.S. spy satellites. Thanks to its fast-developing space program and growing high-tech computing technology, India too will soon be able to monitor from space all Pakistani military movements. Pakistan has no satellites and, at least for now, no access to space recon data from friendly nations. India's spy satellites will not, however, be able to detect Pakistani missile launches.

If a full-scale war erupts, and Pakistan is unable to prevent its defenses from being torn open, Islamabad's last recourse may be to fire tactical nuclear weapons at the advancing Indian armoured corps, and the logistic bases that support them. This, of course, would cause India to retaliate, possibly with a nuclear attack on cities such as Lahore, Multan, Karachi, and Islamabad. Pakistan would use its new medium-range ballistic missiles to strike Delhi, Amritsar, Bombay, Jaipur, Ahmadabad, and even as far south as Bangalore.

As previously noted, a RAND Corporation study estimated that an India-Pakistan nuclear exchange would cause two million immediate casualties, and a further one hundred million in ensuing weeks.

Adding to the risk of nuclear war, India has repeatedly threatened air and missile strikes against Pakistan's nuclear reactors, weapons assembly facilities, and bases from which nuclear-armed aircraft or missiles can be launched. Indian strategists were greatly impressed by Israel's destruction of Iraq's Osirak reactor in 1981, and have reportedly been encouraged by Israeli advisers to "surgically" remove Pakistan's nuclear capability. Israel has been actively aiding India's secret nuclear program since the 1980s, and sending counter-insurgency specialists to aid Indian forces in Kashmir.

Any Indian attacks on Pakistani nuclear plants would invite immediate retaliation by Pakistan. Even without the danger of enemy attack, India's eleven reactors devoted to production of weapons-grade uranium-233 and plutonium-239 are ticking time bombs, often denounced by critics as little Chernobyls, because of their poor maintenance and a shoddy safety record.

An attack on Pakistani or Indian reactors would release clouds of radioactive dust and debris that would blanket southern Asia, spreading, eventually, around the globe. The explosion of just one nuclear reactor would pollute the groundwater and food chain in the region for many decades. The proximity of Indian and Pakistani reactors to heavily populated areas makes a potential "reactor war" all the more dangerous.

The recent introduction by India and Pakistan of short- and medium-range ballistic missiles configured to carry nuclear warheads sharply increases the reach of any potential nuclear exchange. The missiles have a flight time to target of as little as three minutes. Recent nuclear tests conducted in India in the Thar Desert were designed to validate new tactical nuclear warheads for its missiles, air-delivered bombs, and 155 mm artillery, as well as a precursor thermonuclear, or hydrogen, bomb.

India's acceleration of development of an intermediate version of the Agni-II is clearly designed to strike targets on the Tibet Plateau and deep into western China, including the important industrial cities of Chengdu, Wuhan, Kunming, and Chongqing—and even Hong Kong and Shanghai. In April 1999, India tested the new, solid-fuelled, two-stage Agni-II, which can deliver a one-ton conventional or nuclear warhead over a distance of 2,500 kilometre (1,554 miles), making it a true intermediate-range ballistic missile (IRBM). Indian defense officials claimed Agni-II would eventually be deployed on rail cars.

Pakistan responded only three days later by test-firing its 2,300-kilometre (1,430-mile) Ghauri-IRBM, and a new, single-stage missile, the 750-kilometre- (466-mile-) range Shaheen.

While Delhi and Islamabad rattled their missiles, India's then defense minister, George Fernandes, warned, "With today's launch, we have reached a point where no one from anywhere will dare threaten us." "Anywhere" clearly meant China and even the United States.

Development of strategic arms by India's Defense Research and Development Organization (DRDO) will not end with the Agni-II. The DRDO is expected to introduce the 2,175-mile- (3,500-km-) range Agni-III, a version capable of striking targets anywhere in China.

India is also developing a true intercontinental ballistic missile (ICBM), likely by adding a third solid-fuel stage to Agni-II. This 6,000–7,000-kilimetre- (3,728–4,350-mile) missile will be capable of reaching parts of North America, Japan, and Europe. In addition, DRDO is working on a submarine-launched ballistic missile, Sagarika, and an air-breathing cruise missile. These long-range systems have alarmed not only China, but all of Asia and even American defense planners.

Equally worrying, neither India nor Pakistan has effective surveillance systems capable of giving early warning of enemy missile launches. As a result, their new ballistic missiles create a hair-trigger, use-them-or-lose-them situation—meaning that they might be launched on warning, under fear enemy missiles were incoming, or after a false report of nuclear attack. The necessary civilian and military command-and-control authority to effectively handle nuclear weapons and, *in extremis*, to decide on their use or non-use, are lacking in both India and Pakistan, though the two nations are working to create such strategic organizations.

Right now, the nuclear arsenals of India and Pakistan are under a complex, even uncertain, chain of command that could break down in a crisis, or even produce a false warning of an enemy nuclear attack.

Chronically poor telecommunications and frequent breakdowns in command-and-control on both sides create a further threat of unauthorized or mistaken launches. Agreement by India and Pakistan to advise their neighbour of test launches has in no way lessened this danger. In South Asia, telephone communications are so poor, most senior government officials rely on cellphones. In the event of war, even primitive jamming techniques by the enemy would disrupt the radio transmitters and relay stations on which cellphones depend to function, as well as other radio and microwave transmissions. The fog of war would thicken then grow opaque: in this dangerous miasma, Indian and Pakistani leaders might have to make nearly instant decisions that could mean death for millions of their citizens and a catastrophe for the entire earth.

A more dangerous situation cannot be imagined—and Kashmir could very well be the fuse that ignites a nuclear holocaust on the continent.

13
PARADISE LOST

SRINAGAR

After the usual harrowing flight north from Delhi, I arrived at fabled Srinagar. Kashmir may be the jewel of the subcontinent, but Srinagar is rather disappointing. In spite of its legendary lakeside setting, quaint wooden buildings, clusters of houseboats, and Mogul gardens, Srinagar has the same overcrowded, scruffy, haphazard air as most other South Asian cities. Traffic jams, heaps of refuse, and a miasma of polluted air belie the beauty that surrounds this city of 450,000. Spoiled by the steady influx of tourists for the past century, Srinagar's natives have gained a well-deserved reputation for fleecing, harassing, and abusing visitors. Even the famous houseboats that ply Dal Lake are infested with rats and armies of roaches that are almost as aggressive and annoying as the swarms of touts that incessantly cajole and importune tourists.

Before the uprising, Srinagar's narrow streets, dark, winding alleys, and colourful bazaars offering spices, fruits, and handicrafts had some exotic charm. But the intifada turned the once vibrant, colourful city into a semi-ghost town. As I walked through the grim, deserted streets I met wary patrols of Indian Army, police, and paramilitary troops. Sandbagged Indian checkpoints, manned by nervous, trigger-happy troops, guarded important intersections and government buildings. I had seen a similar pall of fear and raw tension fall over other cities at war: Beirut, Luanda, Algiers, San Salvador, Bogota, Kabul. Srinagar was clearly a city under siege.

At dusk, a curfew went into effect, leaving the streets empty and sinister. Indian troops in Jeeps and light trucks scanned the wooden buildings, their automatic weapons at the ready, on the alert for any movement on the roofs that might mean snipers. The Indians never knew when a grenade would be tossed at them or, worse, an RPG rocket fired at one of their vehicles. Any unusual or unexpected activities after dusk could trigger volleys of fire from the edgy Indian soldiers; they would shoot first and investigate later. The large numbers of innocent civilians shot by accident were simply classified as "terrorists," or "caught in crossfire."

Outside Srinagar, security was even more tenuous. Roads to the once-popular tourist resorts at Gulmarg and Pahalgam were often closed by small bands of mujahedin. Military and police vehicles were routinely ambushed, forcing the Indians to travel in large convoys. The heavily wooded slopes along the roads and narrow defiles provided ideal guerrilla cover, where even the amateur fighters of the various mujahedin groups could operate with some measure of effectiveness.

Wars fought among civilian populations are always a dirty, bloody business. Guerrilla wars, in which the insurgents often receive support from the local populace, are even more so. As the French discovered four decades ago in Algeria, the most effective way to crush guerrilla forces is to separate them from the civilians who sustain them.

•••

Is there a solution to the problem of Kashmir? Half a century of wrangling between India and Pakistan, two wars, and a national uprising have so far changed nothing. Until 1998, the outside world was content to regard Kashmir as a festering, but strategically contained bilateral dispute between India and Pakistan. Like Afghanistan, the area was so remote, so little known, that it was impossible to rouse international public opinion over its travails, even among Islamic nations. Even the United Nations, which had originally called for a referendum to settle the state's future, lost interest in the seemingly intractable issue, and skillful Indian diplomacy thwarted Pakistan's attempts to internationalize the problem.

While other remote conflicts, like East Timor or Tibet, attracted enough media attention to cause popular indignation in the West, the suffering and aspirations of Kashmir's people were largely ignored. The distorted but widely held view that all Muslim liberation movements are terrorists, or at least dangerous troublemakers, contributed to the general lack of concern for Kashmir. Human rights groups that raised the issue received scant attention. Desultory efforts by the United States, Britain, and the Soviet Union to resolve Kashmir soon petered out after being overtaken by more pressing matters. Leave bad enough alone was the world's view of Kashmir.

This international nonchalance abruptly changed in mid-1998 when India detonated five nuclear devices. The nuclear tests, intended to bolster India's security, backfired on Delhi by shocking the outside world and focusing its attention on long-neglected Kashmir. The immediate result for India was opprobrium and temporary financial sanctions. Badly needed foreign investors were scared off, China and Pakistan were deeply alarmed, and the world was furious at India. Pakistan's riposte—a nuclear test of its own—deepened international concern and forced the entire matter of Indo-Pakistani relations and Kashmir onto the diplomatic docket—precisely what India had so long laboured to avoid.

Alarm bells began to go off from Washington to Tokyo, as strategists who had previously written off Southwest Asia as an unimportant geopolitical backwater abruptly realized that two deeply inimical nuclear powers, at scimitars drawn over Kashmir, could very easily get themselves into an advertent, or accidental nuclear war that would kill millions and pollute the planet with radioactive fallout. The dirty secret everyone had chosen to ignore was suddenly out in the open.

Delhi, stunned by unexpected international condemnation, attempted to furiously backpedal, claiming its nuclear explosions were merely a response to threats from China, a contention few believed. India's conditional offers to sign the Non-Proliferation

Treaty did little to allay concern that the subcontinent was at the edge of a nuclear abyss.

Kashmir could no longer be safely forgotten. Without a settlement of the dispute, which focuses and magnifies all the historical, religious, and political hatreds between the two estranged sister-nations, the dangerous impasse would persist indefinitely, subject to perilous escalation at any time.

The confrontation came just as the United States was rapidly expanding its influence into energy- and resource-rich Central Asia. A second Great Game was afoot in the vast steppe and mountain region stretching from China to the Caucasus. Whereas in the nineteenth century, railroads had been the conduits of trade and empire building, at the very end of the twentieth century, oil and gas pipelines had become the new arteries of geostrategic power projection and economic exploitation. A long list of countries, including Russia, the United States, Pakistan, India, China, Iran, Turkey, Saudi Arabia, Japan, and South Korea, and Europe, were all vying to grab a portion of the new oil and gas reserves in the Caspian Basin and, further west, in the semi-independent former Soviet republics. It looked like the world's next gold rush.

The festering civil war in Afghanistan blocked the shortest pipeline routes south and forced the United States to alter its bitterly hostile policy toward Tehran and seek accommodation with Iran, through whose territory lay the next best export route for Central Asia's riches. Just as a laboriously achieved detente was beginning to develop between the United States and Iran, there was a new upsurge of hostility between nuclear-armed India and Pakistan; Kashmir, the focus of Indo-Pakistani rivalry, suddenly intruded into the Central Asian issue, threatening to create a second Afghanistan and possibly draw China and India into direct conflict.

While the need for a comprehensive settlement is evident, the means remain elusive. Neither India nor Pakistan will allow the other to dominate a unified Kashmir, and the majority of Kashmir's people strongly reject Indian domination and aspire to the right of self-determination enshrined in the United Nations Charter. After the bloody intifada, and India's ruthless repression, it seems unlikely most Kashmiris would voluntarily consent to continued direct rule by India.

India insists that the resolution of the Jammu and Kashmir problem

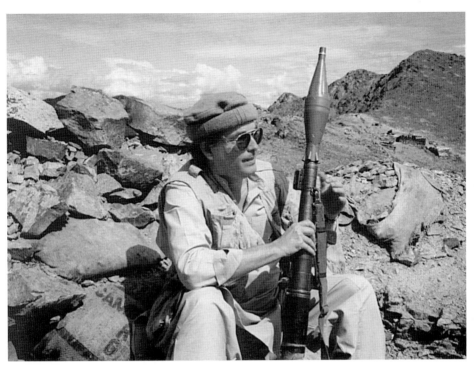
Margolis holding RPG anti-tank rocket at Battle of Jalabad.

Khyber Pass.

Hajji Ajab.

Mujahedin leader Gulbuddin Hekmatyar—later prime minister of Afghanistan—today wanted dead or alive by the U.S.

Watching incoming enemy shells.

The sacred Potala Palace in Lhasa, Tibet.

The fabled Khyber Pass.

Siachen Glacier. A Pakistani 130 mm howitzer goes into action against Indian positions.

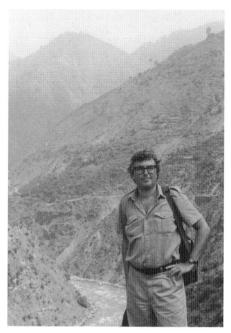

Colonel Musa "the Warrior" points out
Indian positions to Margolis on Siachen
Glacier.

Gorge of Jehlum River in Kashmir,
on the Line of Control facing Indian
positions.

On the road to Siachen, 30 kilometres from the Tibet border.

Lake in Tibet on the way to Lhasa.

Bodyguards supplied me, thanks to Hajji Qadeer.

Wounded Pashtun mujahedin in Peshawar.

President Zia ul-Haq in his home in Rawalpindi, 1986.

Burhanuddin Rabbani—later president of Afghanistan.

Prime Minister Nawaz Sharif in his home.

The road to Siachen. Guard rails not included!

The deadly Karakoram Highway to China.

is an internal matter, in which outside powers and the UN have no business. (The Jammu portion of Kashmir has a Hindu majority and thus will opt for continued union with India.) Pakistan has never been troubled by outsiders questioning its continued possession of the Northern Territories, but that may change if the Kashmir issue comes under international arbitration. In fact, it could open a diplomatic Pandora's box, raising the vexing questions not only of the Northern Territories, but also of Gilgit-Baltistan, Indian-held Ladakh, and the Chinese annexation of Aksai Chin.

In spite of these daunting diplomatic rigidities, the original fifty-year-old UN plan for a supervised referendum in Kashmir still remains the best possible solution. There is no political, demographic, or economic reason why Kashmir could not exist as a viable independent state, with the proviso that, as a buffer between India and Pakistan, it would have to establish and maintain absolute neutrality.

An honest vote in a referendum, of course, would produce a majority in favour of accession to Pakistan or independence. India has long understood this fact, and, accordingly, is determined at all costs to block any vote it cannot control and, inevitably, rig. Only intense international political and economic pressure, or a massive upsurge in the insurrection, could change Delhi's mind, though even this seems unlikely. India's politicians, particularly the Bharatiya Janata Parly's (BJP) Hindu chauvinists, have staked their fortunes on crushing the revolt in Kashmir, and would be turfed out of office by angry Indian voters who would see any settlement over Kashmir as a sellout to the hated Muslims, and even more fiercely hated Pakistan. Losing Kashmir would fly in the face of the BJP's loudly stated ambitions to re-create the old raj under Hindu rule, and negate the party's very raison d'être as the spear-point of Hindu revivalism.

If independence is unachievable and union with Pakistan impossible, what about genuine autonomy within the Indian union? Delhi claims Kashmir already has full autonomy under the local state government run by Dr. Farook Abdullah. Few believe this canard, not even, apparently, Dr. Abdullah, who is reportedly considering giving up being an Indian satrap and returning to his residence in the peaceful English countryside. Real autonomy would imply a right to secede from India, or at least, to elect a state government that is closely aligned to Pakistan. Delhi would accept neither. A truly autonomous government in

Kashmir might quickly spark calls for more autonomy from other restive regions that chafe at Delhi's controls and taxation, such as Assam, Mizoram, Nagaland, or worse, even big states like Tamil Nadu and Karnataka, which might choose to emulate independent-minded Russian regions like Tatarstan, Krasnoyarsk, or Udmurtia by keeping their taxes at home, selling resources and exports directly to foreigners, and refusing to any longer subsidize poor regions of the country.

Every potential solution is replete with problems and dangers. But Kashmiris have made plain they will no longer accept the status quo. Their efforts to cast off Indian rule, and India's savage response, threaten war daily between India and Pakistan. A way of cutting through this modern Gordian knot must be found before the world's most populous region stumbles into nuclear conflict. The world can no longer afford to close its eyes to this half-century-old dispute.

India's ambition to attain a seat on the UN Security Council, and gain international respectability as a democratic, mature great power, is being undermined by its continued repression in Kashmir, one of the worst examples of human rights violations. Ironically, while the world condemns China for its harsh repression in Tibet over the past decade, India has been responsible for even more political killings and tortures during the same period in Kashmir.

India would probably be better off without its portion of strife-torn Kashmir. Keeping the mountain state in the union by force is costing Delhi huge sums of money it can ill afford, wearing down the Indian army, and damaging India's reputation.

But the Indian government has got itself stuck in the mountains of Kashmir: it is unable to go either forward or backward, as the voices of its moderate politicians are increasingly drowned out by the rising clamour of Hindu fundamentalism and chauvinism. No Indian politician dares risk being accused of having surrendered the glorious earthly paradise of Kashmir to the hated Muslim enemy. Muslim Kashmiris cannot abide Indian rule. Everything must change, but nothing, it seems, will.

However, just when the impasse over Kashmir appeared immutable, the Bush/Cheney administration's so called war on terror altered the political balance of forces in this dispute. Any Muslim groups that took up arms, no matter how just the cause or brutal the oppression, was immediately branded a "terrorist organization." Nations, like Pakistan, and Islamic charities that supported them were branded "sponsors of terrorism." The new U.S. *Patriot Act*, rushed through Congress after 9/11, even seemed to classify spoken or written support of most Muslim causes as an act of terrorism.

To India's glee, Washington at once branded all the Kashmiri liberation groups as "terrorist organizations" and fully, adopted Delhi's party line that the Kashmir jihadis were dangerous miscreants that had to be eliminated.

Pakistan, which had backed many of the Kashmiri freedom groups, was forced to cease its overt support, brand some "terrorists," expel Afghan and other foreign mujahidin, and close ISI-run training camps in Azad Kashmir. Delhi triumphantly crowed that Pakistan had indeed admitted being the sponsor of "cross-border terrorism," which, India claimed, was the sole case of the troubles in Kashmir. Pakistan had to eat crow. Most Pakistanis were furious at President Musharraf for what they saw as a callous, cowardly betrayal of their nation's most sacred cause that came right on the heels of Pakistan's equally craven abandonment of its creation, the Taliban. Pakistan was clearly on the run, and the cock-a-hoop Indians knew it.

America's backing in the Kashmir dispute made Delhi more determined than ever to dig in its heels over Kashmir and keep Pakistan on the diplomatic offensive. Every time Musharraf mused on TV about a new idea for peace in Kashmir, Delhi would scorn the idea and raise new hurdles. Why not? India wanted no change in the political status quo, felt it was well on the way to crushing the uprising in Kashmir, now had the unfettered backing of the United States, and was taking enormous pleasure in watching the "bloody Pakistanis" squirm with misery, impotence, and humiliation.

U.S. pressure on Pakistan and rejection of Kashmiri independence from India or union with Pakistan undermined the more moderate resistance groups favouring independence, such as the All Parties Hurriyat Conference and the Jammu Kashmir Liberation Front, and initially strengthened the more radical Lashkar-e-Toiba and Jaish-e-Mohammed. But after they staged an airplane hijacking and other notorious terrorist attacks in India, including an assault on parliament in Delhi, both groups were banned by Pakistan and proscribed by the U.S. and Britain, which accused them of links to al Qaeda.

While there is no doubt that many of the more militant Kashmiri mujahidin groups share similar world views with al Qaeda, so far no direct operational or organizational links between them and Osama bin Laden's organization have been discovered. Another indigenous Kashmir resistance group, Hizbul Mujahidin continues waging anti-Indian operations. As of 2005, Indian intelligence estimated about two thousand "terrorists" (or "freedom fighters" to Pakistanis) were still operating in Indian-ruled Kashmir.

PART THREE

WAR IN THE DEATH ZONE

14
THE ROAD TO SIACHEN

My third journey into the war zone at the top of the world took me to one of the strangest conflicts in history. Over the years, I had heard reports that India and Pakistan were engaged in a bitter struggle over a vast glacier called Siachen, somewhere deep in the frozen mountain wastes between northern Kashmir and Tibet. It would be extraordinarily difficult to find a remoter or more hostile place on earth.

"It's madness. Total madness," a Pakistani commando officer told me one night in Peshawar. "Siachen is hell on earth. We're fighting the bloody Indians to prevent them from grabbing what we say is our rightful part of hell. That's how much we hate each other."

As I was later to discover, the major was right. The Siachen Glacier was a frozen hell. What else but burning hatred could drive men to battle over an alien, airless wilderness, so high and forbidding that even skilled mountain climbers spoke of it with awe and fear? Yet the Indians and Pakistanis had been fighting over this icy massif for a decade, and showed no sign of relenting.

It was madness on a grand, militarized scale. I determined to go and see this highest war in history.

•••

The Pakistan Airways Boeing 737 took off smartly from Islamabad and headed northeast over Azad Kashmir. I sat in the cockpit, chatting with the captain and first officer, both veterans of the crack Pakistani Air Force. At first, the mountains of Kashmir offered a splendid panorama beneath us, but soon a heavy layer of thick, low-hanging clouds hid the ground. We flew for about an hour in the bright sunshine, swapping aviation stories and jokes about the infinite perils of India's internal airlines.

Ahead of us, slightly to our right, an enormous peak rose out of the clouds. "That's Nanga Parbat," the first officer announced. "Eight thousand, one hundred, and twenty-six metres."

We turned right around Nanga Parbat and began to descend over the Gilgit Valley. To our left another great snow-crowned peak, mighty Rakaposhi, rose 7,786 metres (25,545 feet) into the sky. Scores of climbers had died on its treacherous, icy, crumbling slopes. The twin peaks were avoided by all save the most accomplished and experienced climbers.

Now the captain's mood abruptly changed; he became serious, focused, and tense. "I've got to get to work," he said, scanning his flight instruments. He put the 737 into a steep descent toward the clouds then slowed. Minutes later we left the safe, sunlit upper world and entered the menacing sea of cloud that hung between Rakaposhi and Nanga Parbat. Darkness enveloped us.

"We will be going through the mountains in one minute," the captain announced tersely. Below and around us, concealed behind blankets of grey cumulus clouds, were jagged peaks. I peered nervously into the thick gloom, expecting to see a wall of black rock come flying at us. Ten very long, tense minutes later, we broke through the clouds to find ourselves flying down a long, treeless valley, dotted with small lakes and moraines of glacial rock. To our left and right, mountains rose almost vertically until they disappeared into the mist and clouds.

As we flew onward, the valley grew narrower. Rising air currents buffeted the heavy jet. The ground appeared to be closing in on the belly of the aircraft, and its wingtips seemed close enough to touch the sides of the snow-covered mountains that pressed in on either side of us. This is what it must be like, I mused, to fly at 30 metres (100 feet) down Park Avenue in a big passenger jet on a stormy night. The experience was both thrilling and extremely frightening. One false move and our plane, hurtling down a funnel of rock at 560 kilometres per hour (350 miles per hour), would either hit the ground or clip a mountainside, sending us cart-wheeling to disaster.

After a short eternity of tension, the pilot threw the 737 into a sharp, ninety-degree right turn down another valley that intersected the one we had been following. We stood on our side: I was looking out the window directly down into a rushing stream. Our right wingtip dropped to within what appeared a few feet of the ground. The aircraft jolted and shuddered alarmingly as the turn bled off speed.

Abruptly, the pilot righted the 737, and we emerged from the narrow valley over a broad, sandy plain, through which flowed a wide, dark river. We had reached Baltistan, Pakistan's other northern province, and sometime part of Kashmir. On the far side of the plain, some 24 kilometres (15 miles) distant, rose mountains, and behind this scarp rose another and another, forming a gigantic wall of vertiginous, snowcapped peaks that thrust their jagged tors into the clouds: these were the Karakorams, or Black Mountains, the western extension of the high Himalayas. In the midst of this majestic panorama, which filled my entire visual horizon, one titanic white peak soared above all the others, shining jewel-bright in the hard, high-altitude sunlight. "Look." The captain pointed. "K2."

Mighty K2 rises 8,611 metres (28,251 feet) over on the mountain border between. Baltistan and the Chinese province of Sinkiang (formerly known as Eastern Turkestan). Though slightly lower than Mount Everest, whose summit is at 8,848 metres (29,028 feet), K2 is much less accessible, far harder to climb, subject to more violent weather, and more notorious as a killer of climbers. Just south of K2, three other towering mountains with raw, serrated peaks stood like attending giants on either side of it: Masherbrum-1 at 7,821 metres (25,659 feet), Gasherbrum-1 at 8,068 metres (26,469 feet), and Mount Godwin-Austen, 8,615 metres (28,265 feet). All three have an evil reputation among professional climbers. The groups of "tourist" or "dude" climbers who take package tours to poor, defiled Everest, leaving behind heaps of garbage, drained batteries, and frozen feces, do not venture into the wild region of K2 or its guardians. Just to reach their bases requires at least twelve days' difficult mountain trek from Skardu, the capital of Baltistan.

K2, Gasherbrum-1, Masherbrum-1, Rakaposhi, Nanga Parbat, and Lhotse are also called the Great Sacred Mountains, along with the mysterious, 8,598-metre (28,208-foot) Kangchenjunga, farther to the east in the Himalayas, which appears only rarely from its veil of clouds (it has always done so to mark the coronation of the royal family of Sikkim). I am not a particularly religious person, but to me these wild, regal mountains are cathedrals that fill me with the deepest reverence and awe; I am certain they are sacred, though to which gods I do not know. Perhaps they are gods themselves: great frozen towers of adamantine power and majesty, crowned by swirling clouds and wreaths of blowing snow, glowing deep gold and russet in the rarefied, frigid air.

We landed at Baltistan's main city, Skardu, at 2,347 metres (7,700 feet), a miserable collection of concrete buildings, huts, stalls, and tea rooms, with six thousand most uninspiring inhabitants.

Skardu was an important stop on the ancient caravan route between India, China, and Central Asia. From Srinagar in Kashmir, the caravan route heads north, crossing the Himalayas at the Burzil Pass; it continues to Astor, just below the massif of Nanga Parbat, and thence northeast along the Indus Valley to Skardu.

From Skardu, caravans would follow the Indus northwest to Gilgit, then up over the treacherous passes leading into Turkestan—the same famed Silk Road taken by Marco Polo. A second important caravan route ran 420 difficult kilometres (260 miles) from Srinagar up over the Himalayas at Zoji La, down into Ladakh to Kargil, then east along the Indus to Leh, or "Little Tibet." From Leh, the caravans would strike north over the next mountain range to the Shyok River Valley, then north again around the base of the Siachen Glacier to the Karakoram Pass that debouches onto the plains of Turkestan. From there, they would follow the ancient Silk Road to the legendary oasis trading cities of Yarkand and Kashgar.

Today, Skardu is the jumping-off point for major mountaineering expeditions to K2 and its sister peaks. Though 25,900 square kilometres (10,000 square miles) in area, Baltistan is thinly populated with a total population of only 224,000 people, some of whom are nomads. The region is sandwiched between three of the world's highest mountain ranges—the Himalayas, Karakorams, and Hindu Kush—and Tibet. In winter all the passes into Baltistan are totally closed by snow, isolating the valley for five or six months annually from the outside world. The only way to reach Baltistan in winter is by air; however, even in spring and summer, Skardu airport is frequently closed by snow, storms, or thick clouds.

Skardu lies on a rise above the great, 3,057-kilometre- (1,900-mile) long Indus River, whose headwaters rise on the Tibetan Plateau, flow westward across Baltistan, into the Gilgit Valley, and then south the length of Pakistan, emptying into the Arabian Sea at the port of Karachi. Without the Indus and its tributaries, most of Pakistan would be lifeless desert.

The Indus is a big, brawny river, dark brown in some places, grey in others, a torrent of frigid water filled with tumbling rocks, boulders, trees, rich mud, and gravel. Like the Nile, it brings down precious alluvium from the mountains to the flood plains of the south. With its five major tributaries—Sutlej, Jhelum, Chenab, Ravi, and Beas—the Indus is the mother of Pakistan, supporting some one hundred million people. Along the Indus's banks in the third millennium CE rose the Mohenjo Daro civilization, which flourished in the region when the ancient Egyptian culture was also at its height.

•••

Skardu's seedy bazaar was filled with heaps of dark, wooly, brown yak hides, mountain-climbing gear, cheap Chinese fans and TV sets, sacks filled with spices of every colour and aroma, huge jute bags of rice and wheat from the south, rusting auto parts, worn tires, cases of tinned milk, and buckets of ghee, or clarified butter.

Dust blew through the streets, propelled by a relentless wind. The sun beat down hard in the thin, dry air, immediately parching the skin and throat. Rainclouds from the south were trapped by the Pir Panjal range and the Himalayas, leaving the long Baltistan Valley arid and barren, like the neighbouring Tibetan plateau to the northeast. Arriving in this vast, lonely desert at the roof of the world, after leaving green, wooded Kashmir, made for a dramatic and disturbing contrast. Cross the col of Zoji La and you suddenly find yourself in one of the bleakest wastes in central Asia, where there is almost no rainfall and even the winter's snows on the loftiest peaks are but a thin dusting of white. Ladakh and Baltistan resemble their geographic sister, Tibet: an arid plateau of granite dust, devoid of trees or pastures, encircled by dark crags and cut by broad couloirs of broken rock.

Baltis, a small people with marked Tibetan-Mongol features, mingled in the Skardu bazaar with fair Kashmiris and Gilgitis, as well as darker-hued Pakistanis from the south. Most Baltis are Shia Muslims. Sunni Muslim tribes to the south consider the Baltis heretics, and used to regularly wage war against them, further isolating the valley from contact with India.

The dilapidated centre of Skardu was also a meeting place for the inevitable latter-day hippies from Europe one always finds in remote mountain towns. Unwashed Dutch girls in blue saris and beads, scruffy young Germans with scraggly blond beards, wearing dirty parkas and pakul hats, and a gaggle of coarse, nomadic Australians sat about in little groups, smoking hash, and trying, without much success, to look like the locals, who rewarded their efforts with polite disdain. A mountain expedition was purchasing canned milk, wooden boxes of tea, and large jute bags of rice.

That night, I left the spartan government guest house where I had lodged, and walked down to the river. I was completely alone; the only sound came from the rushing water and wind. The light of the full moon hanging just above the valley reflected off the snowy mountains above and bathed the river in a flat, soft luminescence. I took a few steps into the icy water, bent over and picked up a rock worn smooth and rounded by the rushing waters. Where had it come from, I wondered? Probably somewhere high up in mysterious Tibet, a land I had never seen. The grey-green basalt rock, which dried quickly in the arid air, felt strangely warm; it moulded into my hand. I stood in the moonlight, experiencing a magical moment of communion with the hidden gods of the roof of the world.

I said a brief prayer for my mother, father, and distant friends.

The next day I arose at dawn and went to breakfast. A cheery Pakistani army officer marched into the dining room, introduced himself with fine courtesy as Captain Aziz, drank a cup of milky tea with me, and announced, "Come, Mr. Eric, it is time to go to Siachen." The Pakistani military had laid on a Jeep to take me to the glacier, which was a closed, highly sensitive military zone, and the theatre of active combat operations. Had I known what ordeals lay in wait, my enthusiasm to embark on this adventure would have been somewhat more restrained.

Baltistan lies on a northwest axis between the world's two highest mountain ranges: the Himalayas to the south and the Karakorams to the north. The Karakorams extend 400 kilometres (250 miles) from the Hunza Valley above Gilgit to the western borders of Tibet, an unbroken chain of soaring peaks and glacier-filled valleys that, unlike the Himalayas, has no intersecting passes, and is thus virtually inaccessible to travellers or commerce. In the nineteenth century, a few hardy British surveyors had roughly mapped the western end of the Karakorams; aside from these tentative efforts, the forbidding mountains remained almost entirely uncharted and unknown.

Two vast glaciers, Baltoro and Siachen, the highest and largest outside of the Arctic and Antarctic regions, extend along the northern flank of Baltistan. These huge seas of ice and deep, lethal crevasses rise to altitudes of over 7,000 metres (22,965 feet). Siachen, which means "wild rose" in the Balti language, is the higher of the two.

Siachen marks the eastern end of Baltistan. Here, the borders of Chinese Sinkiang, Tibet, and Indian-held Ladakh meet in one of the world's most remote, inhospitable places. Just to the north, an ancient caravan route leads over the 5,575-metre (18,290-foot) Karakoram Pass into Chinese-held Aksai Chin. From there, the unpaved track continues to the desert oasis of Haji Langar, where it connects to the major military road built by China that runs northwest from Tibet, through the icy wastes of Aksai Chin, to Yarkand and Kashgar in Sinkiang.

The Karachi Agreement, signed by Pakistan and India at the end of their 1947 war, demarcated the ceasefire line up to a point on the Shyok River near the southern end of the Siachen Glacier. During the 1947 fighting, Muslim Baltistani forces had advanced to the foot of the glacier, clearing the entire valley of Indian forces. North of the Khapalu region and Nubra Valley, however, the ceasefire line was left undemarcated and notional.

At the time, the region's mountainous geography was only poorly mapped, even less understood, and rightly deemed of no earthly use to anyone. Pakistan was later to claim the border should have extended northeast from the Nubra Valley to the Karakoram Pass, but did not press this point after the 1947 ceasefire. The Indian and Pakistani governments had little interest in the area, and were preoccupied with their violent dispute over Kashmir.

So the situation remained until 1950, when China invaded and occupied Tibet. India was initially alarmed by the Chinese invasion, but was unable to confront both China and Pakistan at the same time. India's leader, Prime Minister Jawaharlal Nehru, was an ardent socialist and leading advocate of Third World political unity against the "imperialist" powers. Nehru much admired Mao Tse-tung and his Chinese revolution; he believed India and China should cooperate closely to dominate and guide Asia. Equally important, Nehru's Fabian socialism held that territorial disputes—the evil fruits of capitalism and imperialism—could not occur between "fraternal socialist nations." India had nothing to fear from China, insisted Nehru.

Nehru's remarkably naive view of China became official government policy. Delhi simply closed its eyes to China's occupation of Tibet, hoping the entire nasty business would somehow go away. Nehru seemed to believe that once China had reasserted its ancient political "patronage" over Tibet, Mao would withdraw his troops and allow the remote Himalayan kingdom to slip back into its traditional peaceful obscurity. The 4,000-kilometre (2,500-mile) frontier between China and India was, in Nehru's optimistic phrase, to be "a border of peace."

To Nehru's surprise and chagrin, China did not withdraw its troops, but set about converting Tibet into a Chinese province. Chinese field armies were permanently based in Tibet, supported by new military roads, depots, and airfields, and Han Chinese settlers were brought into Tibet by Beijing. A flood of immigrants followed, eventually turning Tibetans into a minority within their own nation. A brief, abortive effort by the U.S. Central Intelligence Agency and India's intelligence service to mount a rebellion against China's occupation of Tibet was ruthlessly crushed.

Nevertheless, India proclaimed the era of good relations and brotherhood between Delhi and Beijing, known under the charming slogan "Hindi-Chini-Bhai-Bhai," would prevail over mundane questions of borders and territory. Much of India's leadership had only the vaguest notion of the geography of the Himalayas and Karakorams, a region as alien to most Indian plains dwellers as Alaska's mountain ranges would be to residents of southern Alabama.

India's mood of false optimism and the era of Hindi-Chini-Bhai-Bhai was shattered in late 1959 when Chinese troops based in Tibet began to edge into northern Ladakh and disputed regions of Arunachal Pradesh (then called the North-East Frontier Agency, or NEFA) along the high, mountainous frontier above East Pakistan and Burma. Beijing claimed it was merely asserting sovereignty over territory that had always belonged to the Chinese Empire. Delhi finally raised the alarm, accused China of illegally occupying 90,000 square kilometre (34,740 square miles) of its territory in Arunachal Pradesh, and began rushing troops to the endangered northern fronts. China forcefully reasserted its claim to the disputed border region above Assam.

Almost unnoticed by Delhi, China also occupied the barren, uninhabited, but strategically important 40,000 square-killometre (15,440-square-mile) region of Aksai Chin near the end of its western border, which had been historically considered part of Ladakh. India claimed that Pakistan had facilitated the Chinese takeover, in return for diplomatic and military support, which was is likely true. Delhi became acutely alarmed when it learned China been building a highly strategic military road for the past three years through Aksai Chin, linking Tibet with Chinese Sinkiang to the west.

As in so many of the Third World's modern territorial disputes, much of the fault for the growing Indian-Chinese border crisis lay with imperial Britain. The British Raj had demarcated India's northern borders with Tibet and Turkestan (now Chinese Sinkiang) in a haphazard and often slipshod manner. Neither region was deemed a threat to India. The British Raj had no commercial interests in Tibet or central Asia, so both regions were largely ignored, though a wary eye was kept on the Russian Empire, which was slowly expanding south toward the Himalayas and Afghanistan. As a result, the rulers of the British Raj decided to leave the wild mountain ranges and deep valleys of the eastern Himalayas and Ladakh as a sort of no man's land between the two rival empires.

In 1914, Sir Henry McMahon, representing Lord Curzon, the viceroy of India, negotiated a treaty with Tibet that delineated the border between the British Raj, Burma, Tibet, and the lands of the local Muslim rulers of Eastern Turkestan. Chinese representatives only observed these negotiations, and refused to sign the resulting agreement. This abstention allowed them to maintain later that the McMahon Line was invalid, had no legal basis, and was an act of colonial arrogance imposed by British imperialists on Tibet's weak religious leadership—which, in any event (according to China), had no authority to negotiate over borders that were rightfully under the mandate of Beijing, the historic overlord of Tibet.

The McMahon Line was roughly drawn and often geographically vague. Legend has it McMahon used a thick-nibbed pen whose broad strokes left many border regions in question. The British-demarcated frontier failed, in many instances, to follow the region's natural topographical divisions of valleys, watersheds, and ridge lines, creating a confused, ill-defined, and fragmented border, a sort of geographical limbo. India and China subsequently published maps that showed large areas of territory claimed by the other side within their own borders. Both nations claimed that what had previously been mutually accepted as a forgotten no man's land had actually been under their active administration. It was thus inevitable the two great powers of Asia that succeeded the British Raj would eventually clash over the poorly demarcated roof of the world.

Nehru, under pressure from his defense minister, V.K. Krishna Menon, and his cousin Lieutenant General B.M. Kaul, and increasingly hard pressed by noisy opposition parties and the jingoistic Indian media, decided in 1960 to confront China. Menon and Kaul proposed a "forward strategy" to solidify Indian claims on the northern border. This hasty, ill-conceived plan called for Indian troops to advance boldly into the disputed territory, edge around Chinese forward posts, and isolate them from their supply lines.

The Indian Army's swift, bloodless 1961 success in taking over the former Portuguese colony of Goa had emboldened the generals of the high command. Furthermore, Menon claimed China was diplomatically isolated, locked in confrontation with both the United States and the Soviet Union, and reeling from the disaster of Mao's Great Leap Forward, in which up to thirty million Chinese peasants died of starvation. China was in no position to resist India, Menon argued, and would fall back without a real fight. Nehru finally gave in to the pressure, deciding the time was ripe to challenge a weakened China.

China's brilliant foreign minister, Zhou Enlai, sought to head off a clash with India by offering to accept India's claims along the eastern end of the McMahon Line in Arunachal Pradesh, a region of little value to China, in return for India's acceptance of China's claims to all of Aksai Chin. In addition, China proposed to drop its historic claim to 103,600 square kilometres (40,000 square miles) of territory between the McMahon Line and the foothills of the Himalayas above Assam. Delhi, confident in its own military prowess, rejected Zhou's proposal out of hand.

Indian patrols began skirmishing with Chinese units in the high, misty valleys of the North-East Frontier Agency (NEFA). In spite of Delhi's decision to go on the offensive, its military buildup was desultory. Some army units, including the famous Fourth Infantry Division, of North Africa fame, were moved up into the mountains. A single division was not enough to defend the long NEFA border, a task that demanded, at the very least, four divisions. Similarly, a single brigade was sent up to Ladakh, when five would have been the minimum for successful offensive operations.

The Indian troops deployed north had few radios capable of operating in the mountains, were poorly provisioned, lacked warm clothing, and were indifferently led. Worse, the Indians had no accurate military maps of the mountain region. Some Indian units were forced to use old British tourist maps and guidebooks. The Indian troops, or *jawans*, most of whom were lowlanders, quickly became disoriented and depressed at altitudes of 5,486 metres (18,000 feet), and often got lost in the twisting, cloud-shrouded Himalayan valleys as they tried to outflank or envelop Chinese positions.

India's lackadaisical attitude contrasted sharply with China's determination to maintain control of the crest of the Himalayas and cement control of Tibet. The People's Liberation Army (PLA) drove new roads from Lhasa to Ladakh, hard on India's border, established supply dumps, and set up regular communication links to military units deployed along the Himalayan Line of Control. Chinese mountain troops were supplied with accurate maps, and, unlike their Indian opponents, given detailed briefings on the topography around them. The Indians knew almost nothing of what the Chinese were doing; most of Delhi's scant information came from sporadic patrols along the LOC, from nomads, and from misinformed diplomats in far-off Beijing.

By contrast, the diligent Chinese had built a network of spies among local mountain tribesmen, who provided accurate information about Indian deployments in forward and rear areas. According to the Indian writer Rajesh Kadian, the Chinese, with admirable Maoist thoroughness, even built prisoner-of-war camps designed to hold three thousand captives, which he says was a "remarkably accurate assessment as after the war, 3,587 Indian soldiers were taken prisoner."

In one amusing incident, the Chinese set up a little hut of pleasure near the border in which two attractive Mompa tribeswomen played the role of Himalayan Mata Haris by eliciting military information through pillow-talk from lonely, garrulous Indian officers.

By the fall of 1962, tensions between India and China were at the boiling point; clashes and skirmishes were occurring almost daily at both ends of the Himalayas. India's feisty press and the political opposition beat the war drums, demanding Nehru's government take action to "stop Chinese aggression." Nehru was still loath to jeopardize relations with Mao Tse-tung, but wavered in the face of his general's warn ings and rising public clamour for military action. Krishna Menon finally made up Nehru's mind.

The cadaverous and intensely nervous Menon bore a remarkable physical resemblance to Pakistan's consumptive founder, Muhammad Ali Jinnah. Menon was a fiery left-winger who bitterly hated the West and believed India was destined to lead the Third World. Unfortunately, his bombastic oratorical skills far exceeded his knowledge or intelligence. Nehru always put far too much faith in Menon, allowed his erratic and spiteful defense minister to convince him that it was time to launch a full-scale offensive, one the Chinese would not be able to resist or even react to militarily. India's professional generals thought Menon was a loud-mouthed fool; Menon returned the favour by refusing to listen to their views on the Himalayas, or even the information they gave him about the army's glaring lack of combat-preparedness and logistical weakness.

Krishna Menon assured Nehru the Indian Army was ready and able to evict the Chinese from their encroachments in the NEFA and Ladakh. In September 1962, Nehru reluctantly ordered the army to occupy Indian-claimed areas. Nehru and Menon assumed such action would be the work of only a few days. Indian astrologers consulted the stars and assured Menon the offensive would be a triumphant success. Neither the politicians in Delhi nor the Indian general staff understood the military situation. In fact, very few Indians knew anything about the remote Himalayan border, other than the fact that it was being threatened by China.

The Chinese, of course, did not see themselves as aggressors, but as the liberators of territory that was rightfully Chinese. In truth, some of the areas and border posts claimed by India actually lay, according to nineteenth-century British Raj maps, within Tibetan and Chinese territory.

At first, India's offensive advanced without serious challenge. Chinese forces fell back steadily. But a month after Indian troops had occupied substantial portions of the disputed border zones, the Chinese counterattacked. On October 20, 1962, four Chinese mountain divisions attacked points along the eastern border, and in Ladakh. The Indians quickly found themselves outgunned, outmanoeuvred, and outsmarted by the veteran Chinese troops. India's *jawans* had not been trained in mountain warfare, their equipment was obsolete, and their officers were out of their depth.

The Chinese People's Liberation Army (PLA) employed the same tactics in the Himalayas and Ladakh that had proven so successful against U.S. troops in the mountains of Korea. Chinese troops were trained to pin down heavily defended hilltop positions by frontal attacks, then edge around the enemy flanks, and attack from the rear. Thanks to redoubtable marching skill and a light logistical tail that was not dependent on roads, Chinese infantry could cover great distances over rough terrain that would be considered impassable by heavily laden Western armies.

The PLA's ability to move men and supplies swiftly over broken ground by day or night gave it remarkable flexibility and mobility, allowing the Chinese to avoid or bypass enemy strong points. In Korea, mountains proved ideal tactical topography for China's fluid infantry tactics. Time after time, PLA units worked around dug-in UN units, or drove in deep into U.S. defense lines by crossing unguarded mountain ridges where road-bound American troops could not follow or operate. After heavy fighting, Indian forces at both ends of the frontier were thrown into full retreat. In the second week of November, Chinese troops launched a major offensive against Indian positions around the key strongpoint of Bomdi La, the gateway from the high mountains to the wide plains of Assam. Indian units were battered by artillery, pinned down, then outflanked by Chinese thrusts over the mountains. In Ladakh, the PLA assaulted the Indians on a 400-kilometre (250-mile) front. There, however, unlike in the NEFA, the Chinese made slower progress, though they again pushed the defending Indians steadily back.

By the third week of November 1962, Indian defense lines in the NEFA were broken. After the Battle of Bomdi La, the victorious Chinese were poised to debouche from the Himalayas into Assam. Calcutta lay only 800 kilometres (500 miles) to the south. Panic erupted in Delhi. A deeply humiliated Nehru abandoned his most cherished beliefs in anti-imperialism, swallowed his considerable pride, and begged the United States to send aircraft to bomb the advancing Chinese, with nuclear weapons if necessary, he pointedly added.

Then, on November 21, China stunned everyone by announcing a unilateral ceasefire, and a withdrawal of its troops behind the disputed Line of Control: in other words, a return to the pre-war status quo. Chairman Mao, ever the artful psychologist, thus added humiliation to India's military debacle. Beijing announced its army had "taught India a lesson." Indeed it had. The defeat left India reeling in shock, and unwilling to challenge China in the Himalayas or Ladakh for the next thirty years.

Nehru was stunned and emotionally shattered. The disaster left him a broken man, and his health began to fail. He was as devastated as his friend and ally Gamal Abdel Nasser had been by the calamitous defeat inflicted on Egypt by Israel in 1967. Nehru died less than two years later.

The 1962 disaster led India to quickly expand and rearm its military forces. New mountain divisions were formed, and accurate surveys were begun of the hitherto uncharted Himalayan and Ladakh border regions. Disputed Kashmir suddenly assumed heightened strategic importance as Delhi worried that China had designs on the mountain state, or that it might join Pakistan in a coordinated assault on northern India. Most important, India's leaders became convinced China represented a long-term territorial rival. In 1963, India began secret development of a nuclear weapons program.

For the next twenty years, India steadily shored up its defenses in the Himalayas and Ladakh. When Pakistan and China agreed to begin construction of an all-weather road, the Karakoram Highway (not to be confused with the Karakoram Pass), linking Gilgit with Sinkiang, alarm bells began to ring in Delhi. India feared that in time of war Chinese troops would be able to reinforce northern Pakistan via this route, even though the narrow, perilous highway snaked over high mountains and was often blocked by landslides or snow, and could be easily interdicted by bombing or commando raids.

Construction of the Karakoram Highway and Indian anger over the loss of Aksai Chin to China spurred Delhi to begin expanding its military influence in the remote, undemarcated mountain regions north of Ladakh, and around the Siachen Glacier.

In the late 1970s, a series of mountaineering expeditions led by Indian army officers began exploring and surveying the peaks in the Siachen-Baltoro-Kangra region. At first, Pakistan accepted these expeditions as purely scientific and did not react. But in 1983, the Indians lifted an entire mountain battalion by helicopter onto the eastern side of the Siachen Glacier. A series of permanent military posts were constructed there in April 1984, generally at elevations of 2,438 to 4,876 metres (8,000 to 16,000 feet). That same year Indian forces deployed forward, digging in atop the glacier, commanding its highest points and most important features. This gave the Indians an important tactical advantage, but made the task of supplying them extremely arduous and hazardous.

India's military intrusion into what had been an undemarcated no man's land deeply alarmed Islamabad. Pakistan became convinced the Indians were embarked on a grand strategy to advance westward into Baltistan and occupy Skardu. Using Skardu and its large airfield as a main operating base, the Indians, it was feared, would then drive into the Gilgit Valley, thus severing the Karakoram Highway, Pakistan's sole land link to its most important ally, China. Some Pakistani strategists, deeply concerned by India's fast-growing strategic alliance with the U.S.S.R., even claimed India was bent on invading Chinese Sinkiang, capturing the vital road junction of Kashgar, and then linking up in the Pamirs with Soviet forces in the Soviet Socialist Republic of Kyrgyz.

As a result, Pakistan rushed troops to Siachen, and began building bases in the Khapalu Valley to support them. The glacier, 80 kilometres (50 miles) long, and rising to an average altitude of 6,096 metres (20,000 feet), quickly became the world's most improbable and difficult battlefield. Indian and Pakistani mountain units began a dramatic race to occupy the remaining peaks commanding the glacier. Infantry battles, with machine guns, mortars, rockets, and artillery, raged between the two sides in a desperate effort to deny the enemy superior ground. By 1984, the two foes had deployed a total of some ten thousand troops at Siachen. That same year, they fought one of the largest battles on Siachen, supported by heavy artillery and rocket batteries, each suffering losses of around one hundred dead.

The Pakistanis held one important tactical advantage at Siachen. Their troops on the glacier, dug in at elevations from 2,743 to 4,572 metres (9,000 to 15,000 feet), could be supplied by a land route from Skardu to the Khapalu Valley. From bases and depots at Khapalu, men and supplies could be brought up to the glacier by Jeep or truck, then moved to forward positions by mule, or on porters' backs. The Pakistanis were able to move 130 mm guns onto the glacier, bringing many of the Indians' positions atop and behind Siachen within range.

By contrast, the Indians had no land route to their generally higher positions on the glacier: the terrain on the Indian-controlled side was too rough and steep to allow vehicular traffic. The Indians were forced to move men and supplies north from their main operational base in Ladakh at Kargil, up to camps in the Nubra Valley at the foot of the Siachen Glacier. From there, every soldier, bullet and shell had to be laboriously transported by porter, pack animal, or helicopter onto the glacier. Indian artillery was forced to locate at the base of the glacier, putting the guns out of range of the Pakistani logistics bases at Khapalu. Supplying the three Indian battalions deployed at Siachen with ammunition and combat supplies became an arduous and enormously costly operation. Expenditure of heavy-artillery ammunition alone by the two sides at Siachen amounted to some eighty thousand rounds annually.

In early 1999, India began work on a road from its forward supply bases to the glacier, a route that had to cross numerous 5,486-metre (18,000-foot) passes frequently blocked by landslides and avalanches. The cost of such an undertaking is huge, particularly for a nation in which a third of the citizens subsist in dire poverty, but India seemed determined to dominate Siachen at all costs and, just as important, deny it to the hated Pakistanis.

The air at Siachen's altitude is only half as dense as at sea level. This meant helicopters were able to lift only a quarter of their normal load— or even less, depending on the altitude to which they sought to fly. In many cases, Indian helicopters could only carry one or two soldiers or a few boxes of ammunition or food to the glacier's top. Resupply for the Indians, and to a somewhat lesser but still painful degree for the Pakistanis, became an agonizingly slow, tedious process that put men and machines under enormous, punishing strain. Frequent severe weather and violent storms made all air and ground movement extremely risky and unreliable. Accidents killed as many men as enemy fire.

It was, as one Indian officer told me, "like fighting a war on the moon." And that was just the problem of logistics. The terrible cold and extreme altitude atop the glacier was equally and undiscriminatingly murderous to soldiers and journalists alike, as I would shortly discover.

15
MUSA THE WARRIOR

aptain Aziz and I set off at dawn from Skardu in a green Toyota Land Cruiser. Aziz was a thin, wiry Punjabi from Multan, in the south, with a ready smile, a cheerful disposition, and (I happily noted) well-developed driving skills. We followed the mighty Indus for some hours, skirting its banks and its gravelly alluvial plain, over what purported to be a road, at least on the military map he provided me with, but which was in truth no better than a rough dirt track, with occasional patches of gravel where water flowed down, deep, treacherous holes that seemed designed to break axles. Shaky bridges of wooden planking crossed dry water courses, or nullahs, that intersected the track. Land Cruisers are not built for creature comforts; their dour Japanese designers seemed to have forgotten, or never learned, the use of springs.

The view along the Indus was magnificent. To our left extended the unbroken wall of the snow-clad Karakorarns, a gigantic maze of peaks stretching to the far horizon. The thin air and strong sun etched the mountains in sharp detail. Above us, the cloudless sky was an intense cobalt blue. Birds wheeled in rising currents of air as the morning cool dissipated and the day grew warmer.

At Gol, we crossed a swaying wooden plank bridge suspended, from concrete pillars at either end, over the boiling, dark waters of the Indus. Every 16 kilometres (10 miles) or so, a small, decrepit village of mud bricks stood by the side of the track. As we passed, villagers waved to us, or stared in curiosity. All about, the dun-coloured land was parched and sere, a high-altitude desert set beneath the radiant snows of the distant mountains.

After Gol, we continued on a southeast bearing for Khapalu along the wide banks of the Indus. Khapalu is described as the most important town in the region, but it turned out to be no more than another miserable collection of shacks and warehouses, a sort of miniature version of Skardu. A large wooden suspension bridge moored to two imposing concrete arches spanned another, almost equally turbulent river, the Shyok. After clattering over it, Aziz and I stopped to admire the view of the rushing river, then continued our arduous drive, heading in the general direction of the narrow valley of the Saltoro River, which flows down from the Siachen Glacier.

What had been a dirt road along the Shyok soon degenerated into a pitted rock track that seemed to be shaking the life out of the Jeep and its riders. We could drive at no more than 16 kilometres per hour (10 miles per hour) for fear of breaking an axle; even so, clouds of dust and grit covered us, filling our mouths, ears, and eyes. I held on for dear life as the Jeep jolted and swayed violently.

At numerous points, landslides or large boulders obstructed the route. Somehow, the intrepid Captain Aziz managed to manoeuvre the

Jeep over or around them, sometimes with only an inch to spare. We had occasionally to fill deep holes in the track with rocks. Aziz warned me to keep a constant watch for rockslides. It would take only a one or two falling chunks of rock to push us into the river below.

In the afternoon, we entered a fairly flat region with broad, green fields of wheat that offered a welcome contrast to the arid wastes we had lately crossed. Balti women, clothed in gaily coloured yellow and blue robes, were working in the lush fields.

"We are coming to an oasis village I call 'the little paradise,'" announced Captain Aziz. Indeed, after the near-desert landscapes we had seen, the hamlet did seem rather magical. It looked, I thought, like the Koran's vision of paradise, a place of running water, greenery, orchards, and handsome women. Waterfalls cascaded down the sides of a steep cliff bordering the village, becoming rivulets of bubbling silver that coursed around its humble mud-brick buildings and copses of slender trees. The little cultivated plots were intersected by a chessboard of irrigation ditches carrying streams of cold, clear mountain water. Birds and butterflies from many miles around flocked to the oasis, congregating in its fruit trees and willows.

A British adventurer of the last century described the oasis villages of Baltistan as looking like "bits of some other country cut out with a pair of scissors and dropped into a desert: a cloudless region, always burning or freezing, under the clear blue sky."

We reclined and lunched beside a brook, beneath tall, leafy trees that offered shelter from the sun, gratefully relaxing in the cool, moist air. I went to the waterfall and washed off the dust that covered me from head to foot. A group of smiling Balti villagers came to offer us fruits from their orchards, bowls of nuts, and milky-white tea. The women, I noted, were far taller and more attractive than the ones I had seen in seedy Skardu. Children eyed us shyly, pointing at the strange farangi who had come to their little paradise. I drank hungrily and deeply from the waterfall, whose cold, clear waters tasted delicious, an extremely rare luxury in a part of the world where groundwater is almost always perilous to all but the most inured natives.

I wondered if the writer James Hilton had used this village, or one much like it, as the setting of his famed novel, *Lost Horizon*, in which a British diplomat crash-lands somewhere in the Himalayas, and discovers the lost valley of Shangri-La, an Eden whose kind, gentle people never grow old. There must be hidden valleys here in Baltistan, I mused, places no Westerners had ever visited, where the arcane secrets and magic of Tibet's red-hat lamas were still preserved. In some lost lamasery of Baltistan there had to be a sacred text explaining how the legendary high priests of Tibet were able to live for hundreds of years. Still pondering these thoughts, I fell into a deep, gentle sleep beside the rushing stream.

An hour later we set off again along the bank of the river. After two more hours of driving we left the track and worked our way up a long slope. Captain Aziz halted the Jeep, got out, and motioned me to follow him. We climbed up a steep ridge that rose to our right. Just below the crest, Aziz ordered, "Stay low."

I cautiously stuck my head above the ridge and had a quite sudden and horrible attack of vertigo. We were on the edge of an enormous precipice that fell at least 2 kilometres (1.25 miles) straight down into a distant valley below. It was the kind of terrifying drop about which I'd had recurrent nightmares over the years: clinging by my fingernails to the edge of a cliff, slowly loosing my grip, and then falling screaming into the abyss.

We had reached the crest of the Ladakh mountain range, which extends from northwest to southeast along Tibet's western border—and the Line of Control between Indian Ladakh and Pakistani territory. Before us lay a panorama of snow-capped mountains, forested hills, and glittering rivers that reminded me of the glorious vistas of Switzerland's Bernese Oberland—magnified by a factor of ten. From where we crouched, the vast sweep of Kashmir and Ladakh extended below us, framed, to the south, by the soaring range of the Zanskar Mountains. Beyond the Zanskar lay the vale of Kashmir, and below that the flat, endless, steamy plains of northern India. In the thin, dry air, distant objects appear close. One's sense of distance and proportion becomes confused. Yaks on a far-off slope seem but a few minutes' walk away. A single tree that is plainly visible may be a day's walk distant. Sound, too, distorts in the mountains, playing strange tricks on the ears.

"Look, there. Kargil." Aziz pointed to a town at the confluence of three rivers in the valley below us. "Keep your head down," he warned. "The Indians watch this ridge."

Kargil was Ladakh's second-largest town after the capital, Leh, and the main operating and logistics base for Indian army units at the Siachen Glacier. Even from afar, Kargil was unprepossessing, a haphazard collection of wooden buildings and storehouses with a small bazaar in the middle that bore evident signs of occasional shelling by Pakistani artillery during periodic border flare-ups. From Kargil, a narrow Indian military road followed the old caravan route, winding northeast up into the Nubra Valley to the foot of the Indian side of the Siachen Glacier.

In May 1999, some eight hundred Kashmiri mujahedin crossed the LOC and seized the 4,877-kilometre (16,000-foot) ridge line from which we were peering down on Kargil. From their vantage points, the mujahedinn were able to bring down fire, and target Pakistani artillery, on the strategic Kargil-Leh military road. India's main ammunition dump near Kargil was blown up, destroying eighty thousand howitzer shells.

India launched a series of violent counter-offensives to regain the heights above Kargil, Drass, Batalik, and the Mushkoh Valley, employing up to two mountain divisions, Gurkhas, heavy artillery, and round-the-clock air strikes. As Delhi and Islamabad traded threats of war, and Indian generals threatened to attack Pakistan south of Kashmir, Indian strike corps in Punjab and the Thar Desert moved to offensive deployments. Pakistani forces went on full alert. India and Pakistan were within hours of full-scale war. There were reports that both sides had armed and deployed some of their nuclear weapons.

The heavy fighting raged for eight weeks, costing India at least 1,200 casualties, two warplanes, and a helicopter. The worst fighting between India and Pakistan in thirty years deeply alarmed the United States, which brought intensive pressure to bear on Pakistan to pull back the mujahedin, who could not have gone into action without logistic and artillery support from the Pakistani army. Prime Minister Nawaz Sharif was forced to order the mujahedin back; Pakistan was widely blamed around the world for starting the fighting. But as a result of the surprise attack, the Kashmir dispute had suddenly become internationalized, and it dominated international headlines for two months.

We left our lookout and resumed driving. The rising terrain became more alpine, dotted with dark boulders, runnels of grey gravel, and heaps of glacial rock. As we struggled over the terrible, tooth-rattling rock track, I held on grimly as each jolt sent spasms of pain through my tensed, aching back muscles. Once again, we were covered in dust and blasted by the fierce, unfiltered sunlight. The road led up, and then farther up the side of a huge massif of dark, striated rock.

After more agony, we reached the top of the Bilafond Pass at 4,757 metres (15,609 feet). Before me, a wall of sheer, light grey peaks rose about 16 kilometres (10 miles) from our position, raw, serrated and jagged, set against the backdrop of an intensely blue sky and thin wisps of cloud. A vast, utterly still lake, perhaps 10 kilometres (6 miles) in length and 5 kilometres (3 miles) in width, lay at the foot of the mountain wall, reflecting with mirror-like clarity the sharp peaks behind. I had never seen such wild mountains. They bore none of the rounded, weathered maturity of America's or Europe's peaks: they were young, powerful, menacing. Witch's peaks, I thought, a setting that reminded me of Modest Mussorgsky's sinister tone poem *St. John's Night on the Bare Mountain*.

We skirted along a huge mountain that formed the right flank of the motionless lake, edging along the increasingly narrow track that had been hewn into the cliff side. The track was just wide enough for the Jeep: one side was a wall of crumbling rock, on the other a sheer, almost vertical drop some thousand of feet into the water below. There was no guardrail or any sort of barrier to prevent us flying over the precipice. From time to time, the track narrowed. I watched with fascinated horror as we half projected over the void. Captain Aziz inched forward , his knuckles white on the steering wheel.

A boulder lay on the tracks. We stopped to study the new obstacle.

We felt tiny, like ants struggling up the side of an alp. I could see the track as it extended ahead for many miles: it looked like a thread laid halfway up the side of a mountain. Vertigo and agoraphobia—the fear of open space—gripped me. I felt insignificant, minute, a speck of dust in a landscape of titans. There was no sign that any other humans had ever been in this land of the gods.

The dauntless Aziz managed to circumvent the boulder, but not before our Jeep had first the front wheel, then the rear, hanging in the air. "Be ready to jump if we start going over," he cried. At least, I thought ruefully, I will have the world's most beautiful view as I die.

A kilometre (half-mile) farther on, a shower of small rocks peppered us. Soon after, an avalanche of boulders came crashing down in front of the Jeep. There was no shelter. We could not turn around. "Allah keep us safe," exclaimed Aziz. I heartily concurred, as we bounced grimly onward. An hour later, we had to shoo a reluctant bovine—half yak, half cow—off the track where it had decided to spend the afternoon.

We descended into a steep valley, worked our way up over a col between two peaks, then down into another long, narrow valley covered with broken rocks. The air was getting thinner; there was a rising chill. "We are getting close to the border with Tibet," Aziz told me. "It's just there, over that next range of mountains." Mysterious, forbidden Tibet, which I had so longed to visit, lay hidden from our view only by a single range of mountains. We could have hiked there in a few days, I mused.

Darkness was falling. Night always comes early in high mountain valleys. The rapidly setting sun tinged the soaring peaks above us with ocher, a ribbon of gold, magenta, and then red. After another hour of laborious driving, we came to a small village built on either side of a fast-flowing mountain stream. A group of low, evil-looking mud huts with wooden plank roofs held down by large rocks clustered together. Skinny, cranky goats and a few chickens milled about. Faces peered out at us from unlit doorways. An air of abandon and misery hung over this grim little hamlet, lost in the darkening mountains.

Aziz led me into a large hut. An overpowering stink of smoke, sweat, rotting refuse, and goat fat filled the squalid enclosure. It was very dark inside, illuminated only by a single kerosene lantern and a large fire in the stone hearth in the middle of the hovel. At first, I thought we were alone, but as my eyes grew accustomed to the darkness, I discerned six or seven figures standing in the darkness beyond the pool of light thrown off by the fire and flickering kerosene lantern. The figures lurched and stumbled toward us. They were very small men, none over 1.6 metres (5 feet 2) in height, terribly scrawny, and obviously malnourished, with features typical of the Tibetan highlands: broad foreheads; limp, dirty hair; almond eyes; and sallow, yellow skins. The villagers wore an assortment of rags and threadbare shawls. Their faces and hands were covered with dirt and grime.

I was introduced to the village elders, who greeted us fairly warmly, offering thick, oily tea in battered tin cups that had obviously never been washed. As we sat and talked through Aziz, who knew some Balti, I noted other figures, boys and a few women, crouching in the shadows, staring with rapt fascination at the strange visitors from another planet. The fire made the air inside hot and fetid. I longed to escape but could not, as we were being served dinner, an experience that I knew would prove both ghastly and potentially lethal.

A tin bowl of some unidentifiable brown, malodorous sludge was put into my hands, along with a small wheel of flat barley bread. I pushed the Balti stew around in the bowl, pretending to eat it—a trick I had learned in Africa when confronted with "bush stew," and devoured the bread. Soon after we finished, three more figures emerged from the gloom beyond the firelight. They stumbled forward and gibbered at us, their faces contorted, eyes empty of reason, saliva running from their toothless, gaping mouths. One came up and put a filthy hand on my face. I was revolted, but steeled myself lest I insult our hosts and provoke an angry response from these strange Balti mountain people.

Aziz explained to me that this village was notorious for its high number of mental defectives. "But most of the villages here are like this," he said. "There is no iodine in their food or water, and the villagers become crazy or sick as a result."

Iodine deficiency is the curse of high mountain dwellers. Decades earlier, I had seen the same malady in some of Switzerland's remote valleys. Lack of dietary iodine caused thyroid deficiencies and Down's syndrome. Iodized salt had eliminated this affliction in Europe, but here in Tibet, and across the wide sweep of the Himalayas and Karakorams, lack of iodine and other vital nutrients—notably vitamins A, B, and C—caused a wide variety of easily preventable disorders and a generalized weakening of immune systems that left the mountain dwellers vulnerable to other diseases, both acute and debilitating. Virtually all of the inhabitants of the mountain regions from Afghanistan to Burma also suffer from endemic parasites that further weaken them and curtail their short, brutish lives.

After dinner, we crawled into sleeping bags and huddled close to the dwindling fire. From the darkness came strange grunts and scurryings. I wondered if we would be murdered in our sleep for our possessions, and forced myself to sleep with one eye open—or so I thought. In fact, I fell into a deep sleep. Suddenly, I was awakened by a hand on my face. Another of the village defectives was stroking my face. He had never seen a European or North American and was fascinated, I subsequently learned, by my fair skin.

We left the village before dawn, eager to be well away from this pestilential place. For most of a day, we jolted and bumped over a rock track that led ever upward toward the mountain ridges above. The air became thinner still, cold and crisp. At least the clouds of gritty dust that had previously engulfed us were gone. There was almost no vegetation save lichens and green-grey moss. Water poured down the steep slopes of the Saltoro Pass, collecting into frigid pools, splashing around boulders, spraying into the air. I saw almost no sign of animal life but an occasional herd of wooly yaks grazing on high pastures, and, twice, mountain goats on the edge of the snowfields above us.

Toward dusk, we saw the twinkle of electric lights in the distance. They seemed a quite magical apparition in this primitive wilderness. Darkness fell just as we picked our way down into another valley, over which towered an enormous massif of rock, snow, and ice. We had finally reached Dansum, elevation 2,560 metres (8,400 feet), the foot of the mighty Siachen Glacier, a 80-kilometre (50-mile) river of ice that flowed imperceptibly down from the massifs of Masherbrun and mighty K2.

The Pakistani army's main operating base for the Siachen campaign was a collection of whitewashed buildings with metal roofs, barracks, storehouses, munitions depot, a field hospital, and a landing pad for helicopters. A flagpole, neatly surrounded by white stones, stood at the centre of the camp, a cheery reminder of the outside world that we had left so far behind. The camp was a tiny dot of civilization utterly lost in a vast wilderness of mountains and unexplored valleys; it reminded me more of an isolated scientific station on the coast of Antarctica than an army base.

After showering off layers of grime and dust, we went to the officers' mess for dinner. A cheery fire burned and crackled in a large stone fireplace, on whose mantelpiece reposed numerous regimental trophies and plates. A long table filled most of the room, and around it sat about twenty army officers. Military pictures and unit pennants hung on the whitewashed walls. It could have been a British Army regimental mess on the wild North-West Frontier a century ago. The only difference was the location, and the darker-hued faces of tough-looking Pakistani officers.

I was introduced to the colonel commanding the base and to his subordinates. All appeared quite delighted to have some company in this outpost at the very end of the world. Suddenly, a tall officer I had not previously seen came up from behind me, put his hand on my shoulder, and said, "My dear Eric, how nice to see you again. We meet in such strange places!"

Indeed. The first time I met Colonel Youssef was in Peshawar, on the North-West Frontier. The second was inside Afghanistan, when the 1.9-metre (6-foot-4) Pathan officer had been seconded to Pakistan's ISI and was busy directing Afghan mujahedin in the Great Jihad against the Communists. A few years later, we met again in Peshawar, this time with his chief, the courageous soldier and fierce Islamic warrior Lieutenant General Javid Nasser, director general of Inter-Service Intelligence (ISI), Pakistan's military intelligence service. Upon my return from Afghanistan, General Nasser had touched me deeply by giving me his personal, annotated copy of the Koran, a mark of the highest respect and affection among observant Muslims.

Colonel Youssef now bore the silver insignia of the Black Panthers, Pakistan's elite commando unit that was employed in especially dangerous or politically sensitive operations. We joked, swapped war stories, and laughed our way through dinner. I told Youssef and his fellow officers about wars I had seen in other mountain regions: Lebanon, eastern Anatolia, Abkhazia in the majestic Caucasus, northern Yemen, Burma, and Iraqi Kurdistan. All mountain wars, we concluded, were the same: all that mattered was holding the highest ground and ridge lines—and getting adequate supplies up to the troops. Armies that knew how to fight on foot, and march—like the Chinese—were superior to round-bound armies, spoiled by always riding to war on wheels.

Youssef surprised me by recalling an offhand remark I'd made years before in Peshawar. My mother, who was born in northern Greece, grew up in Albania, a tiny, mountainous Balkan land that much resembled in topography, tribal customs, and warlike spirit the uplands of Scotland, and the bellicose Pathans of Pakistan's North-West Frontier. I have no doubt whatsoever that my love for fierce mountaineers and sympathy with their hopeless struggles against invading lowlanders was genetic in origin.

"I've studied the campaigns against the Turks of the great Albanian hero, Skanderbeg," Youssef continued, to my amazement. "He was one of history's finest mountain warriors."

Casually discussing fifteenth-century Albania in a lost valley next to the border of Tibet seemed hallucinatory. As I explained how Skanderbeg and his mountaineers had ambushed and annihilated the Sultan's armies in the mountain defiles of Albania, firelight played over the dark walls of the mess. To these modern warriors, battles fought five hundred years ago had as much to teach, as much importance and passion, as those conducted a year before. War was war. Technology and equipment might change, but the laws and conduct of the art of war are immutable. The campaigns of Skanderbeg and Xenophon held as much relevance for these professional soldiers as Vietnam, or their last war with India.

I recalled the dictum that, compared to war, all man's other efforts seem trivial. Here I was, happily among comrades who were not afraid to avow their love of combat and the profession of arms. We in the West can no longer openly admit the potent appeal war holds for many men. Instead, we hide behind the justification that war is a necessary evil, forced upon our reluctant selves purely for the sake of self-defense.

I finally took my leave of the officers, returned to my simple room, and gratefully crawled into my sleeping bag. It was very cold. My nose clogged up; my breathing grew shallow; and my heart seemed to beat with abnormal force. I had a minor headache. These were the early signs of altitude stress. I'd first experienced these symptoms in Cuzco, Peru, at about 2,743 metres (9,000 feet) in the Andes. We were at roughly the same elevation, exactly the altitude at which oxygen deprivation begins to be felt. It had probably been coming on all afternoon and evening, but our slow ascent, the excitement of the adventure, and the cheery evening in the mess had masked the symptoms from me until now.

High altitude also causes insomnia. I tossed and turned in my sleeping bag for what seemed hours, struggling to take deep breaths of air, and aching all over from the punishing Jeep ride. I drank half a pint of vodka that I had secreted in my bag. Drinking is contraindicated at altitude, but the spirit finally helped send me off to a troubled, fitful sleep. I dreamed of Albania, mountains, and more mountains.

At dawn, Captain Aziz and I breakfasted on hearty porridge and mugs of sweet chai, bade farewell to our previous evening's companions, and set off in our trusty Land Cruiser. We immediately began ascending a steep rock track that began near the camp, zigzagging up the side of the Siachen massif. The Jeep struggled in the thin air over what seemed an endless, mind-numbing series of sharp switchbacks. Soon, the barracks of the camp we had left below appeared the size of match- boxes. Higher and higher we climbed, clinging precariously to the narrow track chiseled into the side of the massif.

Late in the morning, we finally reached our destination. The grey crags opened up, forming a small, flat valley nestled among snow-capped peaks. Clustered in the middle were four low buildings and numerous supply bunkers. A Pakistani flag whipped in the stiff breeze. We had reached al-Badr Camp, the base of the twenty-fifth Punjabi Regiment's "Siachen Angels."

Five officers stood waiting for me. All were burned black by the powerful sun and strong winds. They wore heavy brown sweaters, berets or knitted mountain caps, thick black beards, and mountaineer's sunglasses with one-way, silvered lenses and side flaps. After saluting, the shortest of the officers, a stocky broad-chested man, stepped forward to greet me. He beamed a radiant smile that revealed from the undergrowth of his formidable beard a set of pure white teeth. "Greetings, Mr. Eric, be welcome! You are our honoured guest. I am Colonel Musa of the twenty-fifth Punjabis."

I took an immediate liking to Colonel Musa. He had an infectious smile and a cheerful warmth that seemed not at all in conflict with the awe and fearful respect he inspired in his men. Musa radiated fierce energy. He proudly showed me around his small base, introduced me to the rest of his officers, then took me for a quick lunch of pungent goat curry and tea in the unit's spartan mess.

Musa's men put on demonstrations of rock-climbing, crossing streams on ropes, and live-firing exercises, during which I blasted a distant pile of rock with a medium machine gun, earning praise from the beaming Colonel Musa for my tight, accurate tracer bursts, an art I had learned as an infantryman and combat engineer in the U.S. Army. I also fired a Chinese 12.7mm pedestal-mounted heavy machine gun, watching the big shells sail through the air to their target.

Soon after, we marched forward about a kilometre (half a mile) to another flat open area, where two Chinese-made 130 mm guns were positioned under camouflage netting. Their crews stood at the ready. That morning, Indian artillery on the opposite side of the Siachen massif had been shelling Pakistani positions. Colonel Musa had thoughtfully delayed his riposte until I arrived.

Higher up and farther forward on the glacier, a Pakistani artillery spotter was radioing in the coordinates of the Indian guns. An officer listened intently on headphones, noting the fire coordinates on a grid map, and performing calculations of temperature, wind speed, and humidity. He barked orders. The guns were elevated, and adjusted in azimuth. I looked at the long-barreled, green-painted M-46 130 mm cannon with a certain awe. Originally produced by the Soviet Union and later copied by China, these were the notoriously deadly pieces that had so often routed South Vietnamese army units during the Vietnam War. They were greatly feared by American troops who, until the 130s arrived, had never had to face artillery more powerful than mortars. The guns were old, but deadly accurate, long-range, and fast to reload; they could even fire on a flat trajectory, making them useful for direct combat support and anti-tank defense.

A corporal waved a red flag, giving the order to fire. I was standing about 6 metres (20 feet) behind the first gun. When it was fired, I was blown off my feet. The air atop Siachen was too thin to buffer the concussion of the exploding propellant charges. As I struggled to my feet, the second 130 mm fired. The shock waves again knocked me over. The Pakistani gun crews laughed uproariously. I backed off and braced myself for the next volley.

The 130 mm shells arced up and away from our position, disappearing over a ridge. About thirty seconds later came a dull report as the shells exploded, then echoes and more echoes, and echoes of echoes, bouncing off the sides of the mountains. "In winter, when the snows are thick," explained a gunnery officer, "we must be careful when we fire that we don't cause an avalanche onto our own positions."

The big 130s loosed another dozen rounds, then ceased fire. The officer who had been manning the radio spoke intently to the forward artillery observers on the ridge above. He then jumped up with a big smile, calling out the ancient Islamic battle cry, *"Allah Akbar!"* (God is great!) The forward observer reported five direct hits on the Indian artillery positions, causing two secondary explosions and silencing the enemy guns. Everyone cheered lustily and cried, *"Allah Akbarr!"* Today, Pakistan had won a small skirmish in the long, bitter struggle to control the world's highest battlefield.

The next morning, after a semi-sleepless night induced by the high altitude, I climbed higher up the glacier with Colonel Musa and a party of his men. The ascent over broken, wet rock was extremely steep, and at times perilous. While filming, I accidentally stepped into a deep pool of frigid water. I then had the extremely curious experience of being soaking wet and extremely cold from the waist down while the rest of me was baking in the hot sun.

Above us, the sky was an intense blue. Snow-clad mountain peaks surrounded us on every side. The high-altitude cold was kept at bay by the power of the unfiltered sunlight. As we passed 4,267 metres (14,000 feet), each step became more and more laborious. My heart pounded alarmingly. I gasped for breath and my head began to throb with pain. We stopped often to drink water. High altitudes, like deserts, are lethally dehydrating. Unless one consumes large quantities of water, the kidneys seize up and may cease functioning. Fighter pilots and mountaineers are almost always very thin: they exist in a constant state of semi-dehydration caused by strong sun, heat, and high altitude.

By noon, we arrived at a broad, flat plain of pure white snow. It reminded me of Greenland seen from the air at 10,000 metres (33,000 feet), an enormous, white, featureless nothingness extending away into a hazy infinity. We had finally reached the area of the Conway Saddle, at about 4,876 metres (16,000 feet) one of the higher Pakistani positions on Siachen. The air was extremely thin, bone-dry, and bitterly cold, rather like dry ice. The azure sky above seemed close enough to grasp in my hands. A wave of vertigo overcame me. I felt I might fly upward at any moment and be lost in the blue sea above. The world seemed to spin. I wanted to lie down and cling to the ground with my hands and feet. The altitude and lack of oxygen were numbing my body and brain. It was a beautiful but terrifying place. The world's highest mountain was only 3,962 metres (13,000 feet) higher than where we stood.

My Pakistani companions knelt down in the snow and said their midday prayers. I thought how very odd it was to see men in thick, quilted Arctic parkas and sunglasses bowing down in the snow and praying to the god of the distant Arabian desert, 4,876 metres (16,000 feet) below us and 2,896 kilometres (1,800 miles) away to the west. Colonel Musa led the prayers at the top of the world.... "Bismillah, ar-Rahman, ar-Rahim...in the name of Allah, the most gracious, the most merciful, praise be to Allah, the cherisher and sustainer of the worlds, most gracious, most merciful, master of the Day of Judgement, Thee do we worship, And Thine aid we seek...."

We had tea at a sandbagged Pakistani forward post atop an icy knoll. A kilometre (half-mile) farther on lay Indian positions. During periodic flare-ups, the heavily armed Indians and Pakistanis would use mortars and anti-aircraft weapons, such as 14.5 mm, 37 mm, and 57 mm guns, to fire at one another's positions. The big 37 mm and

57 mm shells were particularly devastating against sandbagged positions, and could chew their way through thick concrete.

Colonel Musa showed me a commanding peak for which the Pakistanis and Indians had fought bitterly. "We spotted a group of Indian soldiers trying to reach the peak, which looks down on our positions and makes a perfect artillery observation post," the colonel explained. "We had to stop them." He told me the story.

A Pakistani helicopter took off from Dansum. However, the contested peak atop Siachen was so high, the helicopter could carry only one soldier up into the thin air. A lone Pakistani commando with a light machine gun was lifted up to the top of the peak. He rappelled down a rope from the helicopter, which was struggling to hover in the thin air and gusty winds. Just as the Indians reached the top of the peak, the Pakistani officer opened fire, killing some, and driving off the rest. They fired at him and threw grenades, wounding him severely. But the Pakistani held on until another soldier was brought up, then another. Thanks to this little Thermopylae, the Pakistanis managed to retain control of the strategic peak, and thus prevent the Indians from directing artillery fire onto their vulnerable rear areas.

The forward Pakistani positions that cover the 77-kilometre (48-mile) front, or line of contact, consisted of snow-covered bunkers and trenches, reinforced by sandbags and piles of rock. Each was garrisoned by a squad of mountain troops whose principal task was to keep watch on the no man's land between them and the Indian advance posts. These front-line posts had to be reinforced and provisioned under cover of darkness. Because of the mountainous terrain, most of the fortified posts were isolated, unable to support their neighbouring positions or join other strongpoints in delivering interlocking fire.

For the soldiers, staring for hours out across the white, snowy wastes was tedious, mind-numbing work that often produced visual distortions and snow-blindness. In spite of the dark snow-goggles worn by everyone at this altitude, retinal and corneal damage from the intense, searing sunlight and lack of filtering ozone was common. Some soldiers had gone permanently blind on Siachen.

The altitude, terrible cold, searing wind, and lack of humidity inflicted a host of ailments on the Pakistani and Indian combatants. Frostbite constantly threatened soldiers who had to remain immobile for long periods in forward positions. In the winter, the temperature, driven down by intense wind chill, could drop to minus 51°C (minus 60°F). Exposed skin would freeze in less than one minute: fingertips, noses, cheeks, and earlobes were particularly vulnerable. Even in the short, more clement summer months, the cold could come unexpectedly, brought by frequent, but unpredictable storms. Heavy-duty lubricants in small arms and artillery would freeze, forcing soldiers to keep the actions of their rifles under their thick parkas.

Howling winds that never seemed to cease produced a deep psychological depression in the soldiers; it was an eerie wailing that distorted sound and frayed the taut nerves of even the hardiest, relentlessly sapping their vitality. Soldiers on Siachen claimed they heard strange, spectral voices on the wind, or cries of agony and torment. Some said these were the calls of the yeti, or abominable snowmen, which by legend roamed the wild heights of Siachen; others that ghosts of the dead, or mountain djinns, wailed their blood-chilling cries in the frozen night.

The effects of high altitude were at least better understood. At 10,000 feet (3,048 m), the oxygen content of air is only half that of sea level. Physical exertion at this level—about the height of the highest ski slopes at Aspen or St. Moritz—produces breathlessness and rapid heartbeat. Many people experience stuffed nose, a sharp metallic taste in the mouth, headaches, and insomnia. Two or three days of rest is generally enough to acclimatize most people. In the high Andes, new arrivals are given frequent cups of coca-leaf tea to help assuage the effects of altitude.

Newly arrived Pakistani troops spend a week acclimatizing at the 3,048-metre (10,000-foot) level, doing light duty before moving to higher positions, up to 4,572 metres (15,000 feet). Above 3,048-metres (10,000 feet), the altitude begins to seriously stress the body and alter its chemistry.

At 5,486 to 6,706 metres (18,000 to 22,000 feet), the highest elevations at Siachen, climbers enter what is known as the "death zone." Physical exertion becomes extremely difficult and laboured. The body constantly gasps for air. The heart furiously pumps blood, but cannot adequately nourish the body's extremities. Low oxygen produces growing disorientation and confusion, making even simple physical or mental tasks excruciatingly slow and tiresome. Hearing and vision become distorted. Dehydration caused by the thin, arid air and strong sunlight further stresses the body, and causes severe constipation. The skin can feel as if ants are running over it. Even eating becomes an ordeal.

Most climbers can acclimatize to the higher elevations, but certain people are particularly susceptible to the two scourges of the mountains: high-altitude pulmonary edema (HAPE), and high-altitude cerebral edema (HACE). In the former, body fluids are driven by high pressure into the lungs. The sufferer quite literally begins to drown in his own fluids. Blood fills the sputum. HAPE comes swiftly and can produce death within hours. The only remedy is rapid descent. There is much wisdom in the old mountain maxim: "Climb high, sleep low."

Cerebral edema is rarer, but equally deadly. Body fluids rush into the brain, causing it to swell against the skull, producing intense pain, hallucinations, stupor, dementia, and then death. Again, rapid descent is the only way to save the sufferer. Both conditions seem to affect men more than women, and middle-aged men, as I was later to discover, in particular. Even those who have become acclimatized to high altitude can suddenly be stricken by either sickness. In effect, both HAPE and HACE are similar to the bends, the deadly condition experienced by divers who go too deep, or ascend and depressurize too quickly.

Altitude sickness on Siachen causes almost as many Pakistani and Indian casualties as enemy action. Ironically, natives to the high valleys of Baltistan, Ladakh, and Tibet often fall ill to a variety of disorders and fevers when they descend to lower altitudes or the plains of northern India. As a final scourge, many of the soldiers stationed for long periods at Siachen also experienced impotence, often lasting for months, after they returned to low altitude.

For Pakistani and Indian troops, most of whom came from the distant, torrid lowlands far to the south, Siachen was a terrifying and demoralizing place unfit for human habitation. Men and machines routinely broke down in the all punishing cold and lethal altitude. Logistics dominated combat: every bullet and shell, each container of water or food had to be laboriously transported from distant supply depots. Loneliness and boredom afflicted everyone; it was, as one Pakistani officer told me, "the worst place on earth to fight a war."

I stood with Colonel Musa, looking out over the sea of peaks that surrounded us, comparing our experiences under fire. He asked me about the wars I had seen—in Angola, the Mideast, Central America, and Indochina. I asked him about the places he had fought in during his long military career. He had seen combat against India in the mountains of Kashmir, the plains of northern Punjab, the and far to the south in the salt marshes of the Rann of Kutch.

"Where, as a professional soldier," I inquired, "do you prefer to fight: mountains, hills, or lowlands?"

Musa looked at me for a moment, deeply serious. I could see my reflection in his one-way sunglasses. Then a big, ferocious smile and a phalanx of perfect white teeth erupted from behind his beard. I was instantly reminded of G.K. Chesterton's marvelous lines about the Ottoman sultan in his poem "Lepanto":

There is laughter like the fountains in that face of all men feared;
It stirs the forest darkness, the darkness of his beard;
It curls the blood-red crescent, the crescent of his lips...

"My dear Eric, I like to fight wherever there are Indians!" he exclaimed, throwing back his head and roaring with laughter.

Musa was a true mujahid, or soldier of Allah. He and his fellow mujahedin were performing their duty before God of defending Islam anywhere it was attacked by *kufir*. The Koran says, "Fight in the way of Allah against those who fight against you but do not yourselves be aggressors; for, verily, Allah does not love aggressors.... Fight against them until there is no longer oppression and all men are free to worship God. But if they [the enemy] desist, all hostility shall cease...."

And of those shaid (martyrs) who have fallen in the sacred struggle known as jihad, the Koran teaches, "Speak not of those who are slain in the way of God as dead: for they are alive...."

To Colonel Musa, India was the deadliest enemy of his faith, Islam, and also of his beloved homeland, Pakistan.

Across the snowy no man's land were three battalions of Indian jawans who bore the same passionate animosity against Islam and Pakistan. What else but incandescent hatred would drive sensible, civilized men to fight for a decade over uninhabitable, desolate wastes that were of no earthly value to anyone save yetis and yaks?

I have seen human hatred expressed in many places over the decades, from the Mideast to Africa and Asia. Growing up in New York, and later living in the Mideast, I was steeped in the bitter struggle between Jews and Arabs. I had experienced the mindless, primitive tribal hatred between Greeks and Turks, Armenians and Turks, Koreans and Japanese. I had seen the heaps of bodies caused by racial hatred between black and white Africans, or between Bantu Africans and non-Negroid Somalis, Ethiopians, and Tutsis.

But no hatred I have ever encountered, save that held by Serbs and Greeks for Muslims, equalled the vitriolic detestation between Indians and Pakistanis, two related peoples who to most outsiders are virtually indistinguishable from one another. The fiercest form of hatred, it seems, is that between brothers and cousins.

For many years, the bitter animosity between India and Pakistan was considered by Westerners a bizarre curiosity of an unimportant part of the world. But now that both old foes have nuclear weapons, and the means to deliver them at long range within minutes, the Indo-Pakistani feud, which focuses on Kashmir and Siachen, has suddenly become a major international concern and a threat to all mankind.

16
THE HATRED OF BROTHERS

The roots of the remarkable hatred between India and Pakistan, Hindu and Muslim, lie buried deep in the past. India is one of the world's greatest and oldest civilizations. During the centuries of high Hindu civilization, India was never a unified political entity, but a dizzying patchwork of princely states and kingdoms that devoted much of their energy and treasure to doing battle with their neighbours.

In CE 713, Muslim armies advanced from Arabia and Iran into India's westernmost regions, Sind and Punjab, permanently implanting their religion and establishing a number of Muslim-dominated states. Islam then spread down the west coast of India, as far as the Deccan, and established pockets of believers across northern and central India.

In spite of partial Islamic penetration of India, Hindu culture and religion continued to dominate the subcontinent, and largely shaped its identity. Like China, Hindu India believed itself to be the centre of the civilized world, and all outsiders were barbarians. Ironically, it was one such barbarian people, the invading British, who would eventually lay the foundation of a truly united India, and preside over this historic birth in 1947.

Hindu civilization eyed and dominated India until the tenth century CE, when successive waves of Turks, Persians, and Afghans invaded the north. During the ensuing three centuries, India was progressively weakened by feudal warfare, dynasty conflicts, political intrigues. But guarded by the seas in the south, and a nearly impassable wall of mountains on the north, India remained largely immune to outside interference, save in Sind, Punjab, and the region around Delhi and Agra.

India was extremely fortunate to escape the greatest earthquake of the Middle Ages, the twelfth-century conquests of Genghis Khan and his Mongol hordes. This warrior king created history's largest empire, which at its zenith extended from China to Palestine and Eastern. Europe. The Mongol armies also occupied Tibet, where they were welcomed, but they failed to penetrate farther south.

By contrast, Islamic civilization, which had reached its glittering apogee in the late thirteenth century, was doomed by the advance of the Mongol hordes. The great eastern Muslim cities of Samarkand, Bukhoro, Khiva, and Merv, and then the magnificent cities of Iran, were taken by storm and laid waste, one after the other. The inhabitants were slaughtered; pyramids of one hundred thousand human heads were erected. Irrigation systems were destroyed, and salt plowed into fields.

Muslim civilization, which led the world in science, mathematics, medicine, architecture, and literature at a time when London was a village of fifteen thousand unwashed people, was almost erased from the map.

In 1258, the Mongols stormed and razed Islam's greatest city, Baghdad, massacring its million inhabitants. For the Muslim world the Mongol invasions were a catastrophe that could be compared only to nuclear war. Entire nations were exterminated, leaving behind nothing but rubble, fallow fields, and bones. Even today, Islamic civilization has not recovered; for example, modern Baghdad is smaller than the thirteenth-century city of Harun ar-Rashid.

The nomadic Mongols did not want cities or captive populations, so they utterly destroyed everything before them to make more pasturelands for their horse armies and flocks. The Great Khans set out to kill until there were no people left on earth except Mongols.

The Himalayas saved India from this nightmare.

India's self-absorbed isolation ended abruptly in 1498, five years after Columbus landed in the West Indies, when the Portuguese explorer Vasco da Gama landed at Calicut on India's southern coast, an event that was to have profound historic consequences for the subcontinent. European powers, having learned to circumnavigate Africa, began to descend on the southern coasts of India and the East Indies in pursuit of the lucrative spice trade. The British East India Company seized Surat in 1612, Bombay in 1661, and Calcutta in 1698, driving out its Portuguese and Dutch competitors. The French established a garrison at Pondicherry, south of Madras.

Equally important, and more immediate, a Chagatai Turkish-Mongol khan from central Asia, Zahiruddin Babur, fashioned a large empire north of the Himalayas and the Hindu Kush. Babur's ambition was to follow in the footsteps of his fourteenth-century predecessor, the great Mongol conqueror Timur the Lame, or Tamerlane, who had occupied parts of northern India, including Delhi. By the fifteenth, century, however, Genghis Khan's successors had lost much of their primitive ferocity, developing a powerful civilization under the tutelage of Chinese administrators. Islam became the official religion of the Turkish-Mongol khans and many of their subjects, supplanting shamanism and Tibetan Buddhism.

Assembling a large army, Babur marched down the traditional invasion route: through Afghanistan, across the Khyber Pass, and onto the plains of Punjab. On April 21, 1526, at Panipat, just north of Delhi, Babur met and defeated a far larger army of the local Muslim ruler. Babur moved his court to Agra, laying the foundation for the subsequent Mogul dynasty that was to rule much of India for the next three centuries.

Weak and debauched, India's feuding Hindu rulers could not withstand the advance of Babur's artillery and Turkic-Mongol horse armies. Within a few years most of northern India fell to Babur's rule; his famed successors, Akbar and Jahangir, Shah Jahan, and Aurangzeb, conquered much of central and southern India, establishing one of history's greatest and certainly most sumptuous empires.

The Turkic-Mongols—who became known in India as Moguls—quickly established a civilization of enormous vitality, strength, and cultural richness. Islam, already well entrenched in the western regions of Sind and Punjab, spread across northern India into Bengal, and down into the south. India's new iconoclastic Muslim rulers destroyed Hindu temples and Buddhist shrines alike, or converted many sacred Hindu places into Muslim shrines and mosques.

For India's Hindu Brahman elite, the Mogul conquest was a devastating political, cultural, and psychological defeat. India's rigidly structured Hindu social order was undermined by the liberating forces of egalitarian Islam. Hindus were left with a sense of powerlessness, second-class citizens in realms they once ruled. Many Hindu maharajas and rajas soon became lieges of India's Muslim rulers, though other Hindus, such as the warlike Rajputs, Marathas, and Jats, resisted fiercely. So, too, did Sikhs in Punjab. From the Red Fort in Delhi and from Agra, the Great Moguls held sway over a rich and vast Indian Empire. The fusion of Muslim energy and politico-military power with Indian culture produced one of history's greatest explosions of art, literature, and architecture.

The Mogul Empire was gradually undermined, then finally overthrown, in the early nineteenth century by a new maritime power, Great Britain, the first major occupier of India to invade from the sea. Once again the proud, haughty Hindus were conquered by a foreign people, who brought yet another robust religion to further vitiate Hinduism. In Punjab, the breadbasket of India, the decline and decadence of Hinduism had sparked the birth of a new warrior faith, Sikhism, three centuries earlier.

The British, following their policy of divide and rule, deftly played India's princely Hindu and Muslim rulers off against each other. In doing so, they often favoured the minority Muslims, whom the British considered more honest, reliable, and industrious than the "shifty" Hindus. Furthermore, the British, who had no doubt whatsoever of their racial superiority, were offended and angered by the pretensions of the "little brown men" of the old Hindu aristocracy, who had the audacity to see themselves as superior to the intruding British.

Equally significant, India's British overlords strongly favoured the warlike "martial races" of the north—Pathans, Punjabis, Sikhs, Rajputs, and Gurkhas—over other Indian peoples, creating a military caste system that persists to this day in both India and Pakistan. The British considered the Hindus of the plains and the Muslims of Sind to be weak, cowardly, and eminently untrustworthy. By contrast, they judged India's light-skinned, Indo-European frontier peoples to be racially, morally, and intellectually superior.

As a result, the ranks of the British Indian Army were filled by mountain races from the north, who returned the favour by adopting the ethos and habits of their British masters. British racism against darker-skinned Indians fitted neatly with similar prejudices held by fight-complexioned, high-caste Hindus, who, not infrequently, dismiss dark-skinned Dravidians of the south as "niggers."

A prime goal of Nehru and the other fathers of Indian independence, many of whom were high-caste Brahmans, was to restore the faded greatness of Hindu civilization, which had been so long eclipsed, first by the Mogul Empire, and then the British Raj. Though the Congress Party founded by Gandhi and Nehru encompassed a sizeable number of Muslims, and was officially dedicated to multiculturalism and religious tolerance, strong currents of Hindu nationalism coursed below its ecumenical surface. To many Indian nationalists, particularly extremists of the Rashtriya Swayamsevak Sangh (RSS), the Vishva Hindu Parishad (VHP), and other Hindu chauvinist groups (who would later unite under the banner of the Bharatiya Janata Party [BJP]), India could only be reborn when pernicious foreign influences, notably Islam, but also Christianity and even capitalism, were either suppressed or entirely eradicated.

Hindu nationalists were raised believing their once-glittering civilization had been raped, pillaged, defiled, and permanently debased by foreign oppressors. The British were gone, but 120 million Muslims remained, "like an asp coiled in the bosom of Mother India," according to one RSS pundit. The Muslim minority was a constant, everyday reminder of historical defeat, shame, and failure. The granting of special civil rights based on Islamic law to India's Muslim community further convinced Hindu extremists that their Islamic neighbours were a subversive foreign people, a fifth column whose loyalty to the nation was at best uncertain, and an ever-present danger to the Hindu polity. The decline of Hindu civilization, invasions by the Moguls and British, and the subsequent colonial period, left many Indians, and particularly Hindus, with a deep sense of national, cultural, and ethnic inferiority.

The British have long been grand masters of snobbery, class distinction, and the fine art of making other people feel inferior. The new British rulers convinced most Indians in ways both overt and subtle that they were a lesser breed, incompetent and morally unfit to govern their own affairs; Hindu India was backward, dirty, steeped in primitive superstition, corrupt, deceitful, and cowardly.

Many upper-class Hindus, educated by the British, came to believe these slanders, and not surprisingly sought refuge from them by trying to become more British than the British—or, as Indians put it, to become pukka like the great white sahibs who ruled them. Mohandas Gandhi in his youth and early career as a lawyer sought to be one of these "brown Englishmen." Even so, Winston Churchill, the quintessential imperialist, would later describe this great moral leader and noble thinker, with typical British racism, as a "half-naked fakir."

How else could imperial Britain have ruled three hundred million Indians with a garrison that never exceeded one hundred thousand white troops (usually far smaller), thinly spread over the vastness of India? Divide and rule played a major role, but inculcation in the Indian mind of the natural superiority of whites was equally potent as a dominating force. This legacy of inferiority still afflicts India today. Indians have an overriding desire to be taken seriously by the outside world, to be seen as the clever, educated, talented people that they are, rather than as a teeming mass of unwashed, hungry beggars or silly, comical "babus," speaking singsong English and putting on airs. The pomposity and arrogance so often displayed by upper-caste Hindus, which makes Indians widely unpopular and the constant butt of jokes by foreigners, is in good part a reflection of their deep psychological craving for respect.

India wants to be seen and treated by the world as a major military, political, economic, and technological power, instead of a quaint, exotic Third World derelict. This urgent desire for respect was the prime force that drove the nationalist BJP-dominated government in 1998 to detonate five nuclear weapons. India's atomic explosions were mighty affirmations of Great India and Hindu national-cultural power, known as Hindutva. In the Indian view, its nuclear tests blew open the door of the exclusionary white man's club of superpowers. India was sending the message it would shortly be the world's newest great power, and the dominant force in South Asia. Delhi thundered it would no longer accept "nuclear apartheid." The time had come to restore India's lost greatness.

The spread of Islam in India had also posed another threat: it undermined the traditional caste system, the power base of the ruling Hindu elite. Caste established an unchanging social order, in which large parts of India's huge population were condemned to perpetual servitude to their betters. In many ways, India's caste system resembles both the serfdom of medieval Europe, by keeping agricultural labourers in permanent thrall to landowners and nobles, and South Africa's former apartheid system, by strictly segregating races, tribes, and social groups.

Indian governments have been committed ever since independence to eliminating the caste system. In spite of massive efforts, education, and creation of special reserved jobs, caste still holds much of rural India in its pernicious grasp. Caste is too deeply ingrained in Indian culture and society to be swept away by government fiat. Besides, caste provides a pliant industrial and agricultural lumpenproletariat for factory and landowners. A combination of Hinduism and tradition teaches that it is impossible for a person to leave his caste and move to a higher one during a lifetime. A soul achieves gradual improvement only through reincarnation. This religious belief, which cements passivity, social immobility, and servitude, provides a potent opiate that numbs the masses into acceptance of their condition. Marx would have found a rich lode to mine in today's India (and, for that matter, Pakistan), two-thirds of whose illiterate, superstition-ridden people still live in semi-feudal conditions.

The advent of Islam to India directly threatened the caste system, and thus the socio-economic order. Over the centuries since the introduction of Islam to India, millions of untouchables and other low castes have embraced egalitarian Islam to escape the prison of caste. Islam offered upward social and physical mobility, the chance to escape the fetters of the past, and even to marry into a higher group. The defection of large numbers of Hindus to Islam not only upset the social order, it menaced the domination of India's ruling Hindu political and landowning elite.

Interestingly, Islam played much the same revolutionary role in Eastern Europe from the thirteenth to the fifteenth century. The invading Ottoman armies overturned the medieval feudal system and freed large numbers of serfs in what was to become Romania, Bulgaria, Greece, Serbia, Hungary, and Albania. Persecuted religious sects, such as the Bogomils of Bosnia and Serbia, converted en masse to Islam to escape savage persecution by their fellow Catholics or members of Orthodox churches. While Christians were busy slaughtering and burning one another, the Muslim Ottomans adopted the more sensible and rewarding expedient of simply levying a special head tax on infidels, and welcoming with favour converts to Islam. The Turks were always a minority within their cosmopolitan, polyglot Ottoman Empire, as were the Moguls in India.

The military prowess of the warlike Moguls and, later, Britain's promotion of the martial races, left India with a deeply imbued belief that Muslims far excelled Hindus in the art of war. Muslims were fiercer, braver, better fighters, went the widely held belief among Hindus, a feeling that was reinforced by Britain's not-so-subtle repetition of the notion that Hindus were soft, unreliable, and very poor fighters. Even within the post-independence Indian Army, there was a widespread feeling that one Muslim Pakistani soldier was worth three Hindu Indian jawans. Pakistan magnified such notions by constantly trumpeting the martial superiority of its soldiers and pilots over the Indians. The only units of the Indian Army considered a match for the Pakistanis, many of whose generals and soldiers were warlike Pathans from the wild North-West Frontier, were the equally ferocious warrior Sikhs and Gurkhas. India's victory in the 1971 war against Pakistan did much to erase the notion of Muslim military superiority, but to this day many Indians remain deeply intimidated by their warlike Muslim neighbours, and fear the sword of Islam.

Muslims also represented a subtler psychological threat to Hindus, though one rarely sensed by outsiders. In spite of India's pornographic temples and the famed *Kama Sutra*, modern India is a far cry sexually from the hedonistic days of the lascivious Hindu courts. Indian society is highly conservative and strict, even puritanical, when it comes to matters of sex. Only in recent years has the steady growth of urban life, the emergence of a strong middle class, and the ubiquitous intrusion of Western pop culture introduced a measure of sexual liberation and moral laxity to Indian urban society.

India's Muslims, by contrast, do not seem to suffer from such problems. Islam encourages a robust sex life, albeit strictly within the bounds of matrimony. Muslims tend to have somewhat more offspring than Hindus, a fact that causes great alarm among Hindu extremists who claim, preposterously, that their Muslim neighbours are about to swamp India with floods of Islamic children. Serbs in the Balkans make the very same lurid claims about Muslim Bosnians and Albanians (the latter do have Europe's highest birth rate). The supposed demographic "green peril" and Islam's easygoing attitude toward sex have given Muslims the undeserved but prevalent reputation of being oversexed. Some Indians believe Muslims are more sexually potent because they are circumcised. There seems everywhere to be a curiously strong animosity between men who are circumcised and those who are not. This canard stokes the always smouldering fires of anti-Muslim resentment or hatred.

A far more important source of anti-Muslim feeling in India comes from economic and social stress. At least a third, and perhaps as much as 40 per cent of India's population of one billion lives below even Delhi's meagre definition of the poverty level. Fewer than 25 per cent of Indians are literate; functional literacy may be closer to 10 per cent. The literacy rate in Pakistan is similar.

Everyday life for most poor Indians still borders on the intolerable, in spite of successful campaigns by post-independence Indian governments to eradicate the famines and pestilence that killed millions in the past. Subsistence farming and gruesome industrial working conditions expose malnourished Indian labourers to hunger, sickness, and daily misery. At least three hundred thousand children die each year of diarrhea. India's infant mortality rate is double that of China.

India's gross domestic product per capita averages only $3,297, as compared with $6,742 per person in China. In spite of its huge population and great size, India's economy is about the same size as that of the Netherlands.

There is almost no social safety net to help widows, orphans, the homeless, or the armies of unemployed. At night the streets of India's cities become giant dormitories. Open sewers are often the only places where people can wash their clothes and bathe. For most people, everyday life is a harrowing struggle to feed large families, tend to sick relatives, scrounge up an adequate dowry for unmarried female children, and simply to move around in the frightful urban congestion and foul pollution of India's cities and towns. Child labour and near slavery are common in India and Pakistan. In January 1999, foreign rights groups even discovered fifty thousand enslaved Pakistani industrial labourers who were chained to their cots at night to prevent escapes.

These punishing economic and social stresses produce constant explosions of communal violence. Frustration, anger, misery, and despair combine into a volatile mixture of barely repressed rage that often focuses on various minority groups, usually Muslims, but also Sikhs, and more rarely India's Christians, who account for only 2.3 per cent of the population. The great Gandhi considered India's unrelenting communal violence to be the nation's worst scourge.

While Indian governments have struggled to damp down communal hatreds, many local politicians, national leaders, and gangster chiefs have incited anti-Muslim riots as a way of diverting public attention from genuine problems, or gaining political support. In recent years, the nationalist BJP has whipped up anti-Muslim feeling and on many occasions incited riots, including one notorious disturbance in which a small mosque at Ayodhya, said to be the birthplace of the Hindu god Rama, was demolished. After the assassination of Indira Gandhi by her own Sikh bodyguards, Congress Party politicians encouraged enraged Hindus to massacre some five thousand Sikhs.

The endless vitriolic conflict with neighbouring Islamic Pakistan has also made India's Muslims a constant target of Hindu nationalist wrath. Yet in spite of Hindu suspicions about potential Muslim disloyalty, spying, and sabotage, there have in fact been remarkably few cases of Muslim Indians betraying their nation for the benefit of Pakistan. To the contrary, Muslim Indians have always held prominent positions in the Congress Party and in the upper ranks of Indian society and the arts. Nevertheless, whenever trouble with Pakistan brews, India's Muslims become a lightning rod for nationalist passions and pent-up social tensions.

The phenomenon of economic and social distress leading to communal violence is not confined to India. Pakistan is racked by the same curse, particularly in strife-torn Sind Province, where descendants of immigrants from India, known as *mohajirs*, are locked in a state of virtual civil war with native Sindis. In 1998, more than eight hundred people were killed in Karachi alone in such communal violence, while the Western world fretted about a handful of sectarian killings in Northern Ireland.

Farther north, another near civil war has erupted in Punjab between Shia and Sunni Muslims. Both civil conflicts are said to be fuelled by agents of India's intelligence service, RAW, in revenge for

Pakistan's covert assistance to Muslim secessionists in Indian-ruled Kashmir and modest support of Sikh independence groups in Indian Punjab. Farther north still, on Pakistan's lawless North-West Frontier, bands of local tribesmen frequently fight pitched battles with heavy weapons. One night, in the mountains between Islamabad to Gilgit, the car I was travelling in came under rifle fire. "Don't worry," said my driver, comfortingly, "they are just local, misguided tribesmen who think all other Pakistanis are heretical Muslims. They are only shooting at us to defend Islam."

India's Muslims live in constant terror of riots and massacres, a huge minority of frightened people swamped in a sea of more than eight hundred million hostile Hindus. A pig's head thrown into a Muslim home, a cow's tongue thrown into a Hindu home, a minor traffic accident, or even a squabble over the price of lentils in the bazaar can ignite the kind of sudden, bloody riot between Hindus and Muslims that often results in destruction of entire neighbourhoods. A favourite method of killing people during such riots is to douse them in kerosene and set them alight.

In the mid-1940s India's Muslim League, led by Muhammad Ali Jinnah, campaigned for the founding of a homeland and refuge for India's Muslims. The result was the founding in 1947 of the Islamic Republic of Pakistan, composed of chunks of western India and Bengal in which Muslims predominated. Divided, and separated into East and West, Pakistan was fated to fail as a unitary state, but at the time of its birth, Muslims hailed the new nation as a beacon of Islam and a haven for the persecuted faithful in India. Most Indians strongly opposed the creation of Pakistan, but Nehru and his Congress allies reluctantly agreed to the sundering of their newborn, and just united nation, under intense pressure from Great Britain and the Muslim

Some Indian Muslims also opposed the creation of Pakistan Muslim League, fearing it would invite even more persecution, and make them a distrusted minority in their own land, vulnerable to accusations of dual loyalty, just as a minority of anti-Zionist American Jews opposed the creation of Israel. Pakistan, to which millions of Muslims fled, was in effect an Islamic Israel, created to secure the future of a persecuted, endangered people. But like Israelis, Pakistanis have never been able to decide whether they should have a secular state, or a theocracy based on religious law. Jinnah, however, wanted and got a secular state that has managed to sputter on for half a century, though dismembered by India and riven by dangerous religious, tribal, and regional dissension that persist to this day. Hopes that Pakistan would become a model nation guided by the Islamic precepts of Koranic law, social justice, civic virtue, governmental honesty, and Muslim brotherhood were quickly dashed. Pakistan turned out to be a clone of corrupt, venal, feudal India, but without India's proudest accomplishment: a rough, deeply flawed, but still functioning democracy, which had endured since 1947.

Both India and Pakistan are composite nations stitched together from a welter of states, regions, and tribes. Many Indians and Pakistanis feel little allegiance to the state. The primary unit of loyalty is the extended family, the village, the tribe or caste, and the region. As the Trinidadian-Indian writer V.S. Naipaul pointed out many years ago in his incisive study of India, *An Area of Darkness*, there is almost no sense of community on the subcontinent. The idea of the common good, of helping others who are not relatives, is largely foreign. In India and, Pakistan, the overriding rule is every man for himself. This national self-ishness ensures that both countries lack social cooperation, a common sense of purpose, or a notion of political compromise for the good of the state. Mao believed that China suffered from the same selfish, family-centred atomism, and sought to force national consciousness and civic altruism upon his hitherto unruly people. His social engineering eventually produced the lunatic Red Guards, who nearly destroyed China in the name of national salvation from "feudalism" and "bourgeois values."

For the past half-century, Pakistan has been ruled by a succession of military regimes interspersed with inept, profoundly corrupt civilian governments. Far from blossoming into a just Islamic state, Pakistan remained a feudal society, in which powerful land barons who paid no taxes ruled like medieval nawabs, buying and selling venal politicians like so many bags of basmati rice. The military was the only Pakistani institution that managed to avoid being fouled in the national swamp of corruption and chicanery, or that succeeded in holding popular respect in a country steeped in poisonous cynicism. Pakistan's ablest, most effective post-independence leaders, Marshal Ayoub Khan and General Zia ul-Haq, both came from the army. The fiery Zulfikar Ali Bhutto was a traditional feudal baron who advocated extreme and unrealistic populist policies that enthralled the ignorant masses, but led the nation into bankruptcy and eventually brought on a military coup. Bhutto's daughter, Benazir, who was much idolized by the Western media, was twice ousted from office for gross incompetence, and is now under criminal indictment for rampant corruption and malfeasance.

The threat of invasion by seven-times-larger India is the dominant feature of Pakistani psychology, which is in turn an extension of India's Muslim minority's original fear of being swamped by a sea of hostile Hindus. Pakistan is a long, thin, strategically vulnerable nation, stretched along the narrow valley of the Indus River, which could be overrun by Indian armies in a matter of days. Nearly every Pakistani believes India has never, and will never, accept the 1947 partition, and is determined to reunite the entire subcontinent by military force, re-creating the old British Indian Raj. India's relentless military buildup, incessant threats by Indian nationalists to "crush Pakistan," and Indira Gandhi's invasion—or "liberation," as Indians call it—of East Pakistan in 1971 are proof positive, in Pakistani eyes, of India's lethal intent to exterminate the irksome and offensive Muslim state.

For many Indians, the very existence of Pakistan is both a military threat and a daily reminder of past national humiliations. Hindu nationalists warn that India faces strategic encirclement by a coalition of hostile states—namely China and its close allies, Pakistan and Burma. "Pakistan," as one Hindu chauvinist puts it, "is a dagger thrust at the heart of India." Or: "The Muslims and China are conspiring to destroy India." Such alarms reflect the persistent inferiority complex many Indians still harbour when it comes to the military prowess of the martial races, and uncertainty about their own considerable military power. Leading Hindu strategists claim the subcontinent can never be stable until its "artificial" divisions are eliminated, an assertion that predictably raises alarms not only in Pakistan, but in Nepal, Bangladesh, and Sri Lanka as well, all of which have experienced varying degrees of Indian intervention or strong-arm tactics.

In effect, Pakistanis feel much as Israelis did in the 1960s, when the Jewish state believed it was "surrounded by a sea of hostile Arabs bent on pushing us into the sea." Neither nation understood just how powerful it really was compared with its hostile neighbours. As a result, both Israel and Pakistan secretly developed nuclear weapons as the ultimate form of national life insurance. An important difference, however, is that Pakistan's small nuclear arsenal is purely defensive, while

Israel's two to four hundred nuclear weapons are clearly configured for offensive, war-fighting operations.

Fear of India among Pakistanis combines with an even more potent force, loathing of Hinduism. Islam, the passionately held credo of 140 million Pakistanis, infuses the daily life, behaviour, and thinking of Muslims in a manner that Westerners, with their fading faiths and perfunctory religious observances, find difficult to comprehend. Perhaps a better comparison of the intense animosity felt between Muslim and Hindu is the former life-and-death struggle between capitalism and communism: the two ideologies could not coexist in the same physical space. They were mutually exclusive: acceptance of one system meant negation or elimination of the other.

Everything about Islam is in direct antithesis to Hinduism. The religion revealed by the Prophet Mohammed in the seventh century CE is the world's youngest major faith, and thus still virile where older religions have become jejune, meaninglessly ritualistic, or spiritually and morally exhausted. Islam is a severe desert faith of stark simplicity, whose intense observance totally fills the life of observant Muslims. In orthodox Sunni Islam there is no church and no official clergy, merely leaders of prayer. Islam sets a framework for family life, society, commerce, and conduct of government. The faith and state are inseparable, at least in traditional Islam. Each man stands alone before Allah, and must pay for his own sins or misdeeds. There is no church to intercede or grant absolution. The main tenets of Islam are: acceptance of the one God and his last prophet Mohammed; prayer; fasting during the holy month of Ramadan; pilgrimage once in a lifetime to Mecca; and payment of *zakat*, or a tithe, to help the community and the needy. In modern times, many Muslims interpret *zakat* to mean creation of a state welfare system and redistribution of income, notably oil income, to the needy, and Islamic polity—a concept that provokes intense alarm among the fabulously wealthy, Western-supported potentates who rule so much of the Muslim world.

The Islamic credo begins, "There is no god but Allah..." and herein lies the primary and most violent clash with Hinduism. Islam's first struggle after birth was against the pagan idolaters of Mecca and Medina, who sought to extinguish the infant Muslim community. Idol-worshiping, or adoration of multiple gods, is the worst of abominations to Muslims. The first act performed by Muslim forces as they swept out of Arabia in the late seventh century was to destroy all idols in their path So intense is Islam's prohibition of idolatry that the artistic portrayal of the human figure is almost unknown in the Islamic art of the Arab world, though it does occur in Shia Iran, India, and Muslim South Asia.

Hinduism is the very opposite of austere Islam. Hindus worship a busy, crowded pantheon of gods, goddesses, animals, and even inanimate objects, all of which can assume different incarnations, forms, and natures. Over several millennia, Hinduism has mutated from the fairly simple faith of India's Aryan invaders into a dizzying collection of schools, sects, cults, and offshoots. Like Islam, Hinduism seeks to impose strictures and guidance on everyday life and the conduct of human affairs. Like Buddhism, it teaches that reality is merely illusion, and truth can be achieved only through meditation and enlightenment. But Hinduism is far more relaxed, flexible, and amorphous than Islam or Buddhism, and subject to varied personal interpretation.

Traditional Brahman-Hindu belief holds that all forms visible on this earth are merely emanations of the sole eternal Entity, like drops of water from a sea, or sparks from a fire. Animate and inanimate objects—humans, fleas, elephants, or mountains—are all part of the upward movement of progressive steps of the infinite evolution of the supreme Entity's being. Man, who is divided into classes or castes as part of the upward progression of life, is the highest earthly emanation of this process.

Hindus hope that through the long, painful cycle of death and rebirth eventually they will gain absorption by the universal spirit of Brahma. While the principal Hindu trinity remains Brahma, Shiva, and Vishnu, who represent creation, destruction, and preservation, over the centuries worship and adoration of the myriad lesser expressions of the supreme entity have grown up. Mythology, superstition, sorcery, and idolatry have widely displaced higher religious thought, particularly among the uneducated. As a result, Hinduism often appears to be a faith in which form has completely supplanted content.

While Islam still retains some of its force vitale, Hinduism has tended to fall into rote and superstition, a decline that modern Hindu fundamentalists and reformers seek to reverse by reinvigorating the early warrior nature of their ancient Aryan faith through Hinduism, and purifying it of the accumulated dross of centuries of misinterpretation, idolatry, and corruption.

For a Muslim, there can be fewer more horrifying experiences than entering a gaudily decorated, richly ornate Hindu temple. Naked sadhus, or holy men, perform bizarre contortions before its portals. Inside are collections of candle-lit idols of every colour, shape, and size: green multi-headed gods; black, many-armed goddesses; man-eating ogres; animal gods; deities, half man, half animal; devil gods; pungent incense; and, everywhere, worshipers praying to their favoured idol.

"I respect many Hindus," one Indian Muslim told me, "but how can I take seriously a senior civil servant who leaves his office, goes home, lights incense, and worships an idol of a blue monkey? How, I ask you? Who can respect a religion that worships sacred rats, and even has a rat god?"

Many Westerners find Hinduism just as bizarre and off-putting. The Hindu belief that the great life force takes many shapes, or avatars, and myriad expressions, that the idols they worship are merely points on which to focus faith and prayer, or a temporary shape in which the gods have chosen to come down to earth, is too alien for most non-believers. So, too, is the concept of reincarnation, in which a soul can progress from insect to nirvana over many, many lifetimes.

Caste, a bedrock of the Hindu faith, is also anathema to egalitarian Islam, which teaches that all men, no matter their birth or race, are equal before the one God. So, too, is belief in reincarnation, which Muslims see as absurd and blasphemous.

Muslims consider Christians and Jews as "peoples of the book," sharing such prophets as Jesus, Moses, and Abraham. In fact, Islam considers itself the direct, lineal extension of Judaism and Christianity, at least in their early form, and it accepts the virgin birth of Jesus. Mohammed was simply the last and most important prophet who was sent to once again reveal God's word to the peoples of the book, who had strayed from the path of righteousness.

But Muslims have no spiritual links at all to Hinduism, only abiding scorn and, more often than not, loathing or contempt. Hindus return the favour by dismissing their Muslim neighbours as violent, primitive, oversexed, and untrustworthy religious fanatics, worshiping a fierce, grim deity, unwelcome alien interlopers from the distant, backward Mideast, who would do well to pack their bags and return to Arabia.

A much cherished mantra of Western liberals holds that misunderstanding is the root cause of international tensions and war. If people only understood each other, goes this roseate credo, they would be able to peacefully settle whatever disputes arise. "We're all alike, just separated by a wall of fear and confusion." Such Panglossian thinkers need only voyage to South Asia to see the folly of such nonsense. Indians and Pakistanis are two peas in a pod. Hindu and Muslim have intermingled for centuries, often in the same villages or towns; they understand one another all too well, and easily anticipate their foe's thinking and reactions. Deep mutual comprehension has bred deep distrust rather than enlightenment. Arabs and Israelis are the same. So, too, are the Greeks and Turks of Cyprus. For men of profound ill will, to know your enemy is to truly distrust him.

Ironically, north Indians and Pakistanis of Punjab, that nation's most populous province, are ethnically almost identical, save by religious profession. North Indians and most Pakistanis have much more in common culturally and linguistically than do Indians of the north with their Dravidian southern co-citizens, who speak languages like Telugu, Tamil, and Kannada, which are unrelated to the northern tongues of Hindi, Punjabi, and Urdu. A north Indian can easily converse with a Pakistani Punjabi in Hindi or Punjabi, while he must usually employ English, India's lingua franca, to communicate with a fellow Indian citizen from Tamil Nadu or Karnataka. The grand ethnic divide on the Indian subcontinent is north-south rather than east-west. The governor of Karnataka once proudly showed me a large rubber stamp he kept on his desk. "Whenever those bloody paper wallahs in Delhi send me a letter in Hindi, I stamp 'English correspondence only' on it, and send the damned thing back!"

Northern Indians and Punjabi Pakistanis are part of the same ethnic family. Like all families, their members need deliver only a few key words or gestures to ignite immediate irritation or instant rage in their relatives. Indians and Pakistanis have turned goading one another in ways both great and petty into a virtual art form. One-upmanship between the two old foes is a national sport that rivals cricket. Probably the most famous and admired example occurred in the late 1980s, when India and Pakistan were on the edge of war, and India had concentrated some three hundred thousand troops on the Pakistani border under the code name "Operation Brass Tacks." Just when war seemed imminent, in a dazzling *beau geste*, Pakistan's leader, President Zia ul-Haq, suddenly flew to New Delhi to attend a cricket match to which he had been invited before the crisis. The Indian government, still trumpeting claims of an imminent Pakistani attack, was left looking extremely foolish and abashed. The crisis quickly defused. The lusty Indian media had a field day heaping ridicule on the red-faced politicians in Delhi.

The media on either side never miss an opportunity to pour criticism, scorn, and vitriol on their neighbour, nor to deliver outrageous accusations unconnected in any possible way to reality. Much of the endless Indo-Pakistani bickering is simply silly and juvenile, but occasionally it blows up into a major crisis that inflames passions and produces dangerous crises.

After fifty-four years of acrimony, India and Pakistan are no closer today than they ever were to peaceful coexistence. Endless ministerial meetings, peace conferences, and outside arbitration have produced scant results. Relations have remained so strained for half a century that inauguration of the first regular bus service between India and Pakistan, in early 1999, was hailed as a major diplomatic triumph Perhaps it was, but a bus service seems a pretty pathetic result of so many decades of sustained diplomatic attempts to improve relations, and make Pakistan and India act like normal, well-behaved neighbours.

So long as neither side in this historic conflict possessed nuclear weapons, the ever-present threat of a major war between the two Asian powers was strictly a regional concern. The end of the Cold War and collapse of the U.S.S.R. eliminated the risk of possible Soviet and American involvement in an Indo-Pakistani conflict, as was nearly the case during the 1971 war. But the deployment of nuclear bombs and missiles by both sides has now made their dangerous feud a matter of the most urgent international concern.

The terrifying threat of mutually assured destruction should have forced nuclear-armed India and Pakistan into the kind of stalemate experienced by the United States and U.S.S.R. during the Cold War, a tense, armed truce in which the two superpowers took great pains to avoid a direct clash. But the United States and Soviet Union had ample surveillance and early warning systems, which would have afforded them a few hours, or at least minutes, of analysis and consideration before igniting a nuclear war. Mobile and submarine-launched missiles gave the United States and U.S.S.R. counter-force nuclear capability that even after a surprise nuclear attack would still deliver a devastating riposte. Counterforce capability made it unlikely that a sudden nuclear attack could decapitate America's or the Soviet Union's deterrent forces and national command authority. And fortunately, there was no common border between the United States and the Soviet Union. After the big scare of the 1962 Cuban Missile Crisis, both antagonists sensibly elected to confine their struggle to proxy wars in remote places. The superpowers took great pains to avoid potentially dangerous incidents or provocative military exercises along the inner German border.

India and Pakistan, which share a 1,600-kilometre (1,000-mile) border, enjoy no such luxury. Their vulnerable nuclear arsenals must remain on hair-trigger alert, lest they be destroyed by a decapitating, surprise attack. Trigger-happiness is a constant feature of Indo-Pakistani relations. As previously noted, a major incursion by either side in Kashmir, or spreading of combat operations south from Siachen, could ignite a major war between the two nations that could quickly escalate into a nuclear exchange.

It would take only three nuclear weapons to destroy most of Pakistan; eight to destroy northern and central India. Besides the millions of deaths and casualties a nuclear exchange would produce, radioactive dust from the explosions would circle the globe, contaminating the major groundwater sources of as much as a third of the world's population on the Indian subcontinent and China. Ensuing famines would kill further tens of millions.

Pakistan's chronic political instability is another constant danger. Half a century after its creation, the strife-racked nation holds together by fraying threads. Sind, Pakistan's southern province on the Arabian Sea, is convulsed by civil war; Shia and Sunni Muslims are slaughtering one another in Punjab; Baluchistan goes its own eccentric tribal way. The North-West Frontier is a no man's land; the disputed Northern Territories are lost in geopolitical limbo. Pakistan's military government, led by General Musharraf, rules through martial law, the nation teeters on the edge of bankruptcy, and politics is little more than tribal warfare. Corruption is all-engulfing. The generals are uncertain whether to watch Pakistan slip into chaos, or seize power and then be stuck running a fractious nation that has more often than not defied most past efforts to govern it, and ruined the careers or ended the lives of many of those who attempted to do so.

A Pakistan coming apart at its seams, or rent by civil war, might well tempt India to intervene, as Delhi did during the civil war in former East

Pakistan. The civil war in Sind bears some disturbing similarities to strife-torn East Pakistan in 1970. Once again, India might decide to seize this opportunity to lop off another large part of its embattled enemy.

In such a dire event, Afghans might also be tempted to proclaim their long-sought "Pushtunistan," detaching the Northwest Frontier and joining it to southern Afghanistan. Iran, too, could be drawn into the fray, either to annex Baluchistan, or to defend Pakistan against India. It should be recalled that Iran began development of nuclear weapons under the shah, in part out of fear of India's infant nuclear program. Iran's government may have changed, but the dangerous geopolitical realities of the region remain the same. Iran sees itself somewhat contradictorily, as both a self-appointed defender of Islamic Pakistan against *kufir* India, and a forceful rival of Pakistan for influence in Baluchistan, Afghanistan, and central Asia.

Nor can we totally discount the remote possibility that India might also splinter, though the possibility of such a dramatic geopolitical event seems much more remote than the potential breakup of Pakistan. While India may appear monolithic to outsiders, this immense nation of two hundred languages and major dialects is an unstable quilt of regions, races, and religions that holds together more by inertia than a sense of common interest. Strong secessionist movements operate in Kashmir, Punjab, Assam, and the eastern tribal states along the Burma border. The ongoing insurrection by Sri Lanka's Tamil minority could spread to the populous Tamil regions of southern India, producing calls for a united Tamil state. The existing Indian state of Tamil Nadu, for example, has sixty-two million citizens, making it about the same size as Italy, in terms of population. Many parts of Dravidian India chafe under what is seen as unfair domination of the union government by Hindi-speakers of the north.

We are entering an age of geopolitical dissolution. The nationalism and concentration that characterized the nineteenth century have peaked and are now beginning to recede under the pressure of rising regionalism and ethnic separatism. Modern telecommunications have sharply lessened the need for centralized governments. Complex modern states are more effectively administered politically and economically at the regional or local level. In North America, the powers of Washington and Ottawa are steadily declining as states and provinces assert control over their own affairs.

The collapse of the Soviet Union was the most dramatic example of this trend toward devolution. India and China, both nuclear powers, are also potentially susceptible to centrifugal forces, driven by economic crisis, regionalism, or civil war between competing political factions. India and Pakistan are only half a century old as united, centrally governed nations. The fragility of these nuclear-armed nations, which make up a third of humanity, should not be underestimated.

Lowering the level of mutual hatred and mistrust in South Asia may take generations. Cultural-religious animosity may never disappear. Even so, possession of nuclear, chemical, and perhaps biological weapons by India and Pakistan now mandates decisive international action to begin reducing tensions between the two enemies.

Kashmir, and to a lesser degree, Siachen, are the two obvious flashpoints that could ignite a war. In spite of the enormous difficulties involved, the world community must press India and Pakistan into a gradual settlement of Kashmir. Once the Kashmir dispute is demilitarized, Siachen will no longer be of strategic value to either side. India's ruling circles must accept—and be seen to accept—that the chimera of reabsorbing Pakistan into a Greater India has been abandoned. The two sides will then be able to set about reducing their grotesquely oversized armed forces. Confidence-building measures along the border, and between the two military establishments, will substantially lessen the threat of accidental war.

Watching two of the world's poorer nations, in which most citizens are malnourished and illiterate, spend huge amounts on arms is truly to observe an act of collective madness. India's defense budget consumes 3.75 per cent or more of GDP, and this official figure does not include its secret nuclear weapons program, which very likely at least doubles the actual figure. Pakistan, with a much smaller GDP, spends over 5 per cent, but, again, when nuclear arms are taken into account, the real figure is likely closer to 10 per cent. Almost 40 per cent of all Pakistani government spending goes to defense. By comparison, the United States, with a huge strategic nuclear arsenal and forces deployed around the world, spends 3.4 per cent of GDP on defense.

Better living conditions and more education would do much to lessen the irrational hatreds and communal tensions on the subcontinent, but the money to achieve these goals is being poured into the arms race. India has embarked on a long-term program to dominate the Indian Ocean by deploying aircraft carriers and nuclear submarines, some armed with nuclear-tipped cruise missiles. At the same time, India is pouring billions of dollars into intermediate- and long-range nuclear missiles and military satellites.

Pakistan, outnumbered, outgunned, and left far behind in the military technology race, strains every sinew and courts bankruptcy just to remain far behind in this accelerating Asian arms marathon. As Pakistan's ability to challenge India recedes, Hindu nationalists have adopted a new tack by claiming India's arms buildup is necessitated by the growing threat to India from China. It has been estimated that if India and Pakistan would end their arms race, the funds saved and reinvested in national development would double their annual rates of growth, India's to 10 per cent and Pakistan's to 6 per cent.

Tragically, but inevitably, politicians on both sides of the ceasefire line keep stoking Indo-Pakistani animosity and mutual fear as a handy way of diverting their citizens from the failure of either nation to resolve the scourge of massive poverty and illiteracy. Like politicians in Greece and Turkey, whenever the economy takes a serious nose-dive, they begin beating the war drums and inflaming the always explosive passions of the illiterate masses. Pampered military establishments in India and Pakistan have little interest in seeing funding diverted to social programs, yet another doleful example of the subcontinent's pervasive I'm-all-right-Jack mentality. For the military and civilian elites on both sides, constant purchases of arms provide a ceaseless flow of secret commissions, bribes, and payoffs.

Seemingly insoluble conflicts *can* be resolved. Observing the Indo-Pakistani conflict, the equally long struggle between Jews and Arabs, and the irrational animosity between Greeks and Turks, one can easily become convinced that there are struggles that are fated never to end. Yet when confronted by such determined pessimism I always refer to the titanic, historic clash between Germans and French that so shaped the course and conduct of the bloody twentieth century. Few, fifty years ago, could possibly have imagined that one day Europe's two great warrior tribes, Teutons and Gauls, would cast aside their weapons and embrace.

I have seen two miracles in my lifetime. The first was on the nightmarish French battlefield at Verdun, where in 1916 a million men died or were seriously wounded in an area that could barely hold two of New

York's Central Park. There, on a cold, rainswept fall day, the president of France, François Mitterrand, and the German chancellor, Helmut Kohl, stood before the Douaumont Ossuary, Verdun's grim bone repository, held hands, and solemnly pledged that forever hence Frenchmen and Germans were brothers and comrades-in-arms who would never fight again.

The second miracle occurred as I was driving with a friend from Germany into France on one of our annual expeditions to explore the magnificent World War II forts of the Maginot Line. We motored across a bridge outside Rastatt that spanned the Rhine, the historic border between the two old foes. There was no customs post; not even a single policeman monitoring the frontier crossing. We stopped on the French side, stunned. After two titanic wars that caused the deaths of millions of Frenchmen and Germans, after enormously costly battles for this river frontier, and over the fiercely contested provinces of Alsace-Lorraine—the Kashmir of Europe—after all the slaughter, Herculean effort, nationalist passions, and killing for this most fought-over of borders, nothing at all remained. A century of Franco-German hatred that brought three wars had completely vanished, to be replaced by the mundane normality of everyday European traffic. There was no watch on the Rhine, only small towns in France twinned to small towns in Germany, exchanging their children for summer holidays, to learn one another's language and be taught mutual admiration and respect.

Wise postwar German and French statesmen fashioned this miracle, but it probably could not have happened without the outside influence of the United States, under whose aegis Europe's old enemies finally found trust and cooperation.

A few years later, I sat in Moscow drinking vodka with two former colonels of the Soviet KGB, swapping our Cold War adventures. After some hours of levity, we stopped, looked at one another, and said, at virtually the same moment, "How could we ever have been so crazy as to think of going to war with each other."

A few days later, I discovered that my driver, a delightful man named Gennady, had served as a Red Army lieutenant colonel with the Communist forces fighting in Angola. I told him I'd been on the opposite side as an observer and a journalist, with their foe, the UNITA rebel army. I asked Gennady where he had served.

"At Cuito and Mavinga," he replied. "I was there, too," I exclaimed, In a remarkable coincidence, it turned out we had both been in the front lines during the battle of Mavinga, at precisely the same time, trading rocket fire at each other's positions. "Gennady!" I cried. "Eric!" he cried. We fell into each other's arms, kissing Russian-style, two old warriors and comrades-in-arms, albeit on opposite sides. Such is the madness of war, at least on the personal level.

I recount these anecdotes to show that peace can come where none thought it possible. One day India and Pakistan may find a way to be rid of the demons that haunt them, to reach a compromise over their territorial disputes, and to realize what the Germans and French have learned: that borders are one of our stupidest and certainly most pernicious inventions. Instead of "Death to the enemy," we should all be crying, "Death to all borders."

Of course, that all depends on the will on both sides to end their long feud. Today, there appears little inclination to do so. In Pakistan, Islamic fundamentalists, who are steadily gaining power as the corrupt traditional parties founder, call for renewed confrontation with India. Across the border, India's chauvinists and Hindu fundamentalists continue demanding their nation's new nuclear muscle be used to intimidate Pakistan and even China. For now, ill will rules supreme on the troubled, volatile subcontinent.

•••

High up on the Siachen Glacier, the wind picked up force. Whirling snow devils, white cousins of the vortices that spiral in the deserts of the Mideast, rose from the steep slopes around us. My nostrils contracted in the cold, dry air. Heat and cold assailed me at the same time. I struggled to comprehend the vastness of the panoramic vista before my eyes. Many hundreds of miles to the south, across impassable mountain ranges, lay northern India and Delhi. North of us, across more mountains and glaciers, the remotest part of China. To the west, Afghanistan; to the northeast, Tibet. We were in a vast, empty, vertiginous nowhere, which had somehow become the epicentre of all the conflicting border claims of the nations that surrounded the Siachen Glacier.

I wondered how large this region would be if it were flattened out; perhaps, I mused, the size of France. It seemed utterly impossible that these mountains had once, in eons past, been beneath the sea, as the geologists tell us. Battling over this desolation reminded me of what had been said of the war that began in 1998 between Ethiopia and Eritrea over their barren, almost uninhabited border regions: "Two bald men fighting over a comb."

A Pakistani officer and I drank mugs of hot chaff in a forward position, looking for movement on the Indian side. There was an occasional flash of metal, nothing more. This was to be a peaceful day on the world's highest battlefield. Both sides would devote the day's struggle to combating cold, altitude, and, the soldier's curse everywhere, and in every war: boredom.

"Could there ever be peace between India and Pakistan?" I asked the captain.

He thought for a while, sipping his steaming tea. Then he shrugged.

"I don't know, Mr. Eric, we have been fighting the Indians all our lives. I'm afraid our children will also end up fighting them...maybe even for this miserable place."

"But don't you think some sort of settlement could be possible over Kashmir and Siachen?" I pressed him.

"How can you settle something that two men want so badly?" he asked. "It's like two men fighting over one woman. One will get her, the other will not."

The struggle over Siachen had gone on for more than ten years. According to the Hindu newspaper, operations at Siachen were costing India $400 million annually. By my estimate, Pakistan spends about half of that. The difference in cost is mainly due to India's need to extensively employ helicopters for resupply and reinforcement. The human cost of the conflict is about one thousand dead, and ten thousand wounded or injured each year in combat and accidents, or from altitude sickness. There was nothing at all to suggest that this bizarre, sterile conflict could end anytime soon. The two old foes would continue battling, each hoping to ensure the other did not gain control of this icy hell.

•••

The descent from Siachen and return to Islamabad were as long and arduous as the ascent. I was suffering from advanced exhaustion, serious dehydration, the beginning of altitude sickness, an ear infection, and a twisted back. Two of my ribs were cracked. I was sunburned, bruised everywhere, contused, and unimaginably filthy. But I was filled with the most profound and passionate elation. I had just lived an adventure that very few others on this earth would ever share.

I had been to war at the top of the world.

PART FOUR

THE ROOF OF
THE WORLD

17
THE FORBIDDEN KINGDOM

India's nuclear tests in May 1998, Pakistan's swift riposte, and the violent upsurge in fighting in Ladakh from May to July 1999 alerted the world to their increasingly dangerous confrontation in South Asia. Meanwhile, barely noticed, another potential conflict is building up to the east in the Himalayas along the Roof of the World.

Two nuclear-armed superpowers, China and India, are locked in a growing strategic rivalry for regional mastery whose outcome will shake not only Asia, but the rest of the world.

Three potentially explosive flashpoints between India and China are clearly evident: strategic Tibet, at the midpoint of their long, disputed Himalayan border; isolated, remote Burma; and the waters of the eastern Indian Ocean.

Of these three, Tibet is the most immediate and volatile flashpoint, and the very epicentre of the looming clash between the colliding ambitions of Asia's two giants. When this collision will occur remains uncertain, though a reasonable estimate is sometime within the coming ten or fifteen years.

What is certain, however, is that the inevitable geopolitical rivalry between India and China, who have already fought one war during the past forty years, is steadily escalating. The first superpower conflict of the twenty-first century could erupt along the disputed 4,000-kilometre (2,486-mile) India-China border, as Asia's colossi vie to dominate the world's most populous region.

To see first-hand the epicentre of this coming conflict, I decided to make the long, arduous voyage to the Forbidden Kingdom of Tibet.

•••

Light. Waves of shimmering light assault the eyes and stun the senses. Such was my first impression after landing on the Tibetan plateau: light, and the pure, cold, bone-dry air.

The second sensation was of having alighted on a different planet, one whose atmosphere and gravity resemble earth's in many ways, yet are unfathomably different. Then I felt myself on a huge, mysterious island, floating high in the ether, somewhere above the earth.

There are only three ways to reach Tibet: by supposedly regular, but in fact, quite erratic flights from Chengdu, the largest city in western China; scheduled, but frequently undependable flights from Katmandu, Nepal; or, for the truly intrepid traveller, a magnificent road journey up the Friendship Highway, a long, exhausting undertaking suitable only for those wholly indifferent to time, squalid conditions, breakdowns, or avalanches, and well inured to miserable rations, evil toilets, and innumerable bureaucratic impediments.

In spite of my long experience in the mountains, I unwisely chose the Chengdu gateway, a decision that would later cost me dearly. I was already in China on other business, and due thereafter to fly to Japan. I thus did not want to waste time on a 3,539-kilometre (2,200-mile) detour through Nepal.

The roughly rectangular region extending east from Chengdu to Tibet, and south to the borders of Chinese Yunnan, Laos, Burma, and Indian Assam, is one of the least-known, most topographically difficult parts of the globe. Mighty Asian rivers that rise on the Tibetan Plateau—such as the Brahmaputra, Salween, Mekong, Yangtze, and Red rivers—surge down like the extended fingers of an open hand from their sources at the top of the world, carving and clawing impossibly deep gorges and steep, narrow valleys into the mountains. East-west communications across this maze of rushing rivers, narrow defiles, and heavily forested or jungle-covered slopes is almost impossible, as the Allies and Japanese discovered during World War II.

The primitive tribe people of this sparsely inhabited region are isolated and unfamiliar even to their neighbours. The writ of distant governments does not extend into this frontier region.

Flying due west from Chengdu aboard a Chinese airliner, I marvelled at the utter wildness of the landscape below, a vista so fascinating I forgot my usual nervousness aboard mechanically questionable Chinese aircraft. Tiny villages, blackened plots of land from slash-andburn farming, and the occasional poppy field clung to the terraced sides of precipitous cliffs. Torrential brown rivers surged south and east through steep gorges, carrying infusions of rich alluvial soil down from Tibet to nourish the fields of Southeast Asia. No bridges or roads marred this near pristine wilderness.

After an hour, low-lying clouds obscured the land below. We flew onward at 11,887 metres (39,000 feet) over a flat sea of unbroken gray and white. Then, thirty or forty minutes later, I looked out the airliner's window and suddenly beheld a scene of the most stunning, incomparable grandeur I had ever encountered in a lifetime of travel around the globe.

Before us, an unbroken line of titanic, snow-capped peaks thrust up from the sea of clouds that completely hid their bases. They extended in perfect linear formation from east to west, as far as the eye could see. Each mountain towered majestically alone, separated by many leagues from its neighbours, enormous towers of ice and snow that thrust their jagged peaks into what seemed like the very top of the clear, azure sky, their near vertical sides glowing in the powerful morning sunlight with shifting hues of gold, russet, and bronze.

We had reached the great wall of the Himalayas, the world's highest and longest range of mountains, which begins in China and sweeps ever westward in an immense arc across the north of Burma, Nepal, and India. At Ladakh and Kashmir, the Himalayas then merge with their ranges, the Zanskar, Karakoram, and, far to the west in Afghanistan, the sinister Hindu Kush.

Breathtaking is too weak a word to describe the spectacle that lay before us. Seeing those great Himalayan peaks thrusting up from a sea of low cloud, glowing like beacons in the morning sun, was without question the closest I had ever come to having a religious experience. I was awestruck. In years past, I had spent much time in the Himalayas, but never before had I seen them from so high a vantage, so fully arrayed in all their glory. Each golden peak looked like an ancient god, standing fixed and immobile, surveying the lower world beneath his adamantine feet. I suddenly understood why the peoples of the Himalayas worshiped these towering mountains as sacred objects, or even deities. Here, for certain, was Valhalla, home of the gods.

The great wall of the Himalayas separates the Indian subcontinent from central Asia, effectively isolating one from the other. Here the heavy clouds from the south break against the mountainsides and pour out their burden of rain onto the slopes, where much of it joins huge rivers and their many tributaries, and returns south to India and Southeast Asia.

To the north, Tibet, Ladakh, and much of central Asia is a vast, arid wasteland, suitable only for the most meager subsistence agriculture and grazing. As a result, the populations of these sere, dusty lands has always remained small, and usually nomadic. Water is the mother of civilization.

Imagine Tibet as a great island set in a sea of high mountains. The Himalayas, crowned by the 8,848-metre (29,028-foot) Mount Everest, form the southern side of the Tibetan plateau. Its western flank is delineated by the Karakorams, Ladakh, and disputed Kashmir, and its north by the Kunlun Shan and various tributary ranges (*shan* means "mountain" in Chinese), beyond which lie the empty wastes of the Takliakan Desert. Tibet's eastern border is slightly less mountainous, though its passage is rendered extremely difficult by broad, turbulent rivers and parallel lines of mountains and deep gorges. A few perilous passes in the region of Khamb, and farther north, at Lake Koko Nor, afford limited access to the Tibetan plateau by the old trading route to western China. To the southeast lie the impassable jungle-covered mountains of Yunnan and Burma.

Behind this rampart of crags lies the lofty plateau of Tibet, twice the size of France, roughly 2,400 kilometres (1,500 miles) in breadth and 800 kilometres (500 miles) in width, at an average elevation of 4,572 metres (15,000 feet), or 5 kilometres (3 miles) above sea level, the highest nation on Earth. Contrary to popular belief, Tibet is not exclusively a land of crags. Most of Tibet consists of barren, undulating plateau, dotted with innumerable tarns, or glacial mountain lakes, often ringed by deposits of mineral salts. Mountains soar up from this table land to altitudes of 4,877 to 7,620 metres (16,000 to 25,000 feet). Tibet was long known to China as "the western treasure house." Beneath its soil lie important deposits of gold, copper, gemstones, and radioactive ores.

The northern portion of Tibet, Chang Tang, is a sweeping plain of rocks, glacial moraines, and salt flats, occasionally cut by glacier-fed rivers, assaulted by snow and bitter cold in winter, and by intense heat and dust storms in the summer months. This is the land of Tibet's nomadic herders, who drive their flocks of brown, wooly yaks between small oases, or search for water on the higher slopes of the mountains.

Central and southern Tibet, with the wonderfully named province U, are somewhat less dry, though more mountainous, as they rise to meet the crests of the Himalayas. In the lower, and thus richer, eastern region of Tibet, the province of Amdo is renowned for its forested mountains and scenic beauty; the province of Khamb for its rich pastures, and fierce, nomadic warriors. Since most of Tibet is above the tree line, all wood used in building must be laboriously dragged up from Nepal, northern India, or Amdo and Khamb.

Like many mountain lands, notably Switzerland, or Canada's British Columbia, Tibet's contorted topography, with its mountain-sheltered small valleys and lakes, produces a remarkable variety of micro-climates. Sun-drenched valleys, where temperatures rise in summer to 33°C (91°F), lie just beneath gelid peaks whose snows never melt, even in July and August. Arid wastelands suddenly give way to fertile fields of barley, oats, and wheat. Green pastures bloom magically in the desert after short summer sprinkles of rain. Tiny patches of verdant land nestle at the feet of towering mountains of snow and ice. Unexpected oases dot the Tibetan plateau, which far from being a land of eternal snow, is actually a vast, cold desert at the very top of the world.

Like so much else about the "Abode of Snows" or "Hermit Kingdom," there is widespread uncertainty and debate over the borders of Tibet. There seem to be three distinct Tibets: geographic, political, and ethnic, each of which has different frontiers. Simply put, few, apart from Tibet's Chinese occupiers, are certain of where Tibet actually begins or ends, or even how many Tibetans exist.

According to most Western specialists, Britain's imperial cartographers, and Tibetans themselves, geographic Tibet extends from Kashmir, in the west, to the eastern edge of the great plateau that ends 100 kilometres (60 miles) from Chengdu, and close to the Chinese frontier outpost city of Xining in the extreme northeast. These are the lands traditionally considered part of Tibet, from its early history until the modern era.

Political Tibet, roughly 1,295,000 square kilometres (500,000 square miles) in size, is the current, truncated, Chinese-ruled Tibet Autonomous Province, an entity largely rejected by the people of Tibet but generally accepted by the outside world, including India and the United States. After seizing Tibet in 1950, China carved away almost half of geographic Tibet, appending a third of its territory to Szechuan, and creating from the remainder a new province, Qinghai.

Ethnic Tibet spans a far larger territory. Peoples of Mongol-Tibetan stock inhabit not only geographic Tibet but also Ladakh, Baltistan, bits of Kashmir, Bhutan, Sikkim, Assam, parts of Nepal, and the Chinese province of Sinkiang. The peoples of Chinese Inner Mongolia have close ethnic, cultural, and religious kinship to Tibet. At no time, however, did past Tibetan governments in Lhasa ever exercise control over more than half of the total population of ethnic Tibet.

No one is quite sure how many ethnic Tibetans there actually are today. Western experts maintain that no reliable census figures for Tibet exist. They dismiss Chinese census counts as unreliable or purposely distorted. The most commonly accepted total number of ethnic Tibetans is about seven million people.

Today, there are an estimated 2.5 million Tibetans within Chinese-ruled Tibet proper, and perhaps an equal number in the neighbouring regions annexed by China. In other words, more ethnic Tibetans may live outside modern Tibet than within its borders. China has purposely obscured Tibetan population figures in order to undermine nationalist aspirations and mask the large numbers of Han Chinese immigrants— perhaps as many as 2.5 million in total—brought in since 1950 to solidify Beijing's grasp on the country. China claims that according to its first national census in 1953, there were only one million Tibetans, a figure that by 1990, according to the fourth national census, had reached 2,196,000.

In the capital, Lhasa, Han Chinese now considerably outnumber ethnic Tibetans.

Completion in 2006 of a new high-altitude railroad running from China's northwestern province of Qinghai to Lhasa, Tibet, was not only an engineering triumph for the People's Republic, it also opened Tibet to a new flood of Han Chinese settlers. The railroad, whose highest point reached 5,072 metres (16,640 feet), clearly marked the final absorption of Tibet into China and an end to the isolation that had guarded its unique character and culture for so many centuries.

•••

My second impression of Tibet, after my eyes had grown accustomed to the searing waves of light, was a sweeping panorama of immensity and stark beauty: broad, flat, dun-coloured stretches of arid land; deep blue, motionless lakes interspersed with rugged hills; and, in the far distance, soaring, snow-capped mountains. A cold, relentless wind blows across this barren landscape, raising sheets of dust that linger in the air like low-lying clouds. Only the sound of the wind, and the occasional cry of blackbirds, breaks the overwhelming silence of this pristine wilderness.

On the way from Gonggar airport, which is a two-hour drive east of mountain-ringed Lhasa, I asked my driver to stop our Chinese Jeep before a high wall of rock set next to a lake. On its surfaces was carved an enormous group of Buddhas, painted in vermilion, light blue, topaz, and gold. As I stood admiring this monument and its perfect reflection in the still waters of the lake, a sense of elation came over me. I took out my camera to take a picture, suddenly lost my balance, and almost fell over backward. I did not know it at the time, but this was the first ominous portent of high-altitude sickness. The relatively rapid, 2,743-metre (9,000-foot) ascent from Chengdu to Tibet was beginning to affect my body.

Entering Lhasa, Tibet's temporal and spiritual capital, produced an electric thrill for even a jaded traveller like myself. Here, at last, was the heart of the Forbidden Kingdom; the ultimate goal of pilgrims, adventure-seekers, and professional voyagers alike.

The capital extends along the Kyichu River, set in an elongated, bowl-shaped valley, surrounded by 4,572-metre (15,000-foot) mountains and rugged brown hills. Turning a sharp corner, one suddenly beholds, atop a steep hill, the great Potala Palace, which entirely dominates the city below. This enormous, flat-roofed, white and red structure, with backward-curving white and red walls, was completed in 1694 under the Fifth Dalai Lama. It rises more than 121 metres (400 feet), about thirteen stories, and contains a bewildering maze of corridors, secret passages, and some thousand rooms. The almost half-mile-long Potala is both the Vatican City of Buddhism and the seat of Tibet's government, a warren of dark, low-ceilinged assembly halls, chapels, libraries, schools, reliquaries, offices temporal and spiritual, and a monastery.

Much of the dark interior is decorated with hundreds of statues of Buddha and various deities, ornately carved and gilded wood, murals, frescoes, rich silk wall hangings, colourful Tibetan carpets, and endless shelves filled with religious scrolls and sacred texts. Dungeons and huge storerooms occupy the lowest levels, reminders that the Potala was as much a functioning palace and seat of government as a religious centre—rather as if Rome's Vatican and nearby Castello St. Angelo had been combined into one enormous edifice.

I stood gazing at the Potala, my senses overloaded by its immensity, majesty, and soaring architecture. Its external design was harmonious yet complex, imposing yet functional. I had the impression of looking at a sort of gigantic, spiritual power plant.

Pilgrims came from all over Tibet to worship the Dalai Lama, their Divine Protector, often taking a year or more to perform the journey to the Potala. In the final stage of their adoration, begun outside Lhasa, pilgrims would crawl forward the final miles on their bellies, praying as they went.

Though moved by the ancient dignity and exotic richness of the Potala, as I walked its dark, narrow corridors, redolent of hundreds of smoking yak-butter candles, I also had a strong sense of eeriness and lurking evil. In the flickering light, shadows played on the walls and tapestries, giving them life and movement. The omnipresent darkness, the statues of fierce, glowering gods, the sound of distant chanting, lent a rather sinister aura to this palace of arcane mysteries and intrigue. Red-robed monks moved silently along the corridors, or clustered about objects of particular veneration, intoning prayers and making obeisances.

I decided that high altitude and persistent cold must induce a sense of lugubriousness and melancholy that promotes the worship of angry, ferocious, unforgiving deities who punish more often than they reward. Here was none of the warm, flower-bedecked beauty of Italian or French country churches, or the charming Buddhist wats of Thailand and Burma. This was the home of the thunder gods and evil spirits of the Himalayas, who were to be feared and placated.

Yet these dark feelings quickly vanished once I left the glowering devil-demons and angry deities inside the Potala and Tsuglakhang. Outside in the bright sunlight, central Lhasa's market was bustling, packed with colourful throngs of shoppers, monks, Muslim butchers, Chinese traders, pilgrims, and nomadic tribesmen. It would be difficult to discover a gentler, more amiable faith than Tibetan Buddhism.

In his epic first sermon, Gautama Buddha promulgated the Four Noble Truths that form the core of Buddhism: sorrow is the universal condition of mankind; the cause of sorrow is desire; sorrow only ends when desire ends; desire can be eliminated by following the path of enlightenment. Once all desire is expunged, man no longer desires life, and passes, in a state of enlightenment, to "nirvana," or pure being. Followers of the Noble Path must practice non-violence and moderate asceticism, reject selfishness, and refrain from taking human or animal life. In its early stages, Buddhism was a faith without gods, and almost agnostic in nature.

In Tibet, the Mahayana sect blended the classic Buddhist teachings of self-denial, compassion, contemplation, and monasticism with important elements of Tibet's earlier shamanistic Mongol faith, including ancient rituals, assorted deities, evil mountain spirits, multi-form gods, and totem worship.

The result is an extremely elaborate, ritualistic, complex faith, which emphasizes the doing of good deeds, avoidance of evil thinking or acts, profound introspection, constant religious observance, and, perhaps most important, non-violence. Tibetans believe man exists on a middle level, above the lower realm of eternal suffering, but well below the ultimate nirvana attained by the Buddha. Through a process of reincarnation, people rise slowly upward or fall, depending on their accumulated good or bad deeds (their "karma").

The First Dalai Lama, Gendun Drupl, appeared as a child in 1419. After his death he was recognized by popular acclaim as the true incarnation of the Living Buddha. The office of Panchen Lama, subordinate to the Dalai Lama in a teacher-student relationship, but still a considerable power, was established during the same era. According to Tibetan belief, each subsequent Dalai Lama has been the direct reincarnation of the line begun by the First Dalai Lama, five centuries ago. The current incarnation, the Fourteenth Dalai Lama, born Tenzin Gyatso, was discovered through the traditional arcane process of divination and ritual after the death of his predecessor in 1933.

Ominously, not long before the Thirteenth Dalai Lama died, he made a chilling prophecy: "Unless we now learn how to protect our land, the Dalai Lama, and the Panchen Lama, the Father and the Son, the upholders of the Buddhist faith, the gracious Incarnations, all will go under and disappear and leave not a trace behind...." The child who succeeded him would inherit this fearsome divination.

•••

I walked about Lhasa's central market, idling my way from stall to stall, taking photos and appearing every inch the average tourist. The shoppers and strollers in the streets wore a mixture of colourful Tibetan native wear and shabby Chinese clothing; the common universal uniform of blue jeans and sneakers one sees from Omaha to Osaka was pleasingly absent. I noted, however, a rank, pungent odour that seemed to permeate everything, a cloying mixture of rancid yak butter and unwashed, sweaty bodies. Tibetans, it is said, wash only three times in their lives: at birth, on their nuptials, and at death. Like other peoples of the Himalayas and Andes, Tibetans rarely have the luxury of hot water for bathing. So everyone smells, a fact that only outsiders seem to find unpleasant. Perhaps we Westerners have grown too sensitive, or too devoted to sterility. I recalled Napoleon's famous message to Josephine upon his return from the Russian campaign: "Arriving in three days. Don't wash!"

Foreign tourists made the Chinese edgy, but their dollars were badly needed by the People's Republic, which charged visitors piratical prices for supervised tours of Tibet. I managed to leave my guides, on the pretext of shopping for souvenirs. After two hours of sightseeing, and dodging into temples, I was reasonably certain agents of the Chinese security police were not following me.

Lhasa looked normal, but to my eyes, trained to watchfulness in a score of nasty Communist or Third World dictatorships, the signs of repression were evident. Large numbers of uniformed and plainclothes Chinese police kept discreet watch on the Tibetan population. Police checkpoints guarded many important intersections. Hidden up back alleys, squads of riot police waited for trouble. My reconnaissance around the capital showed that three regular divisions of the Chinese People's Liberation Army were based just outside Lhasa in a rough circle, ready to intervene on short notice. Military checkpoints carefully monitored traffic in and out of the capital.

Following instructions I had received before coming to Tibet, I entered a small, shabby store selling curios and trinkets. In the tiny back room I met with two Tibetan men, who seemed extremely nervous and wary. While a third kept watch outside, they related to me in broken English how the Chinese were relentlessly destroying Tibet's religion and culture, as well as importing large numbers of Han immigrants in a massive effort to make Tibetans a carefully controlled minority in their own country. One of the men had been in the laogai, the fearsome Chinese gulag that is spoken of only in whispers wherever one goes in China.

There is an underground resistance movement across Tibet, but it is badly fragmented, disorganized, and frequently penetrated by Chinese agents. Lacking arms or foreign support, Tibetan nationalists are compelled to adopt a policy of sullen, passive resistance until the day, however distant, that a miracle occurs, and China's iron grip is somehow broken, or at least relaxed. It had happened before in Tibet's long history, I was told, and, with patience, would happen again.

I returned, after much diversionary walking, to my hotel, a low, modern structure that seemed quite out of place in Lhasa. My head was throbbing with pain, and my labouring lungs could not seem to get enough air. My nose became clogged. A sharp metallic taste filled my mouth. The thought of eating repelled me. Deny it as I might, I knew my body was experiencing the adverse effects of altitude. Having undergone a bout of altitude illness in Cuzco, Peru, I knew what to do. I decided to take to my bed and rest, the recommended treatment for oxygen deprivation.

As the night wore on, the pain in my head grew steadily more intense. My body began to ache. I tossed about, listless, enervated, and increasingly miserable. I called the front desk, asking for oxygen. There was none, but I was told to call room service and ask for an "oxygen pillow." Ten minutes later, I was presented with a swollen brown rubber bladder, from which a clamped tube protruded. I loosened the clamp and sucked greedily on the tube for air. What issued from this strange device may have been oxygen, or it may only have been thin air; whatever it was, the emergency pillow did nothing at all to lessen the painful throbbing in my head. Three more pillows, procured from room service, made no difference.

I spent a night of torment. By morning, however, I felt slightly better and decided to continue exploring Lhasa, albeit with painful slowness and frequent stops to gasp for air. My guides insisted on taking me to the famed Norbulingka, the Dalai Lama's former summer palace built on the banks of the river. Grudgingly, I went.

The wood and masonry palace was as delicate and lovely as the Potala was grim and intimidating. One easily understands why the youthful Dalai Lama preferred to pass his hours here, often in the company of his foreign companion and mentor, the Austrian adventurer Heinrich Harrer, as far as possible from the intrigues and stultifying rituals of the oppressive Potala.

Every room of the sprawling Norbulingka was filled with religious statues, tapestries, and scrolls. The by now familiar palace guard of scowling Buddhas and savage protector deities lined the long, dark corridors. I was finally shown into a modest-sized room with a narrow bed, writing table and lamp, and two hard chairs. This, I was informed, was the private bedroom of the "imperialist, reactionary stooge, the former Dalai Lama."

I was at once filled by a sense of shame and embarrassment at intruding uninvited into the vacated personal quarters of so august a figure.

More to the point, I had once met and conversed at length with the Dalai Lama, a fact that made my discomfort all the more acute.

My encounter with the Living Buddha occurred in Canada three years previously, when he was giving a lecture on Tibet. The Dalai Lama was a gentle, mild-looking man who radiated kindness and warmth. The audience of wealthy donors had come to hear His Holiness explain the meaning of life. Instead, the Dalai Lama delivered a long discourse on the history of the Indian-Chinese border dispute that left his listeners dazed and uncomprehending. During the question period, I asked him a number of questions about his views on the border question.

In retrospect, I believe listening that day to the Dalai Lama speak about the geopolitics of the Himalayas may well have planted the seed for this book in my mind.

After the talk, the Dalai Lama came over to talk to me. We fell into a long discussion on the details of the McMahon Line, a subject that clearly fascinated him and about which he was exceptionally well informed. The Living Buddha demonstrated an incisive grasp of Asian geopolitics and the growing strains between India and China. My heart instantly warmed to this highly intelligent man, who is often—and wrongly—depicted as an unworldly mystic. He also left me with a very personal message, whose simple, profound meaning I would not discover until I had voyaged to Tibet and stood in his personal quarters in the summer palace.

18
INDIA AWAKES

China's concern over the loyalty of its "new Tibetan brothers" was well-founded. On the busy streets of Lhasa, Tibetans would shyly approach me, bow, and whisper, "Please, a picture of the Dalai Lama." All photographs or paintings of the Tibetan leader were banned as "subversive" by the Chinese police. Even possession of a photo can lead to beatings, prison, or even the laogai, the vast gulag created by China in the wastes of Quinghai Province, where the average sentence for political deviation, real or imagined, was fifteen to twenty years' hard labour on subsistence rations. Yet it was plainly evident that Tibetans yearned passionately for the return of their spiritual leader, and sorely chafed under the harsh Chinese "liberation."

This point was amply demonstrated to me by a violent riot that erupted before my eyes in downtown Lhasa. Chinese police had tried to seize a picture of the Dalai Lama from a seller of hides. He had resisted; a melee erupted, as passersby sought to prevent his arrest. In a few minutes, the streets of central Lhasa were filled with demonstrators hurling curses at their occupiers, and attacking Chinese-owned shops.

Truckloads of Chinese riot police and heavily armed troops suddenly appeared, sealing the main intersections and cordoning off the downtown area. Tibetan demonstrators were beaten with rubber truncheons and tear-gassed. More troops took up positions on the outer roads ringing the capital. I was stopped by security police, searched, and forced to return to my hotel, for my "protection against bandits and troublemakers," I was helpfully informed. More riots had erupted, I later learned, in Shigatse, Tibet's second city.

Chinese authorities would subsequently denounce the riots as the work of "splittists, feudal elements, and foreign agents." Clearly, Tibet's liberation was not progressing satisfactorily, in spite of four decades of socialist re-education and ideological purification, Chinese euphemisms for brute force, terror, intimidation, and ceaseless propaganda.

Beijing's insistence that Tibet has been an integral part of the Chinese nation for more than 1,500 years is historically unfounded.

Trade links have existed between western China and Tibet for the past two millennia, but China had no political influence, and thus no valid historic claim over the region of ethnic Tibet, until the late thirteenth century. In 1280, the Mongol ruler of China, Kublai Khan, developed an interest in Tibet and its religion. Mongols and Tibetans shared the same ethnic roots and shamanistic beliefs. A delegation of Tibetan lamas of the Sakya order was invited to the Mongol imperial court. Kublai Khan was so impressed by the wisdom of the Tibetan lamas, he immediately converted to their faith, and ordered his followers to do the same. In a matter of a few years, the mighty Mongol Empire adopted Tibetan Buddhism as its state religion. In doing so, the Mongols assumed the role of protectors of their new Vatican, Tibet.

The vast Mongol empire proved ephemeral, disintegrating and vanishing in the fourteenth century. Rebellion erupted across China, producing the powerful Ming dynasty. The Ming rulers continued the spiritual liaison between China and Tibet, which came to be known as the teacher-ruler or priest-patron relationship. Tibetans paid nominal obeisance to the Chinese emperors who, in turn, granted Tibet's religious leaders a unique position in matters spiritual, and complete temporal autonomy over Tibet.

The priest-patron relationship between the Chinese emperors and Tibet mirrored China's traditional feudal policy toward the vassal regimes around its borders, whose rulers were granted full autonomy—in exchange for obedience and payment of annual tribute. This unique relationship would continue as a principal theme of China's foreign policy right down to the end of the twentieth century, when Beijing would "teach a lesson" to neighbouring states that failed to comply with the will of China's rulers.

This very Asian relationship continued when the First Dalai Lama returned to Tibet in the fifteenth century, unifying thenceforth the powers of church and state under his unquestioned rule, and lessening the danger that China might gain control of Tibet by playing off its many political or religious factions against the others. Whereas before Tibet had had many respected priests and wise men, it now had a pope, of resplendent spiritual power and majesty.

China's Manchu dynasty replaced the moribund Ming rulers in the seventeenth century. The Manchus reasserted China's nominal suzerainty over Tibet, which in turn continued to pay token tribute to

Imperial China. In 1720, a Manchu army marched up into Tibet, but soon departed. In fact, until the twentieth century, China had only sporadic physical control of the remote, far western regions of Tibet and Turkestan to which it laid claim. The best a steadily weakening China could achieve was a few ineffectual military expeditions into the region, and the occasional stationing of a handful of imperial officials, known as *ambans* in Lhasa.

Tibet remained happily isolated from the outside world, thanks to its mountain remoteness, until the dawn of the twentieth century, when various imperial powers suddenly took an interest in the lost kingdom, which had until then escaped their predatory designs. The British grew concerned that the relentless southward expansion by the Russian Empire into Central Asia might penetrate Tibet, as well as Afghanistan, thus threatening the borders of British India. There were rumours of Russian agents operating in Tibet. Besides, British interest in the Himalayas was growing: in 1890 the British Raj detached the ancient Buddhist kingdom of Sikkim from Tibet and made it a protectorate.

Seizing the initiative, the British viceroy of India, Lord Curzon, who had described Tibet as an "anachronism," dispatched a three-thousand-man expeditionary force to Lhasa in 1904 to assure Britain's strategic, political, and commercial interests in the kingdom. The expedition succeeded in making the arduous ascent to Tibet, battling Tibetan tribesmen along the way. On August 4, 1904, the British marched into the Vatican City of Central Asia, forever ending Tibet's splendid isolation. Before withdrawing, the expeditionary force imposed a trade treaty on Tibet, which, as was the case with all such imperial pacts, was really designed to open the way to British political influence over Tibet. A direct diplomatic link had been established between Great Britain and Tibet.

The British incursion greatly alarmed the Manchu court. China's anxiety was deepened by Lord Curzon's curt dismissal of China's claim to Tibet as "fiction." In 1909, the Manchus dispatched an army to reassert their claims to Tibet. The Chinese force marched up into Tibet from Chengdu, deposed the Dalai Lama the next year, and occupied Lhasa in the face of stout and prolonged Tibetan military opposition. In 1911, however, the decayed Manchu dynasty was overthrown by Sun Yat-sen. Revolution swept over China, forcing the Chinese garrison in Tibet to withdraw. Strongly encouraged by the British, Tibet declared independence from China in 1913.

These events finally led to an important conclave in 1914 at the Indian hill station of Simla. The Thirteenth Dalai Lama sought British support for full Tibetan political independence. Britain and Tibet signed the accord, which recognized Tibetan independence, and guaranteed British imperial interests in Tibet. China's nominal suzerainty over the kingdom was acknowledged as a face-saving gesture for China, but the new Chinese Republic refused to sign the Simla Agreement. Britain, distracted by events in Europe, soon lost interest in both Tibet and the alleged Russian threat to the Raj. Tibet slipped back happily into obscurity. The Thirteenth Dalai Lama reaffirmed that Tibet, now freed of Chinese occupation, was fully independent of China, but his declaration attracted neither recognition nor attention from the great powers, who were by then absorbed by the looming threat of a world war. Nevertheless, Tibet was de facto, and to all intents and purposes *de jure*, independent, and would remain so for the next thirty-seven years.

•••

On October 7, 1950, China's First and Second Field Armies, totalling eighty thousand soldiers, crossed the upper Yangtze River and invaded Tibet. Late in the previous year, Chinese military forces had slowly infiltrated Tibet's extreme eastern provinces after Beijing Radio had announced that the "renegade" provinces of Tibet, Taiwan, and Hainan would be reunited with the motherland.

Resistance by Tibet's tiny army and bands of Khampa tribesmen was quickly crushed. Beijing Radio proclaimed Chinese troops had entered Tibet to liberate it from "imperialist oppression." Tibet's frantic appeals for help to the United Nations, India, Britain, and the United States were ignored, or rebuffed with diplomatic evasions. No nation was about to challenge the new People's Republic of China, which had some ten million men under arms, over the fate of an obscure mountain kingdom lost in the Himalayas.

India, the most immediately concerned power, closed its eyes to the invasion. Nehru was preoccupied by Kashmir and Pakistan; he cited the vague 1914 Simla Agreement—which China had never signed—as a legal basis for Beijing's claim that Tibet was, in fact, a part of China, and a strictly internal matter. It was a fateful decision India would live to regret.

Tibet was forced in 1951 to sign a treaty confirming Chinese rule over the nation. The young Fourteenth Dalai Lama saw his nation suddenly turned into a province of Mao's revolutionary China. Chinese troops, police, and settlers poured into "liberated" Tibet.

At first, the Chinese promised Tibet full autonomy, religious freedom, and the preservation of its traditions and customs. The Chinese earnestly attempted to convince Tibetans that communism was a superior way of life, which would free them from superstition and feudalism. When this effort failed dismally, China's occupation forces began a severe crackdown, jailing thousands of "reactionaries" and "wreckers." Increased repression, and forced collectivization of agriculture, led to the outbreak of a major rebellion across Tibet in 1959. China poured troops into Tibet and ruthlessly crushed the uprising, killing nearly one hundred thousand Tibetans. A similar number of Tibetans, and their beloved god-king the Dalai Lama, fled to exile in northern India.

In the early 1960s, the U.S. Central Intelligence Agency began a top-secret operation to form, train, and equip Tibetan exiles in India into anti-Chinese guerrilla bands. In 1998, the Dalai Lama's administration in India for the first time acknowledged receiving $1.7 million a year during the 1960s from the CIA, as well as an annual personal subsidy for the Dalai Lama of $180,000, but this is merely a fraction of the total funds expended by the U.S. to support the Tibetan resistance.

The CIA organized regular airdrops of weapons and supplies to bands of Khampa warriors fighting Chinese occupation in eastern Tibet. India, by then finally aroused to the Chinese threat, joined the effort, directing its foreign intelligence agency, the Research and Analysis Wing (RAW), to cooperate with the CIA in supporting Tibetan resistance forces. This was one of only a few known instances when the normally adversarial CIA and RAW worked together. It was even a rarer example of cooperation, albeit chilly and very limited, between RAW and Pakistani intelligence; the latter was aiding the United States in the effort to supply Tibetan rebels. Bases for Tibetan guerrillas were established in the Indian protectorate of Sikkim and in Nepal, which was equally concerned by the looming Chinese threat.

The 1962 border war between China and India finally spurred Delhi's decision to undermine Chinese rule of Tibet. China was caught in a dilemma. Beijing's official propaganda position was that Tibetans welcomed Chinese "liberation" and were joyously participating in the modernization of their nation. China could not thus openly admit that Tibet seethed with rebellion. Nor could China publicly accuse India of trying to undermine its hold on the kingdom, since Tibetans were supposedly revelling in the joys of Chinese occupation.

Tibetan resistance spread across the nation, tying down over 250,000 Chinese troops in counter-guerrilla operations. Unable to crush Tibetan resistance or stop infiltration from guerrilla bases in Nepal and Sikkim, Chairman Mao finally took decisive action. In the late 1960s, China threatened to invade Sikkim and Nepal unless the rebel bases were closed and guerrilla forces disarmed. At the same time, the United States and China were beginning secret negotiations, through Pakistan, aimed at establishing an entente against the Soviet Union.

Secretary of State Henry Kissinger decided opening the door to Beijing was worth far more than wresting Tibet from Chinese control: all aid to Tibetan resistance would cease forthwith. As a result of combined pressure from the United States and China, India and Nepal abruptly abandoned the Tibetan resistance and arrested its leaders. Tibetan guerrilla units that were not encircled and destroyed by the Chinese PLA were disbanded and imprisoned by Nepal. The betrayal of Tibet was complete.

A second enormous disaster, Mao's Great Cultural Revolution, fell upon Tibet, inflicting untold suffering. Much of Tibet's religious and lay leadership, "bourgeois elements," and its small group of intellectuals were executed or thrown into the laogai.

Armies of Red Guards rampaged across Tibet, destroying vestiges of "feudal culture and superstition." In a barbarous act of cultural genocide, more than six thousand monasteries were razed, their precious art and literary treasures either looted or burned.

The West largely ignored this campaign of terror and vandalism, just as it did the similar, and equally egregious, destruction by Mao's Red Guards of China's own cultural and artistic treasures. The Great Cultural Revolution marked one of history's worst cultural disasters, akin to the barbarian invasions of the Roman Empire, or the destruction of Islamic civilization by the Mongols. Many Western intellectuals and leftists, and much of the media, closed their eyes to the barbaric madness that swept over China, loudly extolling the "social progress" brought by the

Chinese communists. Only a few, notably the courageous Belgian writer and art historian Simon Lys, denounced the monstrous criminal acts of Mao and his demented mobs of Red Guards.

During the same dark period, China continued to pour Han Chinese settlers into Tibet, to the point where they eventually came to outnumber native Tibetans by at least one million. China also pursued this policy of strategic demographic inundation in Sinkiang, Inner Mongolia, and Manchuria.

Chinese propaganda made much of the fact that "liberation" had brought Tibet badly needed modernization and redistribution of land. China constructed roads, bridges, hospitals, and schools in Tibet, where none had existed before. Feudal serfdom was ended, only to be replaced by the more draconian servitude of communist collective farming. Although much of the infrastructure in Tibet was designed primarily for the benefit of the military and Chinese settler population, China did drag parts of Tibet into the semi-modern age and improve the standard of living of many Tibetans—but at a fearsome price Tibetans were clearly unwilling to pay.

By the 1970s, China had firmly cemented its strategic control of Tibet. All-weather military roads crossed the country, enabling Chinese troops to move quickly into Tibet from Sichuan, and to all key points along the long border with India. The PLA built a score of new air bases on the plateau, which for the first time put much of northern India within range of Chinese warplanes. Medium-range missiles capable of striking Delhi, Calcutta, and Bombay were emplaced, for the first time, in Tibet. China also rapidly developed its new nuclear testing centre at Lanzhou, on Tibet's northeast border. Over the past two decades, India and China conducted sporadic negotiations over their border disputes, and announced various plans to lessen mutual tensions, including annual meetings at the ministerial level. India remained preoccupied by the confrontation with Pakistan, unrest in Kashmir and Punjab, and the civil war in Sri Lanka. Indian strategists had no desire to become embroiled in a two-front conflict with Pakistan and its ally, China. For its part, China was focused, under the leadership of Deng Xiaoping, on rapid economic development. China's military was denied funds for modernization. Beijing sought to downplay all regional disputes and adopt a non-confrontational foreign policy that would diminish Western fear of the Communist giant, thus affording

China access to badly needed foreign investment, technology, and export markets.

By the late 1990s, China had achieved remarkable economic growth, and as a result of Deng's enormously successful reformist policies was winning grudging acceptance by the outside world as a new regional superpower. The post-Deng political succession had progressed smoothly: China was economically sound, politically stable, and, save for the always explosive Taiwan issue, generally perceived by the West as non-threatening in its foreign policy. Fears a power struggle among Deng's would-be successors might bring chaos, regional secession, or even national disintegration proved unfounded. The collective leadership under President Jiang Zemin managed a smooth, efficient, peaceful transfer of power from the old guard to a somewhat younger (though still old) and more forward-thinking group of party leaders who were determined to press ahead with Deng's economic reforms, while avoiding at all costs Gorbachev's loosening of Communist political controls, an act of folly, in Beijing's view, that caused the collapse of the Soviet state. In another sign of China's growing political stability, the succession in March 2003, from Jiang Zemin to his successor, President Hu Jintao, went flawlessly and without the usual behind-the-scenes rivalries that marked previous changes in power. The silky-smooth Hu was a water engineer who had steadily risen through party ranks. Interestingly, Hu was an expert on China's westernmost regions and had been Communist Party chief in Tibet. Since being named president of China, Hu has conducted extremely cautious, carefully measured policies that have kept China's economy booming at over 9 per cent annual growth. At the same time, Hu and the collective leadership around him have managed to maintain social order and rigid party control in the face of China's runaway growth and huge movements of rural population into urban areas.

India, too, had made important, if less dramatic, economic progress. During the same period, India also succeeded in developing a substantial military-industrial base, and a world-class computing and software industry around Bangalore, India's "Silicon Valley." In effect, India was really two contrasting nations: a backward agricultural country of some nine hudred million; and a fairly modern, industrial-technological urban society of one hundred million. Modern India and antique Mother India coexisted uncomfortably, pulled in opposite directions in a constant tug-of-war between modernists and traditionalists, and afflicted, like so many other Third World nations, by deep cultural confusion.

China and India, Asia's two most populous states, once relegated to the world's lowest ranks as hopelessly backward, chaotic pauper nations, have attained a state of semi-development, internal stability, and self-respect that now permits, and even encourages, both to look outward and reassess their relative positions in South and East Asia. It was also evident that while China had succeeded in stabilizing its population growth at 1.3 billion, India's population was still growing at a rapid rate: sometime in the first decade of the twenty-first century, India will surpass China to become the world's most populous nation.

To understand how strategic events and conflicts will develop in Asia, it is essential to examine the way its two great powers see themselves, and their rival interests, within the region.

India's view is largely shaped by its Hindu nationalist-dominated political establishment, an influential group of strategic thinkers in Delhi, the military establishment, the intelligentsia, and the nation's powerful business leaders. Since independence, India has been torn between two currents of geopolitical thought. The first, espoused by Nehru, saw India as a champion of Third Worldism, Fabian socialism, and peaceful coexistence with its neighbours—Pakistan excepted.

Asia's problems were largely the fault of British and American imperialism, and could be resolved through negotiation, solidarity, and cooperation. India would be the moral champion and prime motive force of this new, benign, post-colonial Asian order. This thinking reached its apogee during the heady days of the 1960s, when Nehru joined with Egypt's Gamal Abdel Nasser, Indonesia's Sukarno, and Yugoslavia's Tito to proclaim the era of non-aligned nations.

India's 1962 war with China, the massive economic failure of socialist Third World nations, and Israel's stunning victory in the 1967 Arab-Israeli conflict put an end to the pretensions and dreams of the non-aligned movement. After the deaths of Nehru, Nasser, Tito, and Sukarno, the movement lost its most articulate, charismatic spokesmen and with them its moral impetus; from then on it would be fatally undermined by the inflated ambitions, empty rhetoric, and the demoralizing economic and military weakness of its leading members. Hope was replaced by disillusionment and widespread cynicism.

Indira Gandhi's rise to power profoundly altered India's geopolitical thinking. This remarkable iron-willed lady, as strong and decisive as Nehru was weak and dithering, abandoned for good his uncertain, confused policies. She was determined to see India quickly become the great power it inherently was. There would be no more silly talk about nonviolence, or foreign policy driven by high moral concerns. India, in Indira's view, had to meet its destiny as Asia's superpower, the subcontinent's unchallenged master, and overlord of the vast Indian Ocean. This muscular strategy meant building up India's industries, military power, and nuclear capability.

In what soon came to be known as the "Indira Doctrine," Gandhi and her dynastic successors, sons Sanjay and Rajiv, translated the aggressive theories then being developed in India's strategic and political think tanks into concrete policy. In 1970–71, Pakistan was confronted, defeated, and dismembered into Pakistan and Bangladesh. Nepal was warned to bow to India's will and to cease flirtation with China. Indian "peacekeeping" forces invaded Sri Lanka during that nation's civil war in a failed effort to turn the island nation into another protectorate of New Delhi. Indian paratroops were dropped on the Maldive islands to put down a coup. Efforts were intensified to crush rebellions by Sikhs in Punjab, Muslims in Kashmir, Gurkhas in Assam, and tribal peoples in the remote eastern hill states bordering Burma and in the strategically important Andaman Islands that lie in the Indian Ocean south of Burma.

India's wobbly post-Gandhi governments were too consumed by domestic problems to follow their predecessor's aggressive world view. But when the nationalist BJP came to power at the head of a coalition, it dusted off the Indira Policy, making it the party's unofficial foreign policy. BJP militants called for the eventual reunification of the entire Indian subcontinent into Bharat Hind, or Great India. In the view of Indian nationalists, British imperialism had chopped up India, creating an unstable and unnatural group of minor states, in order to undermine independent India's power and maintain Western influence in the region. Pakistan, in particular, was seen as an agent of U.S. imperial interests in the Indian Ocean, and a tool for keeping India on the strategic defensive.

This assertive doctrine held that the entire Indian Ocean and its littoral states were an integral part of India's legitimate sphere of geopolitical interest. In effect, India's maritime sphere of dominance extended in a great pyramid, first east across the Bay of Bengal to the highly important Strait of Malacca between Indonesia, Malaysia, and Singapore, and then as far south as the western coast of Australia. Next, forming the bottom of the great triangle, it followed a straight line from Australia to the coast of East Africa and the Mozambique Channel, between Mozambique and Madagascar. Then around the Horn of Africa, and northward through East Africa, finally encompassing the entire Arabian Sea, including the mouth of the oil-producing Gulf.

To assert dominion over this vast body of ocean, and project power far from its coasts, India embarked in the 1970s on a major program of naval construction, which included deployment of two aircraft carriers with their supporting task forces, submarines, a large number of surface combatants, a squadron of long-range TU-142 Bear maritime bombers, and a nuclear attack submarine leased from the Soviet Union. By 2006, India had sharply accelerated its naval construction program to include a new generation of frigates, conventional submarines and a nuclear-powered submarine designed to carry powerful anti-ship missiles and the long-range Sagarika cruise missile. Some intelligence sources believe the Sagarika is a ballistic missile.

The rapid build-up of India's naval forces is clearly designed to challenge China's development of a true blue-water navy. Indian fears that China's Navy may soon start operating in the Indian Ocean. The U.S. Navy, though officially silent, is quietly concerned that India's large, supersonic anti-ship missiles are designed for one main target: U.S. aircraft carriers. It is clear the U.S. Navy, once master of the Indian Ocean, is facing growing naval challenges from both China and India.

The primary mission of India's growing fleet was to blockade Pakistan's coast and the port of Karachi, in time of war. Secondary but still important considerations were protecting India's maritime commerce and imports of oil coming from the Gulf or through the Strait of Malacca; monitoring Sri Lanka and the island groups of the Andamans, Nicobars, and Maldives; and keeping a weather eye on the coasts of Bangladesh and Burma. Another key unstated mission of the Indian Navy was to deter naval intervention in the Arabian Sea by the U.S. fleet in the event of a conflict with Pakistan. During the 1971 war, deployment in the Arabian Sea of a U.S. carrier battle group in support of Pakistan had caused profound alarm in Delhi, and convinced Indian naval strategists any such future American action had to be prevented.

India's maritime assertiveness provoked widespread concern among the littoral states of the Indian Ocean, and even more from the U.S. Navy, which saw a challenge to its hitherto unchallenged domination of that ocean. The strategic axis between India and the Soviet Union and Moscow's supply of enormous amounts of advanced weapons to India at bargain prices heightened American anxiety. A new war between India and Pakistan, or the spread of the war in Afghanistan, might bring the United States and U.S.S.R., supported by India, into a direct clash in the Indian Ocean.

The collapse of the Soviet Union allayed these fears, but in recent years, the old Delhi-Moscow entente has been largely restored. India remains Russia's leading foreign customer for arms, spare parts, and military and nuclear technology. Russia is selling India its most advanced aircraft, such as the MIG-29 and SU-30MK, conventional Kilo-class attack submarines, surface warfare systems, and technology for India's planned nuclear submarines—some of which will be armed with strategic missiles. India's and Russia's strategic interests in Central and South Asia still remain in concert, particularly with regard to Afghanistan, their enmity to Pakistan and opposition to the spread of militant Islam, mutual concern over China, and the shared conviction that the United States has grown too powerful and aggressive as the world's sole superpower.

Pressure from the United States on India to cease its nuclear weapons program and on Russia to halt the export of weapons and nuclear technology to Iran have produced cries of blackmail from Moscow, and heated accusations by India of "U.S. nuclear apartheid," further pushing Delhi and Moscow into a closer embrace.

India's steady economic development, running at the rate of 9.2 per cent at the end of 2006, has permitted it to continue modernization of its armed forces, the world's third largest after those of China and the United States. India's 980,000-man army has been transformed over the past decade by mechanization and more combat-effective, mobile formations structured around armour- and artillery-heavy strike corps designed for war against Pakistan. India now fields over 4,100 main battle tanks, the most effective being the newly acquired Russian T-90s; updated models of the Soviet T-72, and the locally developed, much troubled Arjun tank. The army's striking power has been substantially enhanced by the addition of self-propelled artillery to supplement its already large force of Swedish and Soviet-supplied guns.

The Indian Air Force's 852 combat planes have been supplemented with the latest Russian strike aircraft, France's excellent Mirage 2000B, and highly effective air-to-air and anti-aircraft missiles. Some of India's large fleet of older MIG-21s are being modernized, with Russian and Israeli assistance. Nevertheless, India's air force has serious problems of training, spare parts, and coordination, as well as a truly awesome record of accidents, leading Pakistanis to claim their best strategy is to defer the next war until the Indian Air Force crashes all its planes.

India's navy currently lists one aircraft carrier (the second is out of service, but due to be replaced in 2008 by the upgraded 40,500-ton Russian *Admiral Gorshkov*), nineteen submarines, twenty-four destroyers and frigates, and an air arm with British Harrier jump jets and Soviet reconnaissance bombers. By comparison, Japan, whose GDP is eleven times as large as India's, and whose maritime commerce is greater by an entire order of magnitude, has no aircraft carriers, sixteen submarines, and fifty-seven major surface combatants. India's new submarines will eventually give it a long-range nuclear-strike capability from the sea, with a very low vulnerability to enemy detection or attack, which will give Delhi a survivable reserve nuclear force that can respond even after a surprise enemy nuclear attack.

To India's 1,175,000-man armed forces must be added its large paramilitary forces, which number 1,090,000 active men. Included in this second army are such units as the Rashtriya Rifles, Indo-Tibetan Border Police, Assam Rifles (twice as many men as the entire Canadian Armed Forces), Central Reserve Police Force of 185,000 men, and state armed police numbering 400,000. Some of these units have heavy weapons, are reasonably well trained and disciplined, and must be counted as active army reserves. Other units, such as the notorious Central Reserve Police Force, which has committed extensive atrocities in Kashmir, are undisciplined thugs of little military value. While these paramilitary forces are designed for internal security, some are mobile and could be trucked to combat fronts in wartime, or at least free up army regulars from internal security duties in troubled regions of India.

India's large conventional forces have clearly been designed to fight a war of movement against their historical enemy, Pakistan. The army's most powerful mobile units, three corps with six divisions, face

Pakistan. China's invasion of Tibet and the ensuing 1962 war, however, compelled the Indian defense establishment to develop a substantial mountain-warfare capability with specially trained divisions. India currently deploys, at least under its nominal order of battle, seventeen mountain divisions on the border with China and Tibet, though some have been moved to Kashmir for counter-guerrilla operations. A large, mobile reserve is maintained for rapid reaction.

The development of India's nuclear arsenal, however, has been aimed at China since the beginning. India has overwhelming conventional military superiority over Pakistan; nuclear weapons were unnecessary, and if used against neighbouring Pakistan would cause enormous civilian casualties in India. Delhi's nuclear arsenal confers great-power status and diplomatic muscle; it also counters China's modest but still worrisome nuclear forces. There is some debate whether it was China or India that first began to develop nuclear weapons, though China tested and deployed nuclear warheads well ahead of India. After the 1962 war with China, India put its nuclear program into high gear, exploding a 12-kiloton nuclear device in 1974.

India adopted a two-track nuclear program using enriched uranium and reprocessed plutonium, based on technology supplied by Canada, France, the United States, and the Soviet Union.

Canada's role was of primary importance. The Canadian government sold India four 220 megawatt pressurized heavy-water reactors at giveaway prices as part of its foreign aid program. Equally important, Canada supplied India with blueprints and technology for nuclear plant design and local production of components, as well as the key technology to produce and enrich nuclear fuel. In addition, Canada also trained a sizeable cadre of Indian nuclear scientists and technicians. When India conducted its first nuclear test in 1974, Canada, deeply embarrassed, cut off all nuclear transactions with India, but it was too late. The nuclear genie was out of the bottle.

France helped India build the heavy-water plants at Baroda and Tuticorin, and the fast breeder reactor at Kalpakkam (all three unsafeguarded), and trained large numbers of Indian nuclear engineers and technicians.

The unsafeguarded heavy-water plants at Nangal and Talcher were supplied by Germany, along with the strategic metals beryllium and lithium, the latter used to produce tritium, an element that boosts the power of nuclear explosions. Norway illegally sold India twenty-six tons of heavy water, which was diverted through Switzerland and Romania. The Swiss helped build the heavy-water plants at Baroda and Tuticorin.

The Soviet Union covertly provided India eighty tons of heavy water and a large cadre of nuclear technicians and advisers for the important Madras and Dhruva reactors. Britain supplied turbine generator pumps and sent repair technicians, Sweden special steel plates and flash X-ray devices. The United States unwittingly supplied heavy water for the Canadian Cirus reactor that produced the plutonium used in India's first nuclear device.

Today, four decades later, India has a highly developed civilian nuclear infrastructure consisting of ten major nuclear reactors, with four more due to come online in the near future, supplying 2 per cent of the nation's power requirements.

Many of these plants are under International Atomic Energy Agency safeguards, and produce only electric power. But India also has a very large military nuclear infrastructure, dedicated to the production of plutonium and uranium weapons, which operates without any international inspection or safeguards: twelve reactors, nine "research reactors" (most clustered in the Trombay complex outside Bombay), a fast-breeder reactor, six uranium-ore processing and refining plants, five nuclear-fuel fabrication plants, four reprocessing plants, and eight heavy-water plants.

According to foreign intelligence estimates, India has a stockpile of 800 kilograms of weapons-grade plutonium-239, sufficient to produce between 80 and 120 nuclear warheads. Annual production of enriched uranium-233 is estimated at 650 kilogram (1,433 pounds), enough for 70 to 100 nuclear warheads. Israel has reportedly been secretly helping India develop the reliability, explosive power, and miniaturization of its nuclear warheads, and supplying guidance technology for their delivery systems, the Prithvi and Agni series missiles. By the end of 1998, India was estimated to have anywhere from 10 to 100 operational nuclear warheads that could be activated within hours by insertion of nuclear cores in the weapon's high-explosive outer shells. Development of this powerful nuclear infrastructure and missile delivery systems is estimated to have cost India at least $40 billion, and could very likely reach $120 billion by 2007, a tremendous expenditure for a nation whose per capita GDP is $3,100, and which still receives substantial development and humanitarian aid from foreign donors.

The underground nuclear tests conducted by India in 1998 were designed to validate the reliability of tactical and strategic warheads for missiles, air-delivered bombs, and 155 mm artillery shells. The most important part of the tests was the validating of the new nuclear warheads for the short-range Prithvi, the medium-range Agni series of missiles. Indian nuclear officials also leaked the news that they had tested the "big bomb," a thermonuclear (hydrogen) weapon. This claim is disputed by some Western nuclear analysts.

On April 11, 1999, eleven months after detonating five nuclear weapons, India staged a test of the new, solid-fuel Agni-II missile. The missile flew some 2,011 kilometres (1,250 miles) in a mere eleven minutes and landed in the Bay of Bengal.

The brief hopes for a thaw in Indian-Pakistani relations that appeared after a much-publicized bus trip to Pakistan by India's prime minister quickly evaporated in the backblast of the Agni-II. Not to be out-rocketed by the Indians, Pakistan promptly launched its new solid-fuel, mobile Ghauri missile, which has a range of at least 1,500 kilometres (932 miles), soon to be extended to 2,500 kilometres (1,553 miles).

China, which had been watching India's nuclear and missile tests with mounting ire, made statements protesting Delhi's "provocative, unfriendly" acts. There were reports that China was moving mobile M-9 short-range and M-11 medium-range missiles toward India's border. All of this missile-rattling raised uneasy memories of the naval race and well-publicized naval war games that led up to World War I.

Any doubt that India's Agni-II and oncoming Agni-III were designed for use against China were dispelled by India's prime minister, Atal Behari Vajpayee, who announced that India would build a "credible" nuclear deterrent. Dropping any pretense of diplomatic language or tact, in late 1998, Defense Minister George Fernandes asserted China was now India's "number one enemy."

Soon after, India formed a new National Security Council, headed by the prime minister, to review and formulate nuclear doctrine, another clear sign India was determined to use its nuclear weapons arsenal to enhance its increasingly muscular diplomacy, and if necessary for war. Pouring fuel on the fire, India's outspoken Home Secretary and BJP stalwart, L.K. Advani, warned Pakistan that in light of India's newly revealed nuclear power, it should back down over Kashmir—or else. Indian voters, however, proved considerably less truculent than the BJP's firebrands. In state elections in November 1988, they kicked the BJP out of three important states: Delhi, Rajastan (where the BJP had recently conducted nuclear tests), and the BJP stronghold of Madhya Pradesh. Though rising food prices, notably that of onions, was a major issue in the election, many Indian voters expressed dismay at the BJP's aggressive policies and nuclear scimitar-rattling. The far more moderate Congress Party, led by Sonia Gandhi, Rajiv's widow, gained many seats. Still, the damage had been done.

To no one's surprise, China denounced India's "provocations," vowing it would counter Delhi's nuclear threats by enhancing its own nuclear forces targeted on India. Beijing warned that India was igniting an Asian arms race. Long-simmering strategic tensions between India and China had finally broken out into the open.

•••

Though hardly anyone noticed at the time, the unveiling of India's nuclear weapons provoked considerable unease in another regional power with nuclear aspirations, Iran. The late Shah Reza Pahlavi had decided in the mid-1970s to begin developing nuclear weapons to counter the threat from the Soviet Union, assure Iran's domination of the Gulf, and underline Iran's self-appointed role—in alliance with the United States—as policeman of the central Mideast. Iran began work on small test reactors, and trained a cadre of nuclear technicians in Europe and America. More important, the shah entered into secret negotiations with Israel to purchase nuclear weapons, associated technology, and the Jericho-1 MRBM (medium-range ballistic missile). The 1979 revolution in Iran ended covert nuclear cooperation with Israel, but the new Islamic government, seeing itself surrounded by enemies, accelerated nuclear development and speeded construction of a large reactor complex at Bushir.

Iran is a geopolitical swing nation, looking both west into the Mideast and east to the Indian subcontinent. In recent decades, Tehran, whether under the shah or the mullahs of the Islamic Republic, has seen itself as a defender of Muslim Pakistan and a key force in the newly independent states of Central Asia. India's nuclear program, and its evident great-power aspirations, considerably worried Iran. The long war with Iraq, and intelligence reports that Baghdad was striving to develop nuclear weapons with secret financial aid from Iran's bitter foe Saudi Arabia, convinced Tehran to accelerate its nascent.nuclear program.

A former director general of Pakistani intelligence told me that, in the late 1980s, Iran offered to underwrite Pakistan's total defense budget for ten years if Islamabad would supply nuclear weapons to Iran. Pakistan refused outright. This forced Iran to follow a slower, more arduous program of nuclear development by covertly acquiring bits and pieces of nuclear technology from abroad.

There seems little doubt Iran will eventually acquire nuclear war heads for its Shahab series of MRBMS, which are currently being tested. Any major Indian invasion of Pakistan, or military intervention in Afghanistan, could very well draw in Iranian forces, raising the danger of nuclear confrontation between Delhi and Tehran.

19
THE CLASH OF THE TITANS

It has long been clear to Indian strategists that their nation and China will one day come into open confrontation; the only question is when. Economic growth has permitted both states to upgrade and modernize their conventional and nuclear forces. At some point in the early twenty-first century, the two powers will be locked in a fierce rivalry for mastery of South Asia and its important resources. China, the Indians believe, will not sit back and allow an ever-strengthening India to assert its domination of the region without a struggle.

In the Indian view, China's long-term strategy is to surround and isolate India in a sort of gigantic version of the Japanese board game *Goh*. China's land strategy is based on two nations: Pakistan and Burma. Pakistan and China have been close allies since the early 1970s: Beijing is Pakistan's principal supplier of weapons, some nuclear technology, and diplomatic support. The Karakoram Highway over the mountains from northern Pakistan to Chinese Sinkiang, the sole land link between the two nations, is China's only opening to the West. In the event of war, India fears, China would move large numbers of troops over the highway into Kashmir, threatening Ladakh and India's northern regions.

Burma, now known officially as Myanmar, is the second prong of China's grand anti-Indian strategy. This isolated, little-known nation of 49.5 million dominates India's eastern flank. During World War II, Burma was called "the back door to India" by both the British and the Japanese, who battled ferociously in its thick jungles and mountains. For the past three decades, China has steadily increased its political, military, and economic influence in Burma. The military regime in Rangoon (Yangon), boycotted and shunned by the outside world because of its deplorable human rights record, has turned increasingly to China, and to a lesser degree, to Japan, for support.

A complex series of rebellions by Shan, Karens, and Kachin ethnic minorities has kept Burma in a prolonged state of civil war for the past forty years. In addition to ethnic rebels, powerful opium armies operate in Burma's wild interior, including the descendants of two Chinese Nationalist divisions that were pushed into Burma from Yunnan in 1949, and then subsequently armed and supplied for many years by CIA airdrops.

Though impoverished, chronically unstable, and riven by ethnic strife, Burma is potentially one of South Asia's richest nations, with huge stores of precious teak and other hardwood timber, gemstones, strategic minerals, fertile land, and, most important, extensive, largely unexploited oil reserves. As a result, Burma receives the attentions of its two powerful neighbours, India and China, who covet both its natural riches and strategic position.

In my view, Burma is destined to join Tibet as a major flashpoint between India and China during the first decade of the twenty-first century. The collapse of Burma's ruling military junta, which until recently was known by the wonderfully sinister Orwellian acronym SLORC (State Law and Order Reconstruction Council), could very likely result in the country dissolving into a chaotic civil war between army units, political supporters of opposition leader Aung San Suu Kyi, and the nation's various ethnic armies. This, in turn, could provoke Indian or Chinese military intervention, and a direct clash between the two powers. Stationing of Chinese ground forces or naval units in Burma would also very likely spark a major conflict.

To the west of Burma, India's remote, little-known northeast region has been in a state of almost constant insurgency since independence in 1947. A mountainous, forested region of 254,000 square kilometres (98,000 square miles), with poor roads and scant communications, the states of the northeast are often called the "Seven Sisters." They comprise Arunachal Pradesh—formerly the North-East Frontier Agency—Assam, Meghalaya, Manipur, Mizoram, Nagaland, and Tripura, with a combined population of some thirty-two million people.

This region is highly strategic and extremely sensitive: it is bounded on the north by China and on the southeast by Burma, and connected to the rest of India only through the narrow Siliguri corridor in the state of West Bengal. To its west lies Bhutan; to the southeast, Bangladesh.

Often termed an "ethnic reactor," the region contains a bewildering collection of five different racial groups, hundreds of tribes—110 in Arunachal Pradesh alone—and three main religions: Hinduism, Christianity, and Buddhism. For the past half-century, major insurgencies and secessionist movements have flared in Nagaland, Mizoram, Manipur, and Assam, fuelled by immigration from neighbouring parts of India. The best-organized and most dangerous rebel groups, in the view of Indian security authorities, are the National Socialist Council of Nagaland and the United Liberation Front of Assam, both of which are seeking to establish independent states.

Most of the tribal groups are Christians, except for those of Arunachal Pradesh, and the leadership of the various insurgent groups is predominantly Christian as well. Christian missionaries have long played a key role in supporting and financing the tribal insurgents, just as they have in southern Sudan. The Hindu fundamentalists of the BJP see a sinister plot by international Christian organizations to detach the tribal states from India.

Indian authorities have long accused China, Pakistan, Burma, and Bangladesh of supplying arms, training, and secure bases to the different rebel groups. China and Pakistan have given the insurgents substantial covert support, and continue to do so; Burma and Bangladesh offer passive assistance by allowing rebel units to cross their porous borders. If relations between Delhi and Beijing worsen, it seems likely China will squeeze India by stirring the pot in the northeast, or even actively supporting uprisings there from Burma, where Chinese influence is rising rapidly.

Tribal peoples make up about 8 per cent of India's population. Many of the tribes of the hill states are ethnically linked to those of neighbouring Burma. These hill states, and rebellious Assam, make up the long salient of India's vulnerable northeast frontier, which is threatened by Chinese forces in Tibet. In the event of another Indian-Chinese war, Chinese forces striking south from Tibet through Bhutan could cut off eastern India. If Chinese armies were stationed in Burma, they could push east through the hill states into Bangladesh, threatening Calcutta, and India's most populous states, Bihar and Uttar Pradesh.

Most worrisome to India, though, is the steady increase of Chinese military power on the Tibetan Plateau, which confronts India with the specter of simultaneously facing serious strategic threats on its western, northern, and eastern borders. This fear has led Indian strategists and politicians to warn that India was being "surrounded" by a hostile coalition of forces directed and armed by China.

By the early 1990s, China had deployed five hundred thousand soldiers, a quarter of its standing army, on the Tibetan Plateau, half of them based on the border between India and Tibet, half in central Tibet. Four additional Chinese armies, each the equivalent of a sixty-thousand-man army corps, were based in Sinkiang and the Chengdu military district, able to support operations from Tibet against India by delivering flanking attacks or providing follow-on reinforcements.

China is reducing its three-million-strong armed forces by 20 per cent, with four hundred thousand men transferred from the army to the paramilitary police. Troop strength in Tibet is also being somewhat reduced. The objective of this massive reduction is to divert funds into modernization and better equipment. China's 8,800 tanks are largely obsolete or obsolescent; it needs to acquire modern artillery and self-propelled guns. The navy is being upgraded into a true blue-water arm. China's huge, 3,566-combat-plane air force is totally obsolete: it has only forty modern, Russian-supplied SU-27 fighters, and two hundred J-8s, an upgraded version of the old MIG-21. The remainder consists of 1950s- and 1960s-vintage warplanes, with short range, poor engines, and primitive avionics.

As a result of this modernization program, China's armies in Tibet are improving their firepower, communications, and mobility, in spite of the decrease in sheer numbers. In addition, China's western armies received, along with those facing Taiwan, some of the newest and most advanced arms and equipment. The collapse in 1991 of China's former principal threat, the Soviet Union, allowed China not only to reduce the size of its armies, but to redeploy some of its most effective units from the Soviet border to the south and west, including the 149th Division of the thirteenth Group Army, specialized in mountain warfare, to Chengdu, and the sixty-second Division of the twenty-first Group Army, configured for mobile desert warfare, to Lanzhou, covering China's Central Asian region north of Tibet. New combined arms divisions with enhanced offensive power are being deployed to western and southern regions.

Ever since occupying Tibet in 1950, the PLA has worked feverishly to build networks of all-weather roads, crisscrossing the kingdom and linking it to the Chengdu military region and to Sinkiang. Two other major roads lead to Pakistan and Nepal respectively. The new road system allowed China to move large military formations swiftly along the entire length of the Indian border, affording Chinese generals the ability to concentrate mutually supporting armies almost anywhere along the frontier. A chain of permanent bases, many with huge underground storage sites and heavy fixed fortifications, linked to rear echelons by good roads, has been extended like a new Great Wall along the length of the border with India.

The militarization of Tibet presented India with serious strategic and tactical problems. China quite literally commands the high ground from the 4,267-kilometre (14,000-foot) Tibetan Plateau. The People's Liberation Army's forward positions are located at the very crest of the plateau; Indian positions are located, in many cases, below them. In the event of war, Indian troops must advance uphill to attack Chinese positions firing down on them. India's topographical disadvantage was piquantly summed up by the late Zhou Enlai, who once quipped that if China wanted to destroy India, it need only march one hundred million of its citizens to the southern edge of the Tibetan Plateau, and wash India away by ordering them to urinate downhill.

This serious tactical disadvantage is compounded by the chain of intelligence-gathering stations established by China along the plateau's southern edge, which allow China to monitor Indian air space, electronic communications, and troop movements south of the Himalayas. Israel enjoys a precisely identical intelligence advantage from another plateau, the Golan Heights, which it seized from Syria in 1967. Israeli ELINT (electronic inelligence) antennas atop Golan can monitor and track every Syrian warplane that takes off from southern air bases from the moment they start their engines. It is a simple matter for them to observe major Syrian troop movements and intercept most of the communications issuing from Damascus.

China has constructed fourteen major air bases on the Tibetan Plateau, and a score of tactical airstrips. These bases give the Chinese air force unquestioned domination of Tibet's air space, the forward edge of battle in the event of war, and the capability, for the first time, to fly sustained combat operations over India's north and strike all India's northern cities, including Delhi, Bombay, and Calcutta. Chinese electronic intelligence atop the plateau, looking down from a height of 4,267 to 4,572 metres (14,000 to 15,000 feet), also confers an important advantage of combat information and battle management in any air war, in part compensating for the technological inferiority of China's aircraft against India's far more modern air arm.

But of all China's military emplacements on the Plateau, by far the most alarming to India is an extensive series of missile bases and nuclear installations. At least half China's force of around fifty CSS-2 and CSS-5 MRBMs are based in Tibet, as well as a sizeable number of shorter-range tactical missiles, all carrying nuclear warheads. In addition, China moved its principal nuclear test and development facility from Lop Nor, in Sinkiang, to Nagchuka, 265 kilometres (165 miles) north of Lhasa. India's heartland and many of its major cities are now in range of Chinese missiles.

Water is another issue of major concern to Indian strategists. South Asia's largest rivers flow down from the Tibetan Plateau. The headwaters of some of India's most important rivers and principal source of the groundwater that nourishes the subcontinent rise in Tibet. China thus controls much of India's main supply of water. India's strategists have long worried that China may at some point dam, divert, or interdict its vital water supplies.

To some, such concerns may seem far-fetched. But they are very real. Egypt has long made clear that any attempt by Ethiopia or Sudan to substantially divert upstream waters of the Nile will be a *casus belli*. India has looked with growing concern as Turkey's massive Ataturk hydroelectric scheme in eastern Anatolia has steadily dammed the headwaters of the Tigris and Euphrates rivers, depriving Syria and Iraq of 50 per cent of their downstream water, those nations' major source of irrigation. Israel has maintained occupation of southern Lebanon and Golan in part because they contain vital headwaters for the Jordan, Litani, and Yarmuk Rivers.

Development of naval power by China and India presents another looming source of conflict between the two Asian rivals. Until the 1980s China's large, but obsolescent, fleets, comprising sixty-three submarines, fifty-three large surface combatants, and 747 patrol vessels, was a strictly brown-water force, able to defend only China's immediate coastal region, and even then not very effectively. In recent years, however, China has embarked on a major program to build a true blue-water navy, capable of projecting power far beyond its coasts. China has introduced modern surface combatants of the Russian Sovremenny class, equipped with SS-N-22 long-range, anti-ship missiles, and the new Luda-class destroyers. It has also upgraded its naval aviation arm, and is struggling to build a fleet of nuclear-powered attack submarines to augment its sizeable number of conventional diesel subs. These new offensive warships are primarily designed to counter U.S. carrier battle groups, but they would be equally effective against the Indian fleet. Beijing is also said to be considering acquisition of a large aircraft carrier.

While China's naval forces remain primarily tasked for operations in the Pacific, South China Sea, and the waters around Taiwan, units of the South Sea fleet have begun operating off Vietnam, in support of China's claim to the disputed Spratly Islands, and in the waters between Malaysia, Singapore, and Indonesia, near the mouth of the strategic Strait of Malacca. The Chinese navy has made occasional patrols west of Malacca into the Andaman Sea, and port visits to China's ally, Burma. India now worries China's growing navy may begin regular patrols in the Bay of Bengal. As a result, India is rapidly expanding its naval presence in the region, forming a fourth naval command in 1998 at Port Blair in the strategic Andaman and Nicobar Islands that extend due south from the coast of Burma.

Oil is a principal factor behind these growing naval tensions. The rapidly developing economies of India and China will need to import increasing amounts of petroleum. China's domestic reserves may be exhausted within the next five years, and India's oil reserves are modest. As a result, the two rival powers will come into direct competition for foreign oil, the principal sources being Indonesia, Malaysia, Burma, and the Gulf. India is determined to develop naval forces capable of ensuring its flow of oil from Southeast Asia and the Gulf; the Indians fear that, in any war with China, the Chinese navy could quickly interdict oil shipments from Indonesia, Malaysia and, by submarine blockade, from the Gulf. China, of course, is equally concerned that its oil imports from Southeast Asia could be interdicted, just as effectively, by Indian naval action.

Navies remain, even in our modern age, the primary tool of power projection and geopolitical influence, as America's long naval presence in the Pacific clearly demonstrates. Now that China and India are bent on expanding their geostrategic interests in Asia, it appears inevitable that naval rivalry between the two antagonists will become increasingly important and active.

Some Indian analysts even fear that the Chinese Navy and the U.S. Fifth and Seventh fleets might combine forces at some future date, perhaps during a conflict with Pakistan, to threaten their coast from both the Bay of Bengal and the Arabian Sea. In the summer of 1998, India's defense minister, George Fernandes, underlined these concerns by publicly warning that China and the United States had embarked on a strategic alliance against India.

Amid all these alarms, Tibet continues to be the focus of Indian fears of encirclement and, eventually, attempts by China to destabilize and then splinter the Indian Union. The breakup of India would leave China the unchallenged master of Asia, much as the collapse of the Soviet Union eliminated any threat to Western Europe and the U.S.-dominated Mideast. Japan, though the object of constant Chinese suspicion, is not deemed likely in the foreseeable future to become an aggressive military power, though it will compete vigorously for oil.

Pakistan's long-range strategy is to encourage, whenever possible, the internal weakening of India, which Islamabad hopes will one day lead to the fragmentation of its huge foe. India is convinced China and Pakistan are colluding in this grand strategy, whose first steps would be encouragement of rebellion in India's eastern hill states, Kashmir, among Sikhs in Punjab, Gurkhas in Assam, and unrest among the large Tibetan refugee population in northern India clustered around the exiled Dalai Lama. Unrest or open rebellion in India's unstable border regions could encourage direct intervention of

Chinese troops based in Tibet, or infiltration of Chinese-directed "volunteers" across India's frontiers.

If a major head-to-head clash ever comes between China and India, Indian strategists are convinced it will eventually be played out along the Tibetan border. For India, Chinese-ruled Tibet looms ominously over their nation, a mighty redoubt in the clouds, bristling with enemy armies, ready to sally forth and pour onto the open plains of northern India like a second Mogul invasion.

20
CHINA UNDER SIEGE

China's strategic appreciation of its growing rivalry with India is, of course, starkly different. Beijing's official policy is that it has no territorial or hegemonistic ambitions in Asia, other than reunification of Taiwan to the mainland. But, in reality, Chinese strategists are keenly aware that the steady growth of their nation's power will accentuate already existing economic and strategic rivalry with India.

The two powers are already competing in Asian markets in the export of low- and medium-tech arms, electronics, and cheap consumer goods. Both vie to attract foreign investment.

The principal focus of rivalry, however, will be geopolitical. China may harbour no territorial designs on Southeast Asia, but it certainly intends to extend its political and military influence across the region that China has regarded, for the past three thousand years, as its natural sphere of geopolitical power and it will certainly compete with India for ever-scarcer oil. Burma and Pakistan, two important Chinese allies, are seen as gravely threatened by India. Some Chinese strategists also believe India has long-term designs on Indonesia's oil, and on the vast resources of the newly independent states of Central Asia.

China has worried since the 1960s about the strategic alliance between India and the Soviet Union (and now Russia). The massive arming of India by the Soviet Union/Russia convinced China that Moscow was forging an anti-Chinese axis designed to contain China's ambitions.

After the collapse of the Soviet Union in 1991, the threat to China of a Moscow-Delhi axis appeared to sharply diminish. Economic chaos in Russia delayed, or even shut off, the supply of tens of thousands of spare parts for India's arsenal of Soviet weapons and industrial equipment. Russia would no longer sell India arms or military material at concessionary "fraternal" prices, nor continue the former system whereby India paid for Soviet arms in soft rupees through "clearing accounts" and barter.

However, in the latter part of the 1990s, Russia resumed arms sales to India at an ever-accelerating pace. India was again allowed to pay for this equipment with a combination of hard currency, barter, and rupees. The Indian Air Force particularly benefited from restoration of military ties with Moscow by acquiring advanced model Sukhoi-30MKs and MIG29s, upgraded Russian avionics for its warplanes, new radars, missiles, and naval armaments. As in the 1970s and '80s, Russia and India resumed close cooperation in defense projects, and, most worrying to China, strategic coordination.

In effect, the Moscow-Delhi axis had been reborn. Its prime objectives were containing China's growing power, domination of South and Central Asia, containment of Islamic political-religious movements that threatened both Indian and Russian regional interests, and joint resistance to American power in Asia.

The particular aims of the renewed entente were first, defeating the Islamic movement in Afghanistan, thwarting Pakistan's influence there, and fashioning a pro-Russian, pro-Indian government in Kabul; second, limiting the expansion of Chinese influence into Burma, Indochina, and their neighbouring waters; third, reducing U.S. strategic influence and ability to move in the Indian Ocean and along its littoral. By combining their strategic interests, Russia and India aimed to counterbalance both China's growing power and the still dominant influence of the United States.

China watched uneasily as the Moscow-Delhi axis was restored, well aware that the entente could blossom into a full-grown military alliance. Russia's grave weakness in its Pacific far east, where its population of only twenty-five million faced one hundred million Chinese in China's three northern provinces alone, would in part be offset by the new threat posed by India to China's southern flank

India, it is feared, might join Russia in a future conflict against China, or even with the United States, if Taiwan ever sparks an American-Chinese conflict in the Pacific.

Just as India believes it is being surrounded by a hostile coalition of neighbouring states, so, too, does China. Military strategists in China have long been concerned over the threat scenario of a multi-front war that would pit against them India in the west, Vietnam in the south, Taiwan in the centre, and possibly Japan, the Koreas, or Russia in the north—a coalition that would considerably outnumber China's forces in troops and weapons. China has long suspected the Japanese, in league with the United States, of financing the armed forces of their hostile neighbours.

After Taiwan, China's most important military concern centres on its far western regions of Tibet and Sinkiang. These two provinces comprise a third of China's total land mass, though only a small fraction of. its population. China's hold over these far western regions, separated by 1,600 kilometres (1,000 miles), mountains, broad rivers, and poor communications from the Chinese heartland, has always been tenuous, and constantly challenged.

Full Chinese control of Tibet was not established until 1950. Sinkiang (Xinjiang), which lies to the north of Tibet, is a problem of almost equal complexity. It did not come under Beijing's unquestioned rule until the last century, though China had maintained trading posts and military garrisons in the region for many centuries.

Until the twentieth century, Sinkiang was known as Eastern Turkestan, an enormous sweep of steppe inhabited by nomadic and settled Turkic peoples, extending from the Great Wall of China to the shores of the Caspian Sea. This region had once been the heartland of the great Mongol Empire. In the eighteenth and nineteenth centuries, the Russian and Chinese empires began expanding south and west, respectively. Russia conquered Western Turkestan, today the former Soviet Central Asia; China reasserted historic claims to the remainder, Eastern Turkestan.

The Muslim peoples of Turkestan thus fell under Russian and Chinese rule, though uprisings were frequent and bloody, continuing in Soviet Central Asia and in Chinese Turkestan right down to the 1930s.

As in Tibet, China moved millions of settlers into Sinkiang in a campaign to turn its native Muslims into a minority in their own land. Beijing has established major military bases and garrisons across Sinkiang, supported by armies of police and security agents. Resentment of the harsh Chinese rule has simmered among the Turkic peoples of Sinkiang for the past half-century. While China's brutal repression of Tibet sparked worldwide outrage, its similarly cruel actions in Sinkiang have received almost no publicity, even in the Muslim world. There is no Hollywood to publicize and romanticize the plight of Turkestani Muslims, and no Muslim version of the Dalai Lama to champion and personify their obscure cause.

Sinkiang's largest native ethnic group, Uighurs, have been particularly resistant to Chinese rule. Emboldened and encouraged by the Islamic victory in Afghanistan and the struggle for independence by Kashmiri Muslims, Uighurs have in recent years demonstrated, rioted, and even formed a number of guerrilla and underground urban resistance groups. In 1998, there were a number of bombings of Chinese targets in Sinkiang's cities. Chinese authorities reacted by arresting thousands of Muslims, and executing scores. The PLA rushed troops and paramilitary police reinforcements to Sinkiang.

According to a 1999 Amnesty International report, the first major study about Sinkiang by an international human rights organization, Chinese authorities have executed 190 Uighurs since 1997 for "subversion" or "terrorism" after summary trials; another thirty were awaiting execution. According to Amnesty International, Uighur prisoners were routinely tortured into signing confessions.

Beijing quickly proposed an anti-Islamic-fundamentalist alliance to the Central Asian states of Tajikistan, Kyrgyzstan, Uzbekistan, and Kazakhstan, designed to isolate the Islamic revolt in Sinkiang, and prevent movement of Muslim rebels and arms across the region's borders. In spite of the newfound semi-independence of these Central Asian states, their dictatorial rulers remain, without exception, old-line Communists. The main opposition to these post-Communist leaders comes from internal Islamic resistance forces and, to a somewhat lesser degree, from the Islamic Taliban movement in Afghanistan. Central Asia's Communist rulers had already formed a regional, anti-Islamic alliance, strongly backed by Russian arms, money, advisers, and troops, to oppose the spread of political Islam within their states, and to intervene in Afghanistan in support of the anti-Taliban Northern Alliance. This alliance was quick to lend China discreet aid in isolating Uighur rebels in Sinkiang.

China fears, with good reason, that growing Muslim unrest will flare into open revolt, thus weakening its hold on Sinkiang and, indirectly, on Tibet. India, which has its own long-term ambitions in Central Asia, has been confused by these developments. On one hand, Delhi would like to undermine China's presence in Central Asia; but, on the other, it is loath to support Islamic forces whom it actively opposes in Afghanistan and Kashmir.

China and India are in dispute over yet another contentious issue in the Himalayas: the mountain kingdoms of Nepal, Bhutan, and Sikkim. Nepal, an overpopulated nation of 27.6 million, occupies a highly strategic position along the Indo-Chinese Himalayan border. Consequently, India has long had designs on Nepal, regarding it as a natural sphere of influence, if not an integral part of India, as some Hindu nationalists claim. China, by contrast, has generally viewed Nepal as a useful buffer state and strategic salient that curbs Indian ambitions in the Himalayas, and renders more difficult India's defense of its northern mountain border. In time of war, China would quickly occupy Nepal in order to benefit from its mountain passes and roads that lead south to debouche on the plains of northern India.

Nepal has played a deft diplomatic game between India and China for the past half-century, alternately flirting with one side, then the other. India has taken alarm and protested to India over China's building of military roads up to the Nepalese border. India has repeatedly warned Nepal over its economic and transit links with China, once going so far as to impose a trade blockade that almost wrecked Nepal's economy.

Over the past decade, Nepal's politics steadily deteriorated into violence and autocracy. An increasingly powerful Maoist insurgency seized much of the countryside. After the mysterious murder of the popular constitutional King Birendra, in 2001, his widely disliked, autocratic brother, Gyanendra, became king. In February 2005, Gyanendra staged a royalist coup, making himself an autocrat.

But the Maoist insurgency surged, with about thirteen thousand killed in the cross-fire between Communist rebels and government troops. Anti-monarchist riots erupted in Nepal's major cities. Finally, under pressure from the army, Gyanendra gave up his powers and was relegated to a figurehead monarch. In a remarkable development, Maoists and republicans agreed to a new, interim parliament, and the Maoists gave up their arms. The threat intervention in Nepal by India, China, or even the United States, ended.

But trouble remains.

An increasingly potent Gurkha nationalist movement, made up of the 2.5 to 3 million ethnic Nepalese living outside Nepal, seeks to detach Indian Assam, and possibly parts of Bhutan, to create a Greater Gurkha nation, or "Gurkhaland," which adds a further dimension of danger and uncertainty to this troubled equation.

The Nepalese are keenly aware their nation exists at the pleasure of India and could share the fate of their neighbouring mountain kingdoms. The Indian Army occupied Sikkim in 1970 without a shot; the tiny mountain state was forthwith annexed to India. In 1975, Sikkim became a state within the Indian union. India's seizure of Sikkim closely resembled China's invasion of Tibet in terms of its questionable legality, though certainly not in brutality, yet this act provoked no protest, and attracted barely any attention, in the outside world, save a brief wave of media sympathy in the United States for its attractive American-born Queen Hope, the Grace Kelly of the Himalayas. Hardly anyone had ever heard of Sikkim, and those few who had were hardpressed to find it on the map.

Farther east in the Himalayas, India made the formerly independent little kingdom of Bhutan, which had been an independent monarchy for 1,300 years, into another protectorate, also without international objection. Though taking no action, China has never formally accepted India's annexation of Sikkim or Bhutan, and could make an issue of it at a time of Beijing's choosing. However, in 2006 Delhi and Beijing appeared to agree that Bhutan and Sikkim would be accepted as an Indian sphere of influence provided India did not make too much fuss over Tibet.

Thus, four long-independent Buddhist Himalayan kingdoms—Tibet, Ladakh, Sikkim, and Bhutan—were absorbed by their powerful neighbours, India and China. Though the religion and culture of the latter three were no less rich and distinctive than that of Tibet, the outside world paid scant notice to the annexation of the other "Little Tibets."

Chinese military intelligence believes India is as intent on fragmenting China's close ally, Pakistan, as Pakistan is on fragmenting

India. Though Beijing has adopted a policy of studied vagueness on how it would react to a major Indian invasion of Pakistan, it is likely China would make a powerful military demonstration on India's northern border, or, if Pakistan appeared close to collapse, might intervene massively in the war.

The main threat from India, the Chinese believe, is directed against Tibet. India would be only too happy to remove the danger to its northern border, and break its perceived encirclement, by either destabilizing or, even better, ousting the Chinese from Tibet, and then from Sinkiang. A direct Indian military assault on Tibet would be exceptionally difficult, very costly, and most likely a failure. India's most effective strategy, therefore, would be to undermine China's hold on Tibet through subversion, covert action, and infiltration.

There is little doubt ethnic Tibetans, who are now only half of Tibet's total population, would welcome liberation from their Chinese "liberators," and joyously receive home the exiled Dalai Lama. But after the long, bloody guerrilla war in the 1960s against Chinese rule, Tibetans see no possibility of mounting a successful revolt. The Tibetan resistance has been abandoned by the United States, and denied bases and sanctuary by India and Nepal. Without outside aid, a rebellion against China's huge occupation forces would fail almost from the start.

But as tensions continue to grow between India and China, India might be tempted to mount a campaign of destabilization against Tibet, particularly if China increases its so far modest efforts to stir up unrest in India's eastern hill states, or if China provides aid to the Kashmiri rebels. The large Tibetan exile community in northern India provides an excellent pool of manpower from which to form guerrilla bands, and the means through which to organize an underground movement inside Tibet. India's intelligence service, RAW, has for the past three decades maintained top-secret special military units composed of Tibetan exiles whose mission is to act as scouts and commandos in the event of war with China, or to form the nucleus of a Tibetan liberation army that would spearhead an Indian invasion of Tibet.

China also remains sensitive to the dangerous possibility that India and the United States might cooperate to undermine its hold on Tibet. Beijing has watched uneasily as American investment has flowed into India, and particularly into its high-tech sector.

The 2006 U.S.-Indian strategic agreement that would provide Delhi with American nuclear fuel and technology, and new, advanced weapons systems, was greeted with considerable alarm in Beijing and held up as clear evidence of India's long-term hostile intentions.

Gradual deterioration of uneasy relations between Washington and Beijing, a new crisis over Taiwan, or a growing conviction in U.S. foreign and military policy circles that China constitutes a strategic threat to U.S. interests, or to North America, could put the two superpowers on a collision course. In recent years, the United States has clearly been building up India as a strategic counterweight to China, particularly as relations between Washington and Beijing soured and tensions rose over Taiwan. In fact, the United States has already aided India in its development of its nuclear arsenal and missile systems by winking at Delhi's acquisition of U.S. computer and nuclear technology. Israel has also played an important role in channeling U.S. military and nuclear technology to India as part of the growing strategic alliance between the two nations. Both developments have caused deep alarm in Beijing.

Washington and Delhi understand that the quickest, most effective way to throw China onto the strategic defensive is by stirring up resistance in Tibet. All of China's rulers have been preoccupied by the threat of regionalism and secession movements. As was the case in Imperial Russia, and later the Soviet Union, the greatest part of Beijing's energies are devoted inwardly to simply holding together and governing its huge, sprawling nation. Throughout Chinese history, regional independence movements and warlordism have broken out whenever the centre has grown weak, through decay or factional in-fighting.

At the very heart of these strategic concerns lies China's deep, historic fear of being weakened, then dismembered by hostile outside powers. Memories are still vivid of the nineteenth century and the early twentieth century, when the Western imperial powers Russia and Japan fell like rapacious wolves on the decaying Manchu Empire and tore away its vulnerable border regions. In the current Chinese view, if Tibet is somehow detached from China, Sinkiang will follow, then Hainan, Inner Mongolia, possibly even Manchuria. China's south, traditionally resistant to domination by the Mandarin-speaking north, is already being tugged away from Beijing's orbit by powerful financial interests from Singapore and other overseas Chinese. Szechuan is as populous as Germany and France combined, and could easily stand alone as an independent, prosperous nation. Russia has never given up its ambition to dominate resource-rich Manchuria. A declaration of independence by Taiwan could begin the unravelling of united China.

The most recent example of such lurking centrifugal forces occurred during the Great Cultural Revolution, which began in the fall of 1965. Mao's internal revolution plunged China into anarchy and chaos as civil war raged between a dizzying assortment of political, military, and regional factions. China came very close to national dissolution at the very time when the Soviet Union was considering a pre-emptive invasion of northern China and, very likely, Sinkiang. It took a military coup, followed by intervention of the PLA, to end the national madness unleashed by the Cultural Revolution, crush the notorious Gang of Four, and reunify badly fractured China under the moderate regime of Deng Xiaoping.

As the Communist Party never tires of warning Chinese, the collapse of the ruling Chinese Communist Party, followed by strife between warring factions in Beijing, could gravely weaken the centre, unleashing regional forces and so destabilizing the nation. China's current leadership is convinced that America's grand strategy in the western Pacific is to gradually undermine the Communist Party's hold on power, while keeping China isolated and surrounded by a coalition of hostile neighbours. Washington is employing the human rights issue, Beijing believes, as its main tool to undermine the regime. At the same time, the United States continues to use South Korea, Japan, Taiwan, Singapore, Thailand, and now, it is feared, India, as a great outer wall to surround and contain China, or even to threaten China's vulnerable peripheral regions. The U.S. Seventh Fleet continues to patrol off China's long coast, providing the final link in the chain of hostile forces surrounding China.

•••

I left my hotel in Lhasa at 4 a.m. for the long drive to the airport. An hour later, the first rays of the rising sun edged the mountains around us with borders of gold and red. I once again marvelled at the flatness of Tibet's central plains, juxtaposed against distant walls of snow-capped mountains. We halted briefly in front of a Buddhist "stupa," or shrine, where I said a brief, silent prayer for the people of Tibet.

My head pulsed with pain. I sat in the cold, barren departure lounge, desperately clutching my ticket, seized by waves of panic. I might be stuck there for hours. The flight might be cancelled or wildly overbooked—normal occurrences in China. One never knows in Third World nations when dignitaries will commandeer a scheduled flight or appropriate seats, leaving unfortunate ordinary travellers marooned, sometimes for days. I knew time was running out: I would likely become comatose soon if I did not get down to a lower altitude.

When, after what seemed an eternity of anguish, boarding was finally announced, an unruly mob of passengers stormed the plane. I staggered onto the tarmac, reeling and dizzy, then painfully struggled up the stairs into the long Boeing 757. As I prepared to sit in my seat, I noticed it held a pool of thick, malodorous vomit from a previous passenger. I looked about for another place: there was none. A vicious little Chinese stewardess, clearly a former Red Guards officer, told me to get off the plane if I did not like my assigned seat. Gritting my teeth, and trying to keep my stomach calm, I sat down in the yellow muck and buckled up.

Once again, the dawn view of Tibet's soaring mountains was overwhelmingly beautiful. Sitting in the pool of vomit while beholding one of this earth's most sublime panoramas seemed a curiously apt metaphor for my journey to the roof of the world.

Two and a half hours later we arrived at the welcome lower altitude of Chengdu. The next day, I flew to Hong Kong. My head had stopped aching and I could again breathe normally. However, for the next seven months, I suffered a nasty series of mysterious upper respiratory disorders, alternately misdiagnosed as bronchitis, allergies, or "airway disease," that I was later to learn were caused by the lingering effects of altitude sickness.

A medical specialist warned that, having once been stricken by severe altitude sickness, I would be highly susceptible to recurrences if I again went above 1,829 metres (6,000 feet). To my dismay, I was later to learn he was correct. A passionate lover of mountains, I was henceforth doomed to the lowlands. I would see no more wars at the top of the world.

It was unlikely I would ever return—Tibet was lost to me, and I mourned. But how much worse it must be for Tibetans, who have lost their homeland; they are exiles, perhaps forever, victims of a remorseless modern industrial world they wanted no part of, yet could not, in the end, escape.

21
THE FATE OF ASIA

Cuina's hold on Tibet is total and, at least for the present, unquestioned. But the real question for Tibetans, Indians, and, indeed, most Asians, is who will end up in power in Beijing. In the first quarter of the twenty-first century, the fate of a full third of the globe's population will be determined, or at least significantly influenced by political, economic, and military developments in the People's Republic of China.

The China we see today is clearly a nation and society in transition, but a transition to what? The answer remains unclear, just as it does in post-Communist Russia. Two "old" Chinas have been left behind in the nation's headlong plunge into Asian capitalism: traditional Confucian China, often described as more a civilization than a nation-state; and Mao's tyrannical Communist China, one of history's more bizarre and disastrous experiments in social engineering.

When future historians look back on our times, they may well conclude that the greatest Chinese revolutionary leader of the twentieth century was not Sun Yat-sen or Mao Tse-tung, but the diminutive, underestimated Deng Xiaoping.

Deng's revolution, which began soon after Mao's death in 1976, and is still under way, was not at first appreciated by the West because it was bloodless, low-key, and gradual. There were no mobs of rampaging demonstrators, no factions fighting in the streets, no political executions or mass movements of people. Aside from the trial and jailing of the widely detested Gang of Four, to outsiders Deng's revolution appeared boring, even humdrum.

But of course, it was anything but that. The brilliant Deng pursued the deconstruction of the Communist system and its moribund ideology with exquisite subtlety, consummate skill, and ruthless determination. Who was better placed to destroy communism in all but name than a communist titan and veteran of Mao's revolution?

In only a decade, Deng transformed China from a totalitarian into an authoritarian state, reducing by an entire order of magnitude government and party control. Great revolutionary Deng also released the deep materialism and commercialism of the mainland Chinese that had been long pent up beneath a veneer of Maoist altruism and dedication to the state. The slogan "Get rich quick" quickly replaced "the East is Red." If fifty-five million offshore Chinese could constitute the world's sixth richest economy, imagine, say Deng's supporters, what 1.1 billion mainlanders could do when freed from the fetters of socialism.

Soon after Deng Xiaoping consolidated power in 1977–78, he made a strategic decision to concentrate the force of his new revolution on building China's economic base and modernizing his nation as quickly as possible. Deng correctly judged that in the modern world, economic and industrial power was the necessary prerequisite to development of military strength and great power status. China "must grow wealthy and strong," Deng exhorted, repeating a slogan used by Japan's Meiji modernizers in the late nineteenth century.

During Mao's rule, China had relied on the vast numbers of its armed forces and regional defense units to produce a veritable nation at arms. China's 4.3-million-man armed forces were configured, during the period spanning the 1960–80s, first to prevent the invasion of China by Taiwan, likely backed by the United States, and then, as relations with the Soviet Union steadily worsened, to be able to resist a massive Soviet invasion of Northern China. The deficiency of the People's Liberation Army in all classes of modern weaponry was to be compensated for by a huge field army of 175 divisions, supported by a lightly armed but enormous 20-million-man militia, designed to defend every city, town, and factory. A small nuclear force would assure China had at least a minimal strategic deterrent capability.

China's brief but bloody 1979 border war with Vietnam came as a nasty shock to the new Chinese leadership. Deng became convinced the U.S.S.R. was attempting to strategically encircle China, using Vietnam to threaten its southern flank. The ill-defined Vietnamese-Chinese border; Hanoi's intervention in Cambodia and defeat of Beijing's ally, the Khmer Rouge; the expulsion by Vietnam of large numbers of ethnic Chinese; and a growing territorial dispute over the Spratly Islands in the South China Sea, all served as *casus belli*. China decided to "teach Vietnam a lesson," as it had taught India one in 1962.

In February 1979, China attacked northern North Vietnam with one hundred thousand soldiers. The combat-hardened Vietnamese army defended its border positions with skill and tenacity. Chinese forces soon became bogged down, and suffered significant problems of command and control, logistics, and tactical maneuver. In some places, Chinese troops were routed by the better-armed, more mobile Vietnamese. After a month of inconclusive fighting, China declared a ceasefire and withdrew its troops to the antebellum border. China had done precisely the same thing at the end of the 1962 border war with India. The difference, of course, was that in 1962 China was victorious, while in 1979 its army had been fought to a humiliating standstill by the hated Vietnamese, whom the Chinese considered a barbarian people.

Official Chinese losses were twenty-six thousand killed and thirty-seven thousand wounded; Vietnamese losses were roughly equal. These were high numbers of casualties for a war that lasted only one month. Unofficial reports, however, put Chinese casualties at double that figure. PLA troops, attacking in poorly coordinated and insufficiently supported human wave assaults, were mowed down by the entrenched Vietnamese. This bloody reversal made it clear that China badly needed to modernize its armed forces, and their tactics, logistics and equipment.

To achieve this goal, Deng almost immediately embarked on a highly successful diplomatic campaign to improve relations with Moscow and Washington. China could not wage a two-front war: it would have to either rearm or modernize its economy. It could not afford to do both. Deng wisely chose to divert funds from the powerful PLA into rapid economic development, and to foster creation of a rudimentary free market. The result was stunning double-digit growth that transformed China in fifteen years from a pauper nation into a semi-developed industrial power, in which per capita gross domestic product soared from around $400 to $3,000. Deng had accomplished what Mao had not: a true Great Leap Forward.

Predictions in the early 1990s that China's ebullient economy would become the world's largest by 2010 now seem overly optimistic. By the late 1990s, China's growth had slowed, though it still remained robust. China was faced by rising unemployment, said to number two hundred million people, industrial over-capacity, and growing financial strains. The bold decision by Deng's successor, Jiang Zemin, to completely desocialize the economy by privatizing money-losing government-owned industries, which still employed the majority of Chinese workers, was a perilous gamble whose outcome remains uncertain. So, too, is China's ability to withstand the ongoing aftershocks of the Asian financial earthquake. China's finances are shaky at best, and barely holding up under the multiple strains of modernization, privatization, a shaky banking system, and lack of capital. Still, China's collective leadership shows no sign of slowing what is by all measures one of modern history's most daring and heroic economic and social adventures.

Deng also made the profoundly important strategic decision to liberalize China's economy before tampering with its authoritarian political structure. In his view, Mikhail Gorbachev and his band of reformers had made a catastrophic error by liberalizing Soviet politics without first freeing and modernizing the economy. As the well-meaning Gorbachev was later to ruefully admit, Russians judged the success of his revolution not by the freedoms it brought, but ultimately by the lack of consumer goods and the nation's excruciating economic sickness and social dislocations.

China was determined to avoid Gorbachev's errors, which caused the fall of the Communist Party from power, the collapse of the Soviet empire, grave military weakness, social unrest, and economic penury that ended up transforming once-mighty Russia into a replica of the dying Ottoman Empire, the new Sick Man of Europe. China's economy was like a runaway locomotive. Without a firm hand on the controls of power, China's leadership concluded, their nation would derail and crash like the wrecked Soviet Union. In fact, after the Tiannmen uprising, Deng told Singapore's prime minister, Lee Kuan Yew, "If two hundred thousand students have to be shot, shoot them, because the alternative is China in chaos for another one hundred years." Lee, who understood China better than most Asian leaders, believed China needed another thirty to fifty years before it was ready for democracy.

Deng's grand strategy to steadily build China's economic power required amicable relations with the United States, Asia, and Russia to allow China to develop its main engine of growth—export industries—and reduce defense spending. Once China had attained economic strength, according to Deng's plan, it would be in a position to begin developing military capability commensurate with its new status as a world superpower. However, China would not likely reach this stage until 2010 at the earliest, and, if the economy slowed down, perhaps even later.

The outside world watched China's economic miracle with a combination of awe, lust, and fear. China offered an enormous market for Western and Asian goods of all sorts. But it also presented a new commercial rival, a fact seized upon by Western unions that feared the loss of jobs at home to cheaper Chinese imports. Whereas few Westerners had cared about human rights in China during the era of Mao—or, indeed, before the Communists—a great hue and cry erupted in the West over this issue.

Many Western intellectuals, socialists, and left-wing opinion-makers seemed unable to forgive Deng and his successors for undoing Mao's Communist system, which in the past they had so often lauded as "progressive" and "humane." It was rather as if Che Guevara had gone to work for General Motors. Western leftists and liberals, feeling deeply betrayed, took their wrath out on China by making the Tiananmen Square uprising and the repression of Tibet into international *causes célèbres*, and demanding that trade sanctions be imposed on Beijing over its poor record on human rights.

China's leadership repeatedly insisted it had no territorial designs or major disputes with China's neighbours, save, of course, the long-running problem of "renegade" Taiwan. Over that problem, China alternated between threats, bluster, and offers of cooperation. There was also the still simmering territorial dispute over the Spratly Islands and their surrounding waters, beneath which oil was believed to lie. In fact, China even went so far as to resolve, through diplomacy, the single most dangerous territorial question, its disputed borders along the Amur and Ussuri Rivers with Russia, which had almost led to full-scale war with the Soviet Union in the 1960s. Two other less important Chinese territorial claims, on Kyrgyzstan and Tajikistan, were barely mentioned.

In spite of China's peace offensive, America's foreign-policy and military establishment still harboured deep doubts of Beijing's sincerity. Many conservatives were convinced a future military confrontation between the two great Pacific powers was inevitable. The relentless growth of China's power clearly threatened America's ability to project strategic influence onto the north Asian mainland, and it was clear that it would inevitably challenge the long, unquestioned U.S. domination of the western Pacific and its tributary seas. The loss of the vital U.S. naval base at Subic Bay in the Philippines was another major blow to U.S. strategic power. The Pacific would no longer be an American lake.

The growth of anti-Chinese feeling among American conservatives and liberals rekindled fears in Beijing that the United States was bent on a long-term strategy to destabilize China, keep it militarily weak, and contain China through a process of strategic encirclement. America's policy of studied ambiguity over Taiwan and the vociferous independence movement on the island raised constant alarms in Beijing. In mid-1999, the enormous furor in the United States over the alleged theft by Chinese intelligence of the crown jewels of American nuclear weapons technology, and the accidental bombing of the Chinese embassy in Belgrade by U.S. warplanes further poisoned already worsening relations.

At the same time, U.S. military planners became convinced China was developing the capacity to challenge the Seventh Fleet by acquiring long-range aircraft, new submarines, and surface warships armed with powerful, Mach 2 SS-N-22 anti-ship missiles capable of sinking aircraft carriers. The sudden emergence of India as a powerful nuclear-armed regional rival to China sharply increased Beijing's sense of being surrounded and threatened. So, too, did Japan's cautious attempts to begin flexing its considerable military muscle by patrolling beyond the Sea of Japan, taking a more active role in providing logistical support to U.S. forces in South Korea, and sending Japanese troops on UN missions. Beijing sought to keep Japan on the psychological defensive by issuing loud warnings against the rebirth of "Japanese militarism."

China's future in the first two decades of the twenty-first century still remained uncertain. "Steady as you go" seemed the national motto, along with Deng's famous admonition to get rich quickly. But rapid economic liberalization and development of modern communications would eventually diminish the political power and pervasive control mechanisms of the Chinese Communist Party. Once the party's iron grip on every aspect of people's lives was loosened, or even broken, it might be swept away by a flood of newfound pluralism. China had already permitted democratic elections at the rural village level in the late 1990s; this process was judged successful and might serve as a model in the future for nationwide free elections.

The Chinese Communist Party was also suffering from the same generational problems that led to the downfall of its sister parties in the U.S.S.R. and Eastern Europe. Chinese revere age more than any other people, but it was also evident that the new generation of young, boisterous, capitalist Chinese had almost nothing in common with the elderly Communist grandees who still held the reins of power in their arthritic hands.

At some point within the first decade of the twenty-first century, when Mao, Deng, and the Long March have become remote historical memories, a generational revolution is likely to occur in China that will consign its wizened party apparatchiks to the dustbin of history. The new generation of leadership may not, as Westerners earnestly hope, be young democrats. The forces of Western-style democracy in China are weak and small in number. China, it must be recalled, has never enjoyed anything even approaching democracy during its five thousand years of history. The nature of Chinese society, philosophy, government, and experience is resolutely authoritarian: ideally, the Chinese prefer a powerful ruler whose actions are somewhat circumscribed by custom, the advice of a consultative elite, and the exercise of sound judgement and wisdom.

While a flowering of Western-style democracy in China cannot be excluded, it is much more likely that China will follow the successful example of authoritarian Singapore. Nearly every Chinese citizen, no matter how lowly, knows the old adage that, whenever the government is weak the nation begins to fray at the edges and secessionist forces rise.

The 1920s and 1930s era of civil war, regionalism, and warlordism is a stark reminder of how quickly China can splinter if not ruled by an iron hand. Few non-Chinese comprehend the sharp linguistic differences in China, a nation with at least ten different languages beside the dominant tongue, Mandarin. Or the regional and ethnic differences between the Mandarin-speaking north and the Cantonese-speaking south.

To outsiders, China may look monolithic, but beneath its smooth surface, deep fissures exist that could quickly open if the central government weakens. The forces of political devolution currently sweeping the globe, weakening the power and raison d'etre of highly centralized governments, will eventually smite China, a nation that has been fragmented as often as not during its long history. This natural political development could be accelerated by the future appearance of a weak democratic or pluralistic government in Beijing—a latter-day version, for example, of the Kerensky regime in post-Czarist Russia—that would lack the power or stomach to keep China together.

The inherent fragility of the Chinese state will tend to produce popular pressure for regimes capable of maintaining national unity and order. Just as hyperinflation during the Weimar Republic seared the memories of all Germans, engendering an intense national aversion to debt or even the slightest sign of inflation, an aversion that persists to our day, so China's bitter experiences during the nineteenth and twentieth centuries—the Opium Wars; colonial rapine and national humiliation; civil war; the somber era of warlords, corruption, and banditry—have created a psychological demand for strong, even heavy-handed governments that put national power and cohesion before human rights and democratic politics.

As far as the West is concerned, its Asian interests may be better served by an authoritarian regime in Beijing—like the current one—than by the kind of half-formed, strife-ridden, mutant democracy that we saw in Russia during the Yeltsin era, in which no one is really in charge, and where various rival factions wage tribal warfare to plunder the nation's wealth. China could easily go the way of post-Communist Russia, but with an even greater danger of regionalism and secession.

A splintering China could tempt Russia to seize Manchuria and Sinkiang (Xinjiang), Vietnam to grab border regions in Yunnan and Guangzhou, and, of course, India to seize Tibet and the South Xinjiang-Aksai Chin region. In short, China has good reason to fear a return to the nineteenth century, when the Celestial Empire was torn apart by foreign powers.

So China is more likely to continue under authoritarian government than to veer toward some form of pluralistic system. In spite of this tendency, the old days of totalitarian thought control in China are fast waning. The coming decades are likely to bring an explosion of freer expression, criticism, and even a certain amount of government-tolerated dissent. China will undergo fierce social pressures caused by the dismantling of state-owned industry, which will result in growing unemployment, dislocation of tens of millions of workers, and growing demands for increasingly scarce resources. Some dissent will have to be tolerated as a safety valve. Whatever form China's future governments assume, they will all end up riding on the back of an economic and political tiger.

How, then, will this ongoing revolution affect China's policies toward its neighbours and the other superpowers?

As presently constituted, China appears to have no major outstanding territorial claims or ambitions save reunification with Taiwan, the relatively minor though still potentially dangerous question of the Spratly Islands, and the dangerous issue of the still disputed border with India in the Karakorams and Himalayas. In effect, China reached the extent of its territorial ambitions in the 1950s when it annexed Tibet and Aksai Chin.

But China's sense of borders has historically been rather fuzzy, particularly in the remote, little-known western regions of Sinkiang and Tibet. China's emperors were content for thousands of years to exercise domination, rather than outright rule, over the vast lands beyond the ethnic Han heartland of central and coastal China. So long as the states around China's distant, vaguely defined borders paid homage and tribute to the emperor, they were left pretty much to their own devices. The many peoples beyond China's frontiers were regarded as irksome barbarians to be kept as far as possible from the imperial realm. When these barbarians failed to deliver their annual tribute, or had the audacity to raid the edges of the Han heartland, the emperors would dispatch large armies to punish the miscreants. These punitive expeditions almost always withdrew after finishing their work, leaving behind occasional garrisons to watch the troublesome nomads and hill peoples on the imperial borders. China's thousand-year relations with Tibet followed this pattern of benign neglect and occasional demonstrations of control—at least until 1950.

It is important to understand this historical policy of hard inner borders and soft outer borders, because China's modern leadership has acted in much the same manner as the emperors of centuries past. Mao sent five hundred thousand "volunteers" to Korea when he feared the United States might defeat his North Korean satraps, or even threaten Manchuria. Once the threat had passed, the expeditionary armies were withdrawn from the Korean Peninsula.

During the Vietnam War, China dispatched 320,000 troops to aid its Vietnamese allies in their war against the United States. In 1962, Mao sent eighty thousand soldiers to drive the Indian Army from Ladakh and the eastern Himalayas. After routing the Indians, and "teaching India a lesson," the Chinese troops abruptly withdrew. In 1979 a Chinese expeditionary force punished North Vietnam for "disobedience," then withdrew. Chinese naval forces were similarly dispatched in the late 1970s to briefly chastise Vietnamese and Filipino forces claiming the Spratly Islands.

China's modern leaders, like the emperors, expect their neighbours to accept Beijing's paramount role in Asia and show proper deference to China's will. Until India's emergence as a nascent world power, the only Asian nation that had defied the will of Beijing was Japan, a nation and people whom China regarded with a combination of disdain, hatred, and fear. China's inimical relations with Japan and frequent outbursts against Tokyo may be viewed as similar to the fury the United States shows toward recalcitrant Arab nations—branded by Washington as "rogue states"—who defy the Pax Americana in the Mideast. China, too, has its own Pax Sinica in Asia and intends to enforce its great-power aspirations in the region.

China appears intent on enforcing its geopolitical will over eastern Asia in the traditional manner for the next two decades at least. Korea, whether united or divided, is expected to show deference to Beijing and refrain from serving as a base for the United States or Japan to threaten Manchuria. Both Koreas have clearly accepted this role. Troublesome Vietnam has yet to be brought to heel, but will likely become the focus of Chinese pressure. The smaller "dragon" states of South Asia know the rules in dealing with Beijing, and have no choice but to comply.

As previously described, China is making a significant effort to extend its influence into mineral-rich Burma, both for economic reasons and, even more important, to create a buffer between its sphere of influence in Indochina and the growing power of India. China is also deeply concerned by what it views as India's long-term designs on Tibet, and the instability of Sinkiang. After Taiwan, the most probable areas of future Chinese military operations are against Korea, Vietnam, and against India in Burma and Tibet.

China has also made clear it considers the waters of the South China Sea to be wholly within its geopolitical sphere of influence, a claim that is challenged by the United States and its Asian allies. A naval confrontation in these contested waters or in the Taiwan Strait is possible within the next decade between the U.S. Seventh Fleet and the rapidly enlarging Chinese Navy.

The steady growth of China's geopolitical power must inevitably bring it into contest in eastern Asia with that of the United States, and to a lesser degree with Japan. But such regional rivalry does not necessarily mean global strategic conflict between the United States and China, as many anti-Chinese alarmists in America have been claiming. Until recently, China has had only a small number of ICBMs with a range of 13,000 kilometres (8,000 miles) that are capable of reaching the continental United States, and twelve unreliable CSS-N-3 missiles aboard China's sole nuclear missile submarine, which has experienced severe technical difficulties and may not be seaworthy. The rest of China's nuclear arsenal consists of about one hundred medium-range missiles and some 150 gravity nuclear weapons delivered by obsolete H-6 bombers.

This is not a force that could even begin to pose a threat to the United States. China is, however, working on a new generation of mobile, solid-fuelled missiles, notably the 8,000-kilometre (5,000-mile) three-stage DF-31 equipped with multiple independently targeted vehicles re-entry warheads (MIRVS) based on technology allegedly purloined from the United States.

These modern ICBMS will have the capability to strike much of the United States. Their ability to be transported by trucks or by rail means greatly increased survivability. U.S. intelligence estimated that the DF-31 would be deployed in small numbers by the year 2002 or 2003. Still, China is years away from possessing significant nuclear-war-fighting potential. Though theft of U.S. MIRV technology and plans for the miniaturized W-88 nuclear warhead have greatly aided and accelerated China's strategic weapons programs, there seems little doubt China would have eventually developed such systems on its own.

However, the new antiballistic missile initiative announced by President Bush in late 2001, when deployed will pose a distinct threat to China's limited ICBM arsenal. China is likely to increase sharply the number of ICBMS it has and place MIRV warheads on them.

China's medium-range nuclear arsenal, notably the new 3,000-kilometre (1,864-mile) DF-21 and growing numbers of conventionally armed tactical missiles, does pose a growing threat to China's neighbours, such as Vietnam, South Korea, Taiwan, and Russia, as well as a major danger to the small island nations of Japan and Taiwan. Both are extremely vulnerable to nuclear blackmail, bombardment by conventional missiles, and maritime blockade. Japan, Taiwan, and South Korea are all considering adopting a U.S. theatre anti-missile defense system.

India has made clear it considers itself particularly menaced by China's missile force, and claims it is deploying the 2,500-kilometre- (1,554-mile-) range Agni-II and -III medium-range ballistic missiles to counter the growing Chinese threat. In turn, India's Agni-series missiles, which can strike all of China's most important cities and industrial centres, have provoked deep concern in Beijing, and sparked an arms race between the two Asian powers. Technologically, the Indian-made Agni-III appears superior to Chinese missiles in terms of accuracy, reliability, speed of launch, and mobility. Both India and China have by now mastered the art of miniaturizing nuclear warheads, China thanks to espionage, and India thanks to covert assistance over many years from Israel, which itself purloined U.S. nuclear technology and materiel.

China's slow but steady development of its conventional power is of far less concern to the United States, though a source of concern in Asia. China's somewhat numerically reduced army has great defensive power, but its lack of sufficient armour, transport, self-propelled artillery, and modern communications severely limits its ability to move or manoeuvre. The Chinese air force has only forty-six modern SU-27s and is developing the F-10 fighter, the latter based on U.S. technology sold to China by Israel, which had originally been destined for the Lavi fighter program. However, China has at least a dozen other tactical fighter projects under development, and is trying to acquire airborne early warning aircraft similar to the U.S. AWAC system. Growing Russian technical assistance is playing an important role in modernizing China's air force.

In short, China's armed forces may be huge in numbers, but they remain obsolescent, immobile, and without the precision arms and instant communications that make modern fighting forces increasingly lethal. China's ground forces are capable of threatening Taiwan, Russia's Pacific region, northern Vietnam, Indochina, and, most important, India's northern and eastern borders. But beyond these places, China has no real strategic clout or reach, and cannot be expected to have any until well into the twenty-first century.

Attempts by American conservatives to paint China as a second Soviet Union are overblown. China lacks the strategic or conventional military power of the old Soviet Union, and is only a force to be reckoned with in its immediate neighbourhood. In fact, unlike the Soviets, with their theory of internationalist duty, China has never shown much interest in events beyond those in its strategic backyard. But there, China expects and demands unquestioned obedience.

It seems inevitable that as China's economic, military, and political power grows, that of the United States—hitherto Asia's greatest power—must decline. A militarily weak China allowed the United States to dominate the Sea of Japan and South China Sea, and when necessary to project power on the Asian mainland. The U.S. Navy will no longer enjoy this freedom of movement or action after China has managed to develop its military capabilities.

Shrinking U.S. defense budgets and heavy strain on inadequate military forces are compelling Washington to re-evaluate its traditional policy of forward deployment in the Pacific. U.S. military forces have reached a breaking point: though one-third smaller than they were at the end of the Cold War, they are being tasked with almost 50 per cent more overseas operations, producing troop exhaustion, falling morale, and deterioration of equipment. The long, sterile conflict with Iraq, followed by the war against Serbia, severely depleted U.S. military capability and sustainability. Washington's efforts to hector Japan into assuming more responsibility for Asian security—meaning maintenance of the status quo—have repeatedly failed.

As U.S. power in Asia recedes, that of China must advance apace. China's neighbours have already recognized this fact and are shaping their policies accordingly. American decision-makers have yet to come to the realization that in Asia their power and authority will no longer be absolute: Washington will have to begin learning to be more accommodating in its relations with China, and more accepting of the fact that Beijing will increasingly make its will felt in Asia. In other words, the United States must eventually accept that China has a legitimate, recognized sphere of influence in eastern Asia.

Old powers always find it difficult to adjust to dealing with arriviste powers; the process is often marked by tension and the danger of open conflict, as in the emergence of Germany at the end of the nineteenth century, and Japan a few decades later. This is a perilous time that demands the highest diplomatic skills.

Even so, aside from Taiwan and the South China Sea's resources, there are no other major disputes that are likely to put Beijing and Washington on a collision course. Those who advocate the containment of China must face the fact that China has always more or less contained itself. In China's view, the United States and Russia are no longer its primary strategic threat: this role is now occupied by India. Nor do China and the United States share any major geopolitical or historical disputes, such as are found in the Mideast or Balkans. Even the most ardent American Sinophobes find it difficult to cite specific examples of how China threatens U.S. security or international interests. In fact, China and the United States have much more in common than most great powers: growing trade and technological exchange, a history of American concern for China and widespread respect for its splendid culture, and a mutual degree of personal comfort and ease that neither finds with other nations, such as Japan or Russia.

The same, however, cannot be said for China's immediate neighbours, Japan, Russia, and India. The balance and nature of relations between Japan and China as yet remain to be decided: will Japan be a junior partner to China and accept Beijing's strategic diktat in Asia? Will a more muscular and self-assertive Japan eventually challenge China for regional leadership? Or will Japan remain, like the Great Britain of Asia, sheltered under America's security umbrella, unwilling and unable to intervene in the region's strategic affairs?

China's future relations with Russia promise to be more contentious. Russians and Chinese harbour deep racial hatred for one another, and share a legacy of historical animosity and fear. When I asked senior officers of Chinese military intelligence in the mid-1980s how long it would take the People's Liberation Army to conquer the Soviet Union's Pacific provinces, their terse reply was "Two weeks." Most Russian military planners are convinced that one day China will either attack their vulnerable far east, which has only twenty-five million people, or swamp the resource-rich region with hordes of Chinese settlers.

The Chinese, for their part, have long feared a Russian attack on industrial Manchuria. It is worth noting that Russo-Japanese rivalry over the riches of Manchuria sparked the twentieth century's first significant conflict, the 1904 Russo-Japanese War. Manchuria could well figure in a future conflict of the twenty-first century.

This Asian strategic *tour d'horizon* brings us back to India, which today is the only Asian power that appears determined to actively contest China's self-appointed domination of the region. India and China are on a geopolitical collision course in the Himalayas, in strategic Burma, and over the waters of the eastern end of the Indian Ocean. These two Asian giants now regard one another as the primary strategic and commercial threat; they have embarked on a nuclear arms race and are preparing their ground forces to fight in the Himalayas. Each sees itself as the rightful master of Asia.

If China's history is any guide to its future actions, whatever leadership emerges in Beijing over the next decade—whether younger, "reformed" Communists of the East European mode, democrats, a military junta, or an authoritarian clique—they may be tempted, as Mao was in 1962, to "teach a lesson" to increasingly self-assertive India. The Indians have made plain they will not be routed a second time, and intend to return any Chinese "lesson" in kind.

According to a 1997 U.S. Defense Department study, cited by the former CIA director James Woolsey, China will continue to build its military power "to the point where it can engage and defeat any potential enemy" in East Asia, and it is developing the capability to fight short-duration, high-intensity wars in the region. In other words, to teach more lessons.

The CIA study goes on to make a fascinating and disturbing point: when India and China reach South Korea's current level of per capita energy use, perhaps within the next decade, their combined demand for oil will amount to 120 million barrels daily. At present, the entire globe consumes 60 to 70 millions barrels of oil each day.

To meet such huge demands, India may be drawn to Iran and the Gulf, while China may look south to Indonesia, Indochina, and the South China Sea. Both superpowers will compete to dominate the vast but so far unexploited oil and gas reserves of unstable Central Asia, at a time when Russia will be seeking to reassert its influence over the former Soviet republics of its "near abroad."

Indian strategists are already speaking of the need for Delhi to "assure future sources of Mideast oil" and to dominate the sea lanes over which the oil must travel. Australia protested to Delhi over increasing Indian naval activity in the eastern Indian Ocean as long as a decade ago. Opening of a new Indian naval base in the Andaman islands at Port Blair signals that Delhi also has its eyes on Indonesia and Malaysia.

The lines of a future major conflict in Asia are thus being clearly drawn. Irresistible geopolitical forces are at work, as Asia's two continental giants, India and China, slowly and relentlessly grind against one another like the massive tectonic plates of eons past, whose mighty collision shook the globe and threw up the Himalayas.

22
WAR WITHOUT END

The arrival of the second millennium in 2000 did not inflict the plagues and disasters on the world that religious and technological Cassandras had predicted. The mighty North American economy continued to roll on, stock markets soared, and Pax Americana maintained order around the globe. Those benighted places where the United States failed to impose its writ—South Asia, the Mideast, and Africa—were simply ignored.

But in the ensuing year, it seemed as if the prophetic Four Horsemen of the Apocalypse had been loosed upon mankind. Perhaps those who insisted that the millennium really began at the end of 2001—and not 2000—were correct. First the United States, then the international economy, slid into a deep recession, producing fears that the global financial system might break down or even collapse in a terrifying repeat of the worldwide depression of the 1930s.

Then came the attacks of September 11 against New York and Washington, an event so awesome, terrifying, and devastating that it seemed almost to reverse the spin of the globe. A new "Mad Mullah" in a cave in Afghanistan had declared jihad against the mighty United States and plunged South Asia into a new round of crises and war.

The refusal of Afghanistan's medieval Taliban regime to disavow Osama bin Laden presented President George Bush with a welcome target for America's wrath. The Pentagon immediately implemented contingency plans for invading Afghanistan. These plans had been updated in 2001 after America's flirtation with the Taliban had failed, and the Kabul regime granted the strategic pipeline route to Central Asia to an Argentine firm, shutting the United States out of the gold rush to exploit the resource riches of the Caspian Basin.

In a remarkable display of U.S. military, logistic, and diplomatic power, Washington quickly massed powerful strike forces around Afghanistan, activated a division-sized intervention force, and arm-twisted most Muslim states into cooperating with what President Bush, in an unfortunate Freudian slip, called America's "crusade against terrorism."

The Bush administration's campaign to kill or capture Osama bin Laden, overthrow the Taliban, and replace it with a more amenable regime required that Pakistan, the Taliban's long-time supporter, be brought on side. The White House gave President Pervez Musharraf a "for us or against us" ultimatum. If Pakistan did not sever ties with the Taliban and aid the impending U.S. campaign in Afghanistan, Washington threatened to destroy Pakistan. Islamabad's non-cooperation would bring immediate foreclosure on its $131-billion foreign debt by the United States, Japan, and the U.S.-controlled International Monetary Fund and World Bank. A total trade embargo would be imposed on Pakistan. These measures would have caused Pakistan's feeble economy to collapse.

Even more ominous, Washington hinted that India's armed forces might "not be restrained" if they sought to attack Pakistan. The United States also warned Islamabad that India might dominate post-Taliban Kabul. The besieged Musharraf, bereft of allies and money and unable to acquire arms, was compelled to bow to America's diktat in spite of deep unpopularity for his actions with his own armed forces and the Pakistani public.

The United States also forced Musharraf to fire three of his top generals and closest allies, including Lieutenant General Aziz Khan and ISI director Lieutenant General Mahmoud Ahmed. These officers, among the most capable in Pakistan's armed forces, had put Musharraf in power after their coup against the corrupt and inept former prime minister, Nawaz Sharif. Israeli and Indian intelligence had warned Washington that the three generals were Islamists who favoured the Taliban.

So Pakistan, which had sharply rebuked the United States for abandoning its mujahedin allies in Afghanistan at the end of 1989, did precisely the same thing with its Taliban allies in 2001. Overnight, Pakistan became the enemy of Osama bin Laden and the Taliban, allowing the United States to base military forces on its territory and, equally important, to totally isolate the Taliban by shutting its border with Afghanistan. ISI officers helped the United States hunt bin Laden and played a key role in bribing Pushtun tribal chiefs to abandon the Taliban.

General Musharraf had saved Pakistan from being "ended" by the United States—to use the bellicose terminology of Pentagon hawks—but his nation was left almost totally isolated in South Asia. Islamabad's two-decade-old strategy to dominate Afghanistan and make use of its strategic depth had utterly failed. Pakistan found itself surrounded by enemies and dependant for economic survival on Washington's continued goodwill. Its military-dominated regime was compelled by the United States to crack down on Islamic opposition parties, curtail criticism of government policies, restrict individual rights and free speech, and limit activities by Islamic militants. In short, Pakistan began to look like another U.S.-backed military regime, Egypt.

As one Pakistani writer noted, the Taliban defied massive bombing by U.S. B-52s for five weeks; Pakistan caved in after one phone call from Washington. "Our name is mud," is how another analyst aptly described Pakistan's regional standing. To help divert popular anger away from the debacle in Afghanistan, Pakistan ratcheted up the military confrontation with India by encouraging various Kashmiri mujahedin groups to attack across the Line of Control into the Indian-ruled portion of the mountain state. India reacted predictably, issuing dire threats that sharply raised tensions between the two old foes.

Meanwhile, the United States was busy overthrowing the Taliban. Pounded by over twelve thousand shells and carpet bombing and assailed by their old foes, the Northern Alliance, the Taliban's resistance showed courage but little military skill. The talibs should have immediately dissolved into the southern mountains instead of holding vulnerable fixed lines.

•••

Watching medieval Taliban forces being pounded into bloody pulp by invulnerable American warplanes eerily and vividly recalled the epic battle of Omdurman that had taken place more than a century earlier.

In 1894, an obscure Islamic teacher in western Sudan named Mohammed Ahmad proclaimed himself the Mandi—a messianic redeemer who, according to Islamic tradition, would revive faith and spread it around the globe. The Mandi gathered about him a motley collection of tribal warriors who became known in Europe as the "Dervishes"—not to be confused with the Sufi dervishes of Turkey—and set about to rid Sudan of its Anglo-Egyptian colonial masters.

The Mandi quickly became the *bete noire* of Victorian Britain and no doubt served as a role model for Osama bin Laden. The Dervishes outraged Britain by storming Khartoum and killing the Queen's proconsul,

General Charles Gordon. "Chinese" Gordon was regarded as something of a saint by Britons for bringing the benefits of Christianity to the misguided heathens of China and Sudan.

A British imperial army led by Lord Kitchener was sent up the Nile to punish the "fiendish" Dervishes. Kitchener's force met the Dervishes outside Khartoum at Omdurman. The Dervish cavalry and their sword-wielding tribal infantry, immortalized by Rudyard Kipling as "fuzzy wuzzies," made repeated suicidal charges against the British artillery, Gatling guns, and massed infantry. The Dervish Army was massacred. There were hardly any British casualties, though a young subaltern, Winston Churchill, was nearly grazed by a musket ball. Sudan became part of the British Empire. One hundred three years later, it was the turn of the Taliban's tribal warriors to be massacred by advanced Western weaponry.

After weeks of air attacks on virtually every conceivable target in Afghanistan and almost anything that moved, Taliban leader Mullah Omar ordered his forces to retreat to their tribal homeland in the south. In a surprise move, Taliban forces abandoned Kabul without a fight, leaving the capital open to Northern Alliance forces poised only 30 kilometres (19 miles) to the north and west. The Taliban was firing its final Parthian shaft at Pakistan for having betrayed it. Kabul was to be handed over to Pakistan's bitter enemy, the Northern Alliance.

At this point in the fast-evolving Afghan War occurred one of the most dramatic but least understood strategic developments: the dramatic reentry of Russia into Afghanistan.

Russia had armed and financed the Northern Alliance since the mid-1990s in order to counter the Taliban, whose revolutionary Islamism was rightly regarded as a dire threat to the post-Communist regimes of Central Asia. Moscow maintained twenty-five thousand troops in Tajikistan, where they battled Taliban-backed Islamic insurgents. Growing internal opposition to the corrupt dictatorships of Uzbekistan and Kyrgyzstan by Islamists and non-Islamists was seen by Moscow as a direct threat to its Central Asian sphere of influence, Russia's "near-abroad."

The real power in the Tajik arm of the Northern Alliance was war-lord Ahmad Shah Massoud. As previously noted, he had gone over to the KGB during the first Afghan War and remained an ally of Soviet, then Russian, intelligence. Members of the old Afghan Communist party joined the Northern Alliance or remained in exile in Uzbekistan and Tajikistan. Moscow and Iran struck an informal pact to back the Northern Alliance, flying in daily shipments of arms, munitions, food, uniforms, spare parts, and medical equipment. Russian pilots flew Alliance helicopters and provided technical and logistic support. In short, the Northern Alliance had become a proxy army for Russia.

However, on September 9, 2001, Massoud was assassinated by two Arabs posing as journalists.

While the Bush administration was busy making plans for war against the Taliban and bin Laden, Russia's leader, Vladimir Putin, a former KGB foreign intelligence officer from the elite First Directorate, was making his own plans for Afghanistan. Putin put the chief of the Russian General Staff, Marshall Victor Kvashnin, and Viktor Komogorov, the deputy head of the Federal Security Service—the KGB's successor—in charge of reorganizing and directing the Northern Alliance.

Russia opened its military depots and reequipped the Alliance with T-54/55 tanks, BMP and BTR armoured vehicles, D-30 howitzers, rocket batteries, trucks, munitions, small arms, radios, and medical supplies. Russian officers in mufti assumed direct control of Alliance troops and continued to oversee its logistical train and communications. Regular troops from the armies of neighboring Tajikistan and Uzbekistan, and possibly Iran, reinforced the ranks of the Alliance, whose combat forces grew virtually overnight from under ten thousand to over thirty thousand soldiers.

My old friend, Burhanuddin Rabbani, was still the nominal president of Afghanistan and head of the Northern Alliance, but he had become a figurehead. The real power in the Alliance was held by two old Communists: the Uzbek warlord General Rashid Dostum and General Muhammed Fahim, a former high-ranking member of KHAD, the notorious Communist secret police. These two major war criminals had been responsible for mass killings and atrocities during the 1980s and 1990s.

The Bush administration was so fixated on killing Osama bin Laden and Mullah Omar that it failed—or chose not to notice—that northern Afghanistan had been handed over to Russia on a silver platter. Another view holds that President Bush agreed to Putin's demands for half of Afghanistan and American support of Russia's savage repression in Chechnya in exchange for Moscow's support against bin Laden and the use of Central Asian air bases. If so, this was an unnecessarily generous concession, since the United States did not in fact need to use

Central Asian bases and required little support from Russia in its Afghan campaign.

I believe that the first theory is correct: the Bush administration was simply gulled and outfoxed by Moscow. After assuring Bush that the Northern Alliance would not occupy Kabul until a government was formed that was acceptable to Washington, Putin seized the opportunity a day after the U.S. president had publicly asked Moscow to stay out.

In a brilliant *coup de main*, Marshall Kvashnin ordered the Alliance to race into Kabul, which had just been evacuated by the retreating Taliban. In effect, Putin advanced his rook onto the empty square of Kabul, so checking the strategic ambitions of the Americans.

•••

This was the second time in three years that Marshall Kvashnin had pulled off a remarkably successful *coup de main*. In 1999, as NATO was preparing to occupy Kosovo after the war against Serbia—and exclude Russia—Kvashnin ordered his paratroopers to race ahead of NATO troops and, in violation of Moscow-Washington agreements, seized Priština airport, where Russian troops remain to this day.

Kvashnin's more ambitious plans to move Russian armoured and mechanized forces into Kosovo and Serbia were thwarted by Hungary and Romania, which refused them passage. Nonetheless, Kvashnin's decisive seizure of Priština airport made Russia a player in Kosovo and assured Moscow's influence in future diplomatic manoeuvring over ex-Yugoslavia.

Similarly, Kvashnin's dash to Kabul decisively thwarted American and Pakistani plans to install their own regime in Kabul. The Alliance was clearly in charge of the Afghan capital and the northern half of the nation. This was a double blow to the United States and Pakistan. They had suffered a sharp political defeat and suddenly found themselves blocked from their principal strategic goal: building a pipeline north from Karachi to Uzbekistan and Turkmenistan to export Central Asia's energy riches. Thanks to the Alliance victory, it appeared that the pipeline would go through Russian-controlled territory and not south to Pakistan. Iran had schemed against the Pakistani pipeline project for a decade, and so was also delighted to see its ally, the Alliance, holding Kabul. President George Bush had been neatly and swiftly outmanoeuvred by the wily

Vladimir Putin, who emerged from the end of the first round of the new Afghan drama as the clear winner.

Interestingly, the U.S. government and the American media, which too often acted as cheerleaders for the war rather than providing diverse views, never informed the public that the Russians had reoccupied Afghanistan while no one was looking. When I raised this issue in TV interviews, the standard answer from Bush administration supporters was, "Well, the Russians are now our friends...the Cold War is over." What they failed to realize, of course, was that in the rough, nasty world of big power politics and oil, there are no friends, only competitors.

Angry as the Bush administration was at being euchred by their "new best friends" in Moscow, they pushed ahead with a compliant coalition government that would at least give the impression of a viable regime in Kabul. This regime would then "invite" in Western "peacekeepers," who would keep the new government in power, receive foreign aid promised to Afghanistan, and assure Western interests in Afghanistan.

After much political theatre designed to play to the Western media, a new "broad-based coalition" regime dutifully emerged and assumed office in Kabul. Its leader, Hamid Karzai, was a respected Pushtun who had no real political base but maintained close connections to the CIA. Two women were named to powerless ministries, to universal praise in the West. This was window-dressing. Few non-Afghans understood that behind the facade of a so-called broad-based coalition, the Northern Alliance controlled the three power ministries—defense, interior, and foreign affairs. They held all the cards.

The new regime sharply curtailed the number of peacekeepers that the United States and Britain sought to bring in. There was a brief, undignified scramble by lesser Western powers and allies to join the peacekeeping force in a show of loyalty to the United States, to assert their own power and pride, and to seize the opportunity for their underused soldiers to gain field experience, combat pay, and promotions.

Canada's armed forces, reduced to impotence by decades of budget cuts and initially rejected for service, were reluctantly accepted after pleas from Ottawa for them to serve as auxiliaries to American troops in a relatively safe zone outside Kandahar. Italy had to beg to be included in the coalition.

Turkey also sought to join the peacekeeping force as a way of expanding its influence in Central Asia, a region it calls "Turania," and regards as part of the greater Turkic nation. France sent troops to stake its claim to Central Asian oil. And so on. In spite of the sprinkling of troops from many nations, the occupation force essentially remained an American and British operation.

The Alliance and their Russian patrons understood full well that in today's world, the term peacekeepers has become a euphemism for foreign occupation troops. If any nation were to do the occupying, it was Russia. Western troops would be limited in number and kept outside of Kabul. The whole business of intervention soon came to resemble the self-serving, mutually suspicious European-Japanese-American military expedition to Peking in 1901 to "rescue" foreign legations from the Boxer Rebellion.

While the Russians were reoccupying northern Afghanistan, the United States was busy in southern Afghanistan—in the words of General Tommy Franks of Central Command—"chasing chickens." The "chickens," to use the general's charming rural idiom, were, of course, Osama bin Laden, his fellow al Qaeda leaders, and Mullah Omar. They were believed to be hiding in the Tora Bora region in caves that had been dug or improved during the war against the Soviets. Washington had raised the price on bin Laden's head to "up to $25 million."

The U.S. media produced highly fanciful drawings of elaborate, multilevel underground complexes that resembled the equally fanciful, wildly exaggerated impressions of the Maginot Line seen in the European prewar press. Having been through some of the rudimentary Tora Bora caves during the 1980s, I was amused by how the media managed to transform them in America's imagination into the lair of a second Dr. No.

More massive bombing and a cave-by-cave hunt by U.S. Special Forces and their Pushtun mercenary tribesmen turned up little of value. After first announcing that their nemesis had been cornered, the United States, to its embarrassment and chagrin, had to admit that bin Laden had somehow escaped—likely into Pakistan's Northwest

Frontier where he was being sheltered by friendly tribesmen. A few hundred Taliban and al Qaeda soldiers were killed or captured around Tora Bora, not the thousands that were believed to be in the mountain stronghold. Some escaped, but the principal reason so few were taken or killed was that the numbers of al Qaeda fighters had been exaggerated by the United States from the beginning. There were never more than three hundred to five hundred al Qaeda fighters. A few thousand muja-hedin from Uzbekistan, Kashmir, Sinkiang, and the Philippines had trained at al Qaeda camps, but they were not part of bin Laden's forces. Many of these non Qaeda mujahedin were killed by the U.S. offensive and listed as al Qaeda casualties. Similarly, al Qaeda fighters and Taliban tribesmen were routinely lumped together by the Pentagon and U.S. media, producing confusing reports of casualties and people captured.

•••

So, as of early January 2002, the "chickens" were not to be found. The United States had failed to accomplish its most important goal in going to war against Afghanistan: killing or capturing Osama bin Laden. Mullah Omar, a villain of much smaller water, also remained at large, though his capture appeared likely. Only one senior al Qaeda leader had been confirmed killed by that date. However, al Qaeda had been scattered and put to flight. It could no longer use Afghanistan as an operational base, refuge, or magnet for discontented young Muslims.

The Taliban appeared to be destroyed as a political-religious move-ment, with thousands of its fighters killed or captured. Some, perhaps eight hundred, had been massacred after being taken by Northern Alliance forces, most around Kunduz and Mazar-e-Sharif by General Rashid Dostuam's Uzbeks. The Pentagon's frequent statements that it didn't care whether Taliban and al Qaeda members were taken dead or alive likely contributed to the slaughter of prisoners in Afghanistan. The denial of Geneva Convention protection to the Taliban prisoners, their novel classification by the United States as "battlefield detainees," and their deportation of some to Cuba raised serious questions about the legality and propriety of such actions from a nation that prides itself as a champion of law and human rights.

The United States dropped over twelve thousand bombs on Afghanistan, including a new range of precision guided munitions and deep-penetration bombs. The U.S. Air Force also used numerous 6,800-kilogram (15,000-pound) "daisy-cutter" bombs, the largest in its arsenal.

For the first time, the CIA employed remotely piloted vehicles (RPVS) armed with air-to-ground missiles, confirming the Air Force's long-held fears that the agency was trying to acquire its own air arm. The extensive use of CIA paramilitary gunmen in the Afghan campaign also angered the U.S. Army, which had no control over these agents and almost no liaison with them.

New U.S. thermal sensor technology revealed in the Afghan campaign showed a remarkable ability to detect targets under foliage or snow, under a few feet of ground cover, and in the dark. U.S. military communications also demonstrated powerful new capabilities to transmit data in real time and link units within a combat area or theatre of operations. American Special Forces finally managed to win some combat victories after the disasters in Somalia and Iran. Special Forces forward air controllers with the Northern Alliance targeted B-52 strikes that broke Taliban lines near Mazar-e-Sharif, Kunduz, and north of Kabul.

As always, the U.S. Navy, America's senior service, displayed an impressive capability to launch and sustain operations halfway around the world that would have warmed the heart of Admiral Chester Nimitz.

America was euphoric over "Bush's war" in Afghanistan. It was just the kind of little war beloved by publics everywhere—a swift, easy military triumph with only a handful of casualties. Those experts who had warned of the dangers of involvement in Afghanistan, including this winter, were dismissed as armchair strategists who didn't understand modern military power. The expected explosion of fury across the Islamic world did not occur.

The scattering of thirty thousand lightly armed medieval tribesmen by a combined U.S. and Russian force was hardly an epic military victory, though it was certainly a logistics feat by the U.S. military. No one expected the Taliban to withstand an American-Russian assault. In 1979, it took the Soviet Union only a few days to occupy most of Afghanistan. Getting into Afghanistan had always been easy, as invading armies have discovered. The problem in Afghanistan is getting out, not getting in.

An estimated five thousand Afghan civilians were killed in the American military campaign, which created 160,000 refugees and caused further destruction to Afghanistan's already battered infrastructure. The region north of the Hindu Kush mountains had become a de facto Russian sphere of influence, leaving the three main northern cities of Mazar-e-Sharif, Kabul, and Kunduz and the western stronghold of Herat under the influence of the Northern Alliance and Iran. Southern Afghanistan remained chaotic, as scores of local Pathan chiefs battled for territory or settled old scores.

In an amazing reversal of fortune, Russia had managed to revenge its defeat in Afghanistan at the end of the 1980s, secure its Central Asian satellites, block the United States from the region, and assure that the new energy pipeline routes would go through Russian-dominated territory, not through Pakistan. This geopolitical triumph had cost Russia only a modest sum of money, perhaps $100 million. This was nothing compared to the billions spent by the United States to mount the Afghan campaign, rent access to bases in Pakistan and Central Asia, buy refuelling and overflight rights, and provide financial inducements to wavering allies to join the anti-Taliban coalition. In addition, the United States had to pay a further price by reclassifying Russia's brutal repression of Chechen independence-seekers as a legitimate war against Islamic terrorism.

The Bush administration failed to take into account the geopolitics of the little-known and less-understood region into which it had charged. While most Americans believed that they had won the war against the "forces of evil" in Afghanistan, they did not understand that their nation was at the beginning, not the end, of the latest Afghan war—a new, low-intensity conflict that will likely be a long, confused, murky struggle in this strategic but chaotic nation.

The growing American military presence in Afghanistan means that its garrison of troops is likely to become embroiled in lethal Afghan tribal politics and may face a low but persistent number of casualties from skirmishes and accidents—just what happened to the Soviet garrison in the 1980s. The United States has bought temporary loyalty from tribal chiefs, but this situation could quickly change as Afghans chafe under the growing American presence and resentment builds over being ordered about by foreigners.

It is clear that the United States is inexorably being drawn deeper and deeper into South and Central Asia. Empires expand through war or trade. The American Imperium—or American Raj, as I have long called it—made a decisive *Drang nach Osten*, or strategic move to the east, at the end of 2001. Just as the United States took advantage of the 1991 Gulf War to compel its Arab clients to permit stationing of permanent U.S. garrisons in Saudi Arabia and the Gulf, so the United

States used the campaign against bin laden and the Taliban to expand its military influence into South and Central Asia.

The reason is both simple and complex: oil. Washington was determined to dominate the world's richest new source of oil, Central Asia's Caspian Basin and its neighbouring states—Uzbekistan, Tajikistan, Kyrgyzstan, Turkmenistan, and Kazakhstan. Well before September 11, the United States already had Special Forces operating in Kyrgyzstan and Uzbekistan. In the spring of 2001, as previously noted, Osama bin Laden had advised the unworldly Taliban regime to turn down a low bid from the U.S. oil firm Unocal to build a pipeline to export Central Asian oil. The contract was awarded instead to a rival Latin American firm. Immediately, the United States cut off discreet financial aid to the Taliban and began updating contingency plans to invade Afghanistan and install a compliant regime. The events of September 11 facilitated and accelerated the decision.

In late 2001, the United States established military bases near Kandahar, where units of its elite 101 Airborne Division replaced Marines as a semi-permanent garrison. Three other permanent bases were set up: in southern Tajikistan; at Khanabad*, Uzbekistan; and at Manas, Kyrgyzstan. The United States took over three air bases in Pakistan. All these new bases are linked to and supplied by much larger U.S. military bases in Arabia and the Gulf. The Manas base was expected to grow to three thousand troops and seventy-two warplanes.

The United States thus plunged headlong into South and Central Asia, bringing a vast new region of the globe under its military and political influence—one that might be termed the "Mideast East." Washington appeared set to use the same formula in South and Central Asia as in its Mideast oil raj: keep friendly dictatorial regimes in power and crush their internal opponents in exchange for military bases, large arms purchases, and cheap oil. Osama bin Laden, who claimed that the West has robbed the Muslim world of $36 trillion dollars in oil profits, pronounced that Muslim nations should get $144 for a barrel of oil, not the paltry $20-odd dollars they now receive. The United States will make sure this never happens.

The Bush administration, encouraged by its powerful oil lobby, was determined to dominate the Caspian Basin gold rush. However, U.S.

*currently under temporary closure by the Uzbek regime

military forces are already stretched extremely thin. Involvement in Central Asia strains them severely, on top of the rising costs of basing U.S. troops in Iraq and the Gulf, from which the United States gets only 7 per cent of its oil. Moscow regards the Central Asian states as part of its sphere of influence and expects that they will one day return with their resource riches into a reformed Russian Union. Any American incursion into Russia's "near abroad" must be seen as a grave, long-term threat to be countered by intelligence work, covert operations,

And—when necessary—limited military action. In other words, a resumption in force of the Great Game.

The Taliban was not the only revolutionary force in the region. Militant Islam in Central Asia is a reaction to the deeply corrupt, dictatorial Communist regimes that run the region—not, as Russia and now the U.S. claim, simply another manifestation of Islamic terrorism. In Central Asia, where religion is still circumscribed and the official Muslim clergy are agents of the security services, small mosques remain the sole free "space" where a wide variety of underground opposition groups can operate and meet.

American bombing in Afghanistan killed Juma Namangani, the leader of Islamic insurgents in Uzbekistan, but his supporters, and Islamic insurgents in Tajikistan and Kyrgyzstan, will continue to battle those nations' post-Communist regimes. Gas-rich Turkmenistan faces political uncertainty after the death of its colorful, eccentric dictator, Saparmurat Niyazov, whose grotesque cult of personality made North Korea's Kim Jong Il look almost modest by comparison.

Kazakhstan, which is half ethnic Russian, has been immune up to now to Islamic ferment.

China is watching the arrival of American troops on its highly sensitive western borders and the new U.S.-Indian strategic alliance with mounting concern. Beijing also remains extremely uneasy over resistance by Sinkiang's Muslim Uighers to "ethnic inundation" by Han Chinese settlers. For a brief period in the late 1990s, the CIA reportedly considered using the Taliban to train and arm Uighur insurgents in Afghanistan, but dropped the idea when relations with Kabul soured. As of early 2002, the Uighurs remain sullen and restive. Without strong foreign backing, however, Uighur independence groups struggling for a free Eastern Turkestan are too small and too weak to pose more than a nuisance to Chinese rule.

•••

While international attention was fixed on the hunt for Osama bin Laden and his al Qaeda supporters, a severe crisis was brewing between India and Pakistan that soon eclipsed in scope and danger the comparatively minor events in Afghanistan.

In December 2000—and then in October 2001—Kashmiri insurgents from a new group, Lashkar-e-Toiba, launched audacious raids on two symbols of Indian authority: the famed Red Fort in old Delhi and the state parliament building in Srinagar. India furiously threatened retaliation against Pakistan, which it once again accused of cross-border terrorism. These attacks went almost unnoticed in the West.

On December 13, 2001, unidentified gunmen attacked India's national parliament in New Delhi, killing thirteen. The suicide attackers, all of whom were killed, apparently intended to attack members of parliament gathered within. India was outraged and vowed revenge against Pakistan. Delhi accused Laskhar-e-Toiba and another new militant group, Jaish-e-Mohammed, of launching the suicide attacks. Islamabad denied any involvement and claimed that India had no proof that these two Pakistan-based groups were involved in the attacks.

India almost immediately began mobilizing troops and preparing for war. India's prime minister, Atal Behari Vajpayee, proclaimed that his nation could no longer tolerate terrorism. If the United States could unilaterally attack Afghanistan to root out terrorists, then, Vajpayee logically asserted, India had just as much right to attack Pakistan and root out the terrorists who were waging war inside Indian-controlled Kashmir. The worldwide hue and cry against the ill-defined forces of international terrorism provided the ideal climate for India to go on the political-military offensive.

As war fever mounted, India demanded that Pakistan end all support for Kashmiri militants. The United States backed India's claims and exerted pressure on Pakistan's leader, President Pervez Musharraf, to further rein in the isi and clamp down on Islamic militants within Pakistani territory.

Meanwhile, India accelerated its mobilization. Its three powerful strike corps were moved to offensive positions on the border, where they were poised to slice Pakistan in half at its narrow, vulnerable waist.

More than three hundred Indian warplanes were forward based in Punjab. The Indian Navy put to sea and prepared to blockade Karachi to cut off all of Pakistan's oil and other strategic imports.

Pakistan also mobilized, moved troops to their forward positions, and dispersed aircraft. By mid January 2002, the two foes had concentrated some 1.2 million troops along the border. Violent skirmishes and exchanges of artillery fire occurred almost daily along Kashmir's Line of Control.

Most ominously, India and Pakistan put their nuclear forces on high alert and began assembling nuclear warheads. India warned that Pakistan's nuclear forces would not be allowed to thwart Indian military action, neither the hot pursuit of Kashmiri rebels into Azad Kashmir, nor a full-scale invasion of Pakistan. India said it was ready to strike back against any Pakistani attack. The two old foes were thus in the biggest military confrontation since 1971—except that this time both were ready to deploy nuclear weapons on a three-minute hair-trigger alert. India and Pakistan were prepared to embark on an exceptionally dangerous game of "nuclear chicken" in the Himalayas.

Unaware of the complexities and subtleties of South Asian politics, the White House was so eager to enlist India in its war against terrorism that it signed a strategic alliance with Delhi. Six months before being elected president of the United States, George Bush had been unable to name the leader of Pakistan, referring to him as "some guy." Now the same man held the fate of India and Pakistan—and 20 per cent of the world's population—in his hands.

The new Washington-Delhi pact upset the delicate balance of enmity between India and Pakistan. India took the pact as a green light to use the military option to go after Pakistan and crush, once and for all, the Kashmiri independence movement. Pakistan was left further isolated and now mercilessly squeezed between the United States and India. President Musharraf somehow had to give in to intolerable pressure to end his nation's support for Muslim Kashmiris—a sacred issue to all Pakistanis and to their army—without appearing to do so.

The December 13, 2001 attack on the Indian parliament was clearly designed to push India and Pakistan closer to war. Al Qaeda suicide commandos may have been the attackers. Indeed, just as military operations in southern Afghanistan were winding down, the United States found itself embroiled in a near war between India and Pakistan.

Pakistan, desperate to avoid a war it could not win, backpedalled furiously. General Musharraf locked up Islamic militants and political leaders, curbed the Islamic press, closed religious schools, expelled foreign mujahedin, and sharply reduced support for "indigenous" Kashmiri liberation groups. The pressing need to bring peace to the embattled mountain state was almost totally forgotten in the border crisis and the U.S. invasion of Afghanistan.

All this was a humiliating climb-down for Pakistan and a painful blow to its national pride and raison d'etre. President Bush's ugly referral to Pakistanis as "Pakis" deeply insulted the already demoralized nation. For its part, India kept increasing the pressure and moving diplomatic goalposts so that Pakistan was constantly forced on the defensive. Each retreat by the Musharraf government caused the general's military regime to lose support both among the public and within the army. It was an impossible position. In fact, as the year 2002 began, the two worst jobs in the world were president of besieged Pakistan and president of bankrupt Argentina.

In spite of Musharraf's concessions, the confrontation between India and Pakistan continued. Profound distrust and made concessions and conciliatory gestures suspect. Worse, the tense standoff between the two nuclear powers could erupt at any time into a full-scale conflict. A false report of incoming enemy missiles or air strikes or another high-profile outrage staged by shadowy militants could trigger war between India and Pakistan.

POSTSCRIPT

The traditional Afghan mode of warfare harks back to the Middle Ages when armies campaigned for only part of the year, returning home for spring planting and fall harvesting seasons. They would go into winter quarters during the coldest months when rough dirt roads became impassable from mud, ice or snow. For the Pashtuns, warfare and raiding were sporadic pursuits, conducted at a leisurely pace often determined as much by mood as weather. Pashtuns believed it was undignified, even cowardly, to run while in combat. They walked into battle. When the felt they had proved their point, or were simply tired of fighting, they would abruptly leave the battlefield, as this writer experienced on numerous occasions.

After the U.S. invaded Afghanistan in late 2001 and smashed Taliban's fixed defensive lines with terrifying B-52 carpet bombing, Mullah Oman commanded most of his tribal warriors to return to their homes, doff their black Taliban turbans, don white ones, and blend back into the civilian population of southern Afghanistan. Small bands of veteran fighters took to the mountains to continue the resistance, but to all extents, Taliban appeared to disband.

Washington's neoconservatives and the U.S. media were cock-a-hoop, hailing the victory over Taliban as the template for future operations in the Muslim World. They insisted the combination of U.S. airpower and information warfare, backed by small numbers of U.S. special forces and local allies or mercenaries, could produce highly efficient, low-cost victories over assorted Islamic malefactors. President George W. Bush was hailed as a great and wise war leader whose vision had given America a triumphant victory, as he put it, "over evil."

The seemingly quick victory in Afghanistan was held forth by neoconservatives as an example of how swiftly and easily Iraq's regime could be overthrown. Iraqi exiles, Shia militias, and Kurdish "peshmergas" would play the same role that the Northern Alliance did in Afghanistan. The American high-tech knights would lead Arab and Kurdish foot soldiers into another speedy victory in Iraq that would put its vast oil fields in American hands and leave Israel unchallenged in the Arab world.

Soon after the U.S. invasion of Afghanistan, I wrote a number of op-ed newspaper pieces warning that Taliban would inevitably return to battle, and urged the U.S. and its allies to open talks with Taliban and cease demonizing it. I reminded readers that after the Soviet invasion of Afghanistan in 1979, it had taken three years before serious resistance was organized and took the field.

My warning was dismissed as delusions or, worse, "support for terrorism." The U.S. media fell over itself in a rush to pen glowing stories about the liberation of Afghan women, the schooling of Afghan girls, the "rebuilding of war-ravaged Afghanistan" and its now inevitable, American-authored "march to democracy." Medieval Islam had been soundly defeated: the light of Western civilization would henceforth bathe the wretched Afghans and guide them to a Western consumer society. The Soviet media had produced the same cheery propaganda fluff after the Red Army occupied Afghanistan. A century earlier, the British press had waxed lyrical about the Empire's mission to bring the light of Christianity and civilization to the savages and heathens of Africa and Asia.

Exactly three years after the U.S. invasion, serious resistance broke out across the southern half of Afghanistan. The supposedly defunct Taliban suddenly re-materialized like an evil genie and began shooting at Afghanistan's self-professed "liberators" and their local stooges. There was enormous consternation in Washington and widespread disbelief. "I thought we won the war there?" was the frequent response this writer heard in Washington.

At first, the Bush administration went into denial, insisting the rising wave of attacks in Afghanistan was the work of "foreign Islamic terrorists." But by early 2006, it was clearly undeniable that Taliban had returned and was attacking U.S. forces and their allies with renewed vigor and élan. Equally disturbing, Taliban appeared to have a seemingly inexhaustible supply of arms and munitions *and* a steady flow of young recruits. It also had advanced knowledge of all impending U.S. and NATO ground operations thanks to the thousands of Afghan interpreters, drivers, guides, and service personnel hired by the invaders. In true Afghan tradition, even the highest officials of the Karzai regime hedged their bets by playing both sides: it was the only way to protect their families and prepare for the day when the Westerners would, like the Soviets, pack up and depart.

Taliban's unwelcome reappearance in the midst of Washington's Afghan victory parade intensified U.S. efforts to create what appeared to be a popular, democratic government in Kabul. Since twenty-seven thousand U.S. regular troops and a small army of CIA agents—ssupported by a constellation of aerial, land, and space-based sensors, legions of informers, and a reward of $25 million for information on escaped Taliban leaders—had embarrassingly failed to locate the elusive Osama bin Laden or Mullah Omar for more than five years, the Bush administration had to devise another justification for continuing to occupy Afghanistan.

The real reason, of course, was to pacify Afghanistan and make it secure for planned oil and gas pipelines that were to run south from Uzbekistan and the greater Caspian Oil Basin to Pakistan's Arabian Sea port of Karachi. Just by coincidence, major "anti-terrorist" U.S. bases in Afghanistan just happened to be built along the projected oil corridor. Afghanistan was the vital gate through which U.S. strategic and commercial influence would spread into resource-rich Central Asia—the "Mideast East." The Soviets had viewed Afghanistan in much the same way: as the route that would take them south to the warm waters of the Arabian Sea and the oil-producing Gulf.

To support and supply the U.S. occupation of remote Afghanistan—in itself a major logistical feat—Washington covertly dispensed several hundred millions dollars to the Communist elites of Kazakhstan, Uzbekistan, Tajikistan, and Kyrgystan—as well as to Pakistan—to lease and upgrade air bases and/or secure landing rights. The semi-Communist governments of Romania and Bulgaria also received large cash payments to allow the U.S. Air Force to use their Black Sea air bases as staging posts—as Britain's Royal Navy had once done with Aden and Colombo—for the American air bridge from Frankfurt to the Mideast and Central Asia.

At the same time, Washington set about shoring the credentials of the Krazai regime in Kabul. The amiable Hamid Karzai, a long-time CIA "asset" who had once worked for U.S. oil interests, was portrayed as Afghanistan's democratic savour. Decked out in a dramatic green cloak at the advice of a leading U.S. public relations firm (it was not typical Afghan wear, but looked impressive on Western TV), Karzai cut an appealing and likeable media figure with his excellent English, eloquence, and earnestness. He was the very model of a modern, pro-U.S. Muslim leader.

Actually, Karzai had not been CIA's first choice to become the figurehead ruler of Afghanistan. My old mujahidin friend, Commander
Abdul Haq, was picked by CIA for the role of Afghan president, but the
courageous Abdul Haq had a fatal flaw: he was an impetuous hothead.
Haq organized a small band of men and slipped into Taliban territory,
vowing "to liberate my nation." Unfortunately, Abdul Haq was caught
by Taliban and promptly hanged as a traitor and spy. So the CIA turned
to its backup candidate, Hamid Karzai.

The Karzai regime proved extremely popular—abroad. At home,
however, Karzai was widely dismissed as a powerless U.S. puppet.
Though he was Pashtun, he had no clan or tribal support. In fact,
Karzai deeply alienated his fellow Pashtuns by working hand in glove
with the hated Tajiks. Karzai was kept in power by Western troops, at
first Americans, then NATO. His writ extended no further than Kabul's
city limits, earning him the sobriquet of "Mayor of Kabul."
Afghanistan's warlords, most of whom received covert CIA stipends,
cooperated with the Karzai regime when it suited them and ignored the
president when it did not.

Worse than being an American figurehead, Karzai was seen as a tool
of the Tajiks. The Tajik and Communist Northern Alliance was the real
power behind Karzai and, though somewhat diminished in influence,
remains so to this day. The Northern Alliance was riddled with Russian
FSB agents, had close links to Indian intelligence, RAW, and had long
dominated the opium trade.

In fact, when Taliban controlled nearly all of Afghanistan, shrinking Northern Alliance's sphere to a small toehold in the northeast, the
Talibs managed to reduce opium cultivation and production by 90 per
cent, according to UN figures.

After the Taliban was overthrown by the Americans, opium production surged to the point where today Afghanistan supplies 90 per
cent of world demand for heroin. In 2006, opium production rose 40
per cent. Under the Karzai regime, drugs came to represent over half of
Afghanistan's economy, making it the world's leading narco-state. The
Bush administration simply shrugged off complaints that it was closely
allied to Afghan warlords who, by comparison, made Colombia's notorious drug barons look like vendors of native handicrafts.

Afghanistan's booming drug trade not only engulfed its economy
and government, it spread tentacles of corruption south into Pakistan,

where much of the raw opium was converted in secret laboratories into heroin. The 2.5 million Afghan refugees in Pakistan, who dominated the trucking business, provided a ready distribution network. The drugs were then shipped through the port of Karachi to the outside world. Every level of Pakistan society became corrupted by the trade, right up to the highest echelons of government, police, judiciary and even the nation's least corrupt institution, the military.

While Afghanistan was being consumed by the drug trade, Washington embarked on a plan to legitimize the Karzai regime. He had earlier been named "interim president" in a U.S.-organized national tribal council, or *loya jirga*, Afghanistan's traditional political assembly. Delegates were screened by the CIA, surrounded by U.S. Special Forces and gun-toting mercenaries, and heavily bribed with suitcases full of $100 bills. To no one's surprise, Hamid Karzai was elected interim president. The best measure of his popularity was the fact that he was surrounded at all times by a ring of two hundred gun-toting American bodyguards. Afghans were not trusted to protect their president.

In October, 2004, the U.S. got the tame UN Secretariat to help stage a supposed presidential election whose outcome was pre-ordained. Karzai won handily against feeble candidates handed-picked to ensure he had no real competition. Strong potential contenders, like former prime minister Gulbuddin Hekmatyar, were excluded. Turnout among Tajiks, Uzbeks, and Turkomen was 60 per cent; among Pashtuns, under 30 per cent. Once again, quantities of U.S. $100 bills changed hands and voters were trucked in and forced to cast ballots for the Karzai camp.

A second election, this time a parliamentary poll, was held in September 2005. Unsurprisingly, this vote also produced the desired "support" for Karzai, which Washington trumpeted as irrefutable evidence that a flourishing democracy had indeed taken root in Afghanistan's formerly barren political ground.

The Soviets had done exactly the same thing when they were occupying Afghanistan, and for the identical reasons. Increasingly concerned by growing resistance, and claims that the Communist regime in Kabul of Najibullah was a puppet of Moscow, the Soviets organized a *loya jira*, then national elections, in 1986 and 1987.

Ironically, these Soviet-run elections, though fundamentally rigged, were actually somewhat freer and more genuine than the faux elections staged by Washington in 2004 and 2005. The Soviets allowed real opposition candidates to run, including militant anti-Communist and Islamic parties. These groups were largely excluded by the U.S. in its own contrived Afghan elections as "Islamic terrorists" or "supporters of terrorism." The Western media ignored the mass bribery, intimidation, vote rigging and general chicanery that characterized the elections, instead producing glowing reports about the "birth of democracy" in Afghanistan.

These elections were a remarkable mirror image of the Soviet and U.S. occupation of Afghanistan. Both superpowers invaded, both set up puppet regimes and held rigged elections, both waged war against what they called "Islamic terrorists," both employed the same Uzbek and Tajik warlords, and both killed large numbers of Afghan civilians by bombing and shelling. Whether Afghanistan proves a humiliating defeat for the U.S. as it did for the Soviet Union remains to be seen. The anti-Soviet jihad was armed, financed, and supplied by the West and oil Arabs; today's Taliban has no major foreign support and must make due with scarce local resources.

Still, one wonders, if the Russians wanted to exact revenge on the U.S. for supplying the Stinger anti-aircraft missiles to the mujahidin that turned the course of the war against them, might not the Kremlin discreetly supply modern Russian portable anti-aircraft missiles to Taliban, such as the SA-16 and SA-18. If Taliban were to receive such modern missiles that could restrict low-level U.S. air support, American, British, Canadian and other NATO troops might well be unable to defend their bases or supply lines and be forced, like the Red Army, to withdraw.

While the U.S. and its allies kept depicting the war in Afghanistan as a straightforward mission to kill Islamic terrorists and implant democracy, the hunt for bin Laden, while remaining in full force, had been pushed into the background as a reason for the continuing occupation. However, the better part of a full U.S. division kept up a twenty-four-hour hunt for bin Laden and Mullah Omar, often probing into Pakistan's tribal agencies.

Afghan resistance to the West's growing presence steadily increased, just as it always had in the past. The core of the resistance remained Taliban, this time reinforced by fresh cohorts of younger fighters, and a handful of left-behind al Qaeda jihadis. New forces kept joining the resistance, including Gulbuddin Hekmatyar's important Hizbi Islami nationalist party, other Pashtun *khels* and clans, and veterans of the first Great Jihad, including mujahidin led by the legendary comman-der, Jalaladin Hakkani.

By the end of 2006, though NATO governments and media kept to the party line that Western forces were fighting "terrorists," it was clear that the Western occupation powers were not just fighting Taliban die-hards or a handful of al Qaeda, but, increasingly, much of the Pashtun people who comprise over half Afghanistan's population.

Almost equally important, the war was seriously destabilizing neighbouring Pakistan and gradually drawing it into the Afghan con-flict. Between 15 and 20 per cent of Pakistan's people are ethnic Pashtuns, many of whom are concentrated in the so-called tribal terri-tories along the border with Afghanistan. Pashtuns are heavily represented in the senior ranks of Pakistan's powerful armed forces and intelligence service, that nation's real government.

The international border that separates the Pashtuns of Pakistan from their relatives in Afghanistan, known as the Durand Line, is one of Imperial Britain's typical malevolent colonial creations designed to divide and weaken powerful tribes that continue to cause enormous trouble right down to our own day. Africa and Asia are covered with these still festering geographical wounds inflicted by British imperialism. While the rest of the world recognizes the Durand Line as the border between Pakistan and Afghanistan, the Pashtuns, whose ancestral lands it sunders, do not and continue to move across it without cease, pro-voking charges of "cross-border terrorism" from Washington and Kabul.

Pakistan's "Frontier Agencies" are a wild, lawless, and mostly road-less region of 27,220 square kilometres (10,510 square miles) with 3.4 million Pashtun tribesmen. This exotic region, straight out of the days of Rudyard Kipling and the British Raj, is one of my favourite parts of Pakistan. It is considered violent and exceedingly dangerous, but I never once felt threatened and, in fact, was quite at home with the heavily armed tribesmen who, provided one treated them with respect and good manners, were welcoming and gracious. Where else in the world could one buy home-made AK-47 assault rifles or grenades in vil-lage gun shops and test them out on the main street?

A basic constitutional understanding that underpins the unity of chronically fragile, unstable Pakistan was agreement that the federal army would never enter the independent tribal belt, whose affairs would fall entirely into the hands of its local *maliks* (tribal leaders). The only Pakistani presence allowed would be a few forts with crenelated walls and towers, garrisoned by small, paramilitary units bearing such wonderfully Victorian names as the "Khyber Rangers" or the "South Waziristan Scouts."

As the war in Afghanistan continued, the resistance made increasing use of these tribal territories as staging and supply bases. The fierce Pashtun tribes of North and South Waziristan, Bajaur, Khyber, Kurram and other agencies, were linked by blood, religion and a common world view to the Pashtun Taliban, consequently lending as much aid as they could give to the Afghan resistance.

However, in 2004, the U.S. put enormous pressure on Pakistan's military strongman, Pervez Musharraf, to send his army into the tribal agencies. This prospect horrified Pakistanis, who feared violating a basic tenet of their constitutional understanding with Pashtuns would lead to potentially catastrophic results and even ignite one of Islamabad's worst nightmares: the specter of Pashtuns from Pakistan and Afghanistan seceding from their respective nations to form a new Pashtun state, "Pashtunistan."

Unable to resist heavy U.S. pressure, Musharraf sent his army, discreetly aided by U.S. Special Forces, the U.S. Air Force and CIA teams, into the tribal agencies, allegedly to hunt down "al Qaeda terrorists and their supporters." In the process, some three thousand tribesmen and around seven hundred Pakistani soldiers were killed, producing outrage across Pakistan. Musharraf was branded a traitor by many of his countrymen. "Fight India, not your own people," screamed Pakistan's media. Musharraf was finally forced to back down and make a deal in 2006 with the tribesmen to prevent Islamic militants from using their territory, but few believed it was more than a face-saving retreat from what was nearly a full-scale tribal uprising against Islamabad.

Meanwhile, the increasing effectiveness and frequency of attacks launched the Afghan resistance sparked furious accusations from Karzai and Washington that Pakistan was sustaining and sheltering the insurgents. When guerilla wars start going wrong for the occupier, it is common for them to begin accusing neighbours of being to blame for their reverses. The French did this in Algeria, blaming Tunisia and Nasser's Egypt. The Americans blamed Cambodia and Laos for their problems in Vietnam. Now the U.S. and NATO are laying blame on close ally Pakistan.

While there is no doubt that Musharraf's regime is an active foe of Afghanistan's Islamic and nationalist resistance, there remains very strong support for them among ordinary Pakistanis as well as the military and intelligence establishment. Some help for the Afghan resistance certainly comes unofficially from Pakistani sources, including members of ISI, both active and retired. At least 85 per cent of Pakistanis and most opposition parties are opposed to the Western occupation of Pakistan.

Equally important, though Musharraf was forced to abandon Taliban and at least temporarily renounce Pakistan's important strategic interests in Afghanistan, the leadership in Islamabad seeks to maintain influence there, shape events to its favour, and be prepared for the day when the U.S. and its allies withdraw. Pakistan must also counter growing Russian, Iranian, Uzbek, and Indian involvement in Afghanistan, deal with problems caused by the drug trade, and prevent the war in Afghanistan from spreading into its own territory.

Consequently, Musharraf has long played a double game, trying to satisfy both Washington's demands on one hand and, on the other, to mollify the growing anger of his own people and military establishment. Every time Washington forces Musharraf to bend over further backwards over Kashmir or Afghanistan, he becomes more isolated from his own people, and more vulnerable. His job is one of the most difficult in the world, as he made plain in his recently published memoir, *In the Line of Fire*.

After six years of low-intensity warfare in Afghanistan, the U.S. has found itself no closer to its goal of pacifying Afghanistan, implanting a widely accepted, legitimate regime that would take direction from Washington, and opening the way for energy pipelines. Nor had it found the elusive Osama bin Laden and Mullah Omar, the original reason for the invasion.

•••

After the 9/11 attacks in 2001, the Bush/Cheney Administration invoked the NATO treaty to demand its alliance partners provide troops for Afghanistan. While there was deep sympathy for the United States after the attack, most Europeans were reluctant to see their soldiers go to far-off Afghanistan. The NATO compact, many European politicians maintained, only covered defensive operations on their continent, not expeditions abroad. As President Bush's so-called war on terror intensified, increasing numbers of Europeans opposed its objectives and brutal, lawless conduct. They wanted no part of Afghanistan or of what many Europeans called "U.S. imperial adventures."

However, the Bush/Cheney administration brought such intense pressure on its NATO allies that many were forced to agree to send troop contingents to Afghanistan. Once the U.S. launched war against Iraq, it began demanding its allies send troops there. European nations chose the lesser of evils by agreeing to send "non-combat" troops to Afghanistan's Tajik/Uzbek northern region or to Kabul, which were relatively peaceful.

The Bush/Cheney administration was still fuming over Canadian prime minister Jean Chretien's sagacious decision not to get involved in Iraq. His ill-fated successor, Paul Martin, responded to political and economic pressure from Washington by agreeing to send a small Canadian troop contingent to perform guard duty in Kabul, while giving Canadians the impression it was a "nation-building" and traditional peacekeeping mission.

But Canada's mostly peaceful mission abruptly changed when, according to former cabinet member Sheila Copps, Washington got on the phone and told Ottawa to either send troops into combat in Afghanistan or to Iraq. Southern Afghanistan, which seemed the lesser of two evils, was chosen.

The new Conservative prime minister, Stephen Harper, who was much influenced by U.S. and Canadian neo-conservatives and sought to emulate President George Bush, had urged sending Canadian troops to join the war in Iraq before he took office. Once in power, Harper lost no time in expanding Canada's combat role in southern Afghanistan even though Canadians kept being told the primary object of their intervention was humanitarian.

In a first in military history, the Harper government also claimed Canada's troops were going into battle to defend "women's rights." Canada's militant feminist groups were thrilled that Taliban's women-abusing male chauvinists would be taught a much-needed lesson by Canada's armed forces in gender equality and proper behaviour.

By 2006, 2,200 Canadian troops were based at Kandahar, in the very heart of Taliban and Pashtun territory, replacing U.S. combat troops who were moved elsewhere. Assured they would be greeted by Afghans as "liberators from Islamic terrorism," Canadian troops were disagreeably surprised to become the targets of suicide bombers, snipers, and regular ambushes. They were confused by the fact that the "good" Afghans veiled their women just like the wicked Taliban.

Many Canadians wondered why Ottawa had agreed to put its troops in Afghanistan's most dangerous region while other NATO allies, like France, Italy, Turkey, and Germany, insisted on keeping their small troop contingents out of combat zones.

Canada's dispatch of troops to the war in Afghanistan bore interesting similarities to its first imperial mission when Canadians went off to fight the British Empire's colonial war in 1899–1902 against Boer farmers in South Africa. Few Canadians at that time understood the complexities of the struggle with the Boers, who were portrayed by the jingoistic English-language press as monsters and crazed killers. In the end, more than 220 Canadians died serving as cannon fodder for the British Empire. This, of course, was merely a foretaste of the horrors to come twelve years later in the Great War.

Few Canadians had any better understanding of events in Afghanistan. The Harper government followed the lead of its mentor, the Bush/Cheney administration, by selling the war to the public as a one-dimensional struggle between good and terrorist evil. The facts that Canada had no interests whatsoever (save possible commercial oil drilling rights at some future date) in the region, or that sending troops to fight in Afghanistan would anger the entire Muslim world, were ignored. A wave of jingoism gripped less thoughtful Canadians, exemplified by General Rick Hillier's vow to "kill the scumbags," though it was unlikely the fire-breathing general could tell the difference between a Pashtun "scumbag" and a Tajik "freedom fighter."

Once Canadians went into combat in Afghanistan, much of Canada's media, which had sneered down its nose at the U.S. media's crudities, biased reporting, and fevered flag-waving during the faked-up Iraq War, quickly duplicated America's yellow journalism.

Canadian reporters rushed to Kabul for photo ops, sending back breathless stories about progress in women's rights, education, and nation building. Unfortunately, all of the media's so-called information came straight from press handouts written by military PR hacks, just as most of the American media's reports from Iraq came from military sources.

There were no Canadian reporters with the resistance to provide a balanced view. So what Canadians got was rehashed government and NATO propaganda, disguised as news. Both the Canadian and U.S. media wholeheartedly adopted the Orwellian vocabulary of their governments in biasing the news. Resistance fighters were all "terrorists." Invasion was "liberation." Occupation was "rebuilding." Civilians killed by bombing and shelling were "suspected Taliban terrorists," "collateral damage," or "people used as human shields by Taliban terrorists," torture was "tough interrogation," and so on.

Many Canadians were thrilled by reports coming back of their troops' dramatic battles with Taliban. In a series of engagements around Panjwei in 2006, "over two hundred Taliban terrorists were killed," gushed military spokesmen. Interestingly, few if any enemy bodies were found after these engagements, once again illustrating that in guerilla wars, enemy casualties are always wildly exaggerated. Canadian military spokesmen trumpeted that they had "occupied Taliban territory," naively unaware that guerrillas rarely hold ground but are taught to retreat before superior forces. As Mao famously advised, "retreat when the enemy is strong. Attack when he is weak." Most of the "suspected Taliban casualties" were killed by U.S. air strikes.

Canada, like the United States, had rushed into what seemed a "jolly little war" against a highly unpopular, medieval foe that was abusing women and children, supporting Islamic terrorism, and blowing up Buddhist idols. That oil and gas were located in the region of this crusade against Islamic evil was a happy coincidence. Neither Washington nor Ottawa had any idea what they were getting into, or that they were interposing themselves in the middle of a tribal war in a remote land that had defeated all invaders since Alexander's Macedonians.

The U.S. and Canadian media acted as mouthpieces and cheerleaders for the war, seriously misleading their readers and viewers and failing their basic role in democratic society of exposing government lies and propaganda. Canada's media and its politicians also entirely missed the significant fact that its military intervention in Afghanistan, followed by Harper's fulsome support for Israel's ravaging of Lebanon, killing a Canadian UN observer, and his adoption of Israel's position vis-à-vis Hamas and Hezbollah had made his nation a target of hatred and anger across the Muslim world. The Harper government put Canada squarely in the crosshairs of numerous terrorist groups. To the Muslim world, Canada had become part of George Bush's anti-Islamic crusade.

In Washington, as in Ottawa, ignorance and arrogance ruled the day. A gasconading President George Bush dared resistance forces in Iraq and Afghanistan with his memorable, "bring' em on." Unluckily for Bush, they came on, and buried his presidency, the worst and most shameful in American history. Undaunted by Bush's fate, Canada's new, inexperienced Prime Minister Harper curiously chose to adopt the exact same policies, world view, and vocabulary as his hero in Washington. Why any politician would seek to emulate what polls showed to be the most disliked, if not hated, man on earth remains a mystery. But responding to criticism over mounting Canadian casualties in Afghanistan and growing unease among Canadians that their troops had no business being there, Harper replied with a vintage Bushism: "we won't cut and run."

But Western forces in Afghanistan would have to cut and run were it not for the protection of U.S. air power. Without this air umbrella, NATO forces in Afghanistan would already have been defeated. NATO and the US have around 57,000 troops in Afghanistan. The Soviets had 160,000 men and a puppet Afghan Army of 200,000 and yet they could not defeat the Afghan resistance. The major difference between the two wars is that in the current one, the U.S. Air Force and naval aviation, successors to Britain's Royal Navy, are able to maintain twenty-four-hour air patrols over Afghanistan that include B-2 heavy bombers with huge loads of precision bombs. The Red Air Force never had this capability. Within three minutes of a mujahidin attack, U.S. airpower can intervene and shower the guerrillas with GPS-guided bombs, deadly cluster munitions, fuel air explosives, huge "daisy cutter" bombs, rockets, and cannon fire.

But what is perhaps even more remarkable an impressive than America's lethal technology is the courage and motivation of Afghan mujahidin who continue to face such devastating attacks from the sky in open terrain where they have very little shelter or top cover. Their continued attacks should tell Westerners a great deal about the fierceness and determination of the Afghan resistance. The Soviets learned it, but the lesson has since been forgotten.

The primary problem facing the U.S. and its uneasy allies in Afghanistan is that they have failed to achieve the basic aim of warfare.

As the twentieth century's finest military thinker, Britain's Major General J.F.C. Fuller put it, the aim of war is not military victory but a favourable political resolution.

The United States has won all the battles in Afghanistan and Iraq, but, so far, it is losing both wars because it cannot develop or implement a favourable and lasting political solution: a stable, pro-American regime obedient to U.S. commands, that fights Islamist influence and rejects political Islam while being accepted as legitimate and representative by a majority of Afghans and Iraqis. In both nations, the dismayed Americans have found themselves caught in vicious tribal warfare that defies rational resolution.

So long as the U.S. and its NATO allies keep a regime in power in Afghanistan that reflects the interests of the Tajik and Uzbek minority, there will be no peace or political settlement in that ravaged nation. But once the West's troops are withdrawn, the Karzai regime will soon swept away unless it can somehow legitimize itself as an authentic Afghan government.

The only way the West can hope to achieve its political and commercial goals in Afghanistan is by dealing with the nation's majority, the Pashtuns, their military wing, Taliban and its nationalist allies. So long as Western leaders continue to demonize Taliban and brand it a "terrorist organization," no political accommodation will be possible and the war, which currently costs the U.S. at least $2 billion monthly (and tens of millions more in secret CIA stipends for warlords and politicians), tying down twenty-seven thousand U.S. troops, will drag on. The Afghan resistance continues to gather strength and is pressing U.S. and NATO forces ever harder. It now controls much of the southern half of Afghanistan and is approaching Kabul. Western commanders are urgently calling for more troops and warning they cannot even defend their own bases and supply lines. But every bombing, every demolished village and every dead civilian turns Afghans more and more against their occupiers and provides ten new recruits for the resistance.

Modern guerrilla warfare is not fought for ground, it is all about controlling civilian populations. In this sense, Afghanistan and Iraq are well lost since the U.S. and its allies control very little of the population, and even the portion they do control is shrinking. More of the same in Afghanistan will produce eventual defeat; it is only a question of how long it will take before the last Western troops are run out of

Afghanistan and their local collaborators strung up from lampposts and cranes as Soviet collaborators were.

The Russians are watching America's growing problems in Afghanistan with undisguised glee and a sense of revenge. Osama bin Laden continues to call Afghanistan the first successful phase of a long war to bleed the U.S. and drive it from the Muslim world.

As for the long-suffering Afghans, war and drugs have become their only growth industries. Those who wonder how long the Afghans will continue resisting Western occupation would do well to review the old Hindu prayer at the beginning of this book. The Afghans, let us recall are legendary for their determination, their courage, and their passion for revenge.

INDEX

A

Abdullah, Farouk, 135, 145–146
"Abode of Snows," 242
ad-Din, Salah, 35
Advani, L.K., 265
Afghan Communist Party, 66
Afghan society, 10
Afghani, 85, 150
Afghanistan
    Afghan Wars, 13
    Canadians in, 324–330
    civil war in, 34, 52, 56
    Communist invasion of, 15–18
    media and, 306, 308
    Northern Alliance rule in, 76
    reoccupation by Russians, 76
    U.S. invasion of, 300
    U.S. war with, 316–324
    women in, 14–15, 69
Afridis, 7, 11
Ahmad, Mohammed, 302
Ahmed, Mahmoud, 301
Ajab, Hajji, 2–6
Aksai Chin, 130–131, 185
al Qaeda
    see also bin Laden, Osama; Taliban
    communications, 103
    creation of, 86
    hunt for leaders, 307
    and Kashmiri groups, 175–176
    Massoud assassination, 76
    media and, 97–101
    monitoring of, 88
    structure of, 102–103
al-Badr Camp, 204
al-Faran, 142
al-Fateh, 142
al-Shifa, 98
Albright, Madeline, 107
Alexander the Great, 7, 10, 25
altitude sickness, 206–209, 248
ambans, 252
American Imperium, 310

Amin, Hafizullah, 15–17, 19
Amin, Idi, 26
Andropov, Yuri, 16
Anglo-Afghan War, 14
Ansar, 61
Arabian Nights (Lawrence), 20, 30
An Area of Darkness (Naipaul), 222
arms race, 231
arms sales, 276
Arunachal Pradesh, 185, 187, 269
Aryan Hindus, 123
Atef, Muhammed, 96
Aung San Suu Kyi, 268
Avnery, Uri, 105
Azad Kashmir, 125, 128
    see also Kashmir
Azzam, Abdullah, 81–85, 87

B

Babar, Naseerullah, 59, 63
Babur, Zahiruddin, 213
Badal, 11
Baghdad, 212
ballistic missiles, 167–168, 266, 295
Baltistan, 183–184, 195–196
Bangash, 11
Bangladesh, 133
Beg, Mirza Aslam, 49
Berger, Sandy, 98
Bharatiya Janata Party (BJP), 215–216,
    259, 265–266
Bhutan, 280
Bhutto, Benazir, 48–49, 58–59
Bhutto, Zulfikar Ali, 41, 45, 134,
    222–223
"bin Laden caves," 85
bin Laden Group, 80
bin Laden, Mohammed Awad, 79–80
bin Laden, Osama, 79–111
    see also al Qaeda; Taliban
    al Qaeda, creation of, 86
    allies of, 73
    "Brother Osama," 110

CIA and, 87
citizenship stripped, 91
crusade, 40
embassy bombings, 98
fatwa issued to all Muslims, 96–97
frozen assets, 92
Great Jihad, joining the, 23, 85
hepatitis and, 86
hero to Afghans, 76
hero to Muslims, 109–111
hunt for, 77, 301, 307–308
influences of, 81–85
Iraq, wrath for, 88–89, 106–108
Islamic studies, 81
Massoud assassination, 76
media and, 98–101
oil profits and, 311
pillars of hatred, 104–108
reaction to U.S. troops in Saudi
    Arabia, 88–89
Saudi Arabia, wrath for, 108
Sudan, flees to, 90
U.S. target, 300
Washington's view of, 69
Birendra, 279
BJP. See Bharatiya Janata Party (BJP)
Black Panthers, 202
Bomdi La, 190
Brahmans, 122–123, 214
Brezhnev Doctrine, 16
Brezhnev, Leonid, 16
British East India Company, 125, 213
British Indian Raj, 42
"broad-based coalition," 306
"brown gold," 58
Brown, Harold, 20–21
Brzezinski, Zbigniew, 16–17
Buddha, Gautama, 247–248
burka, 15, 70
Burma, 268–269
Bush administration, 70, 74, 174–176,
    304
Bush, George W., 76, 300, 315
"Butcher of Dacca," 139
Butler, Lady Jane, 13

C
Calcutta, 270
caliphate, 83

Canada, 263, 306, 324–330
Carter administration, 21
Carter, Jimmy, 16, 20, 45
caste, 121–123, 214, 217, 226
Castro, Fidel, 26
Caucasus, 43
Central Intelligence Agency. See CIA
"chat," 120
Chechens, 43, 73–74
Chengdu, 239
Cherkess, 43
China, 275–299
    see also Taiwan
    air base, 272
    armed forces, 296
    arms race, 266
    border war with India, 254–255
    capitalists in, 290
    claims on Kashmir, 130
    Communist deconstruction, 285, 290
    confrontation with India, 187–190
    deployment of troops, 271
    destabilization of India and, 156–157
    economic development, 287–288
    generational revolution, 290
    human rights issues, 289
    India, rivalry with, 275
    Indian threat, 156–157
    Indian-Chinese war, 270
    land strategy, 267–268
    military installations, 272
    modernization of, 270–271, 286, 288
    national dissolution of, 282–283
    naval power, 273
    nuclear arsenal, 263, 295
    occupation of Tibet, 184–185
    oil and, 273–274
    Russian relations, 298
    slowing economy, 287
    social revolution, 292
    Taliban and, 72, 74
    territorial claims, 186
    unilateral ceasefire, 190
    U.S. relations, 72, 298
    Vietnamese-Chinese border war,
        286–287
Chokoti, 158
"chosen of God," 82
Chretien, Jean, 325

Christians, 269
Churchill, Winston, 216
CIA, 36–37, 46, 53, 55, 57, 87, 254,
    308–309, 318–319
Clinton administration, 71, 98, 106
Clinton, Bill, 74
Communism, 66
Confucian China, 285
Curzon, 252

D
da Gama, Vasco, 213
Dagestanis, 43
Dalai Lama, 245, 246, 248–249,
    250–251, 254
Daoud, Prince Mohammed, 14
"death zone," 208
Defense Research and Development
    Organization (DRDO), 168
Deng Xiaoping, 256–257, 283, 285–287,
    289
Dervishes, 302
Dostum, Abdul Rashid, 52, 54, 56, 65,
    70, 74, 308
Dravidians, 122, 230
DRDO. See Defense Research and
    Development Organization (DRDO)
drug trade, 57–58, 319–320
Drupl, Gendun, 246
Dudayev, Jokhar, 104
Dukagjin, Lek, 11
Durand Line, 13–14
Durand, Sir Mortimer, 13
Durrani, Ahmad Shah, 10
Durranis, 10
Duvalier, François, 26

E
Eastern Turkestan. See Sinkiang
Egypt, civil war in, 93–96
Egyptian Brotherhood, 81

F
Fadil the Kurd, 35–41
Fahim, Muhammed, 74
Fakir of Ipi, 30
farangi, 30
fatwa, 96–97
FBI, 48, 94

Federal Security Service, 304
Fernandes, George, 265, 274
FLN. See Front de Liberation Nationale
Four Noble Truths of Buddhism, 245
France, 307
Franks, Tommy, 307
"free space," 68
"free tribes," 10
Friendship Highway, 239
Front de Libération nationale (FLN), 137

G
Gadhafi, Muammar, 30
Gandhi, Indira, 42, 132, 135, 137, 223,
    259
Gandhi, Mohandas K., 125, 216
Gandhi, Sonia, 266
Gang of Four, 283, 285
Ghilzai, 10, 13
Gill, K.P.S., 135–136
Golan Heights, 272
"goondas," 155
Gorbachev, Mikhail, 46, 50, 288
Gordon, Charles, 303
Grant, Charles, 13
Great Cultural Revolution, 255–256, 283
"Great Game," 43, 78
Great Jihad, 23, 46, 55
Great Leap Forward, 287
Greco-Kashmiri, 124
Gul, Hamid, 51
Gulf War, 63
the Gulf, 20–21, 40, 62
"Gurkhaland," 280
Gurkhas, 11
Gyatso, Tenzin, 246

H
hajj, 3
Hakimullah, Marshal, 49
Haq, Abdul, 6, 319
Harper, Stephen, 325–328
Harrer, Heinrich, 248
Hashernites, 61
Haushofer, Baron Karl, 116
hawala system, 103
Hazara, 12
Hekmatyar, Gulbuddin, 32, 54–55, 59,
    85

"Hermit Kingdom," 242
high altitude. *See* altitude sickness
high-altitude cerebral edema, 209
high-altitude pulmonary edema, 209
Hilton, James, 195
Himalayan Mata Haris, 188
Himalayas, 240, 247, 253
"Hindi-Chini-Bhai-Bhai," 185
Hinds, 33
Hindu Kush, 10
Hindu nationalists, 215–216, 220, 223
Hinduism, 224–226
    caste system, 121–123
    Muslim threat to, 217–219
    restoration of civilization, 215–216
"Hindutva," 216
Hoxha, Enver, 26
human rights issues
    China, 289
    Kashmir, 144–145
    Taliban, 308
    United States, 283
Huntington, Samuel, 82
Hussein, Saddam, 30, 62, 89, 106–108

I
ibn-Saud, Abdul-Aziz, 79
Ikhwan, 61–62
India
    aggressive world view, 259
    air force, 164, 276
    armed forces, 262
    arms race, 266
    border war with China, 254–255
    British racism and, 214–214
    caste system. *See* caste
    Chinese rivalry. *See* China
    Dalai Lama and, 254
    deployment of troops, 159–160, 187,
       191–193, 313–314
    destabilization, 155
    economic advantages, 164–165
    false optimism, 185
    hunt for Pakistani terrorists, 313
    independence from British rule, 125
    Indian-Chinese war, 270
    Islamic threat, 217–219
    Kashmiri resolutions, 128
    legacy of inferiority, 215–216

literacy rate, 219
living conditions, 219
media and, 228
modernization of, 261–262
mujahedin crackdown. *See* muja-
    hedin
National Security Council, 265
naval expansion, 260–261
naval forces, 165, 273
Northern Alliance and, 74
nuclear arsenal. *See* nuclear arsenal;
    nuclear programs; nuclear testing;
    nuclear warfare
oil and, 273–274
partitioning of, 126
rearmament of military forces, 191
rebellion, 52, 150
size advantage, 165
spy satellites, 166
tactical disadvantage, 271–272
Taliban invasion of, 146
technological advancements,
    257–258
territorial claims, 186
torture of suspected militants,
    139–142
unified state of, 154–155
war with Pakistan. *See* Kashmir
weapons, 231
women, torture of, 140–142
"Indira Doctrine," 259
Indus, 181–182
Ingush, 43
Inter-Service Intelligence
    Afghan resistance and, 22
    Benazir Bhutto and, 63
    Communist assault, 53
    Kashmiri resistance and, 148–149
    missile training, 37
    mujahedin and, 59
    Russian invasion and, 45
    secret war, 32
    Stingers and, 46
    Taliban and, 63–64
International Atomic Energy Agency,
    264
International Islamic Brigades, 83, 87
intifada, 52
iodine deficiency, 200

Iran
    geopolitical swing nation, 266–267
    the Gulf and, 62–63
    Taliban opposition, 71–72, 74
Iraq, 88–89, 106–108
ISI. *See* Inter-Service Intelligence
Islam
    expansion of, 213
    insurgents of, 312
    reaction to Mongol invasions, 212
    religious belief examined, 224–226
    revolt, 131–145
    riots, 128
    roots of hatred, 211–236
    Soviet invasion of Afghanistan, 23
    threat to Hindus, 217–219
    threat to India. *See* India
Islamabad, 118
Islamic International Brigade, 39, 40,
    115
Islamic Movement, 73
Islamic nationalism, 40
Islamic Republic of Pakistan, 221
Israel, 104–106, 264
Italy, 306
Ivan IV (the Terrible), 43

J
Jaish-e-Mohammed, 313
Jalalabad, 6, 53
Jamiat Islami, 56
Jammu Kashmir Liberation Front (JKLF),
    137, 146–147, 149
Japan, 294
the jewel of India. *See* Kashmir
Jiang Zemin, 257, 287
jihad, 18
Jinnah, Muhammed Ali, 125, 221
JKLF. *See* Jammu and Kashmir Liberation
    Front

K
K2, 180
Kabul, 6, 305–306
Kafir Kalash, 124
Kama Sutra, 218
Kandahar, 306, 325–326
Karachi, 58
Karachi Agreement, 184

Kargil, 196–197
Kargil-Leh military road, 197
Karmal, Babrak, 15, 17
Karzai, Hamid, 306, 318–321
Kashmir, 114–176
    see also India; Pakistan
    civilian casualties, 138–142
    demilitarization of, 231
    entering, 117
    guerrilla insurrection, 137
    holy war, 127
    human rights issues, 144–145
    Hunza Valley, 124
    independence, 73, 146–147
    Indian takeover, 127
    Indo-Pakistani war, 126, 131–133
    the jewel of India, 121
    media ban, 135, 139
    Pakistani support, 148–149, 315
    potential solutions, 172–174
    raids, 313
    Tibet and, 124
    and United States policy, 174–176
Kaul, B.M., 186
Kazahkstan, 73, 312
KGB, 49–50, 52, 84
KHAD secret police, 19, 49
Khalq, 15, 16
Khan, Akhtar Abdul Rahman, 22, 45, 46,
    48
Khan, Amanullah, 146–147
Khan, Ayub, 118, 222
Khan, Aziz, 301
Khan, Genghis, 213
Khan, Kublai, 251
Khan, Tikka, 139
Khartoum, 92
khels, 11
Khomeini, Ruhollah, 82
Khyber Pass, 7
Khyber Rifles, 7, 9
Kipling, Rudyard, 11, 123
Kissinger, Henry, 51, 134, 255
Kohl, Helmut, 233
Komogorov, Viktor, 304
Korea, 294
Kosovo, 305
Kryuchkov, Vladimir, 50
Kshatriya, 122

kufir, 10, 89
Kurdistan Workers' Party (PKK), 161
Kurds, 35–36
Kuwait, 89
Kvashnin, Victor, 304, 305
Kyrgyzstan, 73

L
Ladakh, 129–130, 185, 280
laogai, 247, 250, 255
Laskhar-e-Toiba, 313
Lawrence of Arabia (Lean), 65
Lawrence, T.E., 79
Lean, David, 65
Lee Kuan Yew, 288
Lhasa, 244, 247
Line of Control (LOC), 127, 133–134,
   144, 158–159
"the Lion of Kashmir," 146
Living Buddha. *See* Dalai Lama
LOC. *See* Line of Control
London Telegraph, 30
Lost Horizon (Hilton), 195
loya jirga, 54
Lumumba, Patrice, 26

M
Mackinder, Sir Halford, 116
McMahon Line, 186–187
McMahon, Sir Henry, 186
"Mad Mullah," 30, 300
Madhya Pradesh, 266
madrassas, 58
Mahrattas, 11
Mahsuds, 11
Manchu dynasty, 251–252
Manchuria, 298
Mandi, 302
"The Man Who Would Be King"
   (Kipling), 123
Mao Tse-tung, 283, 285–286
   guerrilla disarmament, 255
   humiliation of India, 190
   Nehru and, 184–185, 188
   social engineering of China, 222
   Tibetan occupation, 184–185,
      254
   Western opinion of, 289
Martin, Paul, 325

Massoud, Ahmad Shah, 32, 54–56, 65,
   74, 75–76, 303
Mecca, 3
Medecins sans Frontières, 30
media-unfriendly war, 18–19
Menon, V.K. Krishna, 186, 188–189
"Mideast East," 311
Ming dynasty, 251
Mitterrand, François, 233
Moguls. *see* Mongols
mohajirs, 220
Mohmands, 11
Mojadidi, Sibgatullah, 24, 25
Mongols, 212–214, 251
Moscow-Delhi axis, 276
Mountbatten, Lord Louis, 125–126
Mubarak, Hosni, 90, 95, 150
mujahedin
   bands, 2
   crackdown, 139–142
   Inter-Service Intelligence and, 59
Mujahedin Services Bureau, 83
Muree, 119
Musa, 204–211
Musharraf, Pervez, 77, 175, 229, 301,
   313, 315, 323–224
Muslim Brotherhood, 23, 36, 39, 62, 82
Muslim League, 221
Muslims. *See* Islam
Muzafarabad, 120
Myanmar. *See* Burma

N
Nadji, 149–153
Naipaul, V.S., 222
Najibullah, 6–7, 15, 17, 53
Namangani, Juma, 312
Nasser, Gamal Abdel, 82
Nasser, Javid, 6, 202
National Guard, 89–90
National Socialist Council, 269
National Socialist Party, 82
NEFA. *See* North-East Frontier Agency
Nehru, Jawaharlal, 125, 184–190, 215,
   221, 253
Nepal, 279–280
Nixon, Richard, 53
Niyazov, Saparmurat, 307
Noble Path, 245–246

Non-Proliferation Treaty, 171–172
Norbulingka, 248–249
Noriega, Manuel, 58
North-East Frontier Agency, 185, 187
North-West Frontier Province, 10, 28
Northern Alliance, 304–306
nuclear arsenal, 263–266, 282, 314
"nuclear chicken," 314
nuclear programs, 134, 154, 261, 263, 266–267
nuclear testing, 171–172, 216, 256, 263, 265
nuclear warfare, 166–169, 228–229
nullahs, 194

O
Omar, Mullah
    see also Taliban
    hunt for, 78, 307–308
    protection for bin Laden, 76–77, 92–93
    retreat of Taliban, 303
    Talib hero, 58
    unifying Afghanistan, 63–65
"Operation Brass Tacks," 227
opium, 56–58, 68–69
Orakzais, 11
Oxus River, 13, 14

P
Pahlavi, Shah Reza, 266
Pakhtun. See Pathans
"Pakis," 315
Pakistan
    Afghanistan war and, 322–324
    air force, 164
    birth of, 221
    defense budget, 231
    defensive strategy, 165–166
    Indian threat, 223
    Indo-Pakistani war. See Kashmir
    media and, 228
    military regimes, 222
    mobilization of troops, 314
    the Mother of Pakistan. See Indus
    nuclear program. See nuclear programs
    political instability, 229–230
    secret war, 45

Soviet resistance, 48
strategic defenses, 162–163
suicide attackers, 313
U.S., support of, 77
U.S. embargo, 164
U.S. threat, 301
U.S. ultimatum, 301
Panchen Lama, 246
Parchem, 15
Pathans
    territory of, 10
    tribal code, 11, 77
    tribal custom, 66
    tribes of, 11
Patriot Act, 175
Pax Americana, 294, 300
Pax Sinica, 294
People's Liberation Army, 188–190, 286
Peshawar, 28–32
peshmergas, 35
PLA. See People's Liberation Army
PLO, 83
Pol Charki prison, 15
Pope John Paul II, 50
Potala Palace, 244, 245, 248
Powers, Gary, 32
Prophet Mohammed, 3
pukka, 216
Punjab, 214
Punjabi Muslims, 11
    see also Islam
Pushtun. See Pathans
Pushtunwali, 77
Putin, Vladimir, 73, 304–305

Q
Qutb, Mohammed, 81, 82

R
Rabbani, Burhanuddin, 24–28, 32–34, 54, 85, 304
Rahman, Abdul, 84
Rajputs, 11
Ramadan, 224
Raphael, Arnold, 48
Rashids, 61
Rashtriya Swayamsevak Sangh (RSS), 215
RAW. See Research and Analysis Wing (RAW)

"reactor war," 167
Red Fort, 313
Red Guards, 222
remotely piloted vehicles, 308
Research and Analysis Wing (RAW), 48,
   156, 281
The Retreat from Kabul, 13
Riyadh, 91
RSS. *See* Rashtriya Swayamsewak Sangh
Russia
   Afghanistan, reoccupation of,
      303–307
   Chinese relations, 298
   expansion, 43–45
   "near-abroad" borders, 75, 303, 312
   Northern Alliance relations, 304
   threat to Taliban, 75
   war funds, 75
Russian Union, 312

S
Sadat, Anwar, 26, 93–95
Saif-ul-Islam, 48
Saladin. *See* ad-Din, Salah
Saudi Arabia, 62–63, 88–91, 108
Sayaf, Abdul, 85
"Seabees," 85
September 11 attacks, 76–77, 101,
   105–106, 300, 311
Serbia, 305
"settled" tribes, 11
Seven Sisters, 269
sharia law, 27, 59, 68, 81
Sharif, Nawaz, 4, 197, 301
Shevardnadze, Eduard, 49–50
Shia Hezbollah, 13
Shia Muslims, 12–13
Shinwaris, 11
"Siachen Angels," 204
Siachen Glacier, 128, 178, 191–193
Sikandar, 123
Sikh Wars, 125
Sikhs, 11, 29, 135–136
Sikkim, 280
Simla, 133–134
Simla Agreement, 253
Singapore, 291
Sinkiang, 277–279
Skardu, 180–181, 191–192

SLORC. *See* State Law and Order
   Reconstruction Council (SLORC)
South China Sea, 297
South Waziristan Scouts, 7
Soviet Union, 15–22, 25, 42–48, 228,
   231, 260, 264
Srinagar, 143, 169–170, 313
START, 50
State Law and Order Reconstruction
   Council (SLORC), 268
Sudan, 90–92
Sudra, 122–123
Sukarno, Ahmed, 26
Sun Yat-sen, 252, 285
Sunni Muslims, 12
Syria, 272
Szechuan, 282

T
Taiwan, 275, 283, 286, 289, 292
Tajik Jamiat Islami Party, 53
Tajikistan, 73
Tajiks, 12
Taliban, 53–78
   see also al Qaeda; bin Laden, Osama;
      Omar, Mullah
   anti-drug campaign, 68–69
   arming of, 59
   China and, 72
   creation of, 58–59
   deportation to Cuba, 308
   destruction of, 308
   "Great Satan," 69
   human rights issues, 308
   India's support, 74
   isolation, 301
   law and order, 15, 59
   media and, 69, 77–78
   movement, 63–67
   oil and, 97
   opium crackdown, 57, 68–69
   outlawed regime, 61
   Pakistani take over, 303
   resurgence of, 316–330
   threat to Russia, 75
   United States and, 69, 72
   women and, 69–71
Tamerlane, 213
Tamils, 230

Taraki, Mohammed, 15, 16
Tiananmen Square uprising, 288–289
Tibet
    Askai Chin, 131
    betrayal of, 255
    Chinese invasion, 253–254
    Chinese "liberation," 250, 255–256
    entering, 239
    ethnic borders, 242–243
    geographic borders, 242
    Han immigrants, 247, 256
    hygiene and, 247
    independence, 253
    invasion of Ladakh, 129
    Kashmir and, 124
    militarization of, 271
    political borders, 242
    rebellion against China, 254, 281
    repression in, 247
    rituals, 246
    road systems, 271
    U.S. support for, 254
Tibet Autonomous Province, 242
Tibetan Plateau, 129, 270–272
Timur the Lame, 213
Turkey, 307

U
Uighurs, 72, 278, 312
United Liberation Front of Assam, 269
United States
    Afghanistan war, 300, 316–324
    air base, 89
    Chinese relations, 298
    deployment of troops, 297
    eastern strategies, 310
    embassy bombings, 97–98
    human rights issues, 283
    Iraqi biological weapons, 108
    Iraqi sanctions, 106–107
    Kashmir policy, 174–176
    nuclear warfare. See nuclear arsenal;
        nuclear programs; nuclear testing;
        nuclear warfare
    oil and, 311–312
    Pacific domination, 289
    Pakistani embargo, 151, 164
    recession, 300

Soviet Union stalemate, 228
Taliban oil contract, 97
Tibetan support, 254
Unocal, 97
Ustinov, Dmitriy, 16
Uzbeks, 12

V
Vaisya, 122
Vajpayee, Atal Behari, 313
VHP. See Vishva Hindu Parishad (VHP)
Viereck, Peter, 82
Vishva Hindu Parishad (VHP), 215
Vorontsov, Yuli, 47, 49
VX nerve gas, 98

W
Wahhab, Mohammad ibn Abd al-, 60
Wahhabism, 60–62
Walid, Khalid ibn al-, 48
Washington-Delhi pact, 314
Wazirs, 11
women
    mistreatment of, 69–70
    status of, 14–15
    Taliban and, 69–71
    torture of, 140–142
Woolsey, James, 299
"World Islamic Front Against Jews and
    Crusaders," 108
World Trade Center bombings, 74, 84,
    103, 106

X
Xinjiang. See Sinkiang

Y
Yeltsin, Boris, 74
Youssef, 202
Yusufzais, 11

Z
Zahir Shah, King, 14, 27
al-Zawahiri, Ayman, 90, 95–96, 101
Zhou Enlai, 187, 271
Zia ul-Haq, Huhammad, 41–51
    covert defense plan, 22
    India, war with, 227